Washington's Revolutionary War Generals

C&C

Campaigns & Commanders

Gregory J. W. Urwin, Series Editor

CAMPAIGNS AND COMMANDERS

Washington's Revolutionary War Generals

Stephen R. Taaffe

University of Oklahoma Press : Norman

This book is published with the generous assistance of
The McCasland Foundation, Duncan, Oklahoma.

Library of Congress Cataloging-in-Publication Data

Names: Taaffe, Stephen R., author.
Title: Washington's Revolutionary War Generals / Stephen R. Taaffe.
Description: Norman : University of Oklahoma Press, 2019. | Series: Campaigns and Commanders ; volume 68 | Includes bibliographical references and index.
Identifiers: LCCN 2019004056 | ISBN 978-0-8061-6431-1 (hardcover : alk. paper)
Subjects: LCSH: Generals—United States—History—18th century. | United States—History—Revolution, 1775–1783—Biography. | Command of troops—History—18th century. | United States. Continental Army—Officers—Biography. | Generals—United States—Biography. | United States—History—Revolution, 1775–1783—Campaigns. | United States. Army—Biography. | Washington, George, 1732–1799—Military leadership.
Classification: LCC E206 .T33 2019 | DDC 355.0092/2 [B] —dc23
LC record available at https://lccn.loc.gov/2019004056

Washington's Revolutionary War Generals is Volume 68 in the Campaigns and Commanders series.

The paper in this book meets the guidelines for permanence and durability of the Committee on Production Guidelines for Book Longevity of the Council on Library Resources, Inc. ∞

1 2 3 4 5 6 7 8 9 10

To David Ohio Taaffe

Contents

Maps

Acknowledgments

Although writing is a solitary endeavor, this book would not have been possible without the help and support of three people in particular. My wife, Cynthia, tolerated my moodiness with her usual patience and kindness. My colleague and friend Brookford Poston read through the manuscript and offered sage advice. Finally, Mark Lender was kind enough to put me in touch with the good folks at University of Oklahoma Press.

Washington's Revolutionary War Generals

Introduction

On 25 November 1783, nearly three months after the Treaty of Paris officially ended the Revolutionary War, the remaining redcoats in the British army's New York City garrison marched down to the Whitehall Street wharf to board vessels that took them away from the American mainland for good. The evacuation was orderly enough, though some spiteful British soldiers greased the flagpole at the battery on Manhattan's southern tip to hinder subsequent celebratory efforts to haul down the Union Jack and raise the Stars and Stripes. At about the same time the last redcoats embarked, Maj. Gen. Henry Knox led a detachment of American troops into the city. Tipping the scales at about three hundred pounds, the strapping, thirty-three-year-old Knox was hard to miss. Despite his impressive girth and intellect, the prewar Boston bookshop owner and amateur artillerist would perhaps have rather passed his life in obscurity. The American Revolution, however, provided Knox with the opportunity to turn his hobby into his profession. Knox's energy, specialized expertise, and common sense quickly brought him to the attention of George Washington, the American army's redoubtable commander in chief. On Washington's recommendation, Congress eventually put Knox in charge of the army's artillery, and in that capacity he ably served as one of Washington's closest comrades throughout the conflict. It was generals such as Knox who enabled the young republic to outlast the most powerful empire on earth and secure its independence.

Shortly after Knox and his troops took possession of New York City, Washington and New York governor George Clinton rode into town at the head of a contingent of politicians, officers, and assorted civilians. American reoccupation after seven years of British rule touched off prolonged celebrations by its patriot population. Clinton threw an elaborate public dinner for Washington and his high-ranking lieutenants, followed several days later by a fireworks display for everyone else. For the American army's officers such festivities were bittersweet, marking as they did the end of their time together. On the one hand, the officers no longer had to risk life and limb on shot-torn battlefields and in squalid winter camps, or watch their men succumb to hunger, exposure, and wounds. They could instead look back with pride on their shared sacrifices, secure in the knowledge that they had played a critical role in winning the war and gaining their country's independence. On the other hand, the conflict had forged them into a proud, distinct, and tightly knit officer corps. They had lived, trained, fought, and suffered together, in many cases for years, for the cause and a people whose appreciation often seemed fickle and tentative. They had become brothers-in-arms, and their future relationships would never possess the same kind of intense bonds that held them together through the war's many trials and tribulations. As one officer put it, "It is difficult though we most earnestly wish it, that we may return to private life with all the care and comfort that an ungrateful country will permit."[1]

Nine days later, at noon on 4 December, many of the army's officers met in the Fraunces Tavern's Long Room to bid farewell to their commander in chief. Considering all they had been through, emotions ran high when Washington entered the room, greeted his officers, and took his seat. After shakily pouring himself a glass of wine, Washington said in a choked voice, "With a heart full of love and gratitude, I now take leave of you. I most devoutly wish that your latter days may be as prosperous and happy as your former ones have been glorious and honorable." Struggling to control his feelings, Washington invited each of his officers to come say goodbye. Knox, seated closest to Washington, approached first and, with tears streaming down his face, wordlessly threw his arms around his commander. Others followed suit, exercising a rare familiarity with the aloof Washington. After everyone had finished, Washington left the room, passed through the light infantrymen assembled to receive him, and walked down to the Whitehall wharf to board a barge heading southward. His officers followed him silently and, joined by a crowd of well-wishers, saw him off.[2]

The moving scene at Fraunces Tavern indicated the enormous respect that Washington and his officers held for each other. Washington was undoubtedly the key American military figure in the Revolutionary War, but his subordinate generals also played vital roles in the struggle for independence. Although Washington and Congress worked together to establish an army and formulate grand strategy, it was the generals who implemented their directives and ran the army's institutional machinery. Indeed, it is impossible to understand the American army's victories and defeats, from the siege of Boston to the siege of Yorktown, without understanding who these men were, how they attained their positions, and how they performed on and off the battlefield.

Although the Thirteen Colonies produced a remarkable number of highly capable political and intellectual leaders who organized, articulated, and justified the American Revolution, they were less successful at manufacturing equally proficient generals. With a few notable exceptions such as Knox, most of Washington's subordinate generals were mediocre at best, and frequently a good bit worse than that. They failed to demonstrate much strategic, tactical, or administrative acumen. They rarely took sufficient advantage of the local geography, the militia's latent power, British strategic and tactical mistakes, and the inherent strengths in American society. They also bickered constantly with Congress and with each other over issues big and small. Plodding conventionality marked their actions from the war's beginning to end. This ineffectiveness is evident in most of the war's campaigns, as well as in the army's day-to-day management.

The main reason for this mediocrity was the colonies' peculiar decentralized political culture. Although the Thirteen Colonies had fought various American Indian tribes and Britain's European enemies, they did not produce many high-ranking military leaders. This was partly due to the British government's reluctance to appoint colonists to high-level commands, but there was more to it than that. The colonists had an ingrained and long-standing aversion toward standing armies, seeing them as threats to civilian rule and liberty. They instead depended on their militias for defense. Because there were no standing armies in the colonies, there was no professional officer corps that Congress could tap for generals to organize, administer, direct, and fight the Continental army when the Revolutionary War began. As a result, Congress relied on another pool for its generals: the colonial upper class.

Thus, classism hindered Congress's ability to locate good generals. Although there was more social mobility in the colonies than in Great Britain, there were definite limits to how far a man could advance. Even in relatively egalitarian New England, power was concentrated in the hands of a few men based on their surnames, land ownership, and wealth. Within each colony, these elites knew each other personally or by reputation, and they formed tight-knit cliques that were often difficult to break into. The elites filled a disproportionate number of political positions and were mostly the ones elected to Congress. They may have bickered over various issues, but they all shared a similar understanding of the characteristics they believed made for good military leaders. As they saw it, zealousness, courage, authority, refinement, integrity, and self-possession were as important as previous military experience in choosing generals. Not surprisingly, when the Revolutionary War began, congressmen looked within their social circles for men with the proper character to serve as generals. Relying on personal knowledge and the recommendations of trusted colleagues was undoubtedly the most practical and easiest way to go about identifying generals under the circumstances, but it did not always produce competent military leadership. Moreover, by limiting their search to their own thin stratum of society, they overlooked plenty of people with military acumen who might have made good generals had they possessed the proper connections and pedigrees to attract Congress's attention. As one general shrewdly noted, "The merit of officers is doubtless to be recommended by some person or persons. But alas, how much are even the best of men prone to be biased in judgment through particular friendship or connections. We are apt to overrate the merits of our friends, and perhaps scarcely notice the greater abilities of others."[3]

Moreover, the United States during the Revolutionary War was more a confederation than a truly unified nation. Each state was a distinct political entity, with its own history, traditions, culture, and government. State governments dispatched delegates to Congress to coordinate the national war effort, but the primary loyalty of these congressmen was usually to their state rather than to the country as a whole. Congressmen looked sharply after their state's best interests, often placing them ahead of, or confusing them with, the interests of the United States. This bias included the selection and promotion of generals. Congressmen generally insisted that someone from their state command their men, and worked hard to ensure that their state was adequately—and what "adequately" meant was often a matter of prolonged and ongoing debate—represented in the roster of generals. Moreover, congressmen were usually overworked and underpaid, so turnover and absenteeism were chronic problems among their ranks. Long-winded speeches, petty bickering, big egos, exhaustion, inexperience, provincialism, and obstructionism made it difficult for Congress to formulate and follow a consistent, fair, and workable plan for choosing and promoting its generals. Instead, personnel policy often became a political football subject to logrolling, side deals, horse-trading, favoritism, and compromise. Such legislative tactics no doubt helped keep the war's rickety machinery running, but they were not necessarily conducive to producing quality military leadership.

The Revolutionary War did not take place in a vacuum, but occurred within a broader multipolar Eurocentric world. The conflict's international context presented Congress with both opportunities and challenges in finding quality generals. In 1776–77, dozens of European officers, inspired by the American Revolution's rhetoric and seeking career opportunities, crossed the Atlantic Ocean to offer their services to Congress. By doing so, they expanded the talent pool from which Congress could draw for its generals, especially because some of these men possessed specialized skills such as engineering and cavalry that few Americans had. Separating the good foreign officers from the bad, however, was often difficult. In addition, foreign officers frequently sought compensation for their services with rank. Appointing them generals, though, often angered and offended passed-over American officers who believed that their sacrifices, native birth, and experience merited preference. As a result, Congress struggled to strike a balance between properly rewarding quality European officers with the appropriate rank without alienating their American counterparts. Its attempts to do so sometimes disrupted the American command structure and interfered with objective efforts to select the best available men as generals.

Finally, seniority impeded Congress's efforts to supply the army with good generals. The consensus among congressmen was that, generally speaking, the next available promotion or appointment should go to the most senior officer. There was a logic to this. Doing so was predictable and orderly, so every officer knew where he stood, and where he was likely to stand in the future, in the chain of command. The problem was that seniority rewarded longevity at the expense of initiative and ability. Professional advancement therefore frequently depended not on an officer's job performance, but rather on his place in the pecking order. Seniority therefore made it difficult to put the best men in the most important positions. To complicate things, removing substandard generals to make way for their betters required public, time-consuming, and divisive congressional action that might or might not yield the desired results. Although some congressmen recognized the negative impact of the seniority principle, even competent generals who might have benefited from a more meritorious approach to promotions remained wedded to it, seeing it as a matter of honor. As one general explained:

> Where one officer is promoted over the head of another, if he has spirit enough to be fit for service it lays him under the necessity of quitting it. It is a public intimation that he is unfit for promotion and consequently undeserving his present appointment. For my own part, I would never give any legislative body an opportunity to humiliate me but once. . . . For rank is of such importance in the army and so delicate are the sentiments respecting it that very strong reasons ought to be given for going out of the proper channel, or else it will not be satisfactory to the army in general or to the party in particular.[4]

Congress tried several times to circumvent the rigid seniority principle, but it remained a thorn in the side of the American war effort throughout the conflict.

American leaders never completely surmounted the obstacles to appointing and promoting good generals. Consequently, most American generals during the war demonstrated significant strategic, tactical, and administrative shortcomings. Fortunately for the American war effort, Congress managed eventually to cobble together a personnel policy functional enough to supply a small number of quality generals who helped Washington deliver victory—or anyhow to avoid defeat. These men shared youthfulness, a willingness to disregard convention, support from Washington, and an ability to adapt and learn from their mistakes.

During the Revolutionary War, Congress appointed seventy-three major and brigadier generals to serve in its various departments and field armies. Most of these officers spent at least some time in the main American army under Washington's direct command. Since Washington usually exerted considerable influence over the selection, intellectual development, and career trajectory of these officers, their experiences with him in the main army provide the best means by which to examine Congress's difficulties in choosing and promoting generals. These generals' performances during their time with Washington also reveal whether Congress was justified in entrusting them with their military responsibilities. Considering the disadvantages under which the United States labored during the conflict—matériel and equipment shortages, opposition from loyalists, high-level warmaking inexperience, political decentralization, and so forth—it is surprising that Congress succeeded in providing sufficient military leadership for the fledgling republic to win the war and secure its independence.

CHAPTER 1

Adopting an Army

1775–1776

Congress Selects Its First Generals

By the time the Second Continental Congress convened in Philadelphia on 10 May 1775, Great Britain and its thirteen rebellious North American colonies had been at war for three weeks. Although he was three hundred miles from home, crotchety Massachusetts delegate John Adams had kept close tabs on events unfolding in and around British-occupied Boston. He knew that after the battles at Lexington and Concord, thousands of New England militiamen had flooded onto the hills overlooking Boston to besiege the city's British garrison, and that they could not remain there for long without the necessary leadership and logistical support. Artemas Ward exercised general command over this ad hoc American army on behalf of the Connecticut, Massachusetts, and New Hampshire governments, but Adams had received numerous reports that the soldiers lacked organization, cohesion, and discipline. As far as Adams was concerned, the remedy to this military problem was for Congress to assume control over the army and appoint a commander to lead it. He was, however, adamant that whoever Congress chose for the job, it must do so unanimously for the sake of intercolonial harmony. However, personal and sectional rivalries had prevented any such consensus from emerging. Adams strongly suspected that John Hancock, the president of Congress, wanted the post for himself, if for no other reason than to gratify his ego. Other New England delegates believed that Ward should remain in charge. Southern delegates, for their part, insisted on one of their own for the position, but were divided over who it should be. As May turned into June, Adams grew increasingly frustrated by Congress's inability to take timely action to resolve the question.[1]

Eschewing all subtlety and finesse, Adams finally opted to force the issue. On the morning of 14 June 1775 (or perhaps a day or two beforehand), Adams addressed Congress. He stated that military necessity demanded the establishment of a Continental army under Congress's authority with which to wage the war. It was not necessary, he continued, for Congress to appoint a commander for that army today, but when it did, he believed that there was only one man suited for the job: Virginian George Washington. By way of justification, Adams referenced Washington's military experience, independent fortune, obvious talent, and sterling character.[2]

Adams's speech had its desired effect. On 14 June 1775, Congress decided to create a Continental army under its authority, but without yet naming its commander. Although Adams's endorsement certainly helped, the delegates' familiarity with Washington played an even greater role in making him the front-runner for the job. Backroom canvassing in the following day or two indicated that Washington's detractors were few and far between, and were motivated primarily by political concerns. No one doubted Washington's character or ability, but some questioned the wisdom of placing a Virginian in charge of an army still composed mostly of New Englanders. Widespread support for Washington, however, quickly drowned out these tepid reservations and prevented any organized opposition from forming. In addition to the attributes Adams identified, Washington had impressed his congressional colleagues with his maturity, military knowledge, pedigree, and diligence. Choosing Washington to command the army would also firmly bind powerful Virginia to the patriot cause. The more the congressmen discussed the issue over drinks and dinners, the more obvious his selection appeared. On 15 June, Congress voted unanimously to appoint Washington the commander in chief of both the main American army outside of Boston and of all other American forces raised or to be raised. To ensure military subservience to civil authority, Congress also directed him to obey its orders, the first of which was that he go to Boston to assume command there.[3]

As far as most congressmen were concerned, Washington's response to his selection as commander in chief confirmed their conviction that they had made the right decision. He demonstrated a determination, virtuousness, and modesty that reinforced the regard that the delegates already had for him. In his formal acceptance address, Washington stated,

> Though I am truly sensible of the high honor done me in this appointment, yet I feel great distress, from a consciousness that my abilities and military experience may not be equal to the extensive and important trust. However, as the Congress desire it I will enter upon the momentous duty, and exert every power I possess in their service and for the most support of the glorious cause. I beg they will accept my most cordial thanks for this distinguished testimony of their approbation.[4]

Washington was as ambitious as the next man, if not more so. However, he had learned that a feigned reluctance to accept power and authority went a long way toward securing it. Although Washington's humility and reluctance may have appeared self-serving, he repeated and expanded on it in his private correspondence. For Washington, though, his sense of duty trumped any doubts and reservations he may have had. Refusing Congress's offer would have been dishonorable for a Virginia gentleman such as himself. As he explained to his wife, "It was utterly out of my power to refuse this appointment without exposing my character to such censures as would have reflected dishonor upon myself, and given pain to my friends."[5] Instead, Washington relied on Providence to bridge the gap between the high expectations Congress had of him and those deficiencies in talent and ability he claimed to identify in himself.[6]

Washington's behavior reflected the Virginia upper-class cultural environment in which he was raised. He was born in 1732 in Virginia's northern neck into a well-to-do family whose fortunes took a turn for the worse when his father died eleven years later. His lack of formal education contributed to both his youthful awkwardness and his intense desire to fit in with Virginia's aristocracy. He used the money he made as a young surveyor to fund a voracious appetite for land that continued throughout much of his life. Washington also made the connections necessary for him to begin his ascent up Virginia's socioeconomic ladder. One of his sponsors, Virginia governor Robert Dinwiddie, assigned the twenty-one-year-old Washington the job of leveraging the French out of the Ohio River valley. For all the physical courage and endurance Washington demonstrated in trying to do so, his youthful inexperience and clumsiness led him to surrender his small army to the French at Fort Necessity in southwestern Pennsylvania in July 1754. The following year he served as an aide to British general Edward Braddock and survived the disastrous Battle of the Monongahela, which sparked the Great War for Empire between Britain and France (also known as the Seven Years' War or, in North America, as the French and Indian War). Dinwiddie then placed Washington in charge of Virginia's forces along the colony's western frontier. Although he saw almost no combat, Washington learned a great deal about logistics, personnel management, coping with legislators, and making do with little. He also demonstrated an unbecoming quarrelsomeness and pettiness toward politicians in general and Dinwiddie in particular that he eventually overcame. After accompanying the successful British campaign against Fort Duquesne in 1758, Washington resigned his commission and returned home. His marriage to a wealthy widow, Martha Custis, in 1759, catapulted him to the pinnacle of Virginia society. He settled into a comfortable routine of managing his Mount Vernon plantation, engaging in land speculation, and sitting in the colony's House of Burgesses. Whatever his role, he won the respect of those with whom he interacted. His opposition to the British government's efforts to exert its authority over the colonies earned him election to both Continental Congresses, from which he ascended to lead the nascent American army.

Washington was an impressive and imposing man who embodied everything to which an eighteenth-century Virginia gentleman could aspire. Tall and well proportioned, with blue eyes and a prominent forehead, he moved on foot or horseback with an athletic grace that reflected his active lifestyle. When on duty he usually sported a blue coat, cocked hat, black cockade, and an elegant small sword. His strong constitution permitted him to remain at his post throughout the war when so many other officers periodically succumbed to illness and returned home. No one questioned his physical courage, determination, or persistence. Although invariably polite and gracious, he was distant and formal to almost everyone, exuding a natural gravitas that made intimacy impossible with all but a few. He spoke little, but when he did it was direct and to the point. Despite his natural taciturnity, he had a low-key and understated sense of humor that occasionally bubbled to the surface. He possessed incredible self-control that enabled him to check his ferocious temper and touchiness. It also kept his pugnaciousness and aggressiveness within bounds. Washington was not, however, without his foibles and shortcomings. He was proud, conventional, unimaginative, and slow to admit mistakes. Like so many of his class and time, he valued his honor above all else, and reacted badly to anyone questioning or doubting it. As a result, he harbored grudges long after the original bone of contention had lost its relevance.

These traits marked Washington as a fine—or anyhow a stereotypical—Virginia gentleman, but they were not the wellspring of his extraordinary accomplishments. Washington also possessed deeper and less common qualities that made him indispensable to the American Revolution. As a man of moderate intelligence and limited imagination, Washington never sought to use the revolution to fundamentally alter American society. His primary goal was to terminate British authority over the colonies so the Americans could rule themselves. By restricting the scope of the revolution, Washington helped the country avoid the utopian upheavals and bloodbaths that later brought French, Russian, and other societies incalculable grief. Moreover, Washington's belief in the American cause and Providence's role in achieving it permitted him to withstand the defeats, disappointments, discouragements, and criticisms that plagued the American war effort. Time and time again during the conflict, when confronted with the seemingly inevitable dissolution of his army, he fell back on his faith as his last line of defense. As he put it, "I look upon every dispensation of Providence as designed to answer some valuable purpose, and hope I shall always possess a sufficient degree of fortitude to bear, without murmuring, any stroke which may happen to my person or estate from that quarter."[7]

But there was more to it than that. Although Washington personified the revolution, he never confused embodiment with essence. Instead, he saw himself as a cog, albeit a big and important one, in the revolution machinery. He demonstrated this through his altruism, modesty, and honesty. During the war he lived simply in the field with his army, refrained from abusing his powers, and deferred to Congress even when doing otherwise might have been more expedient. Perhaps most importantly, Washington had an indefinable quality that inspired tremendous loyalty from almost everyone around him. He intentionally set himself apart from the rank and file, but his willingness to share in their sufferings and his sincere commitment to their collective well-being won their respect and devotion. His obvious selflessness also gained support from civilians of all stations. As one admirer put it, "Our general [Washington] is a man truly made for this revolution, which could not succeed without him."[8] Indeed, Washington served as the glue that bound together the American people, their leaders, and their cause.[9]

As commander in chief, managing his subordinate generals was one of Washington's most important tasks. He needed to mold them into a tough and responsive team if he hoped to defeat the British army. However, he soon discovered that this was more easily said than done. For one thing, Congress circumscribed his authority over them. Congress not only appointed and promoted the generals but also insisted on a role in determining their assignments, redressing their grievances, disciplining them, and relieving them of their commands. Moreover, most of the generals lacked high-level military experience at the war's start and were therefore unaccustomed to adhering to the chain of command, getting permission, and unquestioningly obeying orders. Indeed, these independent-minded local leaders were more familiar with giving directions and following their own inclinations. Like Washington, they were inordinately sensitive to their honor and often placed satisfying it ahead of military necessity. Finally, they sometimes saw each other as rivals to be bested rather than as brothers in arms. These men were undoubtedly committed to the American cause, but their tendency to conflate patriotism with self-interest was one more burden Washington and Congress had to bear throughout the war.

After Congress appointed Washington commander in chief, its members hurried to assure their constituents of the wisdom of their decision. Doing so not only comforted an anxious public but also reinforced the delegates' conviction that they had made the right choice. As one congressman explained:

> He [Washington] is a gentleman highly esteemed for his military and other accomplishments to that important command. We esteem him well adapted to

> please a New England army and much better suited to the temper and genius of our people than any other gentlemen not brought up in that part of the country. We have no doubt but that he will render himself very agreeable and acceptable to all. His appointment will tend to keep up the union and more strongly cement the southern with the northern colonies, and serve to the removing all jealousies [in an] army composed principally of New Englanders.[10]

Such guarantees had their desired effect. Congress's unanimous and enthusiastic support did much to smooth the way for Washington to assume command of his new army. As one Massachusettsan put it, "We hear General Washington is expected very soon. Almost every tongue is applauding the wisdom of the appointment, and almost every arm is expanded to receive him."[11] Indeed, criticism of Washington's selection was practically nonexistent. Although Washington was grateful for all the confidence expressed in him, he now had to live up to the enormous expectations everyone placed in him.[12]

As things turned out, choosing Washington as commander in chief was one of the easier military decisions Congress made that summer. Washington clearly could not run the new Continental army singlehandedly, so Congress selected subordinate generals to assist him. Although Congress originally intended to assign two major generals, it upped the number to four on 19 June. However, picking these men introduced Congress to some thorny issues that haunted its personnel policies for the duration of the conflict. Reconciling colonial parochialism, political disputes, and petty personal quarrels with military necessity proved so time-consuming and difficult that John Adams wrote, "I have never, in all my lifetime, suffered more anxiety than in the conduct of this business. The choice of officers, and their pay, have given me great distress."[13]

Charles Lee was the leading and most obvious candidate for a major generalship. The son of an army officer, Lee was born in Cheshire, England, in 1732, and educated in Switzerland. There he not only learned the classics and Shakespeare but also acquired a working knowledge of French, Greek, Latin, and Italian. He purchased a commission with his father's help and joined the British army in 1744. During the Great War for Empire, he fought at the Battle of the Monongahela and was later severely wounded during the failed British assault on Fort Ticonderoga in 1758. After recuperating in England, he was sent to Portugal and played an important role in stopping the Spanish invasion at the Battle of Vila Velha in 1762. He was involuntarily retired as a lieutenant colonel on half pay at the end of the conflict and subsequently made his way to Poland and served as an aide to King Stanislaus II. From there he sailed to Virginia in 1773, where he became a vocal and ardent patriot. His zealousness, commitment, and high-level military experience attracted the support of Washington and other southern congressmen, who in turn persuaded the Massachusetts delegation to back him. Unfortunately for Lee, though, John Adams and several New England congressmen argued persuasively that appointing Lee the senior major general would be unfair to Artemas Ward, who was still commanding the army outside of Boston. Although Adams had received reports questioning Ward's competence, he overlooked them in order to keep a Massachusetts officer at the top of the chain of command. As a result, Congress voted to make Ward the first major general, followed by Lee.[14]

Unlike the geriatric Ward, Lee played a major role in the Revolutionary War. Tall, slender, and with a nose so large that soldiers made fun of it, Lee was perhaps the Continental army's most eccentric officer. He traveled everywhere with a small pack of dogs, whose company he claimed to prefer to that of people. He was so outspoken, sardonic, critical, contemptuous, and quarrelsome that he accumulated enemies as a matter of course. Indeed, during the Great War for Empire, the Mohawks nicknamed him Ounewaterika, or "Boiling Water," for his tempestuousness. In an era that valued outward piety, discretion, and fashion, Lee was well known for his blasphemousness and slovenliness. He rarely smiled or laughed but instead projected a morose cynicism that often sucked the energy and initiative right out of a room. Despite these rather formidable character deficiencies, people frequently found his peculiar mannerisms endearing, at least at first, because they indicated a disarming authenticity. This, combined with his military reputation and his strident support for the patriot cause, made him a very popular man at the war's start. As Samuel Adams put it, "I am more and more satisfied in the appointment of General Lee. He is certainly an able officer and I think deeply embarked in the American cause."[15] Unhappily for Lee, though, this adulation was contingent on a selflessness and acumen that in the end was more apparent than real. Without them, he came across as just another disagreeable, selfish, and arrogant blowhard. Congress should have suspected as much when Lee insisted before he accepted his commission that it indemnify him for any loss of property he incurred. Lee himself admitted to another officer that his unexpected willingness to subordinate himself to Ward was motivated partly to bank credit with Congress that he could cash in at the right opportunity.[16]

Intercolonial politics played an even greater role in Congress's choice of the last two major generals. The third slot went to Philip Schuyler, a well-connected and wealthy New Yorker, Great War for Empire veteran, and current congressional delegate. New York was not only strategically located, but its large loyalist population called into question its commitment to the patriot cause. Congress hoped that Schuyler would take command of Continental forces within his colony and rally its inhabitants to the right side. Because Connecticut had provided a disproportionate number of troops to the army outside of Boston, its delegation insisted that one of its officers receive the last major generalship. Congress obliged by appointing Israel Putnam. Recent news of Putnam's role in a successful expedition to Noddle's Island in Boston Harbor on 27–28 May augmented his reputation as a generous, simple, and modest fighting man. Although Connecticut congressmen warned that Putnam's selection would anger two other Connecticut officers with more seniority in the colony's militia who were also serving outside Boston, Congress unanimously opted for Putnam anyway.[17]

After finishing its appointing of major generals on 17 June, Congress engaged in a round of backslapping for a job it considered well done. John Adams, for example, wrote, "Our army will have a group of officers, equal to any service."[18] Such overt self-assuredness, though, obscured murmurings of dissatisfaction among some observers in and out of Congress. John Hancock, for instance, expressed doubts about Putnam's suitability for his rank, while others wondered if Ward was really up to his responsibilities. Although support in Congress for Lee remained strong, one Marylander cautioned, "I wish Lee had not been appointed a general, I do not like his contradicting odd temper."[19] Such forebodings contained more than an element of truth.[20]

Congress's debate over the selection of brigadier generals was more contentious. It had to decide not only the number of brigadiers to appoint but also their names, home colonies, and seniority. Outside lobbying, colonial loyalties, and political considerations once again competed with military requirements in the deliberations. In the end, Congress settled on eight brigadiers, along with an adjutant general of the same rank, and doled them out in proportion to the number of troops each colony had deployed around Boston. This arrangement benefited the New England colonies in general and Massachusetts in particular. Since most congressmen had little knowledge of people outside their particular colonies, they deferred to the recommendations made by colonial delegations. Those colonial delegations, for their part, usually nominated prominent men they knew with military experience. Ranking the designated brigadiers by seniority involved a good bit of give and take, which in retrospect had little discernible rhyme or reason. At any rate, on 22 June Congress chose eight brigadiers, in order of seniority: Seth Pomeroy (Massachusetts), Richard Montgomery (New York), David Wooster (Connecticut), William Heath (Massachusetts), Joseph Spencer (Connecticut), John Thomas (Massachusetts), John Sullivan (New Hampshire), and Nathanael Greene (Rhode Island). As for the adjutant general, that job went to Horatio Gates, an English-born Virginian.[21]

On 23 June Washington, Lee, Gates, and various aides and servants departed for Massachusetts to join the army besieging Boston. A good many congressmen, conscious of the event's historical significance, joined a martial band and some

Philadelphia militia in seeing them off. Although it is possible to criticize the manner in which Congress chose its first batch of generals, it is hard to see how it could have gone about the process much differently. Logrolling, lobbying, parochialism, and compromise are part and parcel of any legislative body, so it is hardly surprising that these factors played a role in Congress's deliberations. Besides, Congress's selections seemed reasonable and astute. All thirteen of the generals Congress appointed were well regarded within their colonies, and ten had prior military experience in the Great War for Empire. Their average age was forty-eight. New England's overrepresentation reflected the region's substantial and disproportionate contribution to the war effort so far. For a variety of reasons, only a few of these men made much of a mark in the Revolutionary War. Ironically, with the exception of Washington, the two most important generals were also the youngest and most militarily inexperienced: John Sullivan and Nathanael Greene. No sooner had Congress's decisions about Washington's subordinate generals become public than some people began criticizing the men for various reasons. Congress, however, opted to wait until it had heard from Washington before it considered any adjustments.[22]

The Siege of Boston

Washington and his companions arrived at Cambridge, Massachusetts, across the Charles River from Boston, on 2 July. By then the American siege of the British garrison in the city had lasted more than two months. The British had driven the Americans off Charlestown Peninsula at the bloody Battle of Bunker Hill on 17 June but had little to show for their victory except for more than a thousand casualties. Despite the Americans' surprisingly stalwart performance at Bunker Hill, Washington quickly realized that he had his work cut out for him. Ward bequeathed to him an army hardly worthy of the name. The American soldiers overlooking Boston lacked supplies, equipment, weapons, training, and discipline. There was not enough gunpowder to fight a major engagement, the sick list was growing, and units were deployed in haphazard fashion. There were no engineers or artillerymen. Each colonial contingent had its own way of doing things, most of which were inefficient and even counterproductive. Indeed, sometimes the men hated each other as much as they hated the British. Soon after he arrived, for example, Washington almost singlehandedly broke up a large-scale riot between Virginia riflemen and New England militia. The upshot was that the American soldiers overlooking Boston were closer to an unruly mob than an organized fighting force.[23]

Washington immediately set to work to bring order out of the chaos. He got out into the field each day to inspect the troops and familiarize himself with the local geography and issued a steady stream of orders on everything

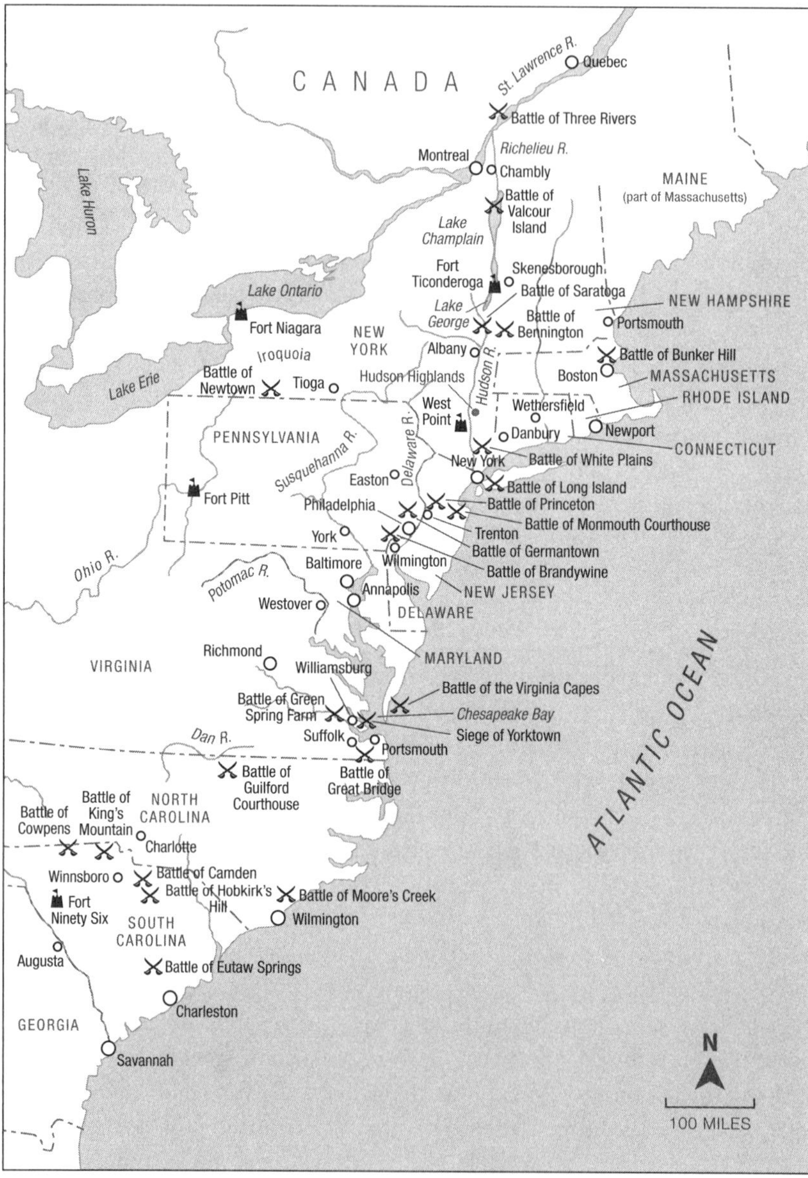

Eastern United States. *Map by Ken Arbogast-Wilson, WTW Design Group.*

from camp sanitation to discipline to rations. As Washington's authority took hold, the situation improved—at least enough for the army to maintain itself. However, Washington understood that an extant army was merely preliminary to the larger goal of defeating the British. Aggressive by nature, Washington was increasingly frustrated by his inability to drive the British out of Boston. The city was practically an island, so successfully assailing it required complicated amphibious operations that Washington's generals insisted were beyond the capability of the American army. The British, for their part, seemed content to remain inert in their stronghold. As the weeks turned into months, Washington could only watch and wait for some creative opportunity to strike a telling blow. Fortunately, Washington's credibility bought him time from Congress and the public. Congress's assurances and his own impressive character had gained him the confidence of the army and the local citizenry. As one person noted to a congressional friend, "I am much pleased with General Washington. He fully answers the character you have given of him."[24]

Washington complained that organizing his new army was his most difficult task. This included accommodating his generals, most of whom he knew only by reputation until he arrived in Massachusetts. As an upper-class Virginian with strongly held views on propriety and decorum, Washington wanted to do everything he could within the bounds of military prudence to gratify his generals' wants and needs. He believed that such an attitude would preserve harmony within the officer corps and maintain morale. However, outside of Boston Washington discovered that this was no easy task. Generals were often inordinately sensitive to questions of personal honor and sometimes seemed more interested in protecting it than in sacrificing for the American cause. Washington could have asked Congress to either relieve or otherwise punish those generals for placing honor above the war effort, but he showed little inclination to do so. For one thing, he was initially uncertain of his authority and his relationship with Congress on such matters. For another, he often sympathized with his generals' desire to safeguard their honor and went out of his way to oblige them. Doing so, however, did not always make the army more effective.[25]

Indeed, throughout the war both Washington and Congress grappled with the role of honor and its proper place in the officer corps. Like so many cultural mores, honor was an amorphous term more easily understood than defined and explained. It extended beyond mere reputation. Honor enabled these men to differentiate themselves from their social inferiors and reaffirmed their ties to their group. The problem was that many officers saw it in zero-sum terms, so that one person's preferment came at the expense of the honor of those passed over. Honor was therefore not dependent solely on one's actions and character but was also at the mercy of events beyond one's control. As an exclusivist group, officers took their honor seriously and zealously protected it from challenges real and imagined. They often placed it above the war effort, arguing that losing it made it impossible for them to serve the country effectively. Considering these realities, it was unsurprising that some congressmen viewed honor as an obstacle to the successful prosecution of the war. Moreover, some believed that it contradicted the republican ideals on which the revolution was based. John Adams explained, "This delicate point of honor, which is really one of the most putrid corruptions of absolute monarchy, I mean the honor of maintaining a rank superior to abler men, I mean the honor of preferring a single step of promotion to the service of the public, must be bridled. It is incompatible with republican principles."[26] Regardless of the truth of such sentiments, neither Washington nor Congress could dismiss honor's impact. They instead sought to accommodate and work around it. As one congressman put it, "What shall we say of this phantom *honor* the soldier's deity and object of worship. I would not have a soldier devoid of it, but I think it a plant better suited for the gardens of monarchy, than those of a republic."[27]

Washington faced his first personnel emergency right after he arrived in Cambridge. Connecticut's congressional delegation had warned that appointing Israel Putnam a major general would anger Brig. Gens. Joseph Spencer and David Wooster, each of whom outranked Putnam in the Connecticut militia. Sure enough, both officers were outraged to learn that Congress had promoted Putnam over their heads. Wooster swallowed his disappointment, remained on duty, and was soon sent to New York City to bolster its defenses. Spencer, on the other hand, left for home without taking leave of or talking with Washington. He bitterly denounced Congress's decision and appealed to the Connecticut assembly, where his good reputation guaranteed him a sympathetic hearing. Although the sixty-year-old Spencer had served in King George's War and the Great War for Empire, he was a lawyer by trade, so he understood the importance of string-pulling and lobbying. Connecticut governor Jonathan Trumbull, however, persuaded Spencer to return to the army and serve under Putnam. In return for Spencer's concession, Trumbull on 13 July wrote to Washington to suggest splitting the Connecticut troops between Putnam and Spencer. Washington responded that there was not much he could do about Congress's arrangements of its generals, but he promised to look into the matter. Despite his accommodating tone, Washington thereafter never trusted or respected Spencer for abandoning his post. When Congress learned the details of the incident, it initially wanted to make an example of Spencer by dismissing him from the Continental army, but the Connecticut delegation dissuaded it from acting. So Spencer stayed in the army, albeit with reduced credibility and a black mark on his record.[28]

There was a similar problem among the Massachusetts generals. The seniormost brigadier, Seth Pomeroy, was a sixty-nine-year-old gunsmith who had served in both King George's War and the Great War for Empire. He joined the American army outside of Boston after Lexington and Concord and fought bravely at Bunker Hill. Soon after, however, Pomeroy left for home after quarreling with the Massachusetts colonial government over his militia rank. Washington therefore arrived at Cambridge with a commission for a man who was not around to accept or decline it. Although Washington was unsure what do to, some Massachusetts officials saw Pomeroy's departure as an opportunity to advance John Thomas. As far as they were concerned, Massachusetts's congressional delegation had erred in subordinating Thomas to Pomeroy and William Heath. Thomas was a fifty-year-old doctor who had, like Pomeroy, participated in King George's War and the Great War for Empire. He had built a reputation in Massachusetts as a judicious, steady, and courageous man with the common touch. People favorably contrasted his handling of his troops outside Boston with Ward's more lackluster performance. By the time Washington assumed command, a consensus had emerged among Massachusetts's leaders that Thomas deserved to be the colony's top brigadier.

Like Spencer, Thomas had his pride and resented that Congress had given Pomeroy and Heath seniority over him. Indeed, he announced his intention to resign his commission. Washington, however, had heard good things about Thomas and sympathized with his grievance, so he urged him to stay on for his country's sake—at least until Congress had an opportunity to review the issue. Although Thomas submitted his resignation, he agreed to remain in camp and kept his gripes to himself. In the end, Congress on 19 July voted to replace Pomeroy with Thomas on the Continental army's roster as the senior brigadier. Thomas withdrew his resignation when he got the news and continued with the army. Thomas's elevation offended the third Massachusetts general, William Heath, but Massachusetts officials persuaded Heath to set aside his pride on this particular matter. Thomas's shenanigans did not hurt his standing with Washington, whose respect for Thomas continued throughout the siege of Boston.[29]

Pomeroy's recusal left an opening in the roster of brigadiers that Washington wanted filled as soon as possible. To replace Pomeroy, Washington on 31 August suggested to Congress one of two officers. The first was John Armstrong, a highly respected Irish-born Pennsylvanian with whom Washington had served in the Great War for Empire. Washington lauded his courage, spirit, and extensive military experience. Although Armstrong was at fifty-seven somewhat old for a combat post, no one questioned his valor, piety, and virtue. Armstrong was obviously Washington's favorite, but, perhaps because some felt that Pomeroy should be replaced by another Massachusettsan, he also put forth Col. Joseph Frye's name. Frye was a sixty-three-year-old farmer, merchant, speculator, surveyor, and community leader, as well as a veteran of King George's War and the Great War for Empire. During the latter conflict, Frye had survived the massacre following the British surrender of Fort William Henry. Washington noted Frye's good reputation but then undercut his own recommendation by commenting that Frye had done nothing during the siege of Boston to set himself apart from other officers. Congress's efforts in September to determine Pomeroy's successor initially failed because both Armstrong and Frye had strong supporters. In December a frustrated Washington complained to Congress that he still needed a brigadier to command one of his brigades. He did not now care who it was, he said, as long as he had someone to do the job. Thus prodded, Congress in January 1776 opted to promote the inoffensive Frye. In all likelihood Congress figured that, unlike Armstrong, Frye was already on hand outside Boston and could be employed immediately.[30]

The war continued while Washington and Congress haggled over generals. Although the American army besieging Boston saw little combat with its British counterpart penned in the city, Washington still had plenty to do. Supplying, equipping, training, and especially recruiting troops was a constant struggle. Indeed, the army remained a work in progress, and Washington was, like everyone else, figuring out his job as he went along. For example, he learned a valuable lesson about discretion when one of his letters disparaging New England soldiers became public. In July Washington organized his army into three divisions, each of which was commanded by a major general (Ward, Lee, and Putnam) and contained two brigades. Brigadiers (Greene, Heath, Spencer, Sullivan, Thomas, and eventually Frye) led the six brigades, most of which contained soldiers from one specific colony. This organization, however, implied a consistency among the rank and file that did not really exist because troops came and went with maddeningly unpredictable regularity.[31]

Henry Knox was among the more welcome additions to the American army that summer. Born in Boston in 1750, Knox apprenticed for a bookstore owner before opening up his own shop at age twenty-one. John Adams, Samuel Adams, and Nathanael Greene were among those who frequented his establishment. Knox developed an interest in all things military, read everything he could on the subject, and joined a militia artillery company. Although he married a woman from a loyalist family in 1774, Knox remained a stalwart patriot. He and his wife slipped out of Boston after Lexington and Concord, and Knox impressed first William Heath and then Washington with his understanding of emplacements. Heath urged Knox to join the army and use his knowledge to assist its fledging and almost gunless artillery corps. Congress had already selected Col. Richard Gridley as both the army's chief engineer and its artillery commander, but Gridley proved too old and indolent for his responsibilities. Indeed, he caused so much dissension that Washington worried that the nascent artillery corps would collapse if he remained at its head. In November, Washington removed the artillery from Gridley's portfolio and recommended Knox to Congress as his replacement. John Adams lobbied on Knox's behalf, and on 17 November Congress appointed Knox a colonel and put him in charge of the artillery corps.[32]

In recommending Knox, Washington demonstrated a hitherto undetected ability to recognize talented people and place them in positions of responsibility. Of course, it was hard to miss the big, brawny, and stout Knox. Despite his impressive girth, he was an energetic man with a booming voice who moved like a ship plying the ocean. He was also one of the army's most personable officers. Urbane, gregarious, and charming, Knox made and kept friends easily. Moreover, he combined this amiability with a strong sense of loyalty, good judgment, physical courage, and a first-rate intellect. His common sense, can-do attitude, and resourcefulness enabled him to maintain the efficiency of the artillery corps when everything else in the army was falling apart. His very presence inspired confidence. On the flipside of his character, Knox's touchiness about honor and rank got him into trouble on more than one occasion during the war. His habit of wrapping a handkerchief around his left hand to obscure two missing fingers, the result of a firearms accident, also bespoke an underlying self-consciousness not immediately apparent. On the whole, though, it is hard to see how Washington and Congress could have made a better choice for the army's artillery chief. Washington certainly saw it this way and came to view Knox as almost irreplaceable, remarking more than a year later, "General Knox who has deservedly acquired the character of one of the most valuable officers in the service, and who combating almost innumerable difficulties in the department he fills, has placed the artillery upon a footing, that does him the greatest honor."[33]

Knox soon proved his value. The previous May American troops led by Ethan Allen and Benedict Arnold had seized Fort Ticonderoga in northern New York from its small and surprised British garrison. Among the captured booty were dozens of cannons of various shapes and sizes, enough to equip an army. Washington and Knox figured that the best way to turn the artillery corps into a truly potent weapon capable of inflicting damage on the British was to procure those cannons. Although hauling the heavy and cumbersome artillery pieces to Boston promised to be an arduous chore, Knox convinced Washington that it could be done. Knox reached Ticonderoga on 5 December after a four-day trip and immediately got to work. He selected about sixty of the best pieces—iron and brass cannons, cohorns, mortars, and a howitzer—lugged them on board flat-bottomed scows, sailed them down Lake George, and then moved them overland to Albany. From there he placed them on horse- and oxen-drawn sleds for the cross-country trek through eastern New York and Massachusetts. Each day brought new problems for Knox to tackle: retrieving a cannon that fell through the Hudson River ice, waiting for and then pushing through heavy snows, traversing rutted and muddy roads, procuring sufficient manpower, and locating enough ropes and saddles and other equipment. Through it all, Knox displayed plenty of ingenuity, persistence, and determination. It took him fifty-six days to pull the cannons three hundred miles, but he finally entered Cambridge on 24 January 1776. With that, he not only gave his artillery corps the wherewithal to do its job but also provided Washington with the lever he needed to pry the British out of Boston. It was a remarkable achievement, and one for which Knox deserved the bulk of the credit.

After Knox returned with his guns, Washington proposed assailing the British garrison in Boston across the ice, but his generals dissuaded him from such a risky undertaking. They instead recommended that the Americans seize the hitherto unoccupied Dorchester Heights. Knox's new cannons, if placed there, would render British occupation of Boston untenable. Doing so successfully, however, required the Americans to quickly deploy the cannons and fortify the heights before the British could react. Because the ground was too frozen for digging earthworks, Washington decided that the Americans should bring their fortifications with them by preparing hay bales, gabions (containers filled with dirt and rocks), and fascines (bundles of sticks bound together) and dragging them up to the heights in oxcarts. On the night of 4–5 March 1776, John Thomas led 1,200 men and their ready-made defenses onto Dorchester Heights. The next morning the British were shocked to discover well-protected cannons pointed down at them. The British had already concluded that Boston was a strategic cul-de-sac not worth holding, but Washington's masterstroke accelerated their preparations to evacuate the city. It took them almost two weeks to get out, during which time Washington refrained from interfering with his artillery. The last redcoats left town on 17 March, thus ending two years of British military occupation.

Boston was the American Revolution's birthplace and heart, so its liberation was something worth celebrating. Washington was overjoyed and relieved by his triumph, which he attributed somewhat inaccurately to the occupation of Dorchester Heights. Indeed, he had good reason to be thankful for the manner in which the siege was conducted. The eight months of minimal combat gave him the opportunity to acclimate himself to his new position without excessive enemy interference. He took charge of a conglomeration of men gathered outside Boston and kept them together until the British left town. In the Great War for Empire, he had commanded hundreds of men, but now he was figuring out how to supply, equip, and arm thousands. Moreover, he was learning to exercise his authority in a decentralized society with uncertain and plastic rules. If he had not exactly created an army by conventional eighteenth-century standards, he had built an organized armed force capable of resisting British power. The public was happy to give Washington credit for both the victory at Boston and the circumstances that made it possible. One person wrote, "His conduct has met with universal approbation, and has gained him the highest applause."[34] Unfortunately for the American cause, these successes fed expectations of Washington that he was unable to fulfill in the following months.[35]

Because there was not much combat during the siege, Washington had little opportunity to see and evaluate his generals in action. However, he could and did form judgments about them based on their ability to perform their housekeeping duties during the army's eight months outside Boston. He found that his major generals were a mixed bag. Like almost everyone else, he maintained his high opinion of Charles Lee. Despite his quirks, Lee's self-confidence and expertise were especially welcome to the large number of inexperienced officers looking for guidance and reassurance. Indeed, Washington thought so much of Lee that he used him as a roving troubleshooter that winter, sending him first to Rhode Island and then to New York City to inspect defenses and offer suggestions. As for Putnam, Washington viewed him as a valuable man and fine executive. It was his predecessor and second-in-command, Artemas Ward, who concerned Washington the most. Ward's health broke down that autumn, and he never really regained it. Ward's inclination was to resign for the good of the cause, but he hesitated to do so because, he said, his officers urged him to remain on duty. Ward's increasing passivity and lethargy did not impress Washington, who wanted him gone and was greatly relieved when Ward finally resigned his commission in April 1776.[36]

Washington was also of two minds about his brigadiers. Spencer did little during the siege to redeem himself in Washington's eyes. Indeed, Washington at one point chastised Spencer for forwarding a petition from some of his officers, calling it unmilitary and detrimental to discipline. Although it is unclear why, Washington was unimpressed with Massachusetts's William Heath too. It is likely, though, that Washington recognized that the army would need more than Heath's plodding brand of mediocrity to win the war. Finally, Washington found minimal value in Joseph Frye, about whom he had never felt much enthusiasm. Frye was, like Ward, increasingly ill, and Washington complained that he shut himself up in his headquarters and did little but fret about his health. To his credit, Frye recognized that he could not contribute much to the army and submitted his resignation after the British evacuated Boston. Washington snidely noted, however, that Frye asked to stay on until April so he could receive three full months' pay as a general.[37]

Washington was more positive about his three remaining brigadiers. Although he admitted John Sullivan's vanity, touchiness, and grandiosity, he also appreciated the New Hampshirite's judgment, energy, and ability. Washington praised Sullivan's New Hampshire troops as among the best in the army. Washington was more vocal and unequivocal in his praise of John Thomas. Unlike Spencer, Thomas had stayed in camp and kept his grievances in house during his tiff with Congress over his rank. Throughout the Boston siege, Washington saw nothing to contradict Thomas's reputation as a brave, capable, and stout-hearted officer well respected by his men. He demonstrated his value by leading the American troops onto Dorchester Heights. Considering his track record, positive standing with Congress, and—not least—his seniority, it was unsurprising that Washington recommended Thomas's promotion to major general in early March.[38]

Of all his brigadiers, the one Washington spilled the least amount of ink discussing during the Boston siege was also the one who became his most important, trusted, and effective officer: Nathanael Greene. Greene was little Rhode Island's contribution to the original roster of Continental army generals. Born in 1742 to devout middle-class Quaker parents, Greene read voraciously and widely as a youth before entering the family's iron foundry business. The Quakers expelled him because of his interest in military science, but he remained sufficiently popular to get elected several times to the Rhode Island General Assembly. Although a slight limp almost prevented him from serving in a local militia company, his military knowledge and familiarity within the assembly secured him a major generalship in the colony's militia. Rhode Island's congressional delegation then successfully nominated him as the colony's brigadier in the new Continental army. He missed Bunker Hill but served in the Boston area for the remainder of the siege. There he earned almost everyone's respect with his energy, cheerfulness, and diligence, despite a bout of illness that kept him housebound for more than two weeks in January and February. Washington was among those impressed. Indeed, Washington saw something in Greene, something that did not become fully evident until several years later. As one of Washington's aides explained a few months after the siege ended, "You have a very just idea of Greene's importance. He is, beyond a doubt, a first rate military genius, and one in whose opinions the general [Washington] places the utmost confidence."[39] Washington started to view Greene not only as his right-hand man but also as an heir apparent. This was so obvious that Washington often refrained from giving Greene the kind of praise and credit he ladled on others out of fear of appearing too partial toward him.

Greene was a tall, somewhat corpulent man with a full and florid face. Mild-mannered, modest, and easygoing, he was hard not to like. In combat he was cool under fire and clear in his thinking. He had a habit of rubbing his upper lip roughly with his forefinger when animated or absorbed in thought. His industriousness, business background, and meticulousness made him a good administrator and differentiated him from so many of his colleagues. Although he never intended to become a soldier, he believed it was his duty to fight for American rights and was convinced that the justness of the cause would compensate for shortcomings in the American war effort. He saw Washington as the personification of that cause and was so completely devoted to him as to sometimes appear sycophantic. Indeed, he named his first son after the commander in chief. Greene was of course not without his faults. He was so well aware of his limitations that he sometimes became overly cautious. He also possessed the usual touchiness about rank and seniority that plagued the American officer corps during the conflict. As time went on, he developed a jaded, negative, and stereotypical view of politicians that often did not serve him well in his dealings with them. He could also be self-pitying and needy, requiring reassurance from Washington of his value. The key to Greene's success, however, was his ability to grow in and adapt to his increasing responsibilities. As time went on, his clear-headedness, deftness, and uncanny ability to balance risk with gain made him one of the great strategists in American military history.[40]

Although Washington had reason to be pleased with the siege of Boston's outcome, the fact was that his generals remained military ciphers. Washington may have formed impressions of them based on their abilities to manage their units on a day-to-day basis, but none of them—or Washington, for that matter—had yet been tested in open battle with the British army. Until they were, Washington's evaluations of his generals remained largely speculative.

An Expanding War

The Revolutionary War may have started in Boston, but it soon spread throughout the Thirteen Colonies and beyond. Colonists had to cope with British incursions, local loyalist uprisings, and American Indian raids from New Hampshire to Georgia. Although militias usually provided the first line of defense against such dangers, colonial leaders frequently called on Congress and the Continental army to repel more serious threats. However, Washington generally preferred to keep his army concentrated and resisted efforts to dissipate his limited resources. Despite Washington's desires, Congress often tapped his army for both troops and generals to conduct campaigns against British, loyalist, and American Indian forces outside the main army's theater of operations. Washington's army, in short, served as both a pool and training ground for generals dispatched elsewhere. On the one hand, this deprived Washington of talented generals and made it difficult for him to establish a coherent, effective, and stable command team. On the other hand, it gave him the opportunity to influence Congress's personnel decisions and to transfer substandard generals to less important areas where their limited skills could do less harm to the war effort. Either way, it was a constant distraction for the beleaguered commander in chief.

While Washington organized his army outside of Boston, Congress in June 1775 authorized a two-pronged invasion of British-held Canada. One prong of about 1,200 soldiers led by Philip Schuyler pushed northward from Crown Point, New York, up Lake Champlain toward Montreal. Schuyler's health, never good, broke down, so his energetic second-in-command, Brig. Gen. Richard Montgomery, took over the army while Schuyler returned to Albany to oversee his administrative responsibilities. Montgomery's troops seized Fort St. Johns on the Richelieu River after an exhausting two-month siege and then occupied Montreal on 13 November 1775. Meanwhile, a second force of about a thousand men under Col. Benedict Arnold left Cambridge on 13 September. After an epic march through the Maine wilderness where they endured hunger and hardship, Arnold and his remaining six hundred soldiers arrived opposite Quebec on 8 November. These accomplishments netted both officers promotions from an impressed Congress—Montgomery to major general in December and Arnold to brigadier the following month. By the time Congress elevated Arnold, however, the campaign had taken a turn for the worse. Montgomery brought a detachment of 350 troops downstream to join Arnold, and their combined force attempted to storm Quebec on 31 December. The attack failed miserably. Montgomery fell in the first minutes of the battle, and Arnold took a bullet in the leg. More than 450 other Americans were killed, wounded, or captured, as opposed to only around twenty British casualties. Despite his injury, Arnold rallied the survivors and hovered outside the city until spring.

When Schuyler fell ill, Congress dispatched Connecticut's Brig. Gen. David Wooster to northern New York to help out. The sixty-four-year-old Wooster had as much military experience as any of the original American generals. He fought so bravely as a militia captain in the colonial/British assault on the French fortress of Louisbourg during King George's War that he was given a commission in the British army. During the Great War for Empire, he led a Connecticut regiment through some of the conflict's heaviest combat. As the colonial relationship with Britain collapsed, Wooster was among the first to recognize Fort Ticonderoga's value and helped set in motion efforts to seize the place. Congress's decision to appoint Israel Putnam a major general offended Wooster, but he remained on duty anyway. He started out the war in New York City and then moved northward to join Montgomery's invasion of Canada. Congress initially approved of his actions there, in part because Montgomery's sensitivity to Wooster's dignity and feelings fostered a good relationship between the two men.

Wooster, who remained behind in Montreal after Montgomery went downstream to reinforce Arnold, therefore became the highest-ranking American officer in Canada upon Montgomery's death at Quebec. Unfortunately, Wooster was not up to the challenge of maintaining and supplying the American army in Canada that winter. Food and equipment shortages, discipline problems, and a smallpox epidemic eroded the army's efficiency. It is hard to see how anyone could have done much better with the limited resources available, but Wooster's abrasive personality exacerbated his difficulties. He alienated Canadians in Montreal with his heavy-handed treatment, costing the Americans valuable local support. His quarrels extended to the officer corps as well, including Schuyler and Arnold. Small wonder that Wooster wrote:

> You observe very justly that every piece of duty is undertaken and executed with a strange indifference that too truly has been the case, ever since I have been here, indeed it has been an arduous task even to keep the troops upon the ground and I have hardly been able to have a single order properly executed, almost every day discovers new traitors even in our bosoms who endeavor to frustrate all our designs.[41]

A visiting congressional delegation put the onus of failure on Wooster and communicated as much to Congress. Although some New Englanders were more inclined to blame Schuyler, the majority of congressmen became convinced that whatever role Wooster was to play in Canada, it should not be in the top spot.[42]

The Canadian campaign and growing evidence of British preparations to crush the American rebellion once and for all persuaded Congress to reorganize and intensify the American war effort. On 4 November 1775 Congress agreed with Washington's recommendation to increase the Continental army to twenty-six regiments containing around twenty thousand men. The following February, Congress also created two new geographic departments: the Middle (Delaware, Maryland, New Jersey, New York, and Pennsylvania) and the Southern (Georgia, North Carolina, South Carolina, and Virginia). Later, in May, Congress added an Eastern Department to encompass the New England colonies. Administering these new departments and commanding these new soldiers obviously required more generals. Congress figured that each department needed a major general in charge and a couple brigadiers to help, except for the Southern Department, which was given two additional brigadiers because of its size and vulnerability to British attack. During several weeks of wrangling, Congress considered character, seniority, colonial/state origins, and merit in making its appointments. On 1 March Congress promoted six men to brigadiers, in order of seniority: John Armstrong (Pennsylvania), William Thompson (Pennsylvania), Andrew Lewis (Virginia), James Moore (North Carolina), William Alexander, Lord Stirling (New Jersey), and Robert Howe (North Carolina). Over the course of the following three months, Congress added several more generals. It elevated Horatio Gates from adjutant general to major general and appointed Frederick William, Baron de Woedtke (Prussia), Thomas Mifflin (Pennsylvania), John Whitcomb (Massachusetts), and Hugh Mercer (Virginia) new brigadiers.[43]

There was an underlying logic behind Congress's selection of this second group of generals, but the usual politicking, parochialism, logrolling, favoritism, and compromise distorted and obscured its reasoning. Congress's determination to balance colonial origins, seniority, and merit sometimes failed to do justice to any of the factors because the importance of each varied from congressman to congressman and delegation to delegation. There was certainly a consensus that the army's expanding size and scope required a more geographically diverse set of generals. As a result, Congress appointed four new brigadiers apiece from the middle and southern colonies. Hitherto overrepresented New England received only one. Since Congress tried to distribute the brigadiers in rough proportion to the colonies' expected contributions to the enlarged army, it was unsurprising that the less populous colonies—Delaware, Georgia, Maryland, and South Carolina—were again left out. Seniority was important in that most delegations recommended their longest-tenured colonels for promotion. This was easy, safe, and predictable not only because almost everyone accepted the seniority principle, but also because very few officers had yet developed the combat records necessary for merit-based advancement. Even so, William Heath chided John Adams for Congress's decision to elevate Horatio Gates over his head. Heath informed Adams that he had fought well at Lexington and Concord, whereas Gates had yet to see action in the war. Adams placated Heath by assuring him that Congress promoted Gates on the assumption that his position as adjutant general gave him seniority over all other brigadiers. The upshot was that although Congress used specific ingredients to come up its second batch of generals, it was difficult to discern them in the resulting sausage.[44]

Congress took it upon itself to assign as well as appoint its new generals. It ordered its southern generals to the new Southern Department: Armstrong to South Carolina, Lewis and Howe to Virginia, and Moore to North Carolina. It also put Stirling and Thompson in charge of the Middle Department, though it was clear that Washington would supersede them once the main army transferred its operations there. Washington's departure from Massachusetts, however, called into question who would command what became the Eastern Department. Washington left Ward in charge until Congress could accept his resignation and select a replacement. Unfortunately for everyone involved, Congress was unable to do either. Ward wanted to do his duty, but he was so ill with smallpox and other maladies that he accomplished very little in overseeing his department and preparing Boston's defenses. Although Ward blamed insufficient resources, others attributed the lack of progress to Ward's poor health, indecisiveness, and inability to cooperate with Massachusetts officials. Ward's repeated letters to Washington and Congress about his status and successor brought no satisfactory response. In May Congress voted to send a major general and brigadier general to Boston, but it left the specific choices up to Washington. Washington, though, claimed that he had no surplus generals and kicked the problem back to Congress. Congress in response promoted Massachusetts's senior colonel, a Great War for Empire veteran named Thomas Whitcomb, to brigadier so he could replace Ward, even though some Massachusetts officials knew that the state roster contained better men for the post. When Whitcomb declined the commission due to age and disinterest—the only reason he joined the army outside Boston in the first place was because his men refused to serve under anyone else—an exasperated Congress on 22 August 1776 asked Ward to stay on until it could get around to addressing the issue. The country's dire straits that winter pushed the issue to the back burner. As a result, a man who by his own admission was not up to this important job remained at his post until the following March.[45]

Meanwhile, many congressmen had concluded that Charles Lee was the man most qualified to lead the American army in Canada. Since the war started, Lee had maintained his reputation as a skilled and experienced general. He had assisted Washington in organizing the army overlooking Boston and then oversaw the defenses of Rhode Island and New York City. Self-assuredness was never a problem with Lee, so his advice and orders seemed authoritative to amateur local military authorities in search of guidance and reassurance. Congress saw Lee in the same light and was convinced that his expertise could redeem decaying American fortunes in Canada. Moreover, his proficiency in French would be valuable in wooing Canada's French majority to the American side. Support for Lee's transfer extended beyond Congress. In mid-January 1776 Benedict Arnold, still nursing his wound and his army outside Quebec, told Washington that he would welcome Lee as his commander. Washington also thought that Canada would be a fine venue for Lee's talents. However, he understood that Schuyler intended to go to Canada and take charge there. That being the case, Washington preferred Lee to stay in New York City and help prepare the city for the British attack that intelligence indicated was in the works.

Lee enjoyed all the attention he received. He informed correspondents that he was ready and willing to go to Canada, but, as usual with him, he attached qualifiers. He noted that he would need reinforcements and heavy artillery to take Quebec. He also added that a bout of gout made it impossible for him to leave immediately. In a letter to Washington, Lee stated that if Congress did send him to Canada, he would like to take either John Sullivan or Nathanael Greene with him because he so respected both men. This of course implied a lack of confidence in Washington's other four brigadiers. Although Congress was informed of Lee's reservations, it overlooked them and on 16 February resolved unanimously to dispatch Lee to Canada as the new American commander. To compensate New York City for Lee's lost services, Congress also ordered Schuyler there as his replacement.[46]

Two weeks later, though, Congress changed its mind and decided to send Lee to command the newly created Southern Department. It did so because of information that the British were planning an offensive in the region. It therefore seemed logical for Congress to dispatch its star general to the point of imminent military danger. Lee thought this was a mistake because his knowledge of French made him uniquely qualified to lead the army in Canada. Washington agreed that Lee would be a better fit in Canada than down south but was comforted with the knowledge that someone of Lee's abilities would defend his regional home. Washington explained to his brother, "[Lee] is the first officer in military knowledge and experience we have in the whole army. He is zealously attached to the cause—honest, and well meaning, but rather fickle and violent I fear in his temper. However, he possesses an uncommon share of good sense and spirit. I congratulate my countrymen upon his appointment to that department."[47]

The military situation in the southern colonies had improved markedly by the time Congress appointed Lee its Southern Department commander. Throughout the region, loyalists rose up before the British army was in any position to help them, enabling the patriots to squash them piecemeal. Continentals and militia defeated local loyalists at the Battle of Great Bridge in Virginia on 9 December 1775 and the Battle of Moore's Creek in North Carolina on 27 February 1776. Despite these welcome successes, Lee was unhappy because he was not sure where the British were likely to strike. As he explained to Washington, "I am like a dog in a dancing school—I know not where to turn myself, where to fix myself."[48]

Lee finally deduced that the British planned to attack Charleston, South Carolina, so he hustled southward with two thousand troops to confront the anticipated threat. His arrival raised morale, even though he struck the locals as an odd duck with his eccentricities and rough manners. Soon, however, Lee clashed with South Carolina officials over the best way to defend the city. The locals, led by Col. William Moultrie, insisted on fighting from a fort on Sullivan's Island at the entrance of Charleston Harbor. Lee believed that doing so would be a mistake because the British could easily isolate and destroy the untrained garrison. He termed the fort a "slaughter pen" and called for its evacuation. Moultrie and his supporters refused to defer to Lee's expertise and continued their preparations. Fortunately for the Americans, the British fumbled their 28 June assault. Unexpectedly high tides prevented the redcoats from reaching the island, and Fort Sullivan's spongy palmetto logs absorbed the impact of Royal Navy cannonballs. Meanwhile, American fire inflicted nearly two hundred casualties on the British fleet. After several additional days of fruitless maneuvering, the British finally pulled up stakes, sailed northward, and did not return for two years. Although in some respects the Americans won the battle in spite of, not because of, Lee's advice, he still garnered a good bit of the credit for the victory. Congress unanimously voted Lee its thanks, and Lee's military reputation glowed more brightly than ever.[49]

While Lee confronted the British down south, John Thomas, the recent hero of Dorchester Heights, hurried to Canada to take charge of the American war effort there. Congress made his appointment official on 6 March, then tacked on a promotion to major general to indicate its confidence in the Massachusetts officer. Thomas was the army's most senior brigadier, so elevating him to a rank appropriate for his new responsibilities did not ruffle feathers among the other generals. Besides, Thomas had impressed everyone since the war's start, including Washington, with his courage, energy, and competence. Although congressmen hesitated to deprive Washington of such a valuable officer, they ultimately decided that Thomas's services were needed more in Canada than around Boston. Thomas left for Canada on 22 March and reached Arnold's little force outside Quebec twenty-four days later. He was shocked and appalled by conditions there. The American army, small enough to begin with, was rapidly melting away due to desertions and expired enlistments. There were not enough provisions, gunpowder was running low, and the Canadians refused to accept what currency was available. Worse yet, on 6 May 1776, newly arrived British reinforcements easily drove American troops away from Quebec. Thomas warned Washington that unless he received substantial help soon, his army would disintegrate. By the time he penned those words, however, he had already come down with the case of smallpox that killed him on 2 June at Chambly. Despite his short and unsuccessful tenure, Thomas's soldiers lamented the passing of such a decent man. One doctor eulogized him in a poem: "Thomas is dead that pious man / Where all our hopes were laid."[50]

Congress responded to the deteriorating situation in Canada by ordering reinforcements to be sent there. These included two brigades under Brig. Gens. John Sullivan and William Thompson. The Irish-born Thompson had emigrated to Pennsylvania and served in the Great War for Empire. After Lexington and Concord, Thompson led a rifle battalion to join the American army overlooking Boston. There he gained Washington's respect as a spirited officer with "liberal sentiments." Indeed, on 7 March 1776 he recommended Thompson's promotion to brigadier, on which unbeknownst to him Congress had already acted six days earlier. Thompson had chafed under the inactivity and politicking outside Boston and looked to Canada as a place to make his mark. As for Sullivan, he also possessed ambition and Washington's confidence. Although Thompson reached Chambly on 14 May, Sullivan did not arrive until two weeks later because he had further to travel, got his orders later, and had to deal with bureaucratic snafus in northern New York. Soon after he reached Canada, Sullivan learned that Congress had recalled Wooster for investigation and that Thomas was dying. That made Sullivan, by virtue of his seniority, the new commander of American forces in Canada.[51]

Both his contemporaries and historians have described John Sullivan as an unlucky general. He was born in Somersworth, New Hampshire, in 1740, the son of a poor teacher. He became a lawyer, embraced the patriot cause, and was twice elected to the Continental Congress. In December 1774 he led a successful raid against Fort William and Mary near Portsmouth, New Hampshire, to acquire weapons and ammunition. This accomplishment, as well as his growing reputation and his seat in Congress, helped secure his appointment as one of the first Continental brigadiers. With his swarthy complexion, black eyes, and dark curly hair, Sullivan cut a dashing figure among American generals. No one doubted his physical courage, restless energy, and commitment to the patriot cause, all of which he demonstrated time and again during the war. People also extolled Sullivan's enterprise, initiative, and sociability. In a letter to her husband, Abigail Adams described him as well as anyone: "He appears to be a man of sense and spirit. His countenance denotes him of a warm constitution, not to be very suddenly moved, but when once roused, not very easily lulled. Easy and social, well calculated for a military station, as he seems to be possessed of those popular qualifications necessary to attach men to him." Unfortunately, Sullivan possessed the vanity, ostentatiousness, and susceptibility to flattery of a stereotypical crowd-pleasing politician. There was in fact a bull-in-a-china-shop quality to him, especially when his honor, rank, or competence were challenged, which did not endear him to many congressmen. Throughout the war his tactlessness and impulsiveness repeatedly undercut his ambition by generating hard feelings among those otherwise inclined to like and support him. Conversely, a well-placed kind word would melt his wrath and indignation. Finally, Sullivan was a chronic complainer full of self-pity. He kvetched that he was unappreciated, overworked, and put-upon. Congress's refusal to recompense him for the four times the British seized his baggage during the conflict was a particular sore topic with him.[52]

Despite these rather significant drawbacks, Sullivan was popular among his colleagues. Officers learned to accept, and even joke about, his less admirable qualities. For example, although Nathanael Greene counted himself among Sullivan's friends, he could not help but poke fun at Sullivan's self-importance by referring to him as "Duke de Sully" behind his back. Washington, for his part, appreciated Sullivan's positive traits and downplayed his less attractive ones. Reassuring Sullivan, defending him from hostile congressional critics, and patiently tolerating his grievances became one of Washington's many chores as commander in chief. In return, Sullivan repaid Washington's forbearance with loyalty, hard work, and intrepidness that should have yielded better results for the American cause.[53]

Like almost every other high-level official sent to Canada that year, Sullivan and Thompson were appalled by the American army's confused state of affairs. Both officers tried to be upbeat, but the continuing smallpox epidemic, declining Canadian support, and insufficient resources made it difficult. Sullivan even suggested that Washington or Lee come to Canada to take his place so he could return home. It did not take long, however, for Sullivan's pugnaciousness to reassert itself. When he learned that the British were at Three Rivers, on the St. Lawrence River's north bank about halfway between Quebec and Montreal, he sent Thompson and about two thousand troops to drive them off. The ensuing battle there on 8 June was a fiasco for the Americans. Everything that could go wrong did. Although Sullivan estimated that there were only around eight hundred redcoats at Three Rivers, there were actually closer to six thousand. American soldiers got lost in the swamps, failed to coordinate their actions, and made no progress against British entrenchments. Thompson was among the nearly four hundred American casualties, captured sword in hand. A future general, William Irvine, was also taken prisoner. British losses were negligible. Fortunately for the Americans, the British did not interfere with their pell-mell retreat upriver to Sorel and Chambly.[54]

Sullivan attributed the defeat at Three Rivers to those British reinforcements whose presence he had failed to detect. The demoralized and panicky American troops who straggled into Sorel and Chambly were in no condition to combat anyone. Even so, Sullivan's initial inclination was to stay put, fight it out, and erase this stain on his record. He explained to Schuyler, "I now think only of a glorious death or a victory obtained against superior numbers."[55] His high-ranking officers, for their part, saw the writing on the wall and persuaded him to withdraw. Sullivan did so with surprising skill, considering the army's condition, and reached an island on the Richelieu River near Lake Champlain called Île aux Noix on 24 June. Once ensconced there, Sullivan received conflicting orders from his superiors. Congress's desire that he maintain a foothold in Canada by all means possible contradicted Schuyler's contention that preserving the American army was Sullivan's top priority. Île aux Noix was a swampy, crowded, fetid pesthole whose diseases soon became as much of a threat as the British army. A mortified Sullivan assured Washington that he was doing his best to restore order, and that the problems he faced were not of his making. Conditions deteriorated to the point that hundreds of men succumbed to smallpox, dysentery, and other ailments. Once again, though, Sullivan's subordinates convinced him that retreat was the only viable option. Sullivan reluctantly agreed, and the last Americans arrived at Crown Point by bateaux on 7 July. From there Sullivan wrote to Congress defending his actions and shifting the blame to forces beyond his control, especially disease. "I never had an idea of pain equal to that which I felt at the evacuation of Canada," he wrote. "I hope Congress will not attribute it to my timidity or want of resolution."[56] While he awaited his fate, Sullivan took comfort knowing that he got away with most of his remaining men and baggage, that his officers fully supported his actions, and that he was making progress in revitalizing his army.[57]

Unbeknownst to Sullivan, Congress never intended his tenure as commander of the American army in Canada to be permanent. Many congressmen concluded that neither Sullivan nor Arnold possessed the necessary stature for such an important post. That being the case, on 17 June Congress placed recently promoted Maj. Gen. Horatio Gates in charge of the northern army. Gates's background was similar to Charles Lee's. Both men were born in England, secured commissions in the British army, and fought as young officers at the Battle of the Monongahela at the start of the Great War for Empire. Although Gates ended the war as a lieutenant colonel, he lacked the connections and resources to move any higher up the army's hierarchy. Thoroughly frustrated by his stagnant career, in 1769 Gates moved his family to Virginia, bought some property, and settled down as a gentleman farmer. He also became a strong supporter of American rights.

Gates's impressive military résumé brought him to Congress's attention. Patriots with Gates's kind of relatively high-level military experience were few and far between, so it made sense for Congress to appoint him adjutant general with the rank of brigadier general. Gates performed this bureaucratic role capably enough during the Boston siege under disorganized and chaotic circumstances. Washington, however, did not seem to think much of Gates one way or another. Later, after their relationship soured, Washington claimed that Gates treated him coldly during their time together. If this was true, it was not in character because Gates was an amiable, honest, and courteous man who tried hard to get along with everyone. He dressed simply and looked older than his years. Indeed, his soldiers referred to him as "Granny Gates" because of his demeanor and the spectacles he wore far down on his nose. Although he was a strict disciplinarian, Gates was liked by his troops because he took care of and looked out for them. These traits made Gates a good adjutant, but unfortunately he lacked that driving killer instinct, that obsession with seizing the initiative and using it to mold events, that separated great generals from the ordinary. Moreover, Gates was too naive and good-hearted to undertake the politicking necessary to prosper in any organization. When thrust into such an environment, Gates sometimes became exasperated and petulant. These less desirable qualities were not readily apparent until the war's pressures made them so. In the summer of 1776, though, Gates seemed like the ideal man to lead the northern army. Virginia congressman Richard Henry Lee, for example, wrote, "His great abilities and virtue will be absolutely necessary to restore things there, and his recommendations will always be readily complied with."[58]

Considering his temperament and pride, Sullivan was, not surprisingly, insulted to learn that Congress had promoted Gates over his head and assigned him to take over the northern army. Sullivan had nothing against Gates personally—not yet, anyway—and was not opposed to someone with greater seniority replacing him, but he believed that Congress's decision to elevate a junior officer at his expense showed its lack of confidence in his generalship. Sullivan therefore felt that it was dishonorable for him to remain in the army and submitted his resignation. His immediate superior, Philip Schuyler, regretted Sullivan's decision but understood the reasoning behind it. Many congressmen, though, were less forgiving because Congress had never intended for Sullivan to lead the northern army on a permanent basis. As far as they were concerned, Sullivan's actions were childish and selfish. They were inclined to accept his resignation and rid themselves of such a troublesome officer. Washington, however, counseled caution. He had warned Congress about Sullivan's likely reaction, stating that Sullivan's resignation would "take from the service a useful and good officer."[59] When Sullivan showed up at Washington's New York City headquarters, Washington did his best to persuade him to stay on and gave him permission to go to Philadelphia and meet with Congress personally. In Philadelphia, the president of Congress, John Hancock, explained congressional thinking to Sullivan and assured him that no offense was intended. After mulling things over, Sullivan withdrew his resignation before more vindictive congressmen could convince their colleagues to accept it. Instead, Congress ordered him to report back to Washington for whatever duty the commander in chief had in mind.[60]

Sullivan's departure, however, did not harmonize the American command structure in the region. Congress's original plan was for Gates to lead the army in Canada while Schuyler remained in Albany to exercise his formidable administrative and logistical talents as head of the Northern Department. By the time Gates arrived, though, his army was back on American soil. Although Gates and Schuyler had both agreed to withdraw the army back to better-situated and smallpox-free Ticonderoga, they each complained about their unclear spheres of responsibility. Congress's solution was to reaffirm Schuyler's precedence and limit Gates's authority to Ticonderoga. The decision made neither man happy. Gates felt like a glorified deputy whose wings had been clipped. Schuyler, for his part, came under fire from locals and congressmen so disenchanted with his starchy patrician attitude that they questioned his competence and even his loyalty. An embittered Schuyler submitted his resignation to Congress in September, but withdrew it when Congress reassured him of its confidence and support. In the meanwhile, Schuyler and Gates tried to remain on civil terms with each other and worked hard to refurbish the army. They established an effective supply line, restored discipline, and oversaw the eradication of smallpox. By the end of the summer, the army contained around nine thousand reasonably effective soldiers. In December, however, Washington ordered Gates to bring most of his troops southward to join the main army making its last stand along the Delaware River, thus removing Gates temporarily from the northern theater.[61]

Command inconsistency was one of the Canadian campaign's defining characteristics. Five generals—Montgomery, Arnold, Wooster, Thomas, and Sullivan—directed the American army at some point during its ten-month sojourn northward. Benedict Arnold, though, was there from beginning to end. He led the expedition from Cambridge through the Maine wilderness to Quebec's outskirts, participated in the failed assault on that city, and then, despite a leg wound, kept together what was left of his little force throughout the winter. Doing so, he said, was akin to making bricks without straw. He asked for and received from Wooster a transfer to take charge of the Montreal garrison after a fall from his horse reinjured his leg, so he missed the battle at Three Rivers. He possessed sufficient strategic acumen to recognize that the defeat doomed American ambitions in Canada. Five days after the engagement, he wrote plainly to Sullivan, "The junction of the Canadians with the Colonies, an object which brought us into this country is now at an end. Let us quit them and secure our own country before it is too late."[62] Arnold and his soldiers slipped out of Montreal on 9 June and rejoined the rest of the army at Île aux Noix, from where they boarded bateaux that took them up Lake Champlain to Crown Point. Arnold emerged from the campaign with the enhanced reputation of someone clearly going places. Congress lauded and promoted him. His most valuable patron, though, was undoubtedly the commander in chief. Washington had assigned Arnold command of the expedition to Quebec because he had suspected Arnold possessed the necessary leadership skills and combat prowess, predicting to Schuyler in December 1775, "The merit of this gentleman [Arnold] is certainly great and I heartily wish that fortune may distinguish him as one of her favorites. I am convinced that he will do everything that his prudence and valor shall suggest to add to the success of our arms."[63] As far as Washington was concerned, Arnold's performance in Canada proved his hunch right.[64]

Arnold was, like Nathanael Greene, a product of New England's merchant middle class. Born in 1741 in Norwich, Connecticut, Arnold apprenticed as an apothecary after his father dissipated the family's wealth through heavy drinking and bad investments. He ran away from home to enlist in the Connecticut army during the Great War for Empire, but he wearied of the discipline, deserted, and returned to his family. With the help of relatives, he became a successful pharmacist and bookseller, and later expanded into overseas trade. Although he was highly successful in his various endeavors, Arnold chafed against the British government's oppressive economic regulations and became a member of the Sons of Liberty. Arnold marched with his militia company to Massachusetts after Lexington and Concord, but quickly grew bored with the tedium of besieging the British garrison in Boston. Instead, he secured permission from the Massachusetts Committee of Safety to seize Fort Ticonderoga. Unfortunately for Arnold, Ethan Allen and his Green Mountain Boys had the same idea, so Arnold had to share the mission and the resulting acclaim with them. Neither Allen nor his Green Mountain Boys treated Arnold very well, leading to hard feelings all around. Worse yet, Arnold also bickered with various government officials, especially over reimbursements for expenses he incurred in the undertaking. Finally, when Arnold returned home he learned that his wife had died, leaving him with a family to support unassisted. Arnold nevertheless headed back to Cambridge, where Washington took a shine to him and appointed him commander of the expedition to Quebec.

Arnold's actions in Canada were merely a harbinger of things to come. In the next year he became one of the war's great combat commanders. Few officers on either side were as capable as Arnold in inspiring soldiers to make the sacrifices necessary to overcome so many obstacles. Fearless, enterprising, and bold, Arnold ruthlessly attained his objectives, military or otherwise. The Canadian campaign also exposed some of Arnold's less admirable qualities. Although he could be ingratiating and polite when it served his purposes, he was often petty, spiteful, arrogant, and arbitrary. For example, he arrested Col. John De Haas for refusing to destroy an American Indian village. Arnold's high-handedness in Montreal prompted one doctor to express the fervent wish that someone would put a hole in his head. Even by the standards of the touchy American officer corps, he was inordinately sensitive to matters of rank, protocol, and seniority. Such views, though, did not prevent him from disregarding orders that he found inconvenient or unwise. Before the Battle of Three Rivers, Sullivan complained that Arnold failed to obey his directives with sufficient alacrity. Indeed, for all Arnold's talk about honor, he defined the notion in such a way as to justify any unscrupulous behavior in which he indulged. His avariciousness got him into trouble on numerous occasions. In Canada some alleged that he used his power to expropriate goods for his own personal use. His quarrelsome nature led to charges and countercharges with Col. Moses Hazen over Hazen's refusal to accept supplies Arnold seized from local merchants. Arnold's imperious attitude toward the officers sitting on one of the resulting courts-martial led the officers to complain to Congress about him. Finally, Arnold's vanity and self-pity fed his growing persecution complex. He often felt slighted, overlooked, and underappreciated by Congress, despite his sterling battlefield record. His resulting bitterness corroded his integrity and commitment to the American cause and ultimately caused him to betray his country.[65]

The American retreat from Canada did not mark the end of the campaign. Schuyler, Gates, and Arnold worried that the British might take advantage of their recent success by invading New York and pushing on to Albany on the Hudson River. Doing so would require control over Lake Champlain to transport and supply their troops. Arnold proposed building a fleet at Skenesborough to keep the lake out of British hands. Schuyler and Gates agreed and put Arnold in charge of the project in part because of his maritime experience. Arnold went about his new job with his usual gusto, but he had his work cut out for him because the Americans lacked the personnel and equipment to construct the warships—carpenters, shipwrights, sailors, saws, nails, sailcloth, cordage, cables, and a hundred other necessary odds and ends. Fortunately, Schuyler's logistical skills provided enough men and equipment to manufacture, equip, and crew sixteen warships of various shapes and sizes by the end of the summer. The British were at the same time creating a navy of their own on the lake. In their case, though, their greater resources and expertise enabled them to more easily overcome many of the problems that plagued their American counterparts. By October they had twenty-five warships with twice the combined firepower of the American fleet. Despite the odds, Arnold took his warships northward and engaged the British off Valcour Island on 11 October. In the ensuing daylong battle, Arnold's superior tactics failed to overcome British advantages in numbers and guns. Although a heavy fog enabled the Americans to escape that night, over the course of the next few days the British captured, sank, or drove aground two-thirds of the American fleet. The Americans lost eighty killed and wounded, and another 120 captured. Arnold and many of his men reached shore and escaped to Ticonderoga to fight another day. British casualties, in contrast, were less than fifty. The way was now open for the British to advance southward, but they decided to return to Canada because it was too late in the year for such an offensive.

The British decision to forgo an invasion of New York in 1776 was one of the most important of the war because it gave the Americans additional time to prepare their northern defenses. For this, Arnold deserved a good bit of the credit. Arnold's contribution was not so much leading his warships into battle off Valcour Island, but rather in building the fleet in the first place. Doing so forced the British to suspend their military operations and construct their own navy on

Lake Champlain. By the time they finished, it was too late in the year to attack northern New York. Despite the strategic uselessness of the engagement, Arnold's performance, even in a losing cause, garnered him considerable praise for his fortitude, energy, and boldness. Even those who criticized his impetuousness had to admire his determination. Sadly, glory for Benedict Arnold was just about the only positive thing the Americans got out of their Canadian campaign. Although the Americans committed thousands of men to try to conquer Canada, many of whom never returned, by the summer of 1776 they were right back where they started. Canada remained under British control as a military bastion they would use for the remainder of the conflict to threaten the new country.

Twelve officers who eventually became Continental generals served in the Canadian campaign in one capacity or another: James Clinton, John De Haas, John Greaton, William Irvine, William Maxwell, Daniel Morgan, John Paterson, Enoch Poor, James Reed, Arthur St. Clair, John Stark, and Anthony Wayne. Although many of them had previous combat experience in the Great War for Empire, the problems they faced in leading, training, equipping, and supplying their units in Canada gave them a greater appreciation for the obstacles the colonies were likely to face in the war than colleagues who had yet been tested by the British military. Their new combat records also brought them to Congress's attention and made their promotions more likely. Finally, the campaign united them in their defense of Sullivan's decision to abandon Canada and in their suspicion of Benedict Arnold's character.[66]

There were many reasons for the American defeat in Canada—insufficient resources, poorly trained and ill-equipped troops, smallpox, logistical problems, and so forth—but inadequate and inconsistent leadership certainly played a role. Although some of the generals Congress dispatched to Canada possessed talent and potential, they did not have sufficient time to make their marks there. Montgomery, Thomas, and Thompson all became casualties less than three months after their arrivals—Montgomery was killed in battle, Thomas died of smallpox, and Thompson was captured. Wooster was overwhelmed by the difficulties he faced. So was Sullivan, but he had sufficient common sense to cut his losses and retreat back to New York. Only Arnold's generalship stood out in any sustained way. In fairness to all six generals, though, it is hard to see how the Americans could have held any of Canada once large numbers of British reinforcements disembarked in the spring of 1776, regardless of the quality of their leadership.[67]

Preparing New York City's Defenses

Long before the British evacuated Boston, Washington zeroed in on New York City as their likely next target. Such a conclusion required little discernment because the city's importance was obvious to everyone. Located in the center of the eastern seaboard at the Hudson River's mouth and containing a population of around 25,000 inhabitants, New York City dominated the region socially, politically, and economically. Its first-rate harbor could shelter as many ships as the Royal Navy cared to build, and the Hudson River provided easy access northward to Albany. As John Adams explained it, New York City was "the nexus of the northern and southern colonies, as a kind of key to the whole continent, as it is a passage to Canada, to the Great Lakes, and to all the Indian nations."[68] It was thus an ideal base and starting point for Britain's subjugation of its rebellious colonies. In January 1776 Washington sent Charles Lee to New York City to oversee the construction of its defenses. Despite a case of gout so severe that he had to be carried around on a litter for a time, Lee did his best to prepare the city for the expected attack. After Lee left in early March to assume command of the new Southern Department, Brig. Gens. William Thompson and William Alexander, Lord Stirling took over until Washington arrived with the bulk of his army in mid-April. Except for a visit to Congress in late May and early June, Washington remained in and around New York City for the remainder of the summer.[69]

New York City's importance made its defense politically necessary, but its peculiar geography undermined efforts to protect it. The city was located on the southern tip of Manhattan, a narrow island of twenty-three square miles separated from the New York mainland by the Harlem River and bracketed by the Hudson and East Rivers. To the immediate east, across the East River, Long Island stretched 118 miles parallel to Connecticut's southern coast. On Manhattan's other side, directly across the Hudson, was New Jersey's shore. Finally, Staten Island sat a half dozen miles to the southwest, across the Upper Bay. British warships could therefore cut off and isolate any American army attempting to protect the city. Tough old Israel Putnam saw the danger immediately and warned, "When they [the British] come up with their ships you'll have your hands full."[70] For his part, Washington was more sanguine. He hoped that his troops and strategically located batteries could keep the British army and navy at bay. On 22 July he wrote to his brother, "I can only say that the men appear to be in good spirits, and if they will stand by me the place shall not be carried without some loss, notwithstanding we are not yet in such a posture of defense as I could wish."[71] His optimism—or, more critically, naivete—reflected that of subordinates such as Greene, who shared Washington's sentiments about American chances of holding the city. Besides, Congress's long-awaited decision to announce American independence heartened patriots and underscored the importance of safeguarding the populace. In fact, while Congress was voting on independence, 130 Royal Navy vessels dropped anchor off Staten Island and began landing the first of thirty thousand British and German mercenary (Hessian) soldiers so they could regain their land legs before prosecuting the campaign in earnest.[72]

To defend New York City, Washington had almost twenty thousand men at his disposal. Providing adequate leadership for all these troops was one of Washington's many responsibilities. In May he complained that he needed more generals for the job, but Congress did not respond because it was wary of again tackling such a politically sensitive issue. In early August, though, Washington increased the pressure by stating that the dearth of major generals was crippling his army's effectiveness. His brigadiers could run their brigades well enough, Washington explained, but his major generals were overstretched by their extensive and numerous duties. This problem would only get worse, he continued, once active campaigning began. Washington figured that he needed three additional major generals for his army, as well as another one for the Eastern Department to replace Artemas Ward. Since most of the major generals would undoubtedly come from the ranks of the brigadiers, Congress would have to appoint their successors as well. Washington therefore asked for six or seven new brigadiers to staff both his main army and its northern counterpart. Although he acknowledged the political difficulties involved, he emphasized that it was militarily imperative.[73]

Thus pressured, on 9 August Congress undertook a third round of promotions. With one exception, Congress elevated the four most senior brigadiers to major generals, in order of seniority: William Heath, Joseph Spencer, John Sullivan, and Nathanael Greene. Congress's original intention was to appoint three major generals, but Washington and others apparently spoke so highly of Greene that Congress included him as well. Congress voted unanimously to promote Greene and Spencer, despite Washington's dislike for the latter officer. Sullivan's and Heath's selections, however, were more contentious. Although Sullivan was still in the doghouse for his petulant response to Gates's appointment as commander of the army in Canada, it is not clear why Heath was so controversial. The following year John Adams noted that many congressmen believed that Heath was in over his head, but he added that they felt the same way about Spencer. At any rate, with Heath the states split six to six in two ballots until a divided delegation swung over to Heath on the third ballot to break the tie in his favor. Initially only one delegation voted for Sullivan, but, for whatever reason, in the end all of them came around to supporting him. As for the brigadiers, Congress promoted six new ones, in order of seniority: James Reed (Massachusetts), John Nixon (Massachusetts), Arthur St. Clair (Pennsylvania), Alexander McDougall (New York), Samuel Parsons (Connecticut), and James Clinton (New York). Determining which states got the new brigadiers was as contentious as expected. Once Congress decided this, though, it usually took the path of least resistance and elevated the most senior colonels within those states' rosters. Therefore, the resulting votes were often more indicative of support for that particular state getting a brigadier than for the individual himself. Parsons received the backing from eleven state delegations, Reed ten, Nixon and St. Clair eight, and McDougall and Clinton seven.[74]

David Wooster's name was glaringly absent from Congress's list of new major generals. In a major departure from the seniority principle, Congress opted not to elevate him even though he was the Continental army's oldest brigadier. Wooster was still under a cloud for his performance leading the American army in Canada earlier in the year. Some congressmen damned him as inefficient and unfit for his duties. After Congress recalled Wooster, he reported to Washington in New York City. There he discovered that Washington's urgent desire for generals did not include him. Washington doubted that Wooster possessed sufficient initiative to be an effective general and therefore did not want him in his army. Instead of employing Wooster, Washington sent him to Congress in Philadelphia. Upon his arrival, Wooster demanded and got a court of inquiry to clear his name. While the court deliberated, Congress ordered Wooster home to Connecticut to see his family. The court and Congress ultimately absolved Wooster of any wrongdoing in Canada, but it was too late to help his career. Warnings from Wooster's supporters that he would resign if Congress failed to appoint him a major general did more to spur than deter his critics, one of whom commented that Wooster's advocates outweighed his talent. Although six state delegations voted in favor of Wooster's promotion, it was not enough. Contrary to his friends' fears and enemies' hopes, though, Wooster remained in the army, and at the end of the year Washington dispatched him to Rhode Island to help defend that state.[75]

Perhaps because of his poor reputation, Wooster's discomfiture generated little comment within the officer corps. However, the larger issue of seniority's proper role in promotions and appointments remained. In fact, as more officers entered the army and built service records, it became increasingly important for everyone to understand Congress's standards for advancement. Most officers continued to believe that seniority should be the default criteria. As they saw things, seniority was the traditional, predictable, stable, and honorable way to rise through the ranks. Almost any other measure, some argued, was dishonorable to bypassed officers because it showed that Congress lacked confidence in their abilities, something sure to demoralize an army and hurt the war effort. Politicians, for their part, found seniority appealing because it removed much of the politicking from the process so everyone could focus on fighting the British. John Adams wrote to one of the newly appointed brigadiers, Samuel Parsons, "Upon the whole I believe it is wisest to depart from the line of succession as seldom as possible." Even so, Adams understood better than some high-ranking officers the weaknesses of the seniority principle. Most obviously, it penalized junior officers who could not rise quickly no matter how much initiative, energy, skill, and success they demonstrated. Adams also noted to Parsons that appointment by seniority was often just plain impractical:

> A colonel is killed in New Hampshire. The next colonel in the American army, to him, is in Georgia. Must we send the colonel from Georgia to command the regiment in New Hampshire? Upon his journey, he is seized with a fever and dies. The next colonel is in Canada. We must then send to Canada for a colonel to go to Portsmouth?. . . . These marches and countermarches must run through all the corps of officers, and will occasion such inextricable perplexities, delays, and uncertainties, that we need not hesitate to pronounce it impracticable and ruinous.[76]

Seniority, concluded Adams, had its place, but was hardly foolproof.[77]

Even those most wedded to seniority did not see it as absolute. Everyone agreed that it was perfectly acceptable to ignore seniority for promotions in cases of meritorious conduct. The difficulty was defining the term. Most officers interpreted meritorious conduct as gallantry on the battlefield. Administrative savvy, tactical and strategic genius, and other exemplary forms of service did not count. John Adams, though, pointed out reasonably enough that an officer needed more than physical courage to be a great, or even adequate, general. In addition, there was the problem of subjectivity; bravery, like beauty, is often in the eye of the beholder. Partiality also made promotions based on merit open to congressional favoritism and prejudice. Nathanael Greene's recommended antidote was that Congress should only elevate someone for meritorious conduct who had Washington's recommendation. Adams responded that the military was just as vulnerable to preferentialism as any other institution. "What then shall we say?" asked Adams. "Shall we leave it to the general and the army? Is there not as much favoritism, as much of nature, passion, prejudice, and partiality, in the army as in an assembly? As much in a general as in a king or minister?"[78] As Adams recognized, the conventional understanding of merit was not the solution to identifying good officers for promotion and appointments.[79]

Finally, state loyalty continued to complicate Congress's efforts to appoint generals. Most congressional delegations wanted their states to have a suitable number of generals, and this desire often trumped seniority and merit. Of course, how many generals a state deserved was as subjective as meritorious conduct. There was a consensus that a state should have generals in rough proportion to its contribution—or promised contribution—to the Continental army. Congressmen also believed that brigadiers should lead brigades composed of soldiers from their home states. Such views seemed reasonable, but they penalized capable officers from smaller states, such as Delaware, that were unable to raise enough soldiers to form their own brigades.

Moreover, the vicissitudes of the war undermined these efforts at fairness. John Adams, for example, complained that Congress did not allot Massachusetts its proper share of generals in its second and third round of promotions. For this Adams blamed himself because he did not know enough about his state's officers to persuasively argue their cases to Congress. In addition, the more Adams thought about it, the more alarmed he became with the insidious consequences of Congress's actions. Massachusetts had received a disproportionately large number of the first batch of generals because so many of the troops outside Boston came from that colony. This put these men near the top of the roster, giving them plenty of seniority in the officer corps. In the ensuing year, however, most of them—Frye, Pomeroy, and Thomas—left the army for one reason or another, leaving only the undistinguished Heath as Massachusetts's representative among the generals. Although Adams and the Massachusetts delegation succeeded in getting James Reed and John Nixon elevated to brigadiers in August 1776, the seniority principle meant that they would probably never rise to the very top of the chain of command. Moreover, not only was Reed more a New Hampshirite than a Massachusettsan, but in September during the Canadian campaign he succumbed to a bout of smallpox so severe that it left him deaf and dumb and eventually compelled him to resign from the army. Massachusetts would therefore be shortchanged in terms of generals and the influence they could exert despite the state's substantial support for the war effort. Disgruntled delegates from many other states could manipulate the data to make similar arguments that Congress's ad hoc system for appointing and promoting generals was unjust to them as well.[80]

Despite all the ambiguities, Congress's promotions that summer did not provoke widespread discontent within the officer corps. After all, Congress generally relied on the seniority principle that most officers understood and supported. Even so, there were pockets of discontent from officers who felt slighted by the process. Henry Knox, for example, believed that Congress should have made him a brigadier because he was artillery chief, and he resented that some regimental colonels were appointed instead. Knox was not the only disgruntled passed-over colonel. New Jersey's William Maxwell and Rhode Island's James Varnum protested that Congress had overlooked them in favor of more junior officers from other states. Maxwell decided that resigning his commission at such a critical time would be dishonorable, but Varnum had no such compunctions and wrote to Washington, "I can no longer command myself, much less can I command others. Disappointment, shame, grief, resentment, all harrow up my soul at once."[81] Although Washington was busy preparing for the British attack on New York City, he found time to dissuade Varnum from quitting by promising to look into the matter and see what he could do. When another Rhode Island colonel, Daniel Hitchcock, learned about Washington's pledge to Varnum, *he* charged Washington with favoritism. Small wonder that Adams concluded that doling out promotions taught him "there is no possibility of giving universal satisfaction to great numbers of men."[82]

On 12 August Washington took advantage of Congress's recent promotions to reorganize his army into five two-brigade divisions, each of which was under one of his major generals: Greene, Heath, Putnam, Spencer, and the recently arrived Sullivan. Although much of his army was composed of militia led by state-appointed generals, his best-trained units were his six Continental brigades commanded by James Clinton, Alexander McDougall, Thomas Mifflin, John Nixon, Samuel Parsons, and William Alexander, Lord Stirling. Washington also dispatched Brig. Gen. Hugh Mercer, a Virginian in whom he had considerable confidence, to New Jersey to organize the state militia there into a "flying camp," meaning a mobile reserve force. Congress did its bit by ordering Charles Lee up from South Carolina to add his expertise to the army, but he did not arrive until after the campaign was well under way. Although the United States had been at war for more than a year, Washington and his Continental generals in and around New York City still had almost no high-level combat leadership experience. Even Sullivan, who had served in Canada, had seen little action. To make matters worse, Washington had little confidence in two of his division commanders, Heath and Spencer. His faith in the remaining three was based on his assessment of their military housekeeping abilities, not on their performance under fire. Indeed, those Continental generals who had commanded their units in battle were either dead (Montgomery and Thomas), captured (Thompson), or otherwise occupied (Arnold and Lee). In short, the American army's leadership on the eve of the war's first large battle left much to be desired.[83]

Washington's deployments reflected his inexperience and naivete. He positioned Heath's division on Harlem Heights in northern Manhattan, Putnam's and Spencer's divisions in and around New York City, and Greene's and Sullivan's divisions across the East River on Long Island's western tip. Dividing his army in the face of British naval supremacy was a bold—even foolhardy—move, but Washington felt that it was politically necessary to fight for the city. While Washington got his ducks in a row, the British remained passive on Staten Island, marshaling their own forces for their big offensive. On the evening of 21 August a terrible storm swept through the region and damaged many of New York City's houses. One lightning strike killed three American officers and melted the tips of their swords. The next morning, large numbers of British troops commanded by General William Howe came ashore at Gravesend Bay on southwestern Long Island. The fight for New York City had begun.[84]

Conclusions

Congress did a great deal to establish military leadership for the new country in the first year and a half of the war. It created the Continental army, developed a primitive bureaucracy to maintain it, and divided the country into military departments. It also unanimously selected Washington as the commander in chief of the army subject to its authority, but with sufficient power to carry out his duties. Finally, Congress appointed major and brigadier generals to help Washington run the army's departments, divisions, and brigades. Although Congress did not codify its criteria for the appointment of and promotion to general, it had determined that the most important factors—beyond character, of course—were seniority, merit, and state origins. By August 1776 Congress selected eleven major generals and twenty-seven brigadiers, most of whom were known and trusted by the delegations of the states from which they came.

The stresses of the war, though, were already taking a toll on these men. Three of the major generals were now gone, or on their way out—one because of illness and stress (Ward) and the other two due to death (Montgomery and Thomas). Of the twenty-seven brigadiers, Congress had elevated seven to major general (Gates, Greene, Heath, Montgomery, Spencer, Sullivan, and Thomas), two declined their appointments (Pomeroy and Whitcomb), two resigned because of poor health (Frye and Reed), one was captured (Thompson), and one had died of disease (Woedtke). Unfortunately for the Americans, those generals who had accumulated the most combat leadership experience also had the highest attrition rate. Of the four generals who had seen significant action in the war so far (Arnold at Quebec, Lee on Sullivan's Island, Montgomery at Fort St. Johns and Quebec, and Thompson at Three Rivers), one had been killed and another captured. Except for Arnold and Lee, the remaining American generals were still untested commanding their units into battle.

Of the twenty-four Continental generals still in the army in August 1776, thirteen were with Washington in and around New York City preparing for the major British offensive. Washington may have been commander in chief, but his authority over these men was not absolute. Congress's power to promote, transfer, or dismiss them hindered Washington's efforts to establish a leadership team to his liking. Washington could and did exert considerable influence over Congress on military matters, but exercising it effectively required time, energy, and persuasiveness that he did not always have. As a result, he was sometimes stuck with generals in whom he did not have complete confidence. For example, he did not think much of Heath or Spencer, even though they both commanded divisions. Despite these obstacles, he had identified officers he liked such as Greene and Knox and had given them increasing responsibilities. Whether they could live up to Washington's expectations, though, remained an open question.

CHAPTER 2

Trying Times

1776–1777

New York Debacle

When Nathanael Greene assumed command of American troops on Long Island on 29 April 1776, he set his men to work augmenting the fortifications along Brooklyn Heights, directly across from Manhattan's southern tip. The position was a good one, with both flanks protected, under Washington's most trusted lieutenant. Although Greene grumbled that he had too much paperwork to get into the field as often as he liked, he was confident that his soldiers were ready to fight, adding, "I have not the most distant apprehensions for this army."[1] In mid-August, though, a series of unfortunate events occurred that rendered American forces on Long Island dangerously vulnerable to enemy attack. First of all, Greene fell seriously ill for several weeks, removing from the scene the general who best understood the terrain and defenses. Washington responded on 20 August by sending John Sullivan to fill in for the convalescing Greene. Pugnacious and impulsive as ever, Sullivan, with Washington's consent, expanded American lines by occupying Guana Heights, about five miles south of Brooklyn Heights. The problem was that Sullivan not only lacked the troops to adequately man his new position, but also left his eastern flank exposed just as the British splashed ashore at Gravesend Bay.

No sooner had Sullivan settled in than Washington ordered Israel Putnam over to replace him. Putnam had complained to Washington that as the most senior major general present, he should have the honor of leading the soldiers in what appeared to be the decisive spot. Washington, always sensitive to such arguments, agreed and dispatched him across the East River. Besides, he had developed second thoughts about Sullivan's deployments. Putnam was about as familiar with the local topography as Sullivan—meaning hardly at all—so his dispositions did little to improve things. Back in New York City, Washington was confused by British movements. He was not sure whether the British landing on

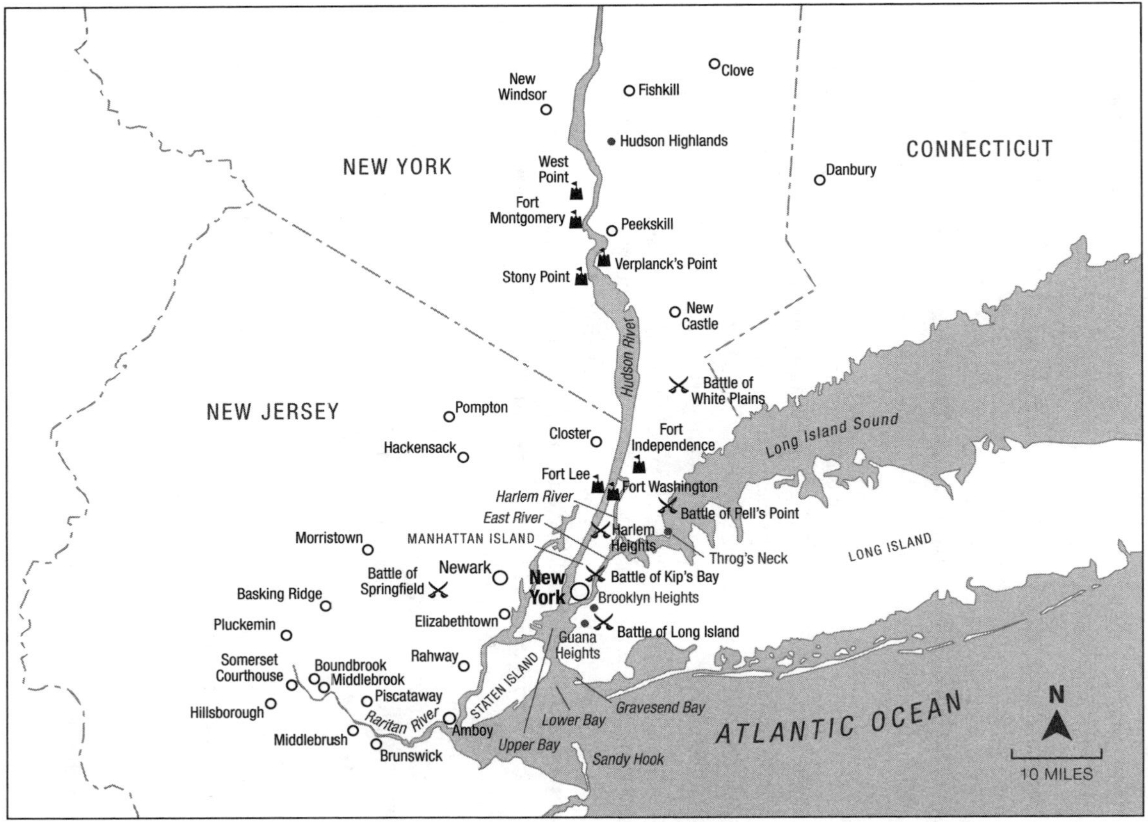

New York City Region. *Map by Ken Arbogast-Wilson, WTW Design Group.*

Long Island was their main effort or a feint to divert American attention from an assault on Manhattan. Splitting the difference, Washington sent reinforcements to Long Island, but not enough to matter. The upshot was that the seven thousand Americans on Long Island were poorly deployed, inconsistently led, and outnumbered in the face of a well-trained British army commanded by an experienced general who had the initiative and knew exactly what to do with it.[2]

On the night of 26–27 August, Gen. William Howe's British army stirred in its Gravesend Bay camp. While two columns of British and Hessian troops pushed north for a diversionary assault on those Americans deployed along Guana Heights, another column of ten thousand redcoats struck out northeastward toward Jamaica Pass to hit the exposed American left flank. The diversionary columns assailed the American units on Guana Heights shortly before sunrise. The Americans there, led by Sullivan on the left and Stirling on the right, initially held their own. However, the British flanking column marched undetected and unopposed through Jamaica Pass, wheeled westward, and in late morning assaulted the Americans on Guana Heights from behind. Washington watched his line crumble from an observation post on Brooklyn Heights, wrung his hands, and exclaimed, "Good God! What brave fellows I must lose today!"[3] Those Americans who could escape the converging British jaws fled to American positions along Brooklyn Heights. Sullivan and Stirling were apprehended, and another general, Connecticut's Samuel Parsons, went missing until he found his way back to American lines next morning. About 1,400 Americans were killed, wounded, or captured by the end of the day, as opposed to around four hundred British casualties.

The British may have won the battle, but the American bastion on Brooklyn Heights remained strong and intact. Its biggest weakness, though, was that once the wind was right Royal Navy warships could ascend the East River and isolate it from Manhattan and the rest of the American army. When Thomas Mifflin and several other officers realized this, they hurried to Washington to warn him. Washington had already dispatched reinforcements across the East River to Brooklyn Heights, but Mifflin's counsel gave him pause. On the evening of 19 August, Washington called a council of war with his generals, including McDougall, Mifflin, Parsons, Putnam, and Spencer. The council unanimously recommended withdrawing from Long Island to Manhattan before the Royal Navy made such a move impossible. Washington had fortuitously ordered Brig. Gen. Alexander McDougall to round up all available boats in the area and send them to the East River. He now directed Col. John Glover and two regiments of tough, disciplined Massachusetts mariners to undertake the evacuation that very night.

John Glover was one of those self-made men who peppered the roster of Continental officers. Born in 1732 in Salem, Massachusetts, but raised in nearby

Marblehead, the short and stocky Glover apprenticed as a shoemaker before becoming a fisherman and eventually a well-to-do shipowner. He served on the Massachusetts Committee of Correspondence, and after Lexington and Concord he led Marblehead's militia contingent to join the troops besieging Boston. Because the Marblehead militia contained a large contingent of sailors, Washington used its troops to crew armed vessels he sent to patrol Massachusetts Bay. Glover's performance here and elsewhere won the respect of officers such as Knox, Lee, and Washington. In fact, Washington later stated that no one in his army was more qualified for brigade command than Glover. Considering his profession, it was unsurprising that Glover was an enterprising man and an excellent disciplinarian. He also possessed a modesty and humility rare in the American army, and therefore displayed little of the touchiness and pride over rank that so frequently embroiled the officer corps. Glover's background and training meant that if anyone was capable of saving Washington's army, he was.[4]

Luckily for the Americans, a storm helped conceal the army's departure in pitch darkness. Although Glover's troops were thoroughly familiar with the water and the teamwork necessary to master it, they had a difficult time rowing across the milewide river until the wind picked up so they could hoist their sails. Along Brooklyn Heights, American soldiers, unit by unit, quietly left their burning campfires and marched through the rainy darkness down to the ferry with their weapons and equipment to wait their turn on the boats. Everyone was dead tired and anxious, a combination conducive to panic. When one group of frightened troops stampeded onto a boat, Washington picked up a large stone, raised it over his head, and threatened to sink the vessel unless everyone calmed down. As it was, Washington was as jittery as the next man. "Good God!" he exclaimed when he learned that Col. Edward Hand's rear guard had mistakenly pulled back to the ferry ahead of schedule. "I am afraid you have ruined us by so unseasonably withdrawing the troops from the line."[5] Fortunately, Hand got his men back into position before the British noticed their absence. As the gray dawn unfolded, many Americans still remained on Long Island, but a dense fog settled in to camouflage the rest of the evacuation. Washington was among the last of the nine thousand Americans to leave, stepping onto a boat around seven in the morning. With that, the American army slipped away to fight another day.

Washington's furtive evacuation from Long Island was an impressive achievement, but retreats do not win wars. Although Washington initially labeled the battle on Long Island a mere skirmish, it was a good bit more than that. The British army not only seized the island and knocked a big chunk out of the New York City defensive perimeter but also demonstrated its superiority over its American counterpart in almost every respect. There were plenty of explanations for the defeat, beginning with Washington. Washington did not spend a great deal of time on Long Island because it was merely one of several possible British targets. He relied instead on his right-hand man, Nathanael Greene, to prepare the Brooklyn Heights defenses. Greene's untimely illness, though, upset Washington's command arrangements. Replacing Greene with first Sullivan and then Putnam led to the unwise redeployments that made British victory easier—redeployments Washington approved without understanding the likely consequences. During the fighting on Guana Heights, Washington was more a passive observer than an active participant. He never really took charge of the army until after the engagement was over. However, once he recognized that the British navy might cut off his soldiers on Brooklyn Heights, he moved quickly, skillfully, and decisively to withdraw them to Manhattan.

The performances of Washington's subordinate generals also left something to be desired. For all the physical courage they demonstrated during the battle, they displayed precious little generalship in deploying and maneuvering their men. Most damningly, neither Sullivan nor Putnam did enough to protect Jamaica Pass. Even so, Washington refrained from scapegoating. He still thought enough of Stirling and Sullivan to encourage Congress to exchange them as soon as possible for captured British generals so they could return to duty. Some questioned the competency of both Washington and those who exerted the most influence over him and wished that Charles Lee was present to provide some much needed professionalism. Others pointed out that while some American soldiers fought well, many others did not, leading to allegations that New Englanders in particular did not cover themselves with glory. It was Henry Knox, though, who put his finger on the reasons behind the American defeat. Knox acknowledged the role played by inadequate intelligence and poor deployment but astutely added, "We are fighting against a people well acquainted with the theory and practice of war—brave by discipline and habit [and] furnished with every implement of war necessary for any enterprise."[6] Until the Americans accumulated the necessary skills and experience, such setbacks would likely remain the rule rather than the exception.[7]

Back on Manhattan, Washington pondered his options. Defeat on Long Island had so damaged morale, especially among the militia, that entire units were decamping for home. The remaining troops suffered from illness, hunger, and declining confidence in their leaders. Washington was almost as discouraged with his men as some of them were with him, but he was not about to give up. To compensate for his declining numbers, he reorganized his thirteen Continental and militia brigades into three divisions under Heath, Putnam, and Greene's temporary replacement, Spencer. The more Washington thought about it, the more he realized that the Battle of Long Island proved that his army lacked the necessary training, equipment, and logistical support to defeat its British counterpart in open battle. That being the case, he decided to avoid such engagements and fight the enemy only on his terms: from well-fortified positions in which his soldiers would possess any topographical advantages. Hopefully such a strategy would suck the British into a war of attrition that they lacked the patience, political will, and resources to sustain. As he explained to Hancock in an oft-quoted passage, "We should on all occasions avoid a general action or put anything to risk unless compelled by a necessity into which we ought never be drawn."[8]

Washington's immediate problem was fitting New York City into his new strategic equation. British naval power and his diminishing numbers made defending the city increasingly problematic, but evacuating it would undermine morale and, he believed, anger some congressmen to whom he was answerable. Washington's generals were divided on the issue. On the one hand, Greene took a hard-hearted approach and recommended abandoning and burning the city, and then retreating to the more defensible northern part of the island. Heath and New York's George Clinton, on the other hand, argued that the political consequences of giving up such an important city outweighed the military risks in trying to retain it. Washington initially tried to square this circle by deploying his army across the island, until he recognized the idea's impracticality. At a 12 September meeting, most of Washington's generals agreed with the necessity of quitting New York City. Before they could implement their plan, though, the British struck again.[9]

On 15 September British troops stormed ashore at Kip's Bay, about a fourth of the way up Manhattan's eastern coast, and halfway between two segments of Washington's dispersed army. The New Englanders defending the beach ran almost as soon as Royal Navy warships opened fire. Two nearby brigades, under Continental brigadier general Samuel Parsons and Massachusetts brigadier general John Fellows, did little to stem the tide, despite Washington's angry and exasperated efforts to rally them. Once on dry land, the British had the opportunity to push westward across the island and cut off Putnam's troops in and around New York City. Fortunately for the Americans, Howe failed to follow up on his advantage, enabling Putnam's men to abandon New York City, escape northward via a road on the island's western side, and join the remainder of the army at Harlem Heights. The next day the Americans repulsed a British probe toward Harlem Heights in a sharp skirmish that did much to raise their flagging morale and provided one of the war's few instances of Washington's tactical skills. However, the fact remained that the Americans had suffered yet another defeat, one that placed New York City in British hands and pushed Washington's army one step closer to dissolution.[10]

Luckily for the Americans, Howe again failed to take full advantage of his victory, instead pausing to take stock. American morale remained shaky even after Washington's little success at Harlem Heights. Washington's ten thousand or so troops in and around Harlem Heights continued to suffer from hunger, desertions, mistrust, low morale, and equipment shortages. In early October, though, the American army received an important addition: Charles Lee. Congress had ordered Lee back north the previous August when it became apparent that the British intended to make their main effort against New York City. That being the case, Congress wanted its star general at the scene of the action. As the American army suffered one setback after another, people in and out of Congress saw Lee as just the man to help Washington turn things around. Indeed, one congressman stated that Lee's presence would be the equivalent of ten thousand reinforcements. Lee was hardly the type to undervalue his worth, but he was unsure whether even his military abilities could compensate for the new country's declining fortunes. Indeed, even before he reached Harlem Heights he suggested that Congress enter negotiations with the British to secure an end to the conflict. Whatever Lee's attitude toward the war, his military acumen was intact. Once he joined Washington's army, he recognized immediately its exposed position. Lee pointed out that the British could land on New York's mainland, march westward to the Hudson River, and isolate the American army in northern Manhattan.[11]

Actually, Lee's observations required little insight. Not only had Howe maneuvered around the Americans twice before, but by the time Lee reached Harlem Heights, Howe's third attempt was already under way. On 12 October British troops landed at Throg's Neck, a spit of land that separated the East River's estuary from Long Island Sound. Unfortunately for the British, the place was more an island than a peninsula, which enabled a small number of nearby American soldiers to bottle them up. While the British floundered on Throg's Neck, on 16 October Washington and his generals met to mull their options. The overwhelming consensus was that the army should abandon Manhattan and withdraw northward before the British struck again. As the army's retreat began, the British on 18 October came ashore three miles up the coast from Throg's Neck at Pell's Point. Four thousand British redcoats and Hessians, marching inland, ran into James Clinton's brigade, temporarily under John Glover. Glover cleverly deployed his 750 soldiers behind a series of stone walls from which they could shoot at the enemy. Glover's brigade inflicted substantial casualties on the British before falling back to Yonkers. Glover's resolute defense helped buy enough time for the rest of the American army to slip away to White Plains, about twenty miles north of Harlem Heights. Glover's stalwart performance won kudos from Washington, Lee, and eventually many congressmen.[12]

Washington's decision to dig in at White Plains on 23 October was motivated in part by its defensible terrain. He deployed his fourteen thousand men astride the Bronx River, with his flanks protected by a lake to the east and Chatterton

Hill and some swamps to the west. However, there was more to it than that. American morale ebbed with each backward step, and Greene for one had advised Washington that unless he turned and fought, the army might evaporate. When Howe arrived five days later and discovered that he could not resort to his usual flanking tactics, he opted to assail Chatterton Hill with a portion of his army. British troops took it after a tough fight in which Alexander McDougall distinguished himself. Each side suffered about two hundred casualties, but Chatterton Hill's loss exposed the remainder of the American line. Before the British could take full advantage of their success, though, heavy rains gave the Americans cover to retreat farther northward to New Castle and dig in again. Rather than continue to pursue the Americans deeper into the Hudson Highlands and away from his naval support and supply lines, Howe broke off his offensive and marched back toward Manhattan.[13]

Because Washington was unsure where the British would strike next, he divided his army into three parts to prepare for any contingency, and assigned their commanders by seniority. He gave Lee five thousand men at New Castle, New York, to guard the approach to New England, ordered Heath and four thousand troops to protect the Hudson Highlands, and took his remaining two thousand soldiers across the Hudson River to New Jersey in case Howe moved toward Philadelphia. When Washington had withdrawn from Harlem Heights, he had left behind three thousand men under Greene to garrison Forts Lee and Washington, which together blocked British access up the Hudson River. Fort Washington, located on a hill near Manhattan's northwestern tip, was so obviously vulnerable that Lee and other generals recommended its abandonment. Washington's gut told him that Lee was right, but he refrained from doing so for a number of reasons. For one thing, Washington was under the impression that Congress wanted it held. Moreover, Greene assured him that the fort could withstand any British assault because of its formidable defenses, stout-hearted garrison, and capable commander, Col. Robert Magaw. Washington greatly respected Greene and hesitated to second-guess the man on the scene. Lastly, Washington desired a firsthand look at things before he made his final decision. On the morning of 16 November, Washington, Putnam, Mercer, and Greene rowed across the Hudson from Fort Lee to look over the place. However, no sooner had they finished their inspection and boarded their boat for the trip back to Fort Lee than the British attacked.[14]

When Washington and his colleagues learned that the British were assailing the fort, Greene, Mercer, and Putnam all offered to remain behind to help Magaw. Washington, for whatever reason, insisted that they all return to Fort Lee. By doing so, the generals escaped death, injury, and captivity, but it was hardly a shining example of moral courage. As things turned out, Fort Washington was not as impregnable as Greene and Magaw attested. Its outer defenses were so extensive that the thirteen thousand British and Hessian attackers swamped them and overwhelmed the defenders in five hours of hard fighting. Magaw and the remaining troops in the inner fort gave up soon after. In addition to 150 killed and wounded, the British took another 2,800 Americans prisoner. The redcoats and Hessians, for their part, lost 450 men.[15]

Fort Washington's sudden fall was a body blow to the American war effort. Strategically, it secured New York City for the British and opened up the Hudson River to Royal Navy operations. It exposed New Jersey and Philadelphia to British attack as well. The Americans not only lost three thousand troops, but also their hard-to-replace weapons and equipment. The battle was equally detrimental to American morale, marking as it did the dismal culmination of a series of British victories from Long Island to Kip's Bay to White Plains. In each engagement Howe had maneuvered with a smooth professionalism that made Washington's actions appear clumsy and amateurish in comparison. Small wonder that Fort Washington's seizure provoked so much hand-wringing among American officers. This was especially true of Nathanael Greene. Greene's assurances to Washington that the fort's defenses were impenetrable proved spectacularly wrong. Greene felt terrible about his mistake, writing to his friend Knox, "I feel mad, vexed, sick and sorry. Never did I need the consoling voice of a friend more than now. Happy should I be to see you. This is a most terrible event. Its consequences are justly to be dreaded."[16] The defeat called into question not only Greene's position as Washington's most capable lieutenant but also Washington's wisdom in selecting his subordinates. Lee, for example, bluntly wrote to Washington, "Oh general, why would you be over-persuaded by men of inferior judgment to your own? It was a cursed affair."[17] Washington was inclined to agree with these sentiments. He blamed his failure to follow his instincts and evacuate the eponymous fort on his misplaced confidence in Greene and his desire to do Congress's bidding and was mortified by the results.[18]

Indeed, poor generalship characterized American operations around New York City, starting at the top with Washington. He was often slow, reactive, overconfident, and detached. This was hardly surprising, considering his inexperience in active campaigning at this level of command, but he clearly needed to demonstrate far greater ability than he had hitherto shown if the Americans expected to win the conflict with him as commander in chief. Fortunately, though, there were glimmers of hope amid the prevailing gloom. When Washington made up his mind to act, he did so with alacrity and decisiveness, as evidenced by his evacuations of Brooklyn Heights and Harlem Heights. He also maintained the loyalty and support of most of his officers and men despite his many mistakes. His instincts were usually right, and he was beginning to recognize that he needed to heed them. Finally, he was getting a grip on the limitations under which his army operated, enabling him to craft a realistic war-fighting strategy. The key to victory, he now understood, was attrition, not one big climactic battle.

Nor did Washington's subordinates have much to be proud of during the campaign. Like Washington, they made their fair share of mistakes, from Sullivan's and Putnam's poor deployments on Long Island to Greene's faulty assurances that the Americans could successfully defend Fort Washington. With the notable exception of Glover's shrewd delaying action at Pell's Point, they demonstrated little tactical skill. Nevertheless, Sullivan's and Stirling's behavior on Long Island and McDougall's actions at Chatterton Hill indicated that there was nothing wrong with the physical courage of most American generals. Their strategic instincts were also generally on target. Many of them, for example, recognized before Washington the folly of attempting to retain New York City in the face of British naval supremacy. These men were, like Washington, learning their trades as they went along, but whether they could do so fast enough to win the war remained to be seen.

Washington's use of his generals was also problematic. Throughout the campaign he struggled to reconcile seniority with perceived merit. For example, he sent Putnam, whose combativeness outweighed his wisdom, to assume command on Long Island at least in part because of Putnam's seniority, with unfortunate results. In addition, two of Washington's divisions were under mediocre men in whom he did not have full confidence, but he was unwilling to exert the effort necessary to replace them. As a result, Heath and Spencer retained their commands. Even when Washington assigned a favored general to an important job, it was no guarantee of success. He put his right-hand man, Nathanael Greene, in charge of first Long Island and then Forts Lee and Washington. In both instances, Greene let Washington down through illness or poor judgment. Even so, Washington maintained his faith in the young Rhode Islander, no doubt seeing these mistakes more as growing pains than evidence of incompetence. Clearly Washington still had a ways to go in effectively assessing and using his chief lieutenants in ways that would benefit the war effort.

Retreat across New Jersey

Fort Washington's fall opened the door for a British invasion of New Jersey. On 20 November British troops under Gen. Charles Cornwallis landed on the New Jersey shore at Closter, six miles above Fort Lee. Since Fort Washington's conquest had rendered Fort Lee useless, Washington ordered Greene to abandon it. Unfortunately, a lack of wagons and ill-disciplined soldiers led to the loss of much of the fort's weapons, equipment, and matériel. Washington and his three thousand men thereupon retreated before Cornwallis's ten thousand redcoats and Hessians. The Americans fell back through Hackensack, Newark, Rahway, Brunswick, Princeton, and Trenton. With each backward step the army sloughed off men, weapons, and equipment. Those who remained in the ranks were dispirited, hungry, ragged, and dirty. Worse yet, large number of New Jerseyans responded favorably to an amnesty proclamation promulgated by Howe, thus undermining local support for the American cause. On 7–8 December the Americans finished crossing the Delaware River just ahead of the British, removed all the boats to the west bank, and put themselves out of harm's way for now.

Washington remained indomitable during his army's dreary retreat through New Jersey, at least publicly. Indeed, Nathanael Greene later commented that he never saw Washington more self-possessed than during those dark December days. His iron will and determination helped maintain the support of his remaining soldiers and kept the army from disintegrating completely. Upon greeting one officer, for example, Washington put his hand to his throat and said, "My neck does not feel as though it was made for a halter."[19] Moreover, Washington was already formulating a plan to finally wrest the initiative away from the British. Since it seemed clear that Philadelphia was the next British target, he wanted to concentrate the reinforcements he had summoned from throughout the region on the Pennsylvania bank of the Delaware River. Once those various units arrived, he would hopefully have enough manpower to take the fight to the British. Washington, however, knew as well as anyone the substantial differences between planning and implementation, and there was little evidence that he would be more successful in protecting Philadelphia than he was in defending New York City. Despite his public stoicism, he was plagued with doubts. He even ordered his Mount Vernon plantation manager to prepare to move his papers inland at a moment's notice if the Royal Navy showed up. Whatever his reservations, he continued to believe that his faith in God and the American cause would ultimately bring victory. "Upon the whole our affairs are in a much less promising condition than could be wished," he observed. "Yet I trust under the smiles of Providence, and by our own exertions we shall be happy. Our cause is righteous and must be supported."[20]

The rapidly changing military situation gave Washington and Congress the opportunity to move some generals to locales and jobs where they could benefit—or, in some cases, do less harm to—the American cause. On 7 December British troops occupied Newport, Rhode Island. Alarmed local officials asked Washington and Congress to send Gates or Greene, as well as some brigadiers, to the region to help organize and lead the militia. Despite Greene's misjudgments at Fort Washington, Washington was not about to part with his favorite and most trusted lieutenant. As for Gates, he had fallen ill while bringing his men down from Fort Ticonderoga, so Washington sent him to Philadelphia to recuperate. Instead, Washington dispatched Joseph Spencer and Benedict Arnold to join David Wooster in defending New England from a potential British offensive out of Newport. Washington had never been impressed with Spencer and was undoubtedly happy to be rid of him. Besides, he was Washington's senior general and therefore entitled to an independent command. Washington thought much more highly of Arnold, who was conveniently on hand and unemployed, and hoped he could compensate for Spencer's shortcomings. Washington also persuaded Congress to dispatch John Armstrong and a new brigadier, William Smallwood, to Pennsylvania and Maryland, respectively, to rally the militias in those states. In this instance, though, Washington respected both officers and expected good things from their presence in their home states.[21]

The war's wear and tear was almost as hard on Washington's generals as on the rank and file. Gates and Greene were not the only generals who fell seriously ill that dismal autumn. Indeed, at one point Washington noted that most of his brigadiers had succumbed to one ailment or another. Washington was usually solicitous of his generals' welfare, but he did not want their misfortune to interfere with the war effort. In December, for example, Alexander McDougall wrote to Washington that rheumatism had made it so difficult for him to perform his duty that he wanted to step down, but that he hesitated to do so at such a critical time. Although Washington desired hale and active generals leading his units, he worried that McDougall's resignation might look akin to a rat abandoning a sinking ship. Besides, he respected the zealous, Scottish-born New Yorker for his stalwart defense of Chatterton Hill and did not want to lose his services. Washington recommended caution, writing, "I think with you, that though your health may require a resignation, that this is not a proper time to make it; our enemies would probably attribute it to the late unfavorable aspect of our affairs, and therefore I would advise you to try whether a little rest might not contribute to the cure of a disorder which is generally brought on by colds and fatigue."[22] McDougall heeded his counsel, recovered by the end of the year, and went on to perform yeoman's service for the American cause for the remainder of the conflict.[23]

Washington's biggest high-ranking personnel problem during the retreat through New Jersey was Charles Lee. When Washington moved to defend Forts Lee and Washington, he left Lee and around five thousand troops behind at New Castle to guard the approaches to New England. Lee was a carping and critical man under even the best of circumstances, so it was unsurprising that since his return from South Carolina he had found fault with Washington's military performance. As far as Lee was concerned, the twin debacles at Forts Lee and Washington proved that Washington was indecisive, irresolute, and easily swayed by incompetent subordinates like Greene. He summed up his feelings in a letter to Gates: "A certain great man is most damnably deficient."[24] In fact, Lee was rapidly losing confidence not only in his commander in chief but also in the entire American war effort.

When it became obvious that the British had focused their efforts on overrunning New Jersey and occupying Philadelphia, Washington ordered Lee and his Continental soldiers to join him and leave New England's defense to the local militia. Lee, however, disliked this idea. He felt that he should use his detachment in northern New Jersey to harass the British army's flank and rear as it marched through the state. Moreover, since Lee believed that Washington's original 10 November instructions gave him the autonomy to act as he saw fit, he was slow to implement Washington's subsequent directives to get moving. Lee proved so dilatory that Washington initially suspected that the British had intercepted some of their correspondence. After some additional back-and-forth, on 27 November a frustrated Washington finally wrote Lee, "My former letters were so full and explicit as to the necessity of your marching as early as possible, that it is unnecessary to add more on that head."[25]

Thus prodded, Lee finally got under way. His efforts to meet Washington's timetable, though, were hindered by continuing shortages, growing local loyalist sentiment—and William Heath. When Washington marched into New Jersey, he left Heath and about four thousand soldiers behind to guard the Hudson Highlands. The thirty-seven-year-old, Massachusetts-born Heath had made his living as a well-to-do farmer before the Revolutionary War. As a colonel in the Suffolk County militia, Heath was among those who harassed the British during their retreat from Concord. His actions there contributed to Congress's decision to appoint him one of the original Continental army brigadiers. Unfortunately for Heath, he failed to impress Washington during the siege of Boston and the fighting around New York City. Indeed, the balding, stiff-necked, and corpulent Heath did not cut an especially dashing or inspiring figure. He was instead the quintessential military bureaucrat. He was a stickler for the rules, enjoyed pomp and circumstance, and possessed little imagination. During the Boston siege, for example, Lt. Col. Rufus Putnam noticed a copy of an engineering book on a table while visiting Heath's headquarters. Since Putnam had been tasked with fortifying Roxbury and knew very little about such work, he asked Heath to borrow the book. Heath replied that he did not lend his books, even though doing so in this instance would clearly benefit the cause in which he and Putnam were both engaged. Putnam had to badger Heath to change his mind. Despite these rather significant drawbacks, Washington eventually grew to appreciate Heath's finer qualities. Heath was so dedicated to the army that he refrained from threats to resign over rank and honor. He also possessed that happy combination of frankness and tact that made him an ideal military diplomat. Finally, his administrative abilities helped reduce Washington's burden as commander in chief. Later in the war Washington wrote to Heath, "It will be impossible that your presence should be dispensed with. And even then, it will be with reluctance, that I can consent to the absence of a gentleman, of such rank, whose services are so necessary, and from whom I have derived such essential aid and assistance."[26]

Because many of his Continentals were in poor shape, Lee wanted to swap them out for an equal number of Heath's healthier men at Peekskill before he continued his march to join Washington's army. As Lee viewed things, Heath was in no immediate danger. Besides, Lee and his troops were marching toward what might well be the war's decisive battle. That being the case, procuring Heath's best soldiers was plain common sense. Heath, however, did not see things that way. Heath was unsure of the overall military situation, but he knew he had orders from Washington to protect the Hudson Highlands that said nothing about weakening his force by trading two thousand of his hale men to Lee. When Heath explained this to Lee, Lee scoffed at Heath's logic and stated that Washington was too remote to warrant a strict interpretation of his directives. "I shall therefore conclude," Lee wrote Heath, "that the commander in chief is now separated from us, that I of course command on this side of the water, that for the future I must and will be obeyed."[27] When Lee arrived at Heath's Peekskill headquarters on 30 November, he renewed his browbeating. Lee admitted that Heath might be technically correct, but he needed Heath's troops and would accept responsibility for taking them. Heath refused to be intimidated, showed Lee Washington's orders, and exclaimed, "Sir, if you come to this post, and mean to issue orders here, which will break those positive ones which I have received, I pray you to do it completely yourself."[28] Although Lee did in fact give the necessary orders, the next day he changed his mind and canceled them. In all likelihood, he had hoped to bluff Heath into voluntarily surrendering his soldiers, but when that did not work he backed down. The irony was that Heath proved almost as much a thorn in Lee's side as Lee was in Washington's.[29]

Having given up on Heath, Lee got his men across the Hudson River on 2 December and marched toward New Jersey. He made good progress and reached Morristown six days later, despite his circuitous route and his soldiers' ragged condition. There Lee paused for three days while he renewed his running debate with Washington over the best use of his force. Lee argued again that he should harass the British army's right flank as is moved west through New Jersey, but Washington finally shut down the discussion once and for all by ordering Lee to join him at the Delaware River immediately. On the morning of 12 December, though, Lee was captured a few miles from his little army in Basking Ridge. Lee was catching up with some of his correspondence when a party of British cavalry, tipped off by a local loyalist, galloped up, dispersed the guards, and threatened to burn down the house Lee was in unless he surrendered. Although the woman of the house offered to hide him, a disgusted Lee shook his head and gave himself up. With that, the jubilant redcoats hustled him off in his slippers and wearing a dirty shirt.[30]

For many Americans, the capture of the army's most experienced general that gloomy December seemed like another nail in the revolution's coffin. Abigail Adams, for example, stated that Lee's misfortune was worse than the fall of Forts Lee and Washington. Congressman Robert Morris wrote, "This is an event much to be lamented. I sincerely pity Lee and feel for the loss my country sustains. His abilities had frequently been immensely useful—the want of them will be severely felt."[31] Some fretted that the British might try and execute Lee as a British army deserter, whereas others worried that his seizure might undermine the rank and file's confidence in its generals. However, scratching beneath the surface of these public dirges reveals a layer of growing discontent with the eccentric Lee akin to that of students who gradually realize that their teacher is not as accomplished as advertised. Lee's second-in-command, the recently exchanged John Sullivan, regretted Lee's bad luck but did not seem terribly broken up about circumstances that catapulted him to the top spot. Although Washington publicly bemoaned Lee's fate, he was more cynical about it in his personal correspondence. He had grown increasingly exasperated with Lee's obtrusiveness and could not have been unaware that this unexpected event neatly resolved his most frustrating personnel problem. Indeed, Washington attributed Lee's discomfiture to his "folly and imprudence." Others echoed Washington's sentiments that as a veteran officer, Lee should have known better than to billet himself so far from his army's lines. Finally, some identified silver linings. One officer related a conversation he had with a colleague: "I told him I was sorry for General Lee because I knew him personally and had a regard for him, but I did not view his capture as unfavorable but as an advantage; that too much confidence had been put in General Lee, that this must have greatly embarrassed the commander in chief, as he was afraid to do anything without consulting Gen. Lee, but now he would be at liberty to exert his own talents."[32]

After declaring American independence, Congress kept busy formulating the Articles of Confederation and addressing the innumerable and seemingly intractable military problems the new country faced. Fortunately for Washington, congressmen were more inclined to blame the deteriorating military situation on the short-term enlistments that deprived the army of a reliable source of manpower than on the commander in chief. As Washington's flagging army fled to the Delaware River, rumors and tension swept through Philadelphia and fueled speculation that the revolution was on its last legs. On 11 December

Congress called for a day of fasting and prayer in hopes of provoking divine intervention to salvage the waning American war effort. Just in case God had other plans, though, the next day Congress accepted Putnam's and Mifflin's advice to adjourn and reconvene in Baltimore. Although the two generals were in town to rally the inhabitants and prepare its defenses, they had almost no troops to lead. Neither general argued that the enemy would reach Philadelphia, but they worried that local loyalists might turn the city over to the British. Putnam in particular seemed to have lost all hope in the cause after the fall of Forts Washington and Lee. Moreover, they agreed with many delegates that it would be easier for Congress to conduct its business away from the stress-filled city. When Congress decamped for Baltimore, it left behind a city of deserted streets, shut-up homes, and a pervading sense of doom. Once in Baltimore, Congress voted to grant Washington extensive powers for six months that included asking the states to call out their militias, appointing all Continental officers under the rank of brigadier, seizing provisions from civilians with compensation, and arresting and confining suspected loyalists. More than ever before, Congress was looking to Washington to salvage a situation that appeared beyond redemption.[33]

Congress appointed eight brigadiers in the last quarter of 1776, but it did so in an ad hoc and sporadic manner based on immediate needs and interests. By now, though, both officers and politicians were becoming increasingly sophisticated and nuanced in manipulating Congress to get the outcomes they sought. Congressmen Benjamin Rush, for example, wrote to Col. Anthony Wayne that their state of Pennsylvania deserved one or two more generals but warned Wayne that he was competing with another colonel, Robert Magaw, for the slot. Rush told Wayne that Magaw had influential friends lobbying on his behalf, so Wayne needed to rally his own supporters to get his name before Congress. "I should not have suggested these ideas to you," Rush explained, "had I not more than once seen the most eminent military merit neglected in our promotions, from ignorance in the Congress or from the want of proper recommendations."[34] Unfortunately for Wayne, he did not receive the promotion he sought—neither did Magaw, who less than two months later lost Fort Washington, his freedom, and his career—but Rush's advice remained sound.

Congress's eight new brigadiers were Adam Stephen (4 September), Christopher Gadsden (16 September), William Moultrie (16 September), Lachlan McIntosh (16 September), William Maxwell (23 October), William Smallwood (23 October), Matthias de Roche Fermoy (5 November), and Henry Knox (27 December). Of these officers, two—Christopher Gadsden and William Moultrie—were South Carolinians who never served outside the Southern Department. Fermoy was a West Indies–born French officer whose hard-to-find engineering skills secured his appointment. Maxwell (New Jersey), McIntosh (Georgia), Smallwood

(Maryland), and Stephen (Virginia) all hailed from states underrepresented in the roster of generals. Finally, Knox owed his promotion to Washington's formidable support. Washington wrote to Congress to recommend Knox's elevation, warning that his irreplaceable artillery chief might resign unless Congress responded positively. Knox later disclaimed soliciting his promotion, and with false modesty added that people praised him more than he deserved. He did allow, though, that his formidable industriousness might have convinced Congress to act on his behalf. Of course, the big question for Knox and his fellow new appointees that December was whether their cause had any long-term future.[35]

Trenton and Princeton

By the time his army retreated across the Delaware River, Washington was a depressed and dejected man. He had in the preceding four months suffered one defeat after another and lost the most strategically vital city in America. Each setback undermined the popular support on which the revolution depended, providing the British with an opportunity to win back the loyalty of their wayward colonists. Washington worried that New York, Pennsylvania, and especially New Jersey were already returning to British allegiance. Moreover, he believed that once the Delaware River froze, the British could cross over and storm Philadelphia. And, since the enlistments of many of his soldiers expired at the end of the year, he would have nothing with which to defend the city and stop the British juggernaut. Small wonder that he lamented to a relative on 18 December, "In a word my dear sir, if every nerve is not strained to recruit the new army with all possible expedition I think the game is pretty near up."[36]

There were glimmers of hope, however, amid the prevailing gloom. For one thing, the reinforcements Washington had summoned during his retreat through New Jersey were appearing. After Lee was captured near Morristown, John Sullivan assumed command of the soldiers, got them on the road at once, and reached Washington's army on 20 December. Two days later, Gates's troops—but not Gates himself, who went to Philadelphia to convalesce from his illness—arrived from northern New York. The local militia, including two thousand men from Philadelphia under Col. John Cadwalader, also rallied to Washington's banner. All these soldiers, when combined with those already at hand, gave Washington slightly more than six thousand troops with which to fight. This number was bound to decrease, but it provided Washington with a window of opportunity to conduct operations. Moreover, Howe suspended his offensive for the winter and returned to New York City. To hold on to New Jersey, he established a string of seventeen scattered outposts across the state. A resurgence of resistance in the state due to British harshness and heavy-handedness, however, soon exhausted the local garrisons and rendered them vulnerable to attack.

Washington was by nature a pugnacious man always eager to seize the initiative, and he had lamented his inability to do so during the army's bleak retreat though New Jersey. Howe's decision to forgo offensive operations finally gave Washington the chance he sought. On 22 December Washington and his generals decided to strike back against the British. Washington's plan called for a three-pronged simultaneous assault across the Delaware River on the night of 25–26 December. One prong, led by Washington and containing 2,400 Continentals, would cross the Delaware at McConkey's Ferry and then march nine miles southeastward to assail the Hessian garrison at Trenton at dawn. The second prong, 800 men under Pennsylvania militia general James Ewing, would cross near Trenton and cut off the Hessians' escape route by seizing a bridge over the Assunpink Creek. Finally, John Cadwalader and 1,800 Philadelphia militia would cross over near Burlington and pin down the enemy garrison at Bordentown. Like many of Washington's designs, it was overly complicated and consisted of too many moving parts, but it promised a dramatic change in the war. Washington certainly saw the potential results in that light. The day of the attack, he wrote one congressman that it was pointless to ruminate over past failures and present misfortunes, but they should instead focus on the future successes he had no doubt were on the horizon.[37]

To preserve secrecy, the American army waited until nightfall on Christmas Day to begin its counteroffensive. Most of the troops with Washington crossed the Delaware in big Durham boats manned by local rivermen and Glover's ubiquitous mariners. Although Knox oversaw loading the boats with his usual cheerfulness and energy, getting the soldiers and their equipment over the ice-clogged and choppy river proved more difficult than anticipated. In fact, conditions were so bad that Ewing and Cadwalader called off their efforts. By the time the last of Washington's soldiers disembarked on the New Jersey shore, the operation was already several hours behind schedule. The march to Trenton was equally harrowing. The poorly clad troops suffered from the cold and snow as they trudged along the slushy roads. As daylight approached, Washington worried that he had lost the element of surprise and the Hessians would be drawn up for battle by the time his army reached Trenton. Undaunted, he pushed on anyway. Fortunately for Washington and his soldiers, the Hessians discounted reports of American activity in the area. Washington divided his army as it approached Trenton, giving Greene one half and Sullivan the other, and at around eight o'clock in the morning he ordered them to assault the town. The attack caught the Hessians unprepared. Hauling Knox's cannons had slowed down the army's march, but now they proved their value by clearing the narrow streets of Hessians attempting to deploy. The battle was over in an hour. The Hessians lost more than one hundred men killed and wounded, as well as an additional nine hundred taken prisoner. Another five hundred or so managed to escape across the Assunpink Creek bridge. As for the Americans, they suffered only a handful of casualties, one of whom was future president James Monroe. An elated Washington shook an officer's hand and exclaimed, "This is a glorious day for our country."[38]

The impact of Washington's triumph at Trenton extended beyond gobbling up one exposed Hessian garrison. Most obviously, it rekindled patriots' flagging morale by demonstrating that defeat was not a foregone conclusion and that the American army was capable of protecting American independence. One civilian explained:

> The news [about Trenton] is confirmed. The minds of the people are much altered. A few days ago they had given up the cause for lost. Their late successes have turned the scale and now they are all liberty mad again. Their recruiting parties could not get a man . . . and now the men are coming in by companies. . . . This has given them new spirits, got them fresh succors and will prolong the war, perhaps for two years. They have recovered their panic and it will not be an easy matter to throw them into that confusion again.[39]

The news had a similar impact on dispirited congressmen. John Hancock, for example, stated, "This may give a different face to our affairs and be productive of very happy consequences."[40] Nor was the officer corps immune from an emotive reaction. Henry Knox wrote, "Providence seemed to have smiled upon every part of this enterprise. Great advantages may be gained from it if he we take the proper steps."[41] Such emotionalism might seem unimportant, but since victory ultimately depended on public and army support for the war, these feelings mattered.

American army leadership at the Battle of Trenton was very good. To be sure, victory required little tactical finesse because the Hessians were so unprepared, but the generals still demonstrated plenty of physical courage and grit. When Brig. Gen. Arthur St. Clair learned that the rain had rendered his officers' weapons useless, he responded, "You have nothing for it but to push on and charge."[42] Washington deserved a good bit of the credit for committing to the offensive and seeing it through to completion despite doubts that the Hessians would be surprised. There was a ruthless determination to his actions that he had not hitherto shown. His lieutenants also performed well. Greene and Sullivan ably led their wings into Trenton, and Glover again overcame the odds to help transport the army across a formidable body of water. Knox's success in loading the boats at the Delaware and handling his artillery during the battle was especially noteworthy. The only sour note, in terms of generalship, was Brig. Gen. Adam Stephen. During the march to Trenton, Washington discovered that Stephen had on his own authority detached a patrol ahead of the army to retaliate against the Hessians for killing one of his men. The patrol's subsequent skirmish with a group of Hessians threatened to alert the Trenton garrison and spoil the attack. An angry Washington allegedly summoned Stephen and yelled at him, "You, sir, may have ruined all my plans!"[43] The Hessians remained inert, however, and the only result from the incident was a black mark in Washington's mental ledger against Stephen.

The American army scurried back across the Delaware River only hours after the last Hessians surrendered at Trenton, but it returned to the town on the last day of the year. Not wanting to give up the initiative he had so recently seized, Washington hoped to build on his success at Trenton by driving the British out of New Jersey. He managed to field an army of almost seven thousand men with which to undertake his campaign by offering a bounty to those soldiers whose enlistments had expired to remain in service, but things did not go as planned. After Howe recovered from the shock of Trenton, he sent Cornwallis with eight thousand Hessians and redcoats to bring Washington to heel. As soon as the British troops left Princeton for Trenton on 2 January, though, they encountered opposition. Washington had dispatched Brig. Gen. Matthias de Roche Fermoy's brigade up from Trenton to delay and hinder the British advance. Although an allegedly inebriated Fermoy abandoned his outfit and scuttled back to Trenton, Col. Edward Hand assumed command and skillfully battled the oncoming British for the rest of the day from behind creeks, walls, and other available forms of concealment. It was almost dark before the British column reached Trenton. Aggressive as ever, Cornwallis immediately assailed the Americans drawn up behind Assunpink Creek. Three times the British assaulted a stone bridge across the creek, and thrice Greene's division and Knox's artillery turned them back. The British suffered 365 casualties, which, when combined with those who fell fighting Hand's brigade, brought their losses for the day to 500 men. The Americans, for their part, suffered around one hundred killed and wounded. The surprisingly fierce resistance, the gathering darkness, and simple exhaustion convinced Cornwallis to suspend his attack until the next morning.[44]

After the fighting died down, Washington summoned a council of war to discuss the army's response to the all-out British assault he was certain would come with the dawn. Washington was inclined to stay put and slug it out with the British because retreating back across the river would be difficult. Besides, withdrawing would be an admission of defeat just when American morale was on the upswing. Giving battle, however, was clearly a risky proposition that might lead to the army's destruction. Although Washington's army was well positioned and had performed credibly that evening, there were reasons to worry that the Americans might crack when Cornwallis renewed the engagement with his veteran redcoats and Hessians.[45]

At this point, Arthur St. Clair offered an alternative. He knew from guarding the Assunpink Creek fords that there was a road around the British left flank. He suggested that the Americans use it to slip away from the British army and plunge deep into New Jersey toward Brunswick, leaving Cornwallis behind holding the bag. Hugh Mercer strongly endorsed the idea, and soon all the officers present but one came around and embraced it.[46]

Washington left behind about four hundred men to deceive the British by minding the campfires while the rest of his army silently filed off down the route St. Clair had identified. Happily for the Americans, a cold biting wind muffled any noise and froze the mucky roads, enabling them to slide away undetected. By dawn the troops were two miles from Princeton when they encountered a column of 750 redcoats on their way to Trenton to reinforce Cornwallis. As each side raised the alarm, Greene dispatched Mercer's brigade to engage the enemy. After an exchange of fire, a British bayonet charge broke Mercer's line and sent his soldiers scurrying away. Mercer was a Scot who had fled his homeland for Pennsylvania after participating in the Jacobite rebellion against Britain. Despite his Anglophobia, he joined a Pennsylvania regiment during the Great War for Empire, amassed an enviable combat record, and ended the conflict as a colonel. He was therefore clearly an officer of great merit with a promising future in the American officer corps. Unfortunately for Mercer, he was mortally wounded while trying to rally his fleeing brigade. While Mercer's soldiers slugged it out with the British, Cadwalader's Philadelphia militia brigade came up, but it too disintegrated under fire. By now Washington arrived and succeeded in reforming both brigades at great personal risk. Mercer's and Cadwalader's men, joined by reinforcements from Greene's division, finally shattered the British. Although Sullivan had to root out some of them from the College of New Jersey's Nassau Hall, most of the surviving redcoats escaped down the road to Brunswick. British losses amounted to 450 men, compared to approximately one hundred Americans killed and wounded.

The Battle of Princeton was Washington's one and only major open field triumph of the war. Although many officers and men contributed to the success, Washington deserved the majority of the credit for rallying his defeated units, leading them back into action, and breaking the British line. As one officer put it, "The fortune of war is reversed, and Providence has been pleased to crown the efforts of our commander in chief with a splendid victory."[47] Washington's accomplishments were facilitated by such lieutenants as Sullivan who aggressively committed their outfits to battle at the right time and place. Even so, Washington's achievement must be qualified. The Americans outnumbered the British by approximately five to one, so victory was almost inevitable once Washington got his soldiers into action. Considering the army's past difficulties and inexperience, though, doing so was a feat that could hardly be taken for granted.

Although Washington hoped to continue on to the major British supply depot at Brunswick, he soon realized that his exhausted soldiers were in no condition for such an undertaking. Moreover, Cornwallis was undoubtedly backtracking as quickly as possible to confront this threat to his rear, so the Americans could not remain at Princeton. Washington therefore opted to head into northern New Jersey's Watchung Mountains. His last troops evacuated Princeton that afternoon just as Cornwallis's vanguard appeared. The Americans trudged along the increasingly muddy roads through Somerset Courthouse to Pluckemin, where they halted to rest and collect stragglers. From there, the hungry and cold soldiers pushed on and just before sunset on 6 January reached their destination: Morristown, a village situated on a triangular-shaped plateau secure from any sudden British attack.

The Trenton-Princeton campaign was remarkable for a number of reasons. In less than two weeks, Washington's seemingly moribund army drove the British out of most of New Jersey and into New York City's environs. Doing so helped reignite American morale and bought the new country time to prepare for future British offensives. In three separate engagements—Trenton, Assunpink Creek, and Princeton—the American army not only inflicted a good many more casualties than it sustained but did so despite being outnumbered much of the time. There is no doubt that the Americans benefited considerably from a series of British strategic and tactical blunders that belied William Howe's hitherto thoroughly professional actions around New York City, but Washington was astute enough to recognize these mistakes and take advantage of them. Indeed, Washington demonstrated considerable aggressiveness, nimbleness, and adaptability from his decision to assail Trenton to his march to Morristown. His successes restored flagging confidence in his leadership in and out of his army. As Delaware politician Caesar Rodney explained, "But while Washington survives the great American cause cannot die, his abilities seem to be fully equal to the public spirit that called him forth. History does not furnish you with a greater piece of generalship than he exhibited [at Princeton]."[48] Washington's chief lieutenants also performed well. Most of them displayed the same bravery and combativeness that they showed in fighting around New York City, but this time to much better effect. Whether they could continue to function at this level when the British resumed the war in earnest remained to be seen.

Conclusions

Congress appointed eight brigadiers in the last quarter of 1776. It did not elevate them all at once, but a few at a time, in an ad hoc manner, and in response to immediate problems and pressures. Congress continued to rely on seniority, merit, and state origins as its criteria for selecting generals, but it had not yet codified these criteria. As usual, the weight Congress allotted to each standard varied from congressman to congressman and state delegation to state delegation. On the one hand, two of the brigadiers, Fermoy and Knox, owed their promotions primarily to merit—or, in Fermoy's case, to perceived merit. On the other hand, seniority and state origins accounted for the appointment of the other five officers. Of the eight new brigadiers, only three served with Washington in the New York City and Trenton-Princeton campaigns: Fermoy, Knox, and Stephen. Although Knox once again proved his worth, Fermoy and Stephen committed military sins that hindered the war effort or angered Washington.

The New York City and Trenton-Princeton campaigns provided the rest of Washington's generals with some hard-earned experience leading their brigades and divisions in action. Their performances ran the gamut between sorely lacking and showing promise. Brigadiers such as McDougall and Stirling demonstrated plenty of combativeness, but this did not yield positive battlefield results. The records of Washington's major generals that autumn and winter were also uneven. No one doubted Putnam's physical courage, but his faulty dispositions on Long Island indicated that Congress had promoted him beyond his intellectual abilities. Heath and Spencer did so little to impress Washington that he took advantage of the changing military situation to transfer both men to regions where he hoped their mediocrity would do less harm to the cause. Greene and Sullivan made serious mistakes around New York City—Sullivan by poorly deploying his men along Guana Heights and Greene by recommending fighting for Fort Washington—but justified Washington's confidence in them by showing considerable improvement during the Trenton-Princeton campaign. Finally, although Lee's strategic instincts were often good, his attempt to impose his plans on Washington hindered Washington's efforts to concentrate his forces behind the Delaware. Lee's capture averted—temporarily, as things turned out—what might have become a damaging and distracting confrontation between the American army's two most important officers.

CHAPTER 3

Turmoil and Strife

1777

Morristown Winter

Although Washington originally saw Morristown primarily as a refuge for his exhausted army, he soon recognized that the town offered additional military advantages. Morristown was not only easily defended and invulnerable to surprise British attack, but it was also well situated for his army to respond quickly to a British drive either across New Jersey toward Philadelphia or up the Hudson River toward Albany. Moreover, Morristown could serve as a base from which American troops could harass British patrols and prevent them from gathering sufficient provisions to feed their horses. Washington had only a few thousand remaining Continentals, as well as the resurgent New Jersey militia, with which to undertake such operations. However, throughout the winter they succeeded in making life miserable for the British garrisons along New Jersey's Raritan River by ambushing foraging expeditions, threatening supply lines, and sniping at exposed sentries. If in the end the Americans failed to cripple the British war machine enough to prevent it from assuming the offensive that spring, they did succeed in maintaining the initiative and keeping the enemy off balance. After more than year as commander in chief, Washington was coming into his own as a strategist.

Paperwork typically occupied a disproportionate amount of Washington's limited time. Working from a local tavern that he appropriated for his headquarters, Washington spilled considerable ink in his efforts to manage and maintain his army. As usual, he struggled to overcome shortages in everything from clothing to equipment to food. Other, less common problems also intruded on his daily routine, such as subduing troublemaking New Jersey loyalists and inoculating his army against smallpox. Although Washington came down with an illness so serious that some feared for his life, he recovered and returned to his never-ending and thankless duties. He could, however, take comfort in his wife's presence and the warm afterglow generated by his recent successes.

Insufficient manpower was among the most persistent and serious difficulties Washington faced at Morristown. Without enough soldiers, Washington knew that there was no way he could stop another sustained British offensive. Congress recognized the problem as well and had already undertaken steps to resolve it. In September 1776 Congress authorized the establishment of eighty-eight new Continental battalions, or regiments—the Americans usually used the terms interchangeably—and in December tacked on an additional sixteen, for a total of approximately 75,000 men. During the winter officers fanned out throughout the states to recruit by means fair and foul. The initial reports to Washington and Congress were positive, and it appeared as if the units were filling up expeditiously. That being the case, Washington moved forward with plans to organize and command all the soldiers he assumed—naively, as things turned out—would pour into Morristown at the end of the winter.

Mulling things over, Washington concluded that his revitalized army would require additional generals. He figured he needed one brigadier for every four-regiment brigade and a major general for every three brigades. He also wanted three lieutenant generals for unspecified reasons, though probably to lead each of the departments. By Washington's accounting, this totaled nine new major generals and twenty-seven brigadiers. He assumed that Congress would promote the three most senior major generals—Philip Schuyler, Israel Putnam, and Horatio Gates—to lieutenant general and would follow a similar logic with the major generals. As for the new brigadiers, Washington recommended that the states furnish them to command their own troops. This would avoid the controversy and contention that usually accompanied the process—or, more accurately, would transfer it to the state level. Washington also wanted the appointments made as soon as possible. When he heard that congressmen were dragging their feet because they worried that all these generals would cost too much money, Washington assured them that the opposite was true. New generals, he noted, would actually save money by uncovering fraud and weeding out ineffective officers from their units. Moreover, since there was not much time before active campaigning began, he hoped the generals were on hand soon to help enlist, organize, train, and discipline their outfits, and to alleviate the enormous paperwork burden under which he labored.[1]

Washington was, with a couple important exceptions, content to leave the selection of these new generals to Congress. Besides, if Congress followed his advice and relied on seniority for the lieutenant and major generals, and on the states for the brigadiers, there should not be much debate or controversy over the promotions. However, he did suggest that Congress appoint two men as brigadiers who were not currently in Continental service. The first, John Cadwalader, was a prominent Pennsylvanian who had done so much to rally the Philadelphia militia for the Trenton-Princeton campaign that Washington marked him for promotion even before he crossed the Delaware to assail Trenton. Although Cadwalader failed to fulfill his part of Washington's plan for that engagement, he played an important role in the Battle of Princeton. In recommending Cadwalader, Washington noted, "I have found him a man of ability, a good disciplinarian, firm in his principles, and of intrepid bravery."[2]

Washington also suggested that Congress appoint Benjamin Lincoln a general. The forty-four-year-old Lincoln had been a well-to-do and well-connected Massachusetts farmer, selectman, member of the General Court, and militia officer before the war. Massachusetts's new state government made him a brigadier general in its militia during the siege of Boston, and in that capacity he impressed Washington. Although he participated in the Battle of White Plains, he remained behind in the Hudson Highlands during the Trenton-Princeton campaign. Despite his broad shoulders and muscular frame, Lincoln did not make a good first impression. He suffered from a speech impediment and narcolepsy, so he sometimes fell asleep in midsentence while dictating correspondence. Nor did he possess much prewar combat leadership experience, having spent the Great War for Empire in Massachusetts. However, people respected Lincoln as an honest, mild-mannered, and modest man who took his Congregationalist Christianity seriously. Others lauded his good judgment, unfailing courtesy, quiet competency, and industriousness. His strength of character drew people to him, making him the perfect officer to rally and organize the militia. Washington certainly saw him in this light and recommended him to Congress by writing, "I should not do him justice, were I not to add, that he is a gentleman well worthy of notice in the military line. He commanded the militia from Massachusetts last summer or fall rather, and much to my satisfaction, having proved himself on all occasions, an active, spirited, sensible man."[3] This may have been true, but Lincoln had not yet had the opportunity to prove himself in battle. As a result, in this instance Washington confused character for generalship. For all his amiability and integrity, Lincoln lacked that ruthless drive, that obsession with winning regardless of others' feelings, that separated extraordinary from average generals. Lincoln had talent and ability, but he was not a great battlefield commander.[4]

Congress was still meeting in Baltimore when it took up the issue of appointing new generals on the last day of January 1777, and discussion continued on and off for the next three weeks. Several state delegations wanted to avoid the contention and controversy that had previously plagued such debates by developing hard-and-fast rules for promotions. The current uncertainty, they argued, was unfair to officers whose futures were held hostage to Congress's whims, prejudices, and subjectivity. Others responded that doing so would tie Congress's hands and therefore interfere with the republican principles on which the revolution rested. In terms of specifics, one proposal called for relying on strict seniority for promotions. It was a simple and clear concept to which officers were accustomed. The Maryland, North Carolina, and Virginia delegations countered by suggesting that states nominate generals in proportion to the number of soldiers they provided. This idea for a quota system generated considerable support among delegates because it rewarded effort—the more men a state provided, the more generals it would get. One person observed, "The rule of succession is most familiar to officers and therefore most agreeable to them, but the proportion would give greatest satisfaction to the states."[5] In each case, though, someone offered an amendment that would give Congress the power to elevate officers outside the usual procedure for acknowledged and meritorious service. The deliberations proved so difficult that one congressman referred to them as "perplexed, inconclusive, and irksome." Just about the only thing that Congress could initially agree on was that the question was a complicated one that extended well beyond an officer's performance.[6]

On 19 February Congress finally resolved the issue with its Baltimore Resolution. In it, Congress decided "that in voting for general officers, a due regard shall be had to the line of succession [seniority], the merit of the persons proposed, and the quota of troops raised, or to be raised, by each state."[7] The resolution codified the practice Congress had generally followed almost from the war's start in selecting its generals. However, like so many compromises, it completely satisfied almost no one and raised more questions than it answered. In particular, it failed to spell out how much weight Congress would give to each criterion. Nor did it define terms such as "merit" and "quota." One congressman later referred to "the mysterious trinity of seniority, merit, and quota."[8] It was guaranteed to feed the discontent some officers already felt about a process they believed was unfairly subjective, unpredictable, and political. Moreover, one North Carolina delegate complained that Congress disregarded it immediately and resorted instead to the usual logrolling, politicking, and favoritism. The important thing, though, was that Congress reserved for itself considerable latitude in making its appointments to general.[9]

Congress rejected Washington's suggestion to create lieutenant generals because the delegates figured that major generals could run the various military departments just as well. They also worried that filling these positions would generate too much favoritism and factionalism within the officer corps. Although Congress originally planned to promote three new major generals, it upped the number to five to facilitate the compromises necessary to settle the issue. On 19 February, after considerable debate, Congress appointed as its new major generals, in order of seniority: William Alexander, Lord Stirling (New Jersey), Thomas Mifflin (Pennsylvania), Arthur St. Clair (Pennsylvania), Adam Stephen (Virginia), and Benjamin Lincoln (Massachusetts). Except for Lincoln, their seniority was identical to that which they held as brigadiers. These men joined Philip Schuyler (New York), Israel Putnam (Connecticut), Horatio Gates (Virginia), William Heath (Massachusetts), Joseph Spencer (Connecticut), John Sullivan (New Hampshire), and Nathanael Greene (Rhode Island) on the roster of active major generals. Congress relied mostly on state quotas and the usual favoritism for its selections, so it passed over several brigadiers who it might have elevated had it used strict seniority: David Wooster (Connecticut), Benedict Arnold (Connecticut), John Armstrong (Pennsylvania), Andrew Lewis (Virginia), Robert Howe (North Carolina), John Nixon (Massachusetts), Alexander McDougall (New York), Samuel Parsons (Connecticut), and James Clinton (New York).

Although it is difficult to completely reconstruct the logic behind Congress's appointments, some things seem clear. Virginia's congressional delegation had committed the state to supply more regiments to the new army—twenty-one—than any other, but it only had one major general: Horatio Gates. Moreover, Gates was an Englishman who had lived in Virginia for less than ten years, so he was hardly a native son. That being the case, it only seemed fair to provide the state with another major general. Congress's decision to select Adam Stephen over the more senior Andrew Lewis was probably due to Stephen's impressive military background and support within Congress. Pennsylvania delegate Benjamin Rush, for instance, had written the previous December, "Stephen must be made a major general. He has genius as well as knowledge."[10] Pennsylvania's congressional delegation, for its part, had promised to raise eighteen regiments, third behind Virginia and Massachusetts. Despite this substantial pledge, Pennsylvania had no major generals. Elevating Thomas Mifflin and Arthur St. Clair rectified this oversight. Congress did so at the expense of another Pennsylvanian, John Armstrong. Armstrong had both an extensive military record in the Great War for Empire and Washington's support, so it is unclear why Congress passed him over. The most likely explanation is that Mifflin and St. Clair had done more to establish personal connections with the delegates. Making New Jersey's Stirling a major general rewarded a medium-sized state with great strategic importance that lacked a major general. Finally, Lincoln was an anomaly because he came directly from the militia, but he had Washington's strong recommendation.

There were also reasons behind Congress's decision to pass over some of the brigadiers. New York had pledged the same number of regiments as New Jersey, but its congressional delegation was down to one man and was therefore ineligible to vote. Without any effective representation in Congress, it was unsurprising that New Yorkers McDougall and Clinton were not elevated. Because Connecticut already had two major generals in Israel Putnam and Joseph Spencer, Congress saw no point in granting it a third by promoting Arnold or Parsons. The same held true with Massachusetts's John Nixon, once Congress opted to appoint Lincoln. Although North Carolina pledged ten regiments to the army, its delegation refused to participate in the selection of major generals because one of its congressmen, Thomas Burke, was angry that Congress seemed to disregard the rules it had just adopted in its Baltimore Resolution. Finally, Maryland, which had committed itself to raising eight regiments, could also claim a major general, but its delegation failed to press for one because the state's Council of Safety had expressed little interest in doing so.[11]

Congress had begun the process of supplying Washington with additional brigadiers even before it appointed its latest batch of major generals. Two weeks earlier, on 5 February, Congress promoted Francis Nash to brigadier. Nash was a forty-four-year-old, Virginia-born North Carolina lawyer, businessman, and legislator. One delegate described him as "brave, modest, sensible, attentive, and good tempered."[12] Congress expected Nash to recruit much of North Carolina's allotment of troops in the western part of the state and then march them northward to join Washington's army with those gathered by fellow North Carolinian Brig. Gen. James Moore. Although Nash carried out his instructions, Moore died of illness on 15 April 1777.[13]

Two days after Congress chose its new major generals, it added ten new brigadiers as well. Although this was a nearly 60 percent increase over the current number of active brigadiers, it was still too few as far as Washington was concerned. They were, in order of seniority: Enoch Poor (New Hampshire), John Glover (Massachusetts), John Paterson (Massachusetts), Anthony Wayne (Pennsylvania), James Varnum (Rhode Island), John De Haas (Pennsylvania), George Weedon (Virginia), Peter Muhlenberg (Virginia), John Cadwalader (Pennsylvania), and William Woodford (Virginia). Because Virginia, Massachusetts, and Pennsylvania together promised to contribute nearly half of the Continental army's regiments, eight of the new brigadiers predictably came from those states. As for specific individuals, Cadwalader, Glover, and Poor all had solid combat records, substantial support in Congress, and Washington's backing. De Haas and Paterson, for their part, had Gates's endorsement. Varnum was from a small state and was not necessarily well liked in and out of Congress, but Washington had promised him the previous summer to look into getting him promoted after Varnum complained that other officers had been wrongly advanced over his head. Washington had also recommended that Congress elevate Connecticut colonels James Wadsworth and Jedediah Huntington, but Congress passed them over because the delegates felt that the state already had sufficient brigadiers in Arnold and Parsons. The same logic prevented Georgia, New Jersey, and South Carolina from attaining any new brigadiers. Maryland's state government had not expressed much interest in securing additional brigadiers for its troops, New York's sole delegate was in no position to lobby for its officers, and Delaware was too small to justify one. For seniority, Congress took the path of least resistance by basing it on the men's prior ranks and dates of commission. The two officers appointed directly from the militia, Cadwalader and Woodford, were placed at the bottom of the roster.[14]

The promotion of someone to general did not necessarily make it so. Although Washington had strongly recommended John Cadwalader's appointment, he knew that getting him to accept it would be a tough sell. On 3 March Washington wrote Cadwalader to urge him to take his commission. Washington noted that now more than ever he needed quality people such as Cadwalader in the army. Cadwalader rejected the offer, however, probably because he worried that Continental officers over whose heads he had been advanced would resent him. A couple years later he told Washington that he deeply regretted his decision, but by then it was too late. Washington was unsurprisingly disappointed by his inability to recruit such a valuable officer, but he maintained his respect and admiration for Cadwalader until the war's end.[15]

Nor was Washington able to secure John De Haas's services. De Haas was a Dutch-born Pennsylvanian who rose to the rank of major in the Great War for Empire. When the Revolutionary War broke out, he led a Pennsylvania regiment in the Canadian campaign. One observer called him an experienced officer, well acquainted with military discipline, and a worthy and honest man. While in Canada he had clashed with Benedict Arnold because he refused Arnold's orders to burn an American Indian village. Later, he impressed first Gates and then Washington during the Trenton-Princeton campaign. De Haas fell ill with gout in February 1777 and returned to his Lebanon, Pennsylvania, home. Washington sent for him several times but heard no response. Finally, on 19 June, Congress informed Washington that De Haas had resigned.[16]

Happily, Washington was more successful in retaining John Glover. Glover was home in Marblehead on recruiting duty when he learned of his promotion. Although he was touched by Congress's and Washington's confidence in him, his initial inclination was to decline because he did not believe he deserved the honor. On 26 April Washington wrote to Glover that he was surprised to hear that Glover did not want the appointment. Washington expressed appreciation for Glover's modesty but noted that there was no one more qualified in the army to lead a brigade. By way of proof, Washington evoked Glover's industry, activity, and ability to get the best out of others. Ratcheting up the pressure, Washington observed that Glover's resignation would also hand the British a public relations coup. Washington's entreaties had their desired effect. Glover was nothing if not loyal to his country and his commander in chief, so he agreed to return to the army and accept his commission, even though this meant leaving behind his eight motherless children.[17]

Congress's explicit decision to take into account state origins in selecting its latest clutch of generals not unexpectedly angered some of those officers who would have been promoted had Congress based its determinations solely on seniority. These included Brig. Gens. John Armstrong and Andrew Lewis, who ranked, respectively, third and fourth on the list of brigadiers. Washington valued both men and did not want to lose their services. He wrote to Lewis:

> I was much disappointed at not perceiving your name in the list of major generals lately made by Congress, and most sincerely wish that the neglect may not induce you to abandon the service. Let me beseech you to reflect that the period is now arrived, when our most vigorous exertions are wanted—when it is highly and indispensably necessary for gentleman of abilities in any line, but more especially the military one, not to withhold themselves from public employment, or suffer any small punctilio to persuade them to retire from their country's service.[18]

Washington added that if Lewis continued to do a good job, Congress would surely recognize his merit and elevate him. Unhappily, Armstrong and Lewis both resigned their commissions rather than submit to this apparent humiliation. A similar discontent extended to some of those colonels passed over. For example, New Hampshire's John Stark was a hard-fighting and well-respected veteran who had seen action at Bunker Hill, Three Rivers, Trenton, and Princeton. Washington thought highly of him and worried that he might not react well to Congress advancing Glover, Paterson, and Poor ahead of him. Indeed, like Armstrong and Lewis, Stark concluded that Congress had lost confidence in him, so he quit the Continental army and returned home.[19]

Benedict Arnold was the most prominent victim of Congress's emphasis on state quotas in appointing generals. Although he was the army's second-most senior brigadier, Congress passed him over because Connecticut already had two major generals in Spencer and Putnam. Neither Spencer nor Putnam, though, had contributed much to the war effort. Arnold, however, was probably the most proficient combat commander the army had yet produced, with a record of distinguished leadership from Quebec to Valcour Island to prove it. He was also one of the army's touchiest, proudest, and most belligerent officers. He was therefore predictably outraged by the congressional decision. He interpreted it as evidence that Congress lacked confidence in his leadership and did not appreciate the many sacrifices he had made for the cause. Indeed, Arnold was so incensed that he asked for a court of inquiry to clear his name. In a letter to Washington, Arnold vented, "Their [Congress's] promoting of junior officers to the rank of major generals, I view as a very civil way of requesting my resignation, as unqualified for the office I hold. My commission was conferred unsolicited, received with pleasure only as a means of serving my country, with equal pleasure I resign it, when I can no longer serve my country with honor."[20]

The thought of losing Arnold's services greatly distressed Washington. As far as he was concerned, Arnold was one of the army's most enterprising, effective, and spirited officers. When he realized that Arnold was not listed among the new major generals, he wrote to him to counsel caution. His omission from the roster, Washington noted, might be an oversight or a mistake. Whatever the cause, Washington promised to do what he could to remedy the situation. Washington was puzzled to learn of Congress's logic for passing over Arnold and urged the delegates to reconsider their decision. In a follow-up letter to Arnold informing him of Congress's rationale, Washington observed that public institutions sometimes act unreasonably, and that Arnold should take comfort in knowing that he deserved better treatment. "I confess this is a strange mode of reasoning," Washington wrote. "But it may serve to show you that the promotion which was due to your seniority was not overlooked for want of merit in you."[21] He did not advise any particular course of action but instead suggested that Arnold think it over. As for a court of inquiry, Washington stated that it was impossible to convene one because no one had leveled any formal charges against Arnold that required adjudication.[22]

On 25 April two thousand British soldiers landed on the Connecticut shore and marched inland toward an American army supply depot at Danbury. There they destroyed large quantities of everything from tents to shoes to barrels of provisions, but on their way back to the coast they were attacked by Connecticut militia commanded by David Wooster. Washington had sent Wooster to New England after his maligned stint in Canada angered many congressmen. Arnold was staying with his family at nearby New Haven when he heard the news, so he rushed to the scene to offer his services. The British escaped after a series of running battles in which Wooster was mortally wounded and two of Arnold's horses were shot out from under him. Although the British severely damaged the American army's logistics, Congress and the public focused instead on the spirited response to the raid. Doing so garnered Arnold additional laurels for his gallant leadership. Congress was so impressed that on 2 May it reversed itself and voted to promote him to major general. Later, it also presented to him an elegant horse properly caparisoned as a gift. As for Wooster, Congress resolved to fund a monument in his honor, thus giving him credit in death that it had denied him in life.

Unhappily for Washington, Congress's decision failed to appease Arnold. Although he was now a major general, he remained junior to those five brigadiers Congress had elevated the previous February. Arnold wanted his seniority restored too. Washington was sympathetic, and even those generals advanced ahead of Arnold's were amenable to the idea. Arnold's insistence and arrogance, though, alienated a good many congressmen who had voted for his promotion. Congress did not take up the issue until August. After a two-day debate, it rejected by a six-states-to-four vote a proposal to grant Arnold his seniority. One delegate explained that many congressmen resented what they perceived as Arnold's efforts to dictate terms to them. As far as many congressmen were concerned, Arnold's conceit threatened civilian control of the military. An outraged Arnold did not resign, but instead he added this latest affront to the increasingly thick mental ledger of wrongs he believed those in authority had inflicted on him.[23]

As for the remaining brigadiers Congress passed over, there is no evidence that Clinton, Nixon, or Parsons ever expressed any resentment to Congress. Nearly two years later, McDougall alluded to the shabby treatment he felt he had received at Congress's hands, but he assured Washington that he would not let such feelings overcome his patriotism. Down in Charleston, Robert Howe told Washington that he disliked Congress's decision, but he never thought about resigning because of it. At the same time, though, Howe lobbied congressional allies to use their influence to get Congress to promote him and restore his seniority. Howe's efforts eventually paid off, but not until eight months later.[24]

In addition to promotions, there were other changes in the American army's high command that winter. After Washington moved his army to New Jersey, he left William Heath behind in New York to guard the Hudson Highlands. Although Heath assumed that campaigning was over and asked for permission to return to Massachusetts to visit family and recruit, Washington instead ordered him to launch a diversionary attack on Fort Independence, a British outpost in Bronx County near New York City. In response, on 18 January 1777, Heath led six thousand militiamen against the fort. Unfortunately for Heath, the outnumbered British garrison holed up behind their fortifications and refused his summons to surrender. Without entrenching tools and heavy artillery, Heath was in no condition to conduct a proper siege. Worse yet, heavy rains ruined much of his ammunition. After mulling over his predicament, on 29 January Heath gave up and retreated northward. Doing so exposed him to innumerable charges of timidity, hesitation, and bluster. When Washington got the details, he rebuked Heath for his performance, focusing in particular on his cautiousness and "farcical" call for the garrison to capitulate. A hurt Heath replied that his councils of war had unanimously agreed with his decisions. If anyone was at fault, he continued, it was one of his subordinates, Brig. Gen. Samuel Parsons.

Heath's failure merely reinforced Washington's conviction that Heath lacked a good combat commander's aggressiveness and forcefulness. In March Washington assigned Heath to replace Artemas Ward as chief of the Eastern Department in Boston. Ward had wanted to step down for months, but Congress and Washington had been too busy to settle on a replacement. Now that the military situation had stabilized, Washington finally got around to fulfilling Congress's orders to name Ward's successor. Washington undoubtedly gave Heath the position not only because he was the senior available major general, but also because his new job would be an administrative one more conducive to Heath's talents. Even after Heath took up his new post, though, Washington continued to find fault with his actions. In early May, for example, Washington complained to Heath about reports that Heath's officers spent too much time loitering, drinking, and gambling.[25]

Heath's departure for Boston meant that Washington had to find a new leader for the strategically vital Hudson Highlands. Washington initially hoped to give the job to Benedict Arnold. Arnold, however, was more interested in traveling to Philadelphia to lobby Congress to restore his lost seniority than in replacing Heath. Washington thereupon turned to Israel Putnam. The fifty-nine-year-old Putnam started life as a farmer but made a name for himself in the Great War for Empire as a company commander. Putnam saw considerable combat in northern New York. At one point he was captured by American Indians and almost burned at the stake until a French officer rescued him from the flames. Putnam was eventually exchanged and returned to duty, and he ended the war as a lieutenant colonel. After the conflict he returned to his Connecticut home and opened up a tavern to supplement his farm income. When he heard about Lexington and Concord, Putnam left immediately for Cambridge to join the fight. Soon after Connecticut made him a brigadier general of its militia, and in that capacity he was the driving force behind fortifying Breed's Hill. After Congress appointed him a Continental major general, Putnam served in the siege of Boston and the fighting around New York City. Later, he took over the Philadelphia garrison while Washington conducted his Trenton-Princeton campaign.

Putnam was a strong and brawny man with a remarkable head of bushy hair. Everyone acknowledged his raw courage and fortitude. Certainly no one questioned his combativeness. According to one story, one night a huge bear carried off one of Putnam's pigs. Awakened by the noise, Putnam crawled into the bear's den on his hands and knees and killed the bear and its cubs with a big stick. Although he possessed little formal education and was barely literate, his cheerfulness, generosity, and honesty enabled Putnam to easily establish rapport with the rank and file. He was tremendously popular at the war's start, but by 1777 there was a growing consensus among congressmen and officers that Congress had promoted him beyond his abilities. On the one hand, he did not understand the intricacies of logistics, personnel management, strategy, and intelligence, leading some to question his judgment. On the other hand, he did possess a rough common sense that helped compensate for his ignorance of these larger issues. Even so, one delegate put it as early as July 1775, "He is totally unfit for everything, but only [for] fighting."[26] Washington was well aware of Putnam's limitations and frustrated with the slowness with which Putnam obeyed some of his orders that winter. This being the case, Washington's 12 May 1777 decision to appoint Putnam to such an important independent command seems odd. However, Washington respected the seniority principle, and as a major general Putnam certainly had claim to the post. Washington could also count on Putnam to fiercely resist any British offensive up the Hudson River. Finally, Washington expected Putnam's new second-in-command, Alexander McDougall, to temper Putnam's impetuousness and provide sound advice.[27]

Putnam was not the only general who left Washington's army that winter and spring. In April Congress directed Arthur St. Clair to take charge of Fort Ticonderoga. The forty-year-old, Scottish-born officer had attended the University of Edinburgh and apprenticed with a doctor before using part of his inheritance to purchase a commission in the British army in 1757. He had fought bravely during the Great War for Empire at the siege of Louisbourg and on the Plains of Abraham outside Quebec. He later married into a well-to-do Boston family, resigned his commission, bought a tract of land in Pennsylvania, and prospered. When the Revolutionary War began, he raised a regiment and participated in the Canadian and Trenton-Princeton campaigns. Washington's willingness to heed St. Clair's advice to sidestep the British army and march into central New Jersey made possible the American victory at the Battle of Princeton. Gates and Thompson both spoke highly of him. St. Clair was a handsome, well-mannered, and honorable man without the cloying ambition of some of his colleagues. His steadiness, prudence, and experience contributed to Congress's decision to promote him to first brigadier and then major general.

Washington regretted losing St. Clair's services not only because he considered him a valuable officer, but also because this left him without a Pennsylvanian to lead the state's Continental brigade now that Armstrong had resigned from and Cadwalader and De Haas refused to serve in the Continental army. To command the Pennsylvanians, in May Washington sent for the man St. Clair was replacing at Ticonderoga, Brig. Gen. Anthony Wayne. Although Wayne had assured the Northern Department commander, Philip Schuyler, that he was making progress readying the fort for operations, he confessed to others that he had not made much headway. Indeed, the immense responsibilities of running Ticonderoga in the winter had almost ruined Wayne's health, so he was happy for the opportunity to assume a more active job conducive to his combative personality.[28]

Moreover, several generals returned home that winter to help recruit the large army Congress had authorized: Enoch Poor to New Hampshire; John Glover, John Nixon, and John Paterson to Massachusetts; and James Varnum to Rhode

Island. When it became increasingly obvious that the British planned an offensive from Canada toward Albany, Washington directed several of them—Poor, Nixon, and Paterson—to take their brigades to Ticonderoga to help Schuyler defend the region. Doing so deprived Washington of several of his most competent officers, men who had proven themselves around New York City and in the Trenton-Princeton campaign. By way of compensation, Washington received new units and new commanders from southward. Virginia, for instance, sent Brig. Gens. Peter Muhlenberg and William Woodford to join the army with their brigades.

In addition to managing his new generals, Washington continued to ride herd over the old ones. Familiarity with them did not necessarily make his job any easier. While no one questioned John Sullivan's loyalty to Washington—in February he warned Washington not to venture east of Morristown because he had a premonition that local loyalists might capture him—disgruntlement remained one of his defining characteristics. He interpreted St. Clair's assignment to Ticonderoga as a personal slight. Sullivan complained to Washington that ever since Congress replaced him as head of the army in Canada, all the other major generals had received independent commands except for him: Putnam at New York City and Philadelphia, Gates at Ticonderoga, Greene at Forts Lee and Washington, Spencer at Rhode Island, and Heath in the Hudson Highlands. As far as Sullivan was concerned, this omission demonstrated Congress's unwarranted lack of confidence in his abilities. Therefore, he staked a claim on the Ticonderoga job, writing to Washington, "I cannot think of the command being given to a young officer without conceiving myself a second time treated with neglect which I well know my conduct has not deserved."[29]

Washington undoubtedly sighed upon receiving Sullivan's letter. His response initially struck a chiding and flippant tone: "Do not my dear General Sullivan, torment yourself any longer with imaginary slights, and involve others in the perplexities you feel on that score. No other officer of rank, in the whole army has so often conceived himself neglected, slighted, and ill-treated, as you have done. And none I am sure has had less cause than yourself to entertain such ideas." Washington then patiently explained that the fact that Sullivan had not attained an autonomous position was pure coincidence, a "mere chapter of accidents," rather than a deliberate affront. Warming to his subject, Washington stated that Sullivan's suspiciousness, if left unchecked, would kill his happiness and sow dissension in the army. Moreover, continued Washington, he did not have time to deal with artificial grievances. Finally, Washington warned Sullivan that even if Congress created new armies, Sullivan lacked the seniority to claim them. However Sullivan felt about Washington's letter, he let the matter drop and continued to perform his duties. This did not stop him, though, from lobbying allies in and out of Congress to secure an independent command.[30]

Washington also had trouble with Maj. Gen. William Alexander, Lord Stirling. The fifty-year-old Stirling was the son of a Scottish nobleman whose participation in the Jacobite rebellion cost him his title and lands. Stirling received a good education and served as aide and secretary to Massachusetts governor William Shirley during the Great War for Empire. After the conflict, Stirling was elected to the New Jersey assembly. He also invested considerable time, energy, and effort into an unsuccessful quest to regain the title and lands his father had forfeited. Despite losing his campaign to reclaim his nobility, Stirling declared victory anyway. He started referring to himself as "Lord Stirling" and maintained a standard of living he could not afford. His expensive lobbying, as well as a series of poor business investments, put him deeply in debt. In fact, cynics charged that his commitment to the American cause was motivated as much by a desire to escape his creditors as by patriotism. In this case, the image made the man because Stirling's contemporaries embraced his new persona. Indeed, his pedigree played as large a role as his limited military background in securing his generalship after the Revolutionary War began. John Adams, for example, explained Congress's decision to appoint Stirling a general: "Lord Stirling was a person so distinguished by fortune, family, and the rank and employment he had held in civil life, added to his experience in military life, that it was thought no great uneasiness would be occasioned by his advancement."[31] Although Stirling was captured at the head of his brigade at the Battle of Long Island, the gallantry he exhibited there won him much acclaim. He was exchanged, rejoined the army, and participated in the Trenton-Princeton campaign. Along the way he accrued enough seniority to rank eighth on the list of major generals by the winter of 1776–77.

The bald Stirling looked like a general's general. He impressed people as disparate as Charles Lee and John Stark. Washington liked him for his gracefulness, geniality, dignity, and mild manner. Despite his inspiring initial appearance, though, there was rather less to Stirling than met the eye. For one thing, he drank too much and suffered throughout the war with gout and rheumatism contracted during the Trenton-Princeton campaign, contributing to a certain lethargy in his makeup. His obsession with his title indicated an unbecoming and superficial pride. One officer remembered that a soldier awaiting execution at the gallows for desertion repeatedly cried out, "The Lord have mercy on me!" Stirling responded angrily, "I won't, you rascal, I won't have mercy on you!" His rashness got him into trouble several times during the war. The fact was that Stirling possessed limited intellect and marginal abilities. One observant Frenchman who met him later in the war summed him up well:

> He is accused of liking the table and the bottle, full as much as becomes a lord, but more than becomes a general. He is brave, but without capacity, and has not

> been fortunate in the different commands with which he has been entrusted.... I conversed a long time with him, and found him to be a sensible man, not ill informed of the affairs of his country. He is old and rather dull; but with all this, he will continue to serve, because the employment, though not lucrative, helps to repair a little the disorder of his affairs; and not having quitted the service since the beginning of the war, he has at least zeal and seniority in his favor; thus he will retain the command of the first line, to which his rank entitles him; but care will be taken not to employ him on particular expeditions.[32]

In early May Susannah Livingston, the wife of New Jersey governor William Livingston, complained to Washington that Stirling was trying to throw her out of his Basking Ridge manor, where she had taken refuge the previous November. Mrs. Livingston protested not only Stirling's decision but also the harsh and tactless way in which he informed her of it. Washington worried that this private dispute might become public and distract from the war effort. Governor Livingston was an influential and important politician whose support Washington needed. Washington wrote to Stirling that if Mrs. Livingston's charges were accurate, Stirling should not have lost his temper and should give her sufficient time to find new accommodations. Stirling regretted that Mrs. Livingston got Washington involved in their personal drama. He explained that he needed the rooms Mrs. Livingston was occupying and had politely asked her to move to one of her four houses six weeks earlier. According to Stirling, he called her bluff when she threatened to leave the next morning. In the end, Mrs. Livingston secured lodgings elsewhere, and the kerfuffle did not seem to affect Governor Livingston's good relationships with Washington or Stirling. Even so, the incident served to remind Washington that revolutions were undertaken and supported by people whose day-to-day concerns can intrude upon higher and more abstract principles.[33]

For all his problems with Sullivan and Stirling, Washington was personally fond of both men. This was not, however, true of his relationship with Maj. Gen. Adam Stephen. Stephen was yet another one of those Scotsmen who filled the upper ranks of the Continental army. Born in 1721, Stephen graduated from King's College at the University of Aberdeen, got a medical degree from the University of Edinburgh, and then worked as a naval surgeon. He moved to the colonies in 1748, settled in Virginia, put out his shingle, and engaged in land speculation and cattle raising. He accompanied a young George Washington on his expedition to the Ohio River valley and was among those who surrendered with him at Fort Necessity in 1754. The following year, he—along with Gates, Lee, and Washington—survived the disastrous Battle of the Monongahela, albeit with two wounds. He was later commissioned a colonel, commanded Fort Cumberland in Maryland, and participated in the successful British campaign against Fort Duquesne in 1758. After the war he ran unsuccessfully against Washington for a seat in the House of Burgesses. His military experience and Virginia background convinced Congress to make him a general, and in that capacity he served in the Trenton-Princeton campaign.

Stephen had his good points. He was a natural and well-educated leader who possessed plenty of ambition. However, years of heavy drinking and partying inhibited his judgment and caused him to question, misinterpret, and subvert orders. Because they went way back, Washington recognized Stephen's limitations from the start. In addition, Washington had over the years grown to dislike Stephen. He had good reasons to question Stephen's military competency. During the march on Trenton, for example, Stephen on his own authority dispatched a patrol that could have tipped off the British to the American army's approach. In April 1777 Washington grumbled to Stephen about his refusal to conduct an inquiry Washington had ordered. His failure to do so, Washington noted, was indicative of Stephen's recalcitrance: "I am very sorry that my orders have been too frequently unattended to, and most certainly wish that in the future no cause for a similar complaint may exist."[34] The following month Washington called Stephen on the carpet for distorting and exaggerating the results of a skirmish Stephen's troops fought with the British near Piscataway, New Jersey. Although Stephen claimed victory, more credible observers stated that it was actually a setback. It was easy for Washington to conclude that Stephen was not an asset, but was rather a hindrance, to the war effort.[35]

Stephen was not the only of Washington's Continental generals who faced military defeat that winter. In mid-April three columns of British troops scattered Benjamin Lincoln's division at Boundbrook, New Jersey, in a sudden and surprise attack. Although Lincoln and most of his soldiers escaped, the British captured three cannons and many of the artillerymen, as well as Lincoln's papers and an aide. It was a damning indictment of American camp discipline. Washington ordered an immediate inspection of the men after they reassembled, but there were no negative consequences for the genial Lincoln. Indeed, most officers blamed negligent militia guards and local loyalists for the unfortunate incident.[36]

Whatever Washington's doubts about and problems with his other generals, he maintained his confidence in Nathanael Greene. Greene still felt humiliated by his performances at Forts Washington and Lee, but he took comfort in Washington's expressions of support and his continuing popularity within the army. Indeed, Washington refused to let Greene go home that winter for fear of losing his services even temporarily. Washington showed his faith in Greene by giving him some of the army's most important and delicate assignments that winter and spring. In late March, for example, Washington sent Greene to Philadelphia to discuss with Congress some issues he was not comfortable putting on paper, but that he trusted Greene to handle. As Washington explained to the president of Congress, John Hancock:

> This gentleman is so much in my confidence—so intimately acquainted with my ideas, with our strength, and our weaknesses—with everything respecting the army, that I have thought it unnecessary to particularize or prescribe any certain line of duty or enquiries for him. I shall only say, from the rank he holds as an able and good officer in the estimation of all who know him, he deserves the greatest respect, and much regard is due his opinions in the line of his profession.[37]

Despite Greene's congeniality, he found Congress's slow pace and byzantine political maneuverings enormously frustrating and was happy to return to Morristown. In May Washington dispatched Greene and Knox to the Hudson Highlands to inspect the posts there and make recommendations. Through it all, Greene remained optimistic that once the Americans raised the big army Congress had authorized, their growing resources, cadre of experienced officers, and logistical network would guarantee victory.[38]

Although Washington's initial reports indicated that recruiting for the new Continental battalions Congress had authorized was going well, as spring approached it became clear that mismanagement, corruption, and a lack of enthusiasm would keep his army far below anticipated strength. As the snow began to melt in the northern New Jersey hills, those men who had enlisted trickled into Morristown, and by mid-May Washington counted 8,100 soldiers available for duty for the upcoming campaign. Washington divided them into five divisions of two brigades apiece. Because he had dispatched his New England brigades to Ticonderoga to deal with the expected British offensive from Canada, most of his units hailed from the middle and southern states. Washington assigned his divisions to his five major generals: Greene, Lincoln, Stephen, Stirling, and Sullivan. As a group, these officers left something to be desired. Greene's solid performance in the Trenton-Princeton campaign helped compensate for his poor judgment at Fort Washington, but whether he fully deserved the confidence Washington placed in him remained to be seen. Sullivan had shown considerable common sense by ordering the retreat from Canada and by hurrying to join Washington's army after Lee's capture. Like Greene, he too fought well in the Trenton-Princeton campaign. If he hoped to become a good general, he needed to overcome his impetuousness, touchiness, and chronic bad luck. Washington may have liked Lincoln and Stirling, but neither had demonstrated much strategic or tactical acumen so far. Finally, Stephen had already proven himself hard to manage, borderline insubordinate, and of questionable character and judgment. These problems, as well as Washington's growing hostility, did not bode well for him or his cause.

In Washington's defense, it is hard to see how he could have selected a better batch of division commanders from the roster. Divisions required major generals, but that spring the Continental army contained only thirteen active officers with that rank. Of those, Washington had found Heath, Putnam, and Spencer wanting and transferred them to jobs more conducive to their skills. Others were already filling important posts: Philip Schuyler was running the Northern Department, Thomas Mifflin was the army's quartermaster, and Arthur St. Clair had been assigned to command all-important Fort Ticonderoga. Gates and Arnold were theoretically available for division command. Gates, however, was embroiled in a long-running dispute with Congress over his tenure in the Northern Department. Moreover, he and Washington had not gotten along well during the siege of Boston. Indeed, Washington was already looking on Gates with a suspicion that eventually metastasized into full-blown paranoia.

Washington would have liked to have the combative Arnold at the head of a division. Doing so would mean finding an equally prestigious post elsewhere for one of the current division leaders because Arnold was junior to them all. Besides, Arnold's attention that spring was focused on regaining his lost seniority. There were some capable brigadiers available, especially up at Ticonderoga, but persuading Congress to promote them and then maneuvering them into a divisional slot would be time-consuming and difficult. The fundamental problems, then, were that Washington's bench was too shallow and the command structure too inflexible.

Foreign Volunteers

In February–March 1776 a thirty-six-year-old, down-on-his-luck former Prussian army cavalry major named Frederick William, Baron de Woedtke crossed the Atlantic Ocean to Philadelphia via Cambridge, Massachusetts. The Prussian government had imprisoned Woedtke in 1772 for overstaying his leave, but he escaped to Switzerland the following year, from whence he made his way to France. While there he learned about the American Revolution and decided that the war presented him with an opportunity to recoup his fortunes. He was so broke that he had to borrow money from friends to book passage to America, but he was lucky enough to possess a letter of recommendation from Jacques Barbeu-Dubourg, Benjamin Franklin's French friend, translator, and publisher. Although Barbeu-Dubourg did not actually know Woedtke, he was familiar with someone who vouched for him, and so wrote his letter based on that acquaintance. Barbeu-Dubourg claimed that King Frederick II of Prussia had unfairly persecuted Woedtke. Woedtke was, Barbeu-Dubourg said, actually an honest and experienced officer who could help the Americans develop a proficient cavalry corps. Barbeu-Dubourg noted that because Woedtke had spent his adult years in the military, he lacked education and polish and knew only how to "burn powder and hew off limbs." Nevertheless, concluded Barbeu-Dubourg, Woedtke's love of liberty and Americans' unpretentiousness would compensate for any of his shortcomings.[39]

Congress was so enamored with Woedtke's credentials that on 16 March it unanimously appointed him a brigadier general. The delegates also ordered him to Canada because they figured his knowledge of French and noble background would impress the Canadians. Regrettably, people soon realized that there was rather less to Woedtke than initially met the eye. He had little understanding of American ideals—at one point he said, "Ah! Liberty is a fine thing. I like liberty. The king of Prussia is a great man for liberty!"[40]—and even less of its culture. Moreover, there were allegations that he drank too much. Upon reaching Canada, he got along with John Sullivan and William Thompson but fell ill at Lake George before he had much opportunity to demonstrate his military abilities. One rainy July day a chaplain named Ammi Robbins found Woedtke very sick and afraid to die. When Robbins returned several days later, Woedtke was so weak he could barely talk, but he had accepted his fate. Although the Roman Catholic Woedtke asked Robbins to administer last rites to him, the Protestant minister assured him that his faith in Jesus Christ was all that was necessary to guarantee his salvation, so they prayed the Lord's Prayer together. Woedtke died a few days later, far from home and for a cause he only dimly understood.[41]

Woedtke was among the first of many foreigners who crossed the Atlantic Ocean to offer their services to the United States during the Revolutionary War. Indeed, at one point Silas Deane, an American diplomatic representative in France, wrote to Congress, "Had I ten ships here I could fill them all with passengers for America."[42] They did so for a variety of interrelated reasons. Some professed a sincere commitment to the republican ideals on which the revolution was based. In joining the Continental army, they were advancing the cause of liberty. Others were adventurers who came to America for fame and fortune. Finally, there were also a number of professional officers eager to ply their trade in what was at the time the only major war in the Western world. In each instance, these men hoped to parlay their unique skills into an important role in the conflict.

At first Congress was very receptive to these foreign offers. The army needed men with specialized skills, such as engineering, that few Americans had. Delegates also worried that rejecting these officers would reflect badly on the American cause in France and elsewhere at a time when Congress was trying desperately to secure foreign support. Disgruntled rejected officers might return home and denounce the American war effort to their influential friends. Moreover, congressmen felt obligated to honor commitments made by their diplomatic representatives in Europe even when they disagreed with the terms. Finally, more than a few delegates were starstruck by ennobled foreign officers who possessed the class, manners, and style to which many Americans aspired. Refusing to employ such refined personages might appear ignorant, churlish, or, worst of all, unsophisticated.

There were as many disadvantages as advantages to using foreign volunteers. The most obvious were the cultural and language barriers these men invariably faced in performing their duties. After all, they could not ply their trade effectively if they were unable to speak or understand English. In addition, Congress had to figure out how to integrate them into the Continental army's command structure. Relying on the traditional criteria of seniority, state origins/quotas, and merit to appoint generals was more problematic than usual. These officers had no seniority in the Continental army and could only accrue it by starting at the bottom. However, most of them expected ranks and positions commensurate with those they possessed—or aspired to possess—back in Europe. Giving these to them, though, tended to antagonize American officers passed over and/or displaced. Allocating generalships based on perceived merit seemed like the best idea in theory, but defining and proving it was an inherently subjective task that rarely satisfied everyone. It was tough to convince battle-hardened American generals of the need to surrender their commands and seniority to a foreigner whose accomplishments were based on secondhand accounts. Congress's initial policy for assigning generalships to foreign volunteers was, as seen in Woedtke's case, founded on hunches, first impressions, and recommendations of uncertain credibility. It was therefore not surprising that although some foreign officers contributed greatly to the war effort, others were more trouble than they were worth because they undermined morale, damaged the army, and disrupted the American high command.

As commander in chief, Washington was usually responsible for finding places in the army for those foreigners Congress commissioned. Throughout the winter of 1776–77, he was sometimes hard-pressed to see the benefits that these insistent and pushy foreigners offered. He complained to Congress that most of these men could not contribute to the American cause because they did not speak English. Their inability to communicate effectively also made it difficult for him to differentiate between competent professionals and unqualified adventurers. He noted that Congress's initial tendency to appoint early comers such as Woedtke generals encouraged subsequent arrivals to expect similar treatment. Although he worried that Congress might upset his generals by promoting foreign volunteers over their heads, he still wanted to retain the services of those with specialized skills that the army desperately needed. To resolve the innumerable problems these foreign volunteers presented, Washington asked Congress to develop a clear policy. Washington recommended that Congress create a separate corps of foreign-born soldiers for the foreign officers to command. Their ranks, he continued, should depend on how many troops they recruited for the unit. Moreover, he wanted Congress to make clear to these foreign volunteers that becoming a general did not guarantee them a command. Washington summed up his frustrations in an 11 February 1777 letter to John Hancock:

> You cannot conceive what a weight these kind of people are upon the service, and upon me in particular. Few of them have any knowledge of the branches which they profess to understand, and those that have, are entirely useless as officers from their ignorance of the English language. I wish it were possible to make them understand when commissions are granted to them, that they are to make themselves masters of the English language in some degree, before they can be attached to any particular corps.[43]

Congressmen were not blind to the dilemmas posed by using these foreign volunteers. Many of them, though, blamed the difficulties Washington encountered on Silas Deane, the secret envoy Congress had dispatched to Europe in March 1776 to secure financial support from the French government. As far as some delegates were concerned, Deane had abused his authority and tied Congress's hands by unilaterally promising commissions, positions, and funds to foreign officers who offered their swords to the Continental army. Deane's December 1776 suggestion that Congress replace Washington as commander in chief with a French war hero, Prince Ferdinand, Marshal Broglie, did little to enhance his credibility. Deane justified his decisions by stating that Congress's instructions to him were too vague to cover all the contingencies he faced. He therefore did what he thought was necessary to attain the assistance of well-qualified foreign officers interested in serving in America.

In early 1777 Congress undertook a number of actions to resolve, or at least alleviate, the problem of foreign volunteers. On 18 February Congress authorized Washington to inquire into the military abilities and conduct of these men to determine how they should be best used. He could dismiss those unworthy of their commissions or unable to contribute to the war effort. The following month, Congress established a three-man committee to review applications from foreigners and investigate the status of French officers already in the Continental army. Congress also directed its Committee of Secret Correspondence to tell its agents abroad to discourage foreign officers from coming to America by warning them they would not be employed unless they spoke English. Finally, Congress's collective attitude toward the foreign volunteers became increasingly chilly, skeptical, and unaccommodating. Taken together, these measures dissuaded—and, in many cases, deeply offended—all but the most committed and determined claimants from pursuing commissions. Even so, as late as July 1778 the president of Congress, Henry Laurens, complained that the issue continued to handicap the war effort. Ultimately, France's entry into the war and its need for competent officers, as much as anything else, ended the stream for foreign volunteers crossing the Atlantic.[44]

The unhappy experience of Philippe Charles Tronson du Coudray best illustrates the disruptive impact that foreign volunteer officers could have on the Continental army's command structure. Born in Reims, France, in 1738, du Coudray joined the French army as a young man, trained as a mining engineer, and then transferred to the artillery. He performed so well during France's war in Corsica in 1768–69 that he was elevated over the heads of 180 other officers to adjutant general of artillery. By the time the American Revolution began, he was a colonel with a reputation as one of the most learned and talented officers in the French army. France's decision to surreptitiously support Britain's rebellious colonies brought du Coudray new responsibilities. Du Coudray dutifully fulfilled his orders to scour French arsenals for cannons for the Americans, but he was bored with peacetime routine and longed for the chance to apply his skills in actual combat. Like so many other French officers, he decided to offer his services to the Continental army. Deane sensed a big opportunity as soon as du Coudray broached the subject with him. Du Coudray did not intend to go to America empty-handed; rather, he planned to expedite the delivery of twenty artillery and engineering officers, two hundred brass cannons, and an enormous amount of supplies and equipment the French government had secretly pledged to Congress. However, du Coudray's services did not come cheap. He wanted Congress to appoint him a major general in charge of the Continental army's artillery, subject only to the orders of Congress, its war committee, and his immediate field army commander. Deane knew that granting du Coudray's demands probably exceeded his authority, but he figured that it was too good a deal to pass up. Besides, when Benjamin Franklin arrived in Paris as Congress's envoy to the French government, he supported the agreement. As Deane explained to Congress's Committee of Secret Correspondence:

> Considering the importance of having two hundred pieces of brass cannon, with every necessary article for twenty-five thousand men, provided with an able and experienced general at the head of it, warranted by the minister of this course to be an able and faithful man, with a number of fine and spirited young officers in his train, and all without advancing one shilling, is too tempting an object for me to hesitate about, though I own there is silence in my instructions.[45]

In May 1777 the ship *Aphrodite* arrived in Boston Harbor from France via the West Indies with du Coudray, his companions, and plenty of supplies, weapons, and equipment on board. After presenting himself to William Heath, du Coudray traveled to Washington's headquarters in Middlebrook, New Jersey, on 31 May to meet the commander in chief. There he informed Washington that he was the Continental army's new artillery and engineering leader, as well as a major general. This was news to Washington, who wrote to Congress immediately after his conference with du Coudray to ask for details. He noted that he already had a first-rate artillery commander in Henry Knox and warned that Knox would undoubtedly resign his commission rather than serve under du Coudray. Nevertheless, du Coudray impressed Washington with his obvious expertise and courtly manner. Washington therefore rather blandly expressed his confidence that Congress could resolve the issue to everyone's satisfaction. When du Coudray reached Philadelphia a few days later and presented his credentials to Congress, though, the delegates were unsure how to respond. On the one hand, Du Coudray clearly possessed skills that Congress wanted to take advantage of, was an honorable man, and had already done much to help the patriot cause by facilitating the transfer of those two hundred cannons to America. On the other hand, congressmen felt that Deane had promised too much on their behalf, and they knew that granting his terms would cause no end of trouble. Moreover, du Coudray's insistence that Congress ratify his deal with Deane quickly drained the pool of goodwill that Congress initially had toward him.[46]

Continental generals were predictably outraged when they learned the details of du Coudray's agreement with Deane. Deane's promise to backdate du Coudray's appointment to major general to the previous August meant that du Coudray would become senior to all generals except Washington, Schuyler, Putnam, and Gates. Battle-hardened officers who had been fighting since the war's start found this tough to swallow. Moreover, many officers did not want to see the popular and respected Knox replaced as artillery chief by a stranger. To many du Coudray represented everything wrong with foreign volunteers. They disliked his arrogance, his otherness, and the special treatment he received. Mulling things over, on 1 July Greene, Knox, and Sullivan each wrote Congress that they would resign their commissions if Congress honored Deane's contract with du Coudray. Although they claimed they worried about placing a foreigner in such an important position, they were motivated more by what they perceived as an attack on their honor and the honor of their colleagues.[47]

The three letters merely complicated the issue for Congress. Most delegates were inclined to disavow Deane's contract with du Coudray, but they felt that Greene's, Knox's, and Sullivan's missives prevented them from doing so. They worried that it would look like they had caved in to army pressure if they reneged on du Coudray's deal. That would set a bad precedent for civil-military relations. As far as they were concerned, the letters constituted a danger to civilian control of the military and the republican ideals on which the revolution was based. In addition, many congressmen disliked the generals' disrespectful tone. John Hancock, for instance, called their comments "highly derogatory to the honor and justice of Congress."[48] Writing to Greene, John Adams noted that if the generals had objections to du Coudray's agreement, they should have expressed them privately to individual congressmen, not publicly to the entire legislative body. Their threats, he continued, showed a lack of judgment on Greene's and Knox's part—but not Sullivan's; Adams apparently had no such expectations from him. On 7 July Congress unanimously resolved that Greene, Knox, and Sullivan should resign if they were unable to accept the principle of civil authority over the army. If Congress expected apologies from Greene, Knox, and Sullivan, they were not forthcoming. Instead, the three men ignored the resolution and carried on with their duties. Congress, having made its point, opted to let the matter drop.[49]

Whatever the outcome of its dispute with the generals, Congress still had to determine du Coudray's fate. On 12 July Congress decided to void Deane's contract with du Coudray because Deane lacked the authority to make commitments on its behalf. Nine days later, a congressional committee recommended giving du Coudray an artillery train separate from Knox. When this proved impractical, Congress on 11 August resolved to appoint du Coudray a major general as of that day and to make him inspector general of ordnance and military manufacturing. Although this made good use of du Coudray's abilities, it was not the combat command he sought. Considering the Kafkaesque circumstances in which he found himself, it was unsurprising that du Coudray grew increasingly petulant and frustrated with Congress's refusal to honor the agreement he had negotiated with Deane in good faith. At one point, for example, du Coudray unsuccessfully petitioned Congress to dismiss Massachusetts delegate James Lovell from any committee related to his affairs because of Lovell's hostility toward him. Despite his increasing alienation, du Coudray tried to be useful. In August he inspected American fortifications along the Delaware River and made recommendations for their improvement. When the British threatened Philadelphia in September, du Coudray offered to accept a captain's commission in order to take a more active role in the war. However, on the morning of 16 September du Coudray drowned when the horse on which he was sitting took fright and galloped off a Schuylkill River ferry into the water. He was buried behind a Roman Catholic chapel at public expense. It was a sad and inglorious end for a man thrust into a politically charged environment for which he was ill-equipped. As for Congress's reaction, John Adams best summed up the feelings of most delegates when he rather cynically wrote, "This dispensation will save us much altercation."[50]

Happily for Adams and his congressional colleagues, for every Fermoy and Woedtke who offered their lackluster services, there were also competent and dedicated foreign volunteers whose presence greatly benefited the American cause. One of the best examples of the latter category was Marie Joseph Paul Yves Roche Gilbert du Motier, Marquis de Lafayette. He was born in 1757 in Chavaniac, France, into one of the country's wealthiest and most renowned families. His father was killed in the Great War for Empire, and his mother died when he was eleven, leaving him a vast inheritance. His 1773 marriage to a member of an even more prestigious family placed him at the pinnacle of French society. His awkwardness and solemnity failed to impress people in those rarified aristocratic circles, leading to what he later termed an "unedifying" youth. He joined the French officer corps in 1771 but lost his commission due to budget cutbacks four years later. He was inspired to support the American cause by, of all people, British king George III's brother, the Duke of Gloucester. At a dinner in Metz, the duke's description of the war fired Lafayette's imagination, such that even before the meal ended he promised himself to go to America and fight for the patriots. He got in touch with Silas Deane, who promised him a commission. Although French king Louis XVI directed him to remain in France, Lafayette ignored the royal order and after many adventures set sail for America in late April 1777 with a gaggle of foreign officers in tow.

Lafayette was about six feet tall, with broad shoulders, an oval face, high forehead, and aquiline nose. He may have been sincerely committed to the American cause, but he also saw the war as a way to quench his almost pathological thirst for glory. This was merely one of several rather serious character flaws. He was touchy and proud of his prerogatives, as were most people of his occupation and standing. As a young man accustomed by wealth to getting what he wanted, he could be immature and impulsive when confronted with personal or professional obstacles. He was also willing to use his fortune, rank, and position to pull strings to secure what he could not otherwise obtain through raw ability. Ingratiation, backstabbing, and petulancy played big roles in his interpersonal relationships. During the conflict his high-strung, voluble, and gossipy personality caused trouble on more than one occasion. Finally, his understanding of American culture and institutions was often at best superficial, and at worst just plain wrong.[51]

Lafayette possessed other attributes that overcame and compensated for his less admirable qualities. When Lafayette and his traveling companions reached Philadelphia via Charleston in July 1777, they received a frosty reception from congressmen jaded by the swarms of grubby foreign volunteers offering their swords to the American cause for often unrealistic prices. Lafayette, though, refused to be deterred or discouraged by this standoffishness. Instead, he used the advantages of his nobility and personality to transform his fortunes. Although Lafayette wanted rank and position as much as other foreign officers, he cleverly informed Congress that he was willing to serve as a major general without salary or command so long as he could work under Washington's tutelage. To congressmen accustomed to pushy and demanding foreigners, this was refreshingly altruistic. Congressmen were equally impressed with Lafayette's nobility, associating it with the refinement, taste, and proper breeding to which they aspired. One noted that Lafayette's "address and manner bespeaks his birth." Besides, they worried that offending such a well-connected and prominent person might undermine efforts to secure French support for the revolution. This was all well and good, but Lafayette's positive traits extended beyond his aristocratic background. He was ready and willing to commit both his time and his considerable wealth to the revolution. Such generosity, even from an affluent person, was attractive and disarming. He also showed an eagerness, cheerfulness, and kindness that won over people inclined to distrust foreigners. He demonstrated the openness of someone accustomed to getting his way who sees no reason why the future will be any different. As time went by, Lafayette revealed tremendous physical courage, an ease with authority, the ability to relate to the common soldier, ample common sense, and a surprising amount of prudence. Finally, he was friendly toward everyone, regardless of station, and seemed bereft of guile and insincerity. Taken together, it was almost impossible to dislike him. As Nathanael Greene put it, "He is an exceeding good hearted youth; and highly deserving the love and confidence of America."[52] That there was undoubtedly a measure of calculation to Lafayette's actions and attitudes does not nullify the overall authenticity of the mystique he created. As he explained to his wife, "I am always even-tempered and easygoing and am happy to be liked by everyone, foreigner or American. I like them all. I hope to merit their esteem, and we are satisfied with each other."[53]

The most important relationship Lafayette established was undoubtedly with Washington. When the two men first met at a public dinner in Philadelphia on 5 August, Washington was sufficiently impressed or intrigued with Lafayette to invite him on an inspection of the city's defenses. Even so, at first Washington was unsure what to do with the young Frenchman. Although Congress had agreed to Lafayette's request for a major generalship, Lafayette did not understand that the rank was an honorary one. Instead, Lafayette expected to command a division as soon as Washington decided he was ready. In the end, Congress left Lafayette's fate in Washington's hands. Fortunately for the Frenchman, Washington was not immune to his charms. Lafayette immediately identified Washington as a surrogate father and treated him as such. He showered Washington with attention and praise, asked for advice and help, and inserted himself into Washington's military family. Washington was ordinarily uncomfortable with excessive displays of affection, but he took Lafayette's adulation in stride. Besides, he appreciated Lafayette's zeal and ardor, as well as the sacrifices he made to join the American cause. He eventually came to see Lafayette as, if not exactly the son he never had, then certainly a favored protégé. He wrote to him a year later, "Your love of liberty—the just sense you entertain of this valuable blessing—and your noble, and disinterested exertions in the cause of it, added to the innate goodness of your heart conspire to render you dear to me; and I think myself happy in being linked with you in bonds of strictest friendship."[54] Such favoritism might have created jealousy and resentment among Washington's other generals, but not in this case. Lafayette's title, wealth, and innate friendliness provided him with an immunity unique within the American officer corps and political establishment. Officers and politicians exhibited a tolerance toward Lafayette such that the usual rules of promotion, rank, and honor did not apply to him. This forbearance paid significant dividends during some of the revolution's darkest days.[55]

Johann von Robais, Baron de Kalb was one of the officers who accompanied Lafayette to America. Lafayette may have possessed wealth, glamor, and youth, but de Kalb was the more impressive soldier and man. Born in 1721 in Bavaria into a peasant family, he secured a commission in the French army when he was twenty-two years old. He fought in the War of the Austrian Succession and the Great War for Empire, rising to brigadier general in 1760. After the conflict the French government sent him to America in 1768 to determine the extent of the colonists' anger with the British government. Like some other European officers, he saw the Revolutionary War as both a struggle for liberty and a professional opportunity, so in November 1776 he offered his services to Deane. Deane was so taken with de Kalb's military background, glowing recommendations, and facility with the English language that he extended him a contract that included the promise of a major generalship. As Deane explained:

> I can by no means let slip an opportunity of engaging a person of so much experience, and who is by every one recommended as one of the bravest and most skillful officers in the kingdom. . . . This gentleman has an independent fortune, and a certain prospect of advancement here, but being a zealous friend of liberty, civil and religious, he is actuated by the most important and generous principles in the offer he makes of his services to the States of America.[56]

Despite its growing antipathy toward foreign volunteers, an impressed Congress opted to honor Deane's commitment and appointed de Kalb a major general on 15 September. De Kalb was unsure whether he should accept the agreement because Congress had rejected most of the other French officers who had crossed the Atlantic with him and Lafayette due to their inability to speak English. De Kalb worried that the French people would reproach him for not showing solidarity and returning to Europe with them. Nor was he happy that Congress was more enamored with the inexperienced Lafayette. However, he did not want to travel all the way to America for nothing. He resolved the dilemma—in his mind, anyway—by striking a deal with Congress that gave him the right to go home if French public opinion turned against him. Congress, though, concluded that de Kalb's reluctance was motivated by its decision to give Lafayette seniority, so to sweeten the pot on 4 October it backdated de Kalb's commission to the same day as Lafayette's.[57]

De Kalb was a stout and well-built man who, according to one congressman, resembled Washington in manners and appearance. What he lacked in formal education, he more than made up for in common sense, courage, prudence, and years of practical military experience. He enjoyed the camaraderie of camp life and impressed people with his frankness, generosity, and modesty. He also possessed an abstentious streak unusual for an eighteenth-century European officer that included refraining from alcohol, living simply, rising and retiring early, and subsisting on a diet of bread and beef. One officer wrote, "No man surpassed this gentleman in simplicity and condescension; which gave to his deportment a cast of amiability extremely ingratiating, exciting confidence and esteem."[58] His biggest eccentricity was an obsessive secrecy about his personal correspondence and diaries. To ensure that his papers did not fall into enemy hands, de Kalb always tried to place his baggage in the center of a marching column. Washington did not know what to make of de Kalb when he joined the American army in October 1777 and initially sent him to inspect the Delaware River fortifications. As time went on, though, Washington grew to respect de Kalb and entrusted him with increasingly responsible positions.[59]

Waiting for the British

Washington's pride in driving the British out of most of New Jersey was tempered by his knowledge that his success was limited in scope. Without greater resources and naval power, there was little chance that the Americans could pry the British out of their New York City stronghold. For all their problems in the winter of 1776–77, the British retained the overall strategic initiative. Unfortunately for them, exercising it created a host of new difficulties to overcome. British resources, while more substantial than those of the Americans, were limited. Accumulating the manpower, supplies, and equipment necessary for another sustained campaign stretched British logistics to the breaking point. Long communications lines, inefficient leadership, and jealousies and mistrust among policymakers also mitigated against the formulation of a coherent and coordinated plan to win the war in 1777. Instead, confusion and mismanagement characterized British grand strategy.

Philadelphia Region. *Map by Ken Arbogast-Wilson, WTW Design Group.*

The first part of the British plan was simple enough, at least conceptually. It called for General John Burgoyne to lead an army of around eight thousand soldiers southward from Canada up Lake Champlain to seize Fort Ticonderoga and then push on to Albany on the Hudson River. It was William Howe's role that was complicated. Lord George Germain, the American secretary and the man most responsible for overseeing the British war effort, wanted Howe to take his army up the Hudson in conjunction with Burgoyne's efforts. Howe, however, spent the winter and spring designing an attack on Philadelphia. Although he initially contemplated marching through New Jersey to get there, he decided that the likely presence of Washington's army on his flank and rear made such an undertaking too hazardous. Instead, he opted to use the Royal Navy to transport his army somewhere south of Philadelphia to assail the city from that direction. Doing so would enable him to tap significant loyalist sentiment supposedly in the region, and it might tempt Washington into a decisive battle out in the open that Howe was sure he could win. By the time Germain learned about Howe's intentions, it was too late to change them. Germain therefore accepted Howe's proposal but did so on the assumption that Howe could wrap up his campaign against Philadelphia quickly and redeploy his forces to the lower Hudson River to support Burgoyne. Germain may have envisioned Howe and Burgoyne coordinating their offensives, but the two generals did not see it that way. As far as they were concerned, they were undertaking two separate and independent operations. As things turned out, it proved to be a recipe for disaster.

Before Howe embarked his army for its seaborne voyage toward Philadelphia, he tried to lure Washington's army out of the New Jersey mountains into a battle on open terrain where the British could prevail. He figured that destroying the American army would make the campaign against Philadelphia easier, or perhaps even unnecessary. His plan was to feint a march toward Philadelphia and then crush Washington's army when it emerged from the hills to block the British advance. On 13 June eleven thousand British troops marched out of Brunswick and set their trap near Hillsborough and Middlebrush. Although Washington initially concluded that Philadelphia was Howe's objective, he opted to remain ensconced around Boundbrook. While Washington waited for events to crystallize, he summoned reinforcements from Putnam in the Hudson Highlands, ordered Benedict Arnold to organize defenses behind the Delaware River, tightened his perimeter, called out the New Jersey militia, and dispatched soldiers to harass the British. Washington's discovery that the British lacked the logistical wherewithal to sustain an overland offensive to Philadelphia removed any incentive he may have had for a direct confrontation with the enemy. After five days in position, Howe concluded that Washington would not take the bait. On 19 June the British withdrew back to Brunswick. Washington sent Greene with three brigades and

Col. Daniel Morgan's riflemen in pursuit, then followed up with the remainder of his army. Morgan's riflemen and Anthony Wayne's brigade inflicted some damage on the British rear guard, but Greene did not display enough aggressiveness to capitalize on it. When Howe discovered that his retreat had provoked the response from Washington he had wanted all along, he turned his men around to seek battle, but Americans scuttled away. By now Howe had burned away two weeks of the campaign season and could not afford to waste any more time. He fell back to Amboy, loaded his troops on ships, and abandoned New Jersey to the Americans.

In foiling Howe's attempt to lure his army to its destruction, Washington confirmed his growing strategic maturity. Washington was under no illusions that his Continentals could defeat the British in an engagement out in the open, so he did not attempt it. Instead, he made full use of the region's topographical advantages to offer battle to the British on terms they were unwilling to accept. He did so with the confidence of a general with a full understanding of the military environment in which he is operating. As for Washington's subordinates, none of them made the kind of mistakes that caused the Americans so much grief the previous summer. Washington singled out Greene and Sullivan in particular for praise—the former for leading the pursuit of the retreating British, and the latter for reuniting his vulnerable division with the rest of the army without loss. In doing so, Washington overlooked Greene's timidity and the fact that Sullivan's actions were not especially extraordinary. At Greene's request, Washington also commended Anthony Wayne and Daniel Morgan for their efforts to inflict damage on the British during their withdrawal to Brunswick.[60]

After a series of logistical and meteorological snafus, the transports carrying Howe's sixteen thousand British, Hessian, and loyalist soldiers finally weighed anchor off Staten Island for Philadelphia on 21 July. Americans speculated endlessly in the ensuing weeks as to the British destination. Philadelphia, Albany and the Hudson River, Boston, and even Charleston were among the most common guesses. The fact was, though, that no one knew for sure. Washington grumbled at this additional evidence of the advantages the British gained from their control of the seas and kept his ten thousand troops marching on the roads between the Hudson River and Philadelphia, depending on the latest sightings of the British fleet. Finally, on 25 August, more than a month after they set out, the British disembarked at Head of Elk at the northern end of Chesapeake Bay, confirming that Philadelphia was indeed their objective. Howe's seaborne voyage not only wasted more than a month of prime campaigning weather, but it had also removed him and his army from the strategic chessboard as much as if they had been on the other side of the planet.

On 24 August Washington and most of his troops paraded through Philadelphia on their way to intercept the British army reportedly preparing to land at the northern end of the Chesapeake. Washington had been reluctant to expose his troops to the variety of temptations the capital offered, but he ultimately decided that a show of strength might encourage the patriots, dishearten the loyalists, and dispel rumors that his army was a ragged mob. Four of his five divisions—the remaining one, John Sullivan's, was on its way south after a marginally successful raid on Staten Island two days earlier—entered the city early in the morning, strode through the streets, and crossed the Schuylkill River before proceeding to Darby Heights to camp for the night. The American soldiers marched in one long column to the sound of fifes and drums, twelve ranks wide, with green sprigs in their hats. To enhance the army's professional appearance, Washington ordered its baggage to bypass the city and meet it on the other side. In addition to the women and teamsters, Nathanael Greene and Henry Knox were also absent. For some reason, they traveled forty miles to Bethlehem on a sightseeing and shopping trip, returning too late to participate. It had stormed the night before, and the morning was overcast and gray, but a good crowd was there to watch the soldiers tramp by. Despite the soldiers' tatterdemalion clothing and haphazard formation, most of the onlookers seemed suitably impressed.

If Washington appeared preoccupied during the parade, he had good reason. He had to worry not only about where and when Howe's army would land, but also about John Burgoyne's campaign in northern New York. Although Washington was not directly responsible for the Northern Department, events there certainly had an impact on his actions. On 5 July Burgoyne and his approximately eight thousand troops seized Fort Ticonderoga by placing artillery on a mountain overlooking the place, rendering it untenable. The American garrison escaped to fight another day, but the fall of the supposedly impregnable fortress opened the way for the British to invade the Hudson River valley and alarmed Americans who had expected Ticonderoga's defenders to hold out indefinitely. Most of the blame for the debacle fell on Ticonderoga's commander, Arthur St. Clair. People accused him of cowardice and even treason. Congress recalled St. Clair and ordered an investigation into his conduct that eventually concluded in his court-martial. Washington was, like everyone else, shocked that St. Clair abandoned the fort. He withheld judgment, though, because he respected St. Clair and figured he must have had a good reason for his decision. As for St. Clair, he insisted that he made the right call because remaining in Ticonderoga after the British occupied the overlooking mountain would have led to the capture of the entire garrison. By withdrawing, St. Clair preserved his three thousand troops for future operations. As he explained to Washington:

> I do not wonder that you should have some doubts about the propriety of my conduct, though it gives me a very painful sensation to know myself, but for a

> moment, the subject of a doubt with you. I have, however, the strongest hopes, when your excellency comes to be fully informed of our situation and force, you will not condemn me; and although I am not solicitous about the opinion of the world (though very far from disregarding it), I wish to hold a character with your excellency something more than merely negative.[61]

Washington tried to be helpful. He reinforced Schuyler's army with two brigades from Peekskill in the Hudson Highlands and later dispatched Col. Daniel Morgan's riflemen as well. He also sent what matériel he could spare. He pointed out to Schuyler that he had an opportunity to strike a crippling blow against the British army now that Burgoyne had abandoned his supply lines and marched inland. Finally, Washington ordered two high-ranking generals northward to help Schuyler. The first was Benedict Arnold. When Washington learned about the British conquest of Fort Ticonderoga, he recommended to Congress that it send Arnold. Washington greatly respected the courage and initiative Arnold had demonstrated at Quebec and at Valcour Island. Moreover, during the British raid on Danbury Arnold showed an ability to rally the local militia that would prove useful in northern New York. Arnold was familiar with the region, having served there the previous year, and he was conveniently nearby and underemployed. Although Arnold was still bickering with Congress over his seniority as a major general, he agreed to set the issue aside while the current crisis unfolded. Arnold left Washington's headquarters at the Clove, New York, on 18 July and arrived in Albany four days later. Schuyler was happy to have such a stalwart fighter on hand to help pick up the pieces after Ticonderoga's fall.[62]

The other general was one of his division commanders, Benjamin Lincoln. Washington thought so highly of Lincoln that he had the previous January recommended his appointment to general directly from the Massachusetts militia. Because Lincoln had impressed Washington with his ability to organize and inspire the militia during the siege of Boston, Washington hoped that Lincoln could put some fight into New England militiamen demoralized by the easy British occupation of Fort Ticonderoga. As Washington explained to Schuyler,

> This gentleman has always supported the character of a brave, active, judicious officer and he is exceedingly popular and much respected in the state of Massachusetts, to which he belongs. [H]e will have a degree of influence over the militia, which cannot fail being highly advantageous. I intend him more particularly for the command of the militia and I promise myself it will have a powerful tendency to make them turn out with more cheerfulness, and to inspire them with perseverance to remain in the field, and with fortitude and spirit, to do their duty while in it. The confidence they have in him will certainly operate forcibly towards producing these desirable ends.[63]

Although Lincoln's health was uncertain, he hustled northward as soon as he got Washington's orders, and on 30 July reached Schuyler's Albany headquarters to report for duty. From there, Schuyler sent him to what is now Vermont to command the militia gathering in the area.[64]

As things turned out, the biggest casualty of Fort Ticonderoga's fall was not Arthur St. Clair, but rather Philip Schuyler. Even before Burgoyne's offensive began, Schuyler's reputation for arrogance and aloofness irked more egalitarian New England soldiers and politicians. Moreover, there were rumors that Schuyler used his position to enrich himself. Congress initially disregarded these allegations, but Burgoyne's easy occupation of Ticonderoga changed the delegates' attitude toward the Northern Department commander. Although Schuyler's defenders pointed out that he could hardly be held responsible for Ticonderoga's evacuation because he was not there, his critics argued that that was part of the problem: Schuyler had not been at the scene of the greatest danger. As a result, he had lost the confidence of his officers and men. Southern congressmen joined their New England colleagues in demanding Schuyler's relief. On 1 August Congress voted to recall Schuyler and investigate his actions. Schuyler was chagrined and humiliated with the news. As far as he was concerned, he had been doing a good job under trying circumstances.[65]

Two days after Congress pulled the trigger on Schuyler, it asked Washington to name his successor as Northern Department commander. Washington was not the kind of man to shy away from tough choices, but in this case he demurred. He explained to Congress that although he appreciated the confidence it expressed in him by its request, he felt that Congress was in the best position to make the call. Congress, he continued, had directly overseen the Northern Department from the war's start, so it was most familiar with the department's personnel requirements. In all likelihood, though, there was a good bit more to Washington's reluctance. For one thing, Washington liked and respected Schuyler and probably would have recommended keeping him at his post. He was no doubt concerned that some might construe his willingness to pick Schuyler's replacement as an endorsement of Congress's decision to remove him. Moreover, Horatio Gates was the obvious candidate to take over for Schuyler. Washington did not think much of Gates, but choosing someone else might provoke a fight with Congress that Washington did not want and might not win. After all, on paper Gates was well qualified for the job; he had plenty of military experience, was popular among New Englanders, had served in the region before, and was, after Putnam, the army's senior active major general. Therefore, Washington figured that punting was his best option in this particular instance.[66]

On 4 August Congress voted to appoint Gates the new commander of the Northern Department. Congressmen hoped that New England soldiers in particular would appreciate Gates's previous experience in the region, his zealous republicanism, and his willingness to share their hardships. Despite his support from eleven state delegations, there were reasons beyond Washington's doubts to question Congress's wisdom in selecting Gates. Just two months earlier, Gates had come to Philadelphia and demanded an audience with Congress. When admitted, he complained in an angry, emotional, rambling, and accusatory speech about the ill-treatment he believed he had received at Congress's hands during his previous stints as head of the Northern Department. He singled out New York delegate James Duane as the chief architect of his woes, much to the outrage of other congressmen. After order was restored, Gates's friends hustled him out of the room before he could cause more trouble. The event should have shown that Gates lacked the temperament and interpersonal skills this new high-level position would require. Once Congress opted to relieve Schuyler, though, Gates was the only viable alternative.[67]

Supporting the Northern Department was one of many issues vying for Washington's attention that summer. Maintaining his army's command structure was another. For example, Washington had to find a new division commander after he sent Benjamin Lincoln northward. To replace Lincoln, Washington turned to Anthony Wayne. He was uncomfortable doing so because Wayne was only a brigadier, but there were no major generals readily available. Wayne was born in 1745 in Chester County, Pennsylvania. He received an education at Philadelphia Academy and then worked in a surveyor's office. After the war began, Wayne took a regiment to Canada. Although he was wounded at the Battle of Three Rivers, he led the survivors up the St. Lawrence River to safety. His actions there and elsewhere convinced Congress to promote him to brigadier general in February 1777. He spent the winter of 1776–77 running Fort Ticonderoga but found his responsibilities so onerous and frustrating that they undermined his health. He was therefore happy to get orders from Washington to join his army. Washington wanted a Pennsylvanian to command the state's brigade, and Wayne was the only brigadier readily available. Wayne arrived in time to make a name for himself by harassing Howe's rear guard during the British retreat back to Brunswick. Washington then directed Wayne to help organize the Pennsylvania militia but changed his mind after he sent Lincoln to assist Schuyler.[68]

With the possible exception of Benedict Arnold, Anthony Wayne was the Continental army's finest combat general. Well-dressed, dark-eyed, and finely proportioned, Wayne cut a dashing figure. He was eventually nicknamed "Mad Anthony" not because of any mental instability but rather because of his ferocious, peripatetic, and impetuous courage under fire. He combined this fierceness in action with sensible planning and freewheeling thinking. He also possessed that commanding presence that characterizes great leaders. His soldiers respected him as a brutal disciplinarian and blunt talker, but officers as diverse as Charles Lee, Nathanael Greene, and Marquis de Lafayette liked him for his cordiality and generosity. Although Washington learned to appreciate and rely on Wayne's abilities, he was not blind to his foibles. Wayne was a braggart, narcissistic, and willing to pull strings to get what he wanted. Years after the war, Washington described Wayne as "more active and enterprising than judicious and cautious. No economist it is feared. Open to flattery, vain, easily imposed upon and liable to be drawn into scrapes. Too indulgent (the effect perhaps of some of the causes just mentioned) to his officers and men."[69] The Continental army had its fair share of brave generals, but Wayne's resourcefulness raised him above the rest.[70]

John Sullivan was, not surprisingly, another of Washington's personnel challenges that summer. In addition to his threat to resign over du Coudray's appointment, Sullivan caused Washington difficulties in other ways. Never one to overlook a challenge to his competency or authority, regardless of its source, in early summer Sullivan became embroiled in a petty dispute with an army surgeon who had badmouthed him. More seriously, on 25 July Washington complained to Sullivan about the quality of his division. Washington stated that Sullivan's troops had engaged in more wanton destruction than any other division in the army by stealing horses, burning fences, and so forth. A week later, one of Sullivan's brigade commanders, French volunteer Brig. Gen. Philippe Hubert Preudhomme de Borre, provided more evidence that not all was right in Sullivan's outfit by hanging a suspected loyalist civilian. Washington's concerns about Sullivan's division also dovetailed with a claim made by Brig. Gen. William Smallwood several weeks later. Having recently resumed temporary command of Sullivan's other brigade after a spell rallying the Maryland militia, Smallwood discovered that it had become noticeably less disciplined during his absence.

To make matters worse, Sullivan fell seriously ill in late July and early August. His doctor ascribed the breakdown in Sullivan's health to alcohol—it is unclear whether he meant excessive consumption or contamination—but the fact that he bled Sullivan four times may have prolonged his ailment. When Sullivan rejoined his division on 4 August, he warned Washington that he was so weak that he night never completely recover. He pledged, though, to continue to do his duty. On 22 August Sullivan led his division on a raid of British-occupied Staten Island that accomplished little. Washington's congratulations did not prevent Congress from ordering an inquiry into Sullivan's conduct in the operation. Washington did not want any distractions from his upcoming confrontation with the British, so he informed Congress that such an inquiry was impossible right now because William Smallwood, one of the participating brigade commanders, was not available to give his testimony. Even so, the issue remained in play throughout the autumn campaigning.[71]

Sullivan was not the only general who caused the army trouble that summer. In late August Stirling hurt himself in a fall from his horse. Rendered bedridden for about a week, he was unable to get around much until early September. While Stirling convalesced, Washington put one of his brigade commanders, Brig. Gen. Thomas Conway, in charge of the division. However, Stirling and Conway did not get along. The Irish-born Conway had spent twenty years in the French army before he crossed the Atlantic to offer his services to Congress. He made no bones about his disrespect for the inefficient Stirling and the low quality of his understrength brigade. Stirling complained to Washington that Conway's refusal to obey his orders was becoming increasingly blatant. This discontent extended beyond Stirling's division. Stephen's excessive drinking that summer continued to raise eyebrows because it sometimes interfered with his performance of his duties. Finally, overwork and a lack of sleep so aggravated Nathanael Greene's asthma that he could only with difficulty oversee his division as effectively as he wanted.[72]

In late August Washington made an important change to his army. He ordered each of his brigade commanders to supply one hundred marksmen for a light infantry corps that would screen his army and harass the enemy. Daniel Morgan's riflemen had done this job well during Howe's incursion into New Jersey earlier in the summer, but Washington had sent them northward to help stop Burgoyne. Washington had found the unit useful and wanted to re-create it for upcoming operations against Howe. Leading such an elite outfit was a plum job that Washington believed required a brigadier general, even though the army was short of men of that rank. Washington gave the new light corps to Brig. Gen. William Maxwell, head of the New Jersey brigade in Stirling's division. Although born in Ireland in 1733, Maxwell was of Scottish descent. He and his family came to Philadelphia in 1747, from whence they moved to New Jersey and became farmers. He worked as a schoolmaster, served in the Great War for Empire, and afterward got a job as a post commissioner responsible for provisioning various British forts on the frontier. After the Revolutionary War began, he took a New Jersey regiment northward to fight in the Canadian campaign. The courage he showed at the Battle of Three Rivers, as well as support from New Jersey's congressional delegation, secured his promotion to brigadier general in October 1776. He played a prominent role in harassing British foraging parties in New Jersey in the winter of 1776–77. His success in handling small units in unpredictable situations undoubtedly contributed to Washington's decision to give him the light corps. Besides, he was the senior available brigadier.

Tall and rawboned, with a florid complexion, large gray eyes, and brogue, Maxwell seemed the epitome of a stereotypical Scottish farmer. His old threadbare coat, shabby hat, and hearty and bluff manner placed him much closer to the rank and file in appearance than the officer corps. One person called him "the most ungentlemanlike-looking fellow I ever saw."[73] Although people lauded his character, patriotism, and honesty, some felt that he lacked the necessary intellect and decorum for a general. Washington may have sensed this as well because he gave Maxwell detailed instructions for using the light corps. More damningly, Maxwell was yet another officer who drank excessively, though he insisted he never did so while on duty. Nevertheless, this all too common affliction undoubtedly hindered his ability to do his job well. Maxwell's new light infantry corps possessed plenty of potential, but its members did not get much opportunity to work together before they encountered the British.[74]

Congress remained in session throughout the spring, summer, and fall to oversee the war effort. Part of its oversight included tinkering with the army's command structure. On 25 March it promoted George Clinton to brigadier general. Clinton was Brig. Gen. James Clinton's younger brother, as well as a well-connected and prominent New York politician. Congress elevated him on the strong recommendation of New York's legislature. In June Clinton was also elected the state's first governor. He was reluctant to take either job because of ill health, but, as usual with Clinton, his sense of duty prevailed. Despite his political position, he held on to his commission until the end of the war, which gave him the unique distinction of being the only man to serve as governor and Continental general simultaneously during the conflict. His divided authority, though, did not interfere with his military relationship with Washington. For one thing, Washington greatly respected Clinton as an officer and friend. Moreover, Washington no doubt figured that having one of his generals in the governor's office might prove beneficial. Defending the Hudson River valley became Clinton's primary military responsibility for the remainder of the conflict.[75]

A week later, on 1–2 April, Congress appointed three new brigadiers to meet the continuing need for generals. It selected Edward Hand (Pennsylvania), Charles Scott (Virginia), and Ebenezer Learned (Massachusetts). All three officers came from states that had contributed a disproportionately large number of men to the Continental army. Hand was an Irish-born former British army surgeon who gave up his commission in 1774 and settled on a farm near Lancaster. He sided with the patriots when the war began, became a lieutenant colonel, and impressed Washington during the siege of Boston. He later participated in the fighting around New York and at the Battle of Trenton. When Fermoy abandoned his brigade on the road from Princeton, Hand took it over and led it in a skillful delaying action against the British army on its way to recover Trenton. In the winter of 1776–77, though, his failure to recruit effectively disappointed Washington. Even so, his record and seniority made him an obvious candidate for general. Shortly after Congress elevated Hand, it ordered him to assume command of the new Western Department at Fort Pitt in western Pennsylvania. As for Scott, he was a rough Great War for Empire veteran who had seen action at Trenton. Unlike Hand, he went on to participate in Washington's operations around Philadelphia in 1777–78. Finally, Learned owed his promotion mostly to his seniority among the Massachusetts colonels. Although he took part in the siege of Boston, he resigned soon after due to illness. Congress picked him anyway and then ordered him to northern New York to help stop Burgoyne's invasion.[76]

In addition to Marquis de Lafayette and Philippe Charles Tronson du Coudray, Congress created several more generals that spring and summer. On 11 April Congress promoted French volunteer Philippe Hubert Preudhomme de Borre—the same man who several months later ordered a civilian executed for suspected loyalist proclivities—to brigadier and backdated his commission to 1 December 1776. Congress did so mostly to honor a commitment Silas Deane had made to Preudhomme de Borre on its behalf, even though this gave Preudhomme de Borre seniority over Knox, Nash, Poor, Glover, Paterson, Wayne, Varnum, Woodford, Muhlenberg, Weedon, Clinton, Hand, and Scott. The following month, on 12–13 May, Congress elevated Connecticut's Jedediah Huntington, Pennsylvania's Joseph Reed, and French volunteer Thomas Conway to brigadier. Washington had recommended Huntington's appointment partly because he thought he was a good officer, and partly to compensate Connecticut for Arnold's resignation. As things turned out, Arnold agreed to remain in the army when Congress gave him his major generalship. That still left Connecticut short a brigadier, so Congress filled the slot with Huntington. Reed was Washington's military secretary and then adjutant general. The two men's once close relationship chilled after Washington discovered that Reed had badmouthed him in his correspondence with Charles Lee before Lee's capture. Even so, Washington on 20 January 1777 suggested Reed's advancement to brigadier with the idea of putting him in charge of the army's nascent cavalry. Congress did so, but Reed declined the honor on 9 June because he was offended by Congress's delay in acting on Washington's endorsement. As for the Irish-born Conway, Congress's Committee on Foreign Applications advised his selection because of his long experience in the French army, Deane's urging, and, not least, his fluency in English.[77]

Despite Congress's efforts, Washington approached his confrontation with Howe shorthanded in generals. Washington had major generals for four of his five divisions, but brigadiers led only eight of his twelve Continental brigades. Although a number of generals had left the service for various reasons, the main problem was that the Continental army's manpower and organizational charts were expanding more rapidly than Congress could create generals for them. To be sure, it is conceivable that units the size of brigades and divisions, which rarely exceeded one thousand and two thousand men, respectively, did not need generals to lead them, but Washington, Congress, and tradition expected it. Washington directly commanded five of the Continental army's fifteen active major generals that summer: Greene, Lafayette, Stephen, Stirling, and Sullivan. Of the remaining ten, Schuyler and St. Clair had been relieved and were under investigation for their roles in Fort Ticonderoga's fall; Mifflin was serving as quartermaster; Putnam was commanding in the Hudson Highlands; Spencer was watching the British garrison in Rhode Island; Heath was overseeing the Eastern Department in Boston; Arnold, Gates, and Lincoln were facing Burgoyne in northern New York; and du Coudray was inspector general of the artillery. As for the twenty-eight active brigadiers, Washington had only ten of them: Conway, Knox, Maxwell, Muhlenberg, Nash, Preudhomme de Borre, Scott, Wayne, Weedon, and Woodford. Six were either in northern New York or on their way there (Fermoy, Glover, Learned, Nixon, Paterson, and Poor), four were down south (Gadsden, Howe, McIntosh, and Moultrie), six were in the Hudson River valley region (George Clinton, James Clinton, Huntington, McDougall, Parsons, and Varnum), Hand was at Fort Pitt, and Smallwood was back in Maryland organizing the state's militia.

The quality of those generals who were with Washington on what many expected to be the conflict's decisive campaign also left something to be desired. Burgoyne's operations had drawn away some of the army's most battle-hardened men, such as Arnold and Glover, to northern New York. Most of the brigade commanders had little or no combat experience in the war. This included not only the Virginia contingent, but also Conway, Nash, and Preudhomme de Borre. All of Washington's division commanders were veterans, but their records were mixed, so it was anyone's guess how well they would perform in the next battle. Knox was the only general who had consistently fought well. The upshot was that the multipronged British offensive had stretched American military leadership as thinly as it had stretched its material resources.

The Battle of Brandywine and the Fall of Philadelphia

After two weeks of maneuvering, on 11 September Washington's and Howe's armies met along Brandywine Creek, about twenty-five miles southwest of Philadelphia near the Delaware border. Although the two armies contained around fifteen thousand men apiece, it was the first time since the New York City campaign that the British army had such a good opportunity to destroy its American counterpart because the terrain was relatively flat. Washington had learned the hard way to avoid engagements with the British on open ground, but Philadelphia's political importance convinced him that in this case it was a risk worth taking. He deployed his troops behind the creek in the hopes of repelling a British attack. He stationed Greene's and Wayne's divisions at Chadd's Ford, with

Stephen's division, Stirling's division, and Francis Nash's recently arrived and unattached North Carolina brigade nearby in support. To guard his flanks, he sent General John Armstrong's Pennsylvania militia downstream and Sullivan's division upstream. Finally, he ordered Maxwell's light corps across the creek to delay and hinder the British advance.

By taking up a defensive position along the Brandywine, Washington surrendered the initiative to Howe. In response, Howe repeated his tactics that had proven so successful on Long Island the previous year by attempting to outflank the American army. He sent about 6,400 of his troops against Chadd's Ford under German general Wilhelm Knyphausen while he and Cornwallis took his army's remaining 7,500 soldiers on a roundabout march upstream to strike the American right flank. Howe hoped that crumbling the American flank would open the way for Knyphausen's men to charge across Chadd's Ford to deliver the coup de grâce to Washington's army. It was a simple enough concept, but one that took time to implement. While Howe, Cornwallis, and their troops undertook a grueling eight-hour hike to reach their objective, Knyphausen's contingent pushed toward Chadd's Ford in the face of stubborn opposition from Maxwell's light corps. Unfortunately for Washington, intelligence lapses and snafus prevented him from spotting the British flanking column until it was almost too late. At the last moment, though, Sullivan reoriented his division near Birmingham Meeting House to face the British, and Washington rushed Stirling's and Stephen's divisions over to deploy on Sullivan's right. The men in the three American divisions barely had time to brace themselves before Howe and Cornwallis sent their soldiers charging across the swale separating the two sides.

Sullivan was trying to bring his division into line with Stirling's and Stephen's when the British attacked. Caught by surprise, his two brigades disintegrated under the sudden pressure in almost the blink of an eye. Sullivan's attempts to rally them failed, so he galloped over to the right with his aides to contest that part of the battlefield. Although Sullivan's division's disappearance left them vulnerable and exposed, Stirling's and Stephen's divisions held on in the face of determined British assaults. Thomas Conway's brigade put up a particularly fierce fight. In the end, though, British numbers and training gradually told. First Woodford's and then Scott's brigades broke, triggering a general American retreat in the gathering twilight. As the Americans fled, Nathanael Greene's division arrived after trotting four miles in forty-five minutes. Greene's troops, especially George Weedon's brigade, brought the British advance to a jarring halt and enabled Sullivan's, Stirling's, and Stephen's soldiers to escape. Down at Chadd's Ford, Wayne's division and Maxwell's light corps turned in good performances, but they were unable to stop Knyphausen's troops from crossing the creek and driving them off.

The Battle of Brandywine was a clear-cut American defeat. Although each side committed about an equal number of men, the British demonstrated their superior combat skills by outmaneuvering and outfighting the Americans at almost every turn. For all of Washington's growing strategic maturity, Howe remained the better tactician. American losses in killed, wounded, and captured probably topped one thousand, though excessive desertions and straggling after the battle made exact numbers hard to calculate. Among the American generals, Lafayette was wounded in the leg and Woodford in the hand. British casualties, on the other hand, amounted to 577, including 89 killed. The strategic consequences for the Americans were equally damaging. Most obviously, the setback opened the door for the British to continue their advance on Philadelphia. In a strategic sense, however, Brandywine did not advance the British war effort all that much. Howe failed to destroy Washington's army or break its morale. Indeed, in this light Brandywine appears more as a missed opportunity for the British than a conclusive victory. Howe had a rare chance to engage the main American army on relatively open ground, and he failed to make the encounter decisive. Instead, Washington's army remained more or less intact, and so long as it existed so did the cause that sustained it.

After Washington collected and reformed his beaten army, he fell back across the Schuylkill River to Germantown on 14 September. He was heartened that his troops remained in good spirits despite their setback at Brandywine. His soldiers' resilience, as well as Howe's lethargy in following up on his victory, convinced Washington to recross the Schuylkill on 15 September to challenge the British again. Washington was not inclined to blame anyone for the Brandywine defeat. Instead, he attributed the loss to contradictory intelligence that enabled the British to reach his right flank undetected and unopposed. This was true enough, though Washington was ultimately responsible for the failure to accurately process the information he received. His inability to do so led to a tactical paralysis that may have cost him the battle. Whatever the reasons for the American army's misfortunes at Brandywine, Washington remained focused on protecting Philadelphia.[78]

There were others who were far more willing than Washington to ascribe blame for the American army's setback at Brandywine. This was especially true of North Carolina congressman Thomas Burke. Burke's seven months in Congress had convinced him that Washington's many ineffective officers were one of the American army's biggest problems. His determination to keep a close eye on them was undoubtedly one reason why he joined Washington's army as an observer just before Brandywine. No sooner had the battle ended than Burke concluded that Sullivan was most responsible for the American defeat. Burke believed that Sullivan had had plenty of time to familiarize himself with the local geography, so he should have been able to accurately evaluate the available intelligence and quickly deploy his army to withstand the British onslaught. To Burke, Sullivan's failure was symptomatic of Washington's substandard major generals. Burke wrote of Sullivan, "This unfortunate general has ever been the marplot of our army, and his miscarriages are I am persuaded owing to a total want of military genius, and to one of that sort of understanding which is unable to take a full comprehensive view of an object, but employs its activity in subtle senseless refinement. Thus persuaded, I thought it my duty to endeavor to have him removed from his command."[79] In the elevated emotions Brandywine generated, Burke on 14 September persuaded Congress to order Sullivan's recall and an inquiry into his conduct. When Washington protested that the military situation was too critical to jettison Sullivan, Congress agreed to leave Sullivan's fate in Washington's hands. To augment Sullivan's embarrassment, some Maryland officers also complained about his performance. The Maryland delegation introduced a resolution to withdraw Maryland soldiers from Sullivan's division, but it failed by a vote of eleven states to two.[80]

Sullivan had courted more than his fair share of controversy in the course of his military career. Although by now he should have been inured to the criticism Burke and others directed at him for his actions at Staten Island and Brandywine, Sullivan remained as thin-skinned as ever. He had no intention of meekly accepting the blame for this most recent American defeat but instead zealously protected his reputation. As a former lawyer, he was willing and able to generate the necessary paperwork and verbiage to clear his name. Despite the continuing campaign against the British to protect Philadelphia, Sullivan found the time to refute the charges leveled against him. He complained to Congress that it had condemned him on the basis of a few disaffected officers and one unhappy delegate, and without giving him the opportunity to present any evidence in his own defense. He was hard put to understand why Congress was singling him out for censure when other generals had participated in other defeats without retribution. Sullivan admitted that his performance at Brandywine was not perfect but noted that he was hindered by conflicting intelligence, ignorance of Stirling's and Stephen's whereabouts, and unfamiliarity with the local geography. He did not want to resign his commission, he stated, but was willing to do so to preserve his honor unless he got a court of inquiry to clear his name. To enhance his rebuttal, Sullivan also secured statements of support from sympathetic officers such as Conway, Lafayette, Stephen, and others who attested to his courage. These men emphasized that Sullivan fought well in a poor situation not of his own making. Sullivan even got backing from Maryland officers to repudiate the allegation that the Maryland rank and file opposed him.[81]

Sullivan also turned to Washington for support. In this case, though, he laced his appeal with a dollop of emotional blackmail. Sullivan told Washington that he intended to resign his commission unless a court of inquiry was empaneled. Sullivan informed Washington that he did not want to abandon him or their mutual cause, but that he needed to protect his honor and reputation from a congressional faction that was obviously out to get him. For all the headaches Sullivan had caused him since the war began, Washington still respected Sullivan as a general and a person. He made it clear to Congress that he did not want to lose Sullivan's services at such a critical military juncture. Washington also assured Sullivan of his backing but noted that the precarious military situation precluded immediately convening a court of inquiry to look into his conduct. Although Washington acknowledged criticisms of Sullivan's deployments at Brandywine, he added that no one had questioned his courage and energy. Washington himself could not pass judgment on the matter because he did not reach that part of the battlefield until the fighting was almost over. Summing up his feelings, Washington wrote, "Upon the whole then no part of your conduct, preceding the action, was, in my judgment, reprehensible. What happened on your march to the field of battle, your disposition there, and behavior during the action, I can say nothing about, no part till the retreat commenced having come under my immediate observation. I can only add therefore, that the whole tenor of your conduct, so far as I have had opportunities of judging has been spirited and active."[82] As for Sullivan's desire to quit, Washington warned him that doing so would prevent the establishment of a court of inquiry because Sullivan would no longer be subject to military authority. When the campaign's tempo slowed down in mid-October, Washington appointed a court of inquiry chaired by Stirling that met from 10 to 12 October. The court heard testimony about Sullivan's conduct during the Staten Island raid the previous August and ruled unanimously that Sullivan performed his duties responsibly. It attributed the problems Sullivan encountered there to happenstance.[83]

By the time Stirling's court of inquiry cleared Sullivan of any wrongdoing in the Staten Island raid, congressional anger about Sullivan's role in the Brandywine defeat had begun to dissipate. South Carolina delegate Henry Laurens, for example, wished Sullivan was as wise as he was brave and complained about Sullivan's "long catechistical letter" to Congress threatening to resign. At the same time, though, Laurens blamed Burke for the current hullabaloo because he meddled in a field in which he had no expertise. Washington's unwavering support also dampened congressional enthusiasm for scapegoating Sullivan. Finally, Stirling's court of inquiry ruling indicated that Congress could not count on the officer corps if it continued to pursue its vendetta against Sullivan over Brandywine. On 11 October Connecticut delegate Eliphalet Dyer admitted to Sullivan that Congress had been too hasty in its actions against him. He added that Sullivan now had plenty of allies in Congress and urged him to continue his campaign for vindication. Eleven days later, Dyer assured Sullivan that Congress was no longer targeting him, so he should now focus on that other war with the British. Although Sullivan was usually as quick to cool as to anger, in this case his resentment festered. The following April, in an exchange of letters with Burke, Sullivan noted that he could not challenge him to a duel because he was an officer, adding ominously that he would not remain in the army forever. Despite all this residual drama, the fact remained that Sullivan had survived yet another controversy to fight another day against enemies on and off the battlefield.[84]

Sullivan's professional survival was due in large measure to astute politicking and Washington's support. Philippe Hubert Preudhomme de Borre, by contrast, lost his career because he lacked these advantages. Preudhomme de Borre had served in the French army for more than thirty-five years before he crossed the Atlantic Ocean to offer his services to Congress in March 1777. Congress appointed him a brigadier general and backdated his commission to the previous December to honor the agreement Silas Deane had made on its behalf with Preudhomme de Borre in Paris. Although Washington worried about Preudhomme de Borre's inability to understand English, he assigned him a brigade in Sullivan's division because he was short of generals and assumed that Preudhomme de Borre knew his business. Sullivan initially approved of Preudhomme de Borre, but the Maryland and exiled Canadian soldiers in his brigade viewed him as an arrogant foreigner with little desire to learn American ways. Preudhomme de Borre's unauthorized execution of a suspected loyalist underscored his cultural ignorance.

At Brandywine Preudhomme de Borre's brigade broke and ran at the very start of the British assault on the American left flank. While Preudhomme de Borre was hardly the only general whose men buckled under British pressure, his unpopularity among his troops and his foreign birth made him an even more convenient scapegoat than Sullivan. Two days after the battle, Congress ordered his recall and an inquiry into his conduct. As with Sullivan's case, Washington responded that he was too busy to convene a court. In the meantime, Preudhomme de Borre concluded that since Congress had questioned his competency, to resign was his only honorable course, which he did. The more Preudhomme de Borre thought about it, though, the more convinced he became that he needed a court of inquiry to clear his name and return to duty at the head of his brigade. On 1 October Preudhomme de Borre wrote to Congress to ask for both a court of inquiry and a promotion to major general. Three days later, Congress rejected Preudhomme de Borre's requests because he was no longer in the Continental army. Whereas the officer corps was largely supportive of Sullivan, it did very little to help Preudhomme de Borre. At his court of inquiry the following week, Sullivan criticized Preudhomme de Borre's performance during the Staten

Island raid, stating that the Frenchman had disobeyed his orders. Washington, for his part, did nothing to assist Preudhomme de Borre either. Preudhomme de Borre remained in America at loose ends until January 1779, when he returned to France absent the glory and reputation he had sought.[85]

Brandywine destroyed Preudhomme de Borre's Continental army career and almost ruined Sullivan's as well. Nevertheless, several generals emerged from the battle with enhanced reputations because of their stalwart performances in that losing cause. Among the division commanders, both Greene and Wayne earned kudos for their actions—Greene for marching his division so rapidly to the beleaguered right flank, and Wayne for his tenacious defense of Chadd's Ford. As for the brigadiers, people praised Conway for fiercely contesting the British assault on the American right flank and Weedon for stymieing the British breakthrough in the gathering darkness so the remainder of the army could get away to fight another day. Finally, Lafayette impressed many observers. Although he did not have a command, his reckless courage while trying to rally and encourage the soldiers showed that there was more to the young French officer than money, titles, and geniality. He got a bullet in his leg for his efforts, but he felt it was a price worth paying to further differentiate himself from the other foreign officers.[86]

Howe's victory at Brandywine may have opened the door for the British to march on Philadelphia, but Washington moved quickly to slam it shut again by recrossing the Schuylkill River with his army on 15 September. Washington's willingness to confront the British for a second time out in the open in less than a week was a bold gamble. In northern New Jersey he had avoided direct field engagements because he recognized that his poorly trained and ill-equipped army probably would not win under those circumstances. He fought at Brandywine because he understood Philadelphia's political and symbolic importance, and losing there had not changed his mind. On 16 September he offered battle to the British at White Horse Tavern, but a sudden torrential thunderstorm ruined his ammunition, forcing him to retreat before the British committed themselves. Reaching into his bag of tricks, Washington then dispatched Smallwood's militia, Maxwell's light corps, and Wayne's division to harass the British army's flanks and rear. Such tactics had worked well in northern New Jersey in confounding the British, and Washington hoped they would yield similar benefits in southern Pennsylvania. Unfortunately for Washington, southern Pennsylvania lacked the mountains and hills that had provided refuge and protection for American troops in northern New Jersey, so Maxwell, Smallwood, and Wayne achieved little. Worse yet, on the evening of 20 September, the British surprised and scattered Wayne's division at Paoli with a ferocious bayonet attack. The British killed or wounded three hundred Americans and captured seventy or eighty more. British casualties came to less than a dozen.

Wayne was shocked and humiliated by the Paoli debacle. The fact that Washington had two days earlier warned him to guard against a British surprise attack only compounded his embarrassment. Condemnation rapidly replaced the praise that Wayne had received for his role at Brandywine. Detractors accused him of carelessness and dereliction of duty. One congressman, for instance, denounced Wayne's "unpardonable negligence." The fact that a good deal of this criticism came from within his own division added insult to injury. Impetuous and proud, Wayne rarely admitted mistakes, so he not unexpectedly denied both responsibility for and the extent of the fiasco. He minimized the setback by noting that his division lost little by way of artillery, stores, and ammunition. He also insisted that he was not taken by surprise but rather had posted pickets who did not sound the alarm in time. He blamed one of his brigade commanders, Col. Richard Humpton, for not responding quickly and efficiently enough. Wayne's dislike of Humpton made him an obvious and convenient target. Finally, on 27 September Wayne asked Washington to convene a court of inquiry to investigate Paoli. Wayne did so not only to clear his name but also to bring his critics out into the open. As he explained to Washington, "Conscious of having done my duty I dare my accusers to a fair and candid hearing. Dark insinuations and insidious friends I dread, but from an open and avowed enemy I have nothing to fear."[87] Washington obliged and put Stirling in charge of it. Although the court of inquiry cleared Wayne of most of the allegations swirling around his performance at Paoli, it did note that he had established his camp too close to the British and that his pickets had been taken unawares. This was not the full exoneration Wayne wanted, so he demanded a court-martial. Washington again agreed and assigned Sullivan to preside over it. After hearing testimony for six days at the end of October, the court ruled unanimously that at Paoli Wayne did everything that could be expected of a brave, active, and vigilant officer, acquitting him with "highest honor." Whatever satisfaction Wayne gained from the verdict, though, did not remove the stain of the defeat from either his record or his conscience.[88]

The British army reached the Schuylkill River on the same day it routed Wayne's division at Paoli. Washington's men were deployed on the other side, with artillery emplaced at all the fords, ready to bloody the water if the British attempted to storm across. Howe instead feigned a march upstream as if he planned to attack the important American supply depot at Reading. Washington took the bait and moved northwestward to protect Reading. In doing so, he loosened his grip on the downriver fords, enabling the British army to cross unopposed on 22 September, which placed Howe's army squarely between Washington and Philadelphia. Four days later, the British marched into Philadelphia without resistance. Congress fled first to Lancaster, and then to York, a small town one hundred miles west of Philadelphia, where it reconvened on 30 September. Philadelphia fell exactly one month after Howe's men splashed ashore at Head of Elk, and only fifteen days after the Battle of Brandywine.

The Battle of Germantown

One of the reasons for Washington's unsuccessful defense of Philadelphia was that the British maintained the initiative throughout the campaign. Washington spent all of September reacting to Howe's well-orchestrated maneuvers, and as a result he was almost always one step behind. This was hardly an effective way to wage war; it was in fact generally a surefire path to destruction and defeat. From this perspective, it was not so much surprising that the American army lost all its battles and the city in its charge, but rather that it survived the experience at all. As a pugnacious man, Washington understood the problem almost instinctively. He tried to regain the initiative by marching on White Horse Tavern and dispatching Maxwell, Smallwood, and Wayne to harass the British flank and rear, but neither effort succeeded. As Washington's army took up station at Pennypacker's Mill the day after the British marched into Philadelphia, Washington continued to watch and wait for an opportunity to strike a blow against them. The questions, of course, were where and how.

Washington got his chance when Howe divided his army soon after the British seized Philadelphia. The British general sent part of his force to open up the Delaware River to British shipping, garrisoned another segment in Philadelphia, and deployed the remainder to Germantown, a village about seven miles from the former American capital. Because Washington estimated—incorrectly, as things turned out—Howe's total strength at only eight thousand men, he concluded that he finally had an opportunity to defeat him in detail. Moreover, Washington was receiving reinforcements to make up for losses sustained at Brandywine and elsewhere. Alexander McDougall and a brigade of nine hundred Connecticut Continentals arrived the day after Philadelphia fell, followed by Smallwood's one thousand Maryland militiamen on 28 September and General David Forman's six hundred New Jersey militiamen the next day. This gave Washington a total of eleven thousand troops, of which eight thousand were Continentals. Although more Continentals and militiamen were on the way, Washington decided to assault Germantown before circumstances changed.

Washington's typically complicated plan called for four separate columns to simultaneously assail the British Germantown garrison in the predawn darkness of 4 October. He assigned Sullivan to lead his and Wayne's divisions directly into the town, with Conway's brigade from Stirling's division out in front to clear the way. Washington may have removed Conway's brigade from Stirling's division because of the bad blood between the two officers, or because Conway's well-trained outfit was best suited for its difficult mission. Stirling's job was to follow behind Sullivan and Wayne with the New Jersey brigade, now back under Maxwell's command, and Nash's North Carolina brigade. For the second column, Washington directed Greene to attack to the east of Sullivan with his and Stephen's divisions, with McDougall's newly arrived brigade out in front. Because Continentals composed both columns, Washington expected them to provide the punch he needed to carry the day. Even so, he found secondary roles for the militia units. He ordered Smallwood's Marylanders and Forman's New Jerseyans to assault on the far left, next to Greene. On the other end of the line, near the Schuylkill, Washington expected John Armstrong's Pennsylvania militia to perform a similar service there.

Although the British had warnings of an impending attack, Washington's assault out of the predawn mist still caught them by surprise. There were, however, nine thousand veteran British troops in Germantown, and they rapidly recovered from the initial shock to put up a good fight. Conway needed support from Sullivan's and Wayne's divisions to break through the outer crust of the British defenses, which took up time. From there the Americans swept past the burning British camp and into Germantown, huzzahing loudly as they overcame knots of British resistance. An encouraged Washington ordered Nash's North Carolina brigade to reinforce Sullivan and Maxwell's New Jersey brigade to assist Wayne in exploiting their initial success. To Sullivan's left, Greene was a half hour late because of bad roads and a confused guide, but he got his men into formation as quickly as possible and sent them charging forward. The British were more prepared along this part of the line, but here too the Americans made good initial progress across the fields toward the town.

Unhappily for the Americans, a number of unforeseen factors turned their apparent victory into bitter defeat. A detachment of retreating redcoats barricaded themselves into a large stone two-story mansion called Chew House. Sullivan's and Wayne's divisions swept past it on their way through town with scarcely a backward glance. When Washington came up, though, he heeded Knox's advice that it would be unwise to leave a fortified stronghold in the army's rear. He therefore diverted Maxwell's New Jersey brigade from reinforcing Wayne to an attempt to storm the mansion. The attack consumed valuable time, energy, and resources and was ultimately unsuccessful. To further complicate matters, the thick smoke and fog that settled over the battlefield made it difficult for officers to orient themselves, coordinate with neighboring units, and direct their men. Jittery troops depleted their ammunition by firing blindly into the haze to clear out real or suspected pockets of British opposition. The two militia columns accomplished little because their soldiers lacked the necessary fortitude to come to grips with the enemy in a meaningful way. Because of these problems, Washington's army was already succumbing to the laws of entropy even before the British launched their counterattack from south of the town. Wayne's division, which had fought fiercely to redeem its Paoli-stained reputation, was the first to unravel. Some of its men began falling back because they mistakenly interpreted the gunfire around Chew House as evidence that the British had cut them off. As they did so, they encountered and exchanged fire in the fog with elements of Stephen's division. Stephen ordered a withdrawal just as the British moved forward against him. The retreat became contagious, infecting Sullivan's and Greene's divisions, as well as the militia. Exhausted, nervous, and disorganized Americans ignored pleas from their officers and left the field, some in good order and others without any discipline whatsoever. Although the Americans managed to lug off most of their cannons and wounded, the army's collapse was as sudden as it was unexpected. Three hours after the engagement began, the beaten Americans were on their way back to Pennypacker's Mill.

Considering its short duration, the Battle of Germantown generated considerable bloodshed. The British suffered 534 casualties, of whom 70 were killed. American losses probably topped 1,000, including 152 killed, 521 wounded, and around 400 taken prisoner. North Carolina brigade commander Francis Nash was among the dead. A cannonball shattered his thigh while he was riding through Germantown, and he succumbed to his injury three days later. Although Nash had only been with the army a short time, he had impressed observers as an officer of great potential. Washington's army may have lost the engagement, but it demonstrated that it retained its sting even after Brandywine and Philadelphia's fall. There were numerous explanations for the American defeat: the holdup at Chew House, ammunition shortages, the weather, the inability of officers to control their men, and Washington's complicated plan. Washington refrained from blaming any one person but instead attributed the setback to the fog and the resulting confusion. One officer, though, came closer to the truth when he later wrote that the reverse "must be ascribed to deeper causes: to the yet imperfect discipline of the American army; to the broken spirit of the troops, who, from day to day and from month to month, had been subjected to the most trying and strength-wasting privations."[89]

Washington may have declined to indulge in scapegoating for the Germantown defeat, but others were more willing to provide that particular service. In the days following the battle, a growing chorus identified Adam Stephen as someone who bore a disproportionate share of the blame for the setback. Even before Germantown, there were persistent rumors that Stephen drank too much. Making what some interpreted as disparaging remarks about his soldiers' performances during the battle did not create much goodwill for Stephen either. His chief denouncer was one of his brigade commanders, Brig. Gen. Charles Scott.

Scott and others charged Stephen with drunkenness, incompetency, carelessness, and behavior unbecoming an officer. Specifically, they stated that during his division's march from the Hudson River to Philadelphia, an intoxicated Stephen had issued in front of his men confusing and contradictory orders. At Germantown he allegedly refused to rally his troops to stop the British advance but instead left the field under the pretense of reconnoitering. Without proper leadership, Stephen's division was unable to function effectively on or off the battlefield.

On 9 October Stephen wrote to Washington to refute the rumors circulating about him. He claimed that if anyone was responsible for the defeat at Germantown, it was Scott. According to Stephen, Scott marched his brigade away from an advantageous position without Stephen's knowledge or consent and then failed to deploy his men in a timely manner. Stephen added that Scott had done the same thing at White House Tavern a week earlier, but he had overlooked Scott's behavior in the hope that it would not happen again. Now that Scott was badmouthing him, though, Stephen felt that he had no choice but to inform Washington because Scott's rumormongering was undermining morale in his division. To put an end to these rumors, restore unit efficiency, and clear his name, Stephen asked Washington for a court of inquiry into his conduct.

Washington agreed to Stephen's request and constituted a court of inquiry headed by Greene that convened on 26 October and heard testimony for six days. The court concluded that there was evidence that Stephen had issued contradictory and confusing orders during the march to Philadelphia, and that he was often intoxicated. The court also determined that Stephen failed to adequately supervise his division at Brandywine and Germantown. In response to this ruling, Washington ordered Stephen's court-martial. He put Sullivan in charge of it, with Brigadier Generals Conway, Huntington, Muhlenberg, and Weedon among its members. It met on and off from 3 to 17 November in Whitemarsh, Pennsylvania. Brig. Gen. William Woodford and especially Scott provided damning testimony against Stephen. Stephen had his defenders, including members of his staff, who stated that they never witnessed him inebriated, but their claims were not persuasive. After deliberations, the court found Stephen guilty of unofficer-like behavior during the retreat from Germantown due to his inattention and poor judgment, and it noted that his frequent drunkenness had undermined the good order and discipline of the army. The court sentenced Stephen to be dismissed from the service. Washington agreed with the decision. Although Stephen appealed to Congress to overturn the verdict, it declined to act because his reputation among congressmen was now no better than it was within the officer corps. Stephen returned to Virginia and played no further active role in the conflict.[90]

Stephen was the only Continental army general court-martialed and immediately dismissed from the service during the war. Considering the army's often dismal combat record, it is surprising that more generals were not cashiered. Washington was partly responsible for this forbearance because he usually refrained from scapegoating. Besides, a zero-tolerance attitude toward failure would have exposed the defeat-prone Washington as a hypocrite and stripped the officer corps bare. Moreover, slews of courts-martial and inevitable appeals to Congress after guilty verdicts might have undermined public confidence in the Continental army and hurt morale. Stephen's case, though, was an anomaly. For one thing, Washington did not like him and never expressed any confidence in him to Congress. This was in sharp contrast to the lengths Washington went to support the contentious Sullivan during his travails after Brandywine. In addition, Stephen's shortcomings were well known and serious. The officers on his court-martial clearly believed that his continued presence as a division commander jeopardized the army's well-being. Stephen had backed Sullivan when Congress sought to blame him for Brandywine's outcome, but instead of returning the favor, Sullivan chose to put the army's welfare first and joined his colleagues in condemning Stephen. Although whistleblowers and complainers are frequently shunned by their colleagues even when they are right, neither Woodford nor Scott suffered for denouncing Stephen. Stephen's incompetence, in short, extended beyond the ordinary, and that more than anything else accounted for his unique fate.

William Maxwell was another general who came under fire for his actions before, during, and after the Battle of Germantown. Washington had put Maxwell in charge of the light corps because of his successes in northern New Jersey earlier in the year. He disbanded the light corps and sent Maxwell back to lead the New Jersey brigade at Germantown. After Brandywine, one of the light corps officers, Lt. Col. William Heth, complained that Maxwell's drunkenness impaired his ability to command. Washington responded by ordering a court of inquiry into Maxwell's conduct presided over by Greene and including Brig. Gens. Peter Muhlenberg and James Varnum. The court heard testimony on 26 October and concluded that while there was no evidence that Maxwell was intoxicated at the time Heth charged, there was evidence that Maxwell had been under the influence of alcohol on several other occasions. The court left it up to Washington whether or not this information warranted a court-martial. Washington decided that it did. The court—the same one that went on to try Stephen—met from 30 October to 2 November at Whitemarsh. After gathering and weighing the evidence, it ruled unanimously that Maxwell had never been too incapacitated by alcohol to disqualify him from doing his duty. If that was a backhanded acquittal, it was enough to keep Maxwell in the army.[91]

Finally, some held Nathanael Greene partly responsible for the defeat at Germantown. People pointed out that he was late to the battle and then failed to effectively coordinate his units. However, jealousy of Greene's close relationship with Washington accounted for at least some of this criticism. Detractors claimed that Greene's timidity stifled Washington's natural aggressiveness and initiative. Greene admitted that the Germantown setback deeply disappointed him. Although Greene congratulated his troops for their efforts in the engagement, he also complained that they needed to learn to retreat, reform, and counterattack. Fortunately for Greene, Washington's obvious confidence in him, as well as his popularity within the officer corps, prevented such mutterings from hurting his standing and reputation in the army.[92]

Sullivan, for his part, emerged from Germantown with an enhanced reputation. This was not so much due to his stellar combat performance—he fought bravely and doggedly, as usual, but not brilliantly—but because of Washington's shrewd politicking. Washington saw an opportunity to use the battle to resuscitate Sullivan's Brandywine-scarred reputation. The day after the engagement, he wrote to Congress, "In justice to General Sullivan and the whole right wing of the army whose conduct I had an opportunity of observing, as they acted immediately under my eye, I have the pleasure to inform you, that both officers and men behaved with a degree of gallantry that did them the highest honor."[93] The strategy worked; Washington's narrative became the accepted version of Sullivan's role at Germantown in and out of Congress. One officer wrote, "I am happy that General Sullivan . . . [was], among others, gloriously distinguished."[94] Word from Washington that Sullivan had redeemed himself for any alleged shortcomings at Brandywine undoubtedly helped dissipate some of Congress's anger toward him.[95]

Saratoga and the Delaware River

On 17 October 1777 General John Burgoyne surrendered his approximately five thousand remaining redcoat, Hessian, provincial, American Indian, and Canadian soldiers to Horatio Gates at Saratoga in northern New York. Burgoyne's invasion had started auspiciously by the seizure of Fort Ticonderoga, but his subsequent efforts to push on to Albany ran into increasing opposition, cumulating in defeats at the Battle of Freeman's Farm on 19 September and the Battle of Bemis Heights on 7 October. The engagements left his soldiers surrounded, hungry, and demoralized. Saratoga was perhaps the greatest and most important American victory of the war, one that yielded both short- and long-term benefits. It snapped off one thick spike of Britain's multipronged offensive, eliminated an entire British field army, secured New York from invasion from Canada, raised American morale, and eventually helped persuade France to enter the conflict on the side of the United States.

The Saratoga campaign produced its share of heroes and controversies. As overall commander of the northern army, Gates was in line for the bulk of the credit for the triumph. Congress voted him its official thanks, and its new president, Henry Laurens, wrote to Gates on 5 November, "Your name sir will be written in the breasts of the grateful Americans of the present age and sent down to posterity in characters which will remain indelible when the gold shall have changed its appearance."[96] Some people, though, argued that American success at Saratoga came in spite of, not because of, Gates and his cautious tactics. In their interpretation of events, it was Benedict Arnold's ferocious assaults on the British, undertaken more or less against Gates's wishes, that ultimately compelled Burgoyne to surrender. Congress was sufficiently aware of Arnold's contribution to officially express its gratitude and restore the seniority he lost the previous February. Arnold also emerged from the campaign with a hatred of Gates and another serious wound in the same leg that was injured outside Quebec. John Stark, for his part, gained kudos for eradicating a large German foraging party at the Battle of Bennington on 16 August at the head of a conglomeration of Massachusetts, New Hampshire, and Vermont militiamen. Congress rewarded him with an appointment to brigadier general, thus rectifying its failure to do so the pervious February. Finally, Congress acknowledged Benjamin Lincoln for his role in rallying the Massachusetts militia. In this case, Congress was motivated more by Lincoln's good nature, commanding presence, and the serious wound he received in his right leg while reconnoitering than by any brilliance he demonstrated on the battlefield.

Washington received the good news about Saratoga at Worcester, Pennsylvania, on 18 October, four days after Gates and Burgoyne opened negotiations. In response, he ordered his entire army paraded that afternoon in a ceremony that included homilies by chaplains, the discharge of cannons, and three loud huzzahs by the troops. The cannonade startled Stirling's horse and threw its rider to the ground, but Stirling, according to one observer, "got up and shook himself like a great water dog."[97] Washington was happy for all the usual and expected reasons, noting a month later that he did not care where the Americans were winning so long as they were beating the British. However, he also had a more immediate and selfish purpose for celebrating Saratoga. Now that Burgoyne's army had disappeared from the strategic chessboard, Washington could tap Gates's dormant force for reinforcements he needed to keep the British penned in Philadelphia. With that in mind, he dispatched an aide, Lt. Col. Alexander Hamilton, to Albany to facilitate the transfer of units to his army. However, doing so proved more difficult and time-consuming than Washington had imagined. Gates was one problem. He wanted to hold on to two Continental brigades in case the British repeated their early October thrust up the Hudson River toward Albany. Moreover, Gates resented that Washington was dictating his deployments from three hundred miles away. It took all of Hamilton's persuasive powers to pry Continental brigades away from Gates, but by mid-November there were more than 5,000 Continentals and 2,500 Massachusetts and New Hampshire militia on their way southward.[98]

In order for these reinforcements to reach Washington, they had to march through the Hudson Highlands. This was Israel Putnam's bailiwick. Like Gates, Putnam worried about another British offensive up the Hudson River and wanted to retain as many soldiers as possible for such a contingency. As far as Hamilton could tell, Putnam seemed in no particular hurry to help Enoch Poor's and Ebenezer Learned's brigades get across the Hudson and on the road to Pennsylvania even after Hamilton pointed out that he had positive orders from Washington directing the moves. Moreover, Putnam combined this operational obstinacy with administrative inefficiency. Hamilton was appalled by the disorganization and neglect he found when he arrived at New Windsor, New York. Both Poor's and Learned's brigades were in deplorable shape due to insufficient funds and equipment, but Putnam was unwilling or unable to provide much help. Although Hamilton praised Poor and New York governor George Clinton for their efforts to get the units moving, he viewed Putnam as part of the problem. On 12 November Hamilton wrote to Washington about Putnam, "I owe it to the service to say that every part of this gentleman's conduct is marked with blunders and negligence, and gives general disgust."[99] Washington responded a week later in a letter to Putnam that he needed those soldiers as soon as possible and wished that Putnam would obey orders promptly without arguing their propriety. As for Putnam's fears of a British attack, Washington assured him that he would accept full responsibility for denuding the Hudson Highlands of troops. Not surprisingly, Putnam saw things in a different light. He believed he was doing the best he could under unfavorable circumstances to comply with Washington's directives. He did not, however, appreciate a young lieutenant colonel such as Hamilton bossing him around, even if he was clothed in Washington's authority.[100]

Washington wanted these reinforcements as soon as possible because he believed he still had an opportunity to win the campaign. Although the British had occupied Philadelphia, they did not yet control its access to the sea because the Americans had constructed an interlocking, intricate, and formidable defensive network along the Delaware River. Its components included Fort Mercer on the New Jersey shore, Fort Mifflin on Mud Island, a small fleet of Pennsylvania and Continental warships, and a series of underwater obstacles. If the Americans there could hold out until winter froze the Delaware, then Howe would be unable to import enough supplies into Philadelphia to feed his army through the winter. If that happened, Howe would have to either evacuate the city or starve in it. Considering the stakes involved, it was hardly surprising that Howe and the Royal Navy wasted no time in committing significant resources to clearing the Delaware after Philadelphia fell.

Washington's initial inclination was to let the local militia bear the brunt of manning the static defenses along the Delaware River while his Continentals maneuvered around Philadelphia from their camp at Whitemarsh, Pennsylvania. As winter approached, though, Washington dispatched a limited number of Continentals to the Delaware to stiffen the militia. On 7 October, three days after the Battle of Germantown, Washington ordered Brig. Gen. James Varnum to send two of his brigade's regiments to reinforce Fort Mercer. Varnum's brigade was on its way from the Hudson Highlands to join Washington's army, so it was a simple matter to divert part of it to the Delaware. These two regiments helped the militiamen, sailors, and a few Continentals stymie a major British offensive against Forts Mercer and Mifflin on 22–23 October. Col. Christopher Greene and his Fort Mercer garrison repelled a Hessian assault, inflicting more than four hundred casualties in one of the most lopsided American victories of the war. A Royal Navy attack on Fort Mifflin the next day also came up short, costing the British two warships, including a ship of the line. After this setback, the British redoubled their efforts to emplace a series of artillery batteries on the boggy shore to bombard the forts into submission before time ran out and the river iced over.

Insufficient manpower and bickering leadership hindered American efforts to defend the Delaware River. In late October Washington attempted to rectify both problems by dispatching Varnum and the balance of his brigade to the Delaware. Washington gave Varnum full authority to arbitrate disputes among officers and hoped that these reinforcements would be enough to hold on to the forts until winter arrived. Even so, Washington warned Varnum that preserving his men was more important than the forts in his charge. Varnum was Rhode Island's sole brigadier. At twenty-eight years old, he was also among the youngest of the Continental army's generals. Varnum was born in Massachusetts and attended Harvard, from which he was expelled for unknown reasons. He transferred to Rhode Island College and graduated in 1769. He worked briefly as a teacher before becoming a lawyer. His education, status, and active membership in the Rhode Island militia made him an obvious candidate to lead one of the state's regiments. In that capacity he fought at Long Island, White Plains, and Trenton. Although he was a firm disciplinarian, he was a difficult man to like because of his hypersensitivity, tactlessness, quarrelsomeness, and impatience. Before the New York City campaign, he threatened to resign his commission because Congress appointed as brigadiers officers junior to him. Washington placated him by promising to put in a good word on his behalf to Congress, which paid off when Congress promoted him to brigadier in February 1777. His friendship with fellow Rhode Islander Nathanael Greene soured when Varnum allegedly treated Greene's wife brusquely. Greene wrote of Varnum, "He is as unfeeling as he is unpolite. That gentleman has the least gratitude of any person I ever saw that claims so much."[101] Several years later, a congressman elaborated on Varnum's shortcomings: "General Varnum of Rhode Island is a man about thirty, of florid habits. He has read some little in books, is fond of speaking and spouting out everything that his reading has furnished him with whether apt or not to the purpose. His temper and council are very precipate [*sic*] and but little calculated to be useful in such an assembly."[102] Because half of Varnum's brigade was already at the Delaware, it made organizational sense to send Varnum with the remainder there. Whether Varnum possessed the proper temperament for the job was a more difficult question to answer. Washington, however, hoped that the stubborn and high-handed Varnum could quell dissension among officers and withstand the growing pressure the British were exerting on Forts Mercer and Mifflin.[103]

Varnum reached the Delaware on 2 November. After inspecting Forts Mercer and Mifflin, he concluded that he could keep them out of British hands for the remainder of the campaign season. However, he was dismayed with the supply shortages, lackluster militia turnout, and infighting he encountered. Varnum used his authority to induce more cooperation from the navy, but he was unable to do much to resolve his logistical and militia difficulties. On 10 November the British launched another major assault on Fort Mifflin. Their shore batteries and warships bombarded the place continuously for six straight days, knocking out the American cannons one by one until all of them were destroyed or dismounted. The around-the-clock barrage, as well as the defenders' inability to fight back, took an increasing psychological toll on the fort's five hundred defenders. Varnum's immediate solution was to rotate units through the fort every day so the troops would not be exposed to enemy fire for very long. Although Varnum visited the fort twice to experience firsthand his men's travails, he was more stressed by responsibility than by flying cannonballs. Washington left it up to Varnum to decide whether or not to evacuate Fort Mifflin, but Varnum found this autonomy unnerving. He complained that he did not know enough about events outside of his immediate area to make an informed decision. In fact, he asked Washington to send a more senior general to assume overall command and relieve him of some of his burdens. Despite his anxiousness, he retained the power of decision. On 15 November he ordered Fort Mifflin's garrison withdrawn to the mainland because he did not believe it could hold out much longer. The evacuation came off without a hitch, leaving a devastated and wrecked fort for the British to occupy. Varnum's disappointment at losing the fort was somewhat counterbalanced by his conclusion that he could still maintain a chokehold on the Delaware from nearby Fort Mercer.[104]

Once Fort Mifflin fell, however, the British moved to seize Fort Mercer as well by sending more than six thousand troops across the Delaware River into New

Jersey. In response, Washington committed more Continentals to the area. He dispatched Nathanael Greene and four more brigades, as well as Daniel Morgan's riflemen, to reinforce Varnum's beleaguered soldiers. Two of the brigades, John Glover's and Jedediah Huntington's, were Saratoga veterans, as were Morgan's riflemen. Greene's two brigades, Peter Muhlenberg's and George Weedon's, had for their part recently seen action at both Brandywine and Germantown. Although Greene was Washington's most trusted lieutenant, Washington probably gave him the mission by process of elimination. Stephen, Sullivan, and Wayne were busy defending their reputations in and out of court, and Stirling was recovering from an injury that made it impossible to ride a horse or even travel by carriage. Washington hoped that Greene could use Fort Mercer as bait to lure the British into a battle in which the Americans had an advantage, but he left the details up to Greene.[105]

Unfortunately for the Americans, Greene's vacillation and communication problems prevented his foray into New Jersey from accomplishing anything. By the time Greene's division got over the Delaware River, Varnum had already decided to abandon Fort Mercer before the British column arrived to overwhelm his isolated brigade. Although on paper Greene had around seven thousand soldiers at his disposal, he had considerable difficulty locating, concentrating, and supplying them all. In addition, the same indecision that had plagued Varnum afflicted Greene as well. Unsure under what circumstances to engage the British, he wished Washington would provide more guidance. He wrote plaintively to the commander in chief, "For your sake, for my own sake, and for my country's sake, I wish to attempt everything which will meet with your excellency's approbation. I will run any risk or engage under any disadvantages if I can only have your countenance if unfortunate."[106] In the end, Greene did not have to make that decision. Once the British occupied and demolished Fort Mercer, they recrossed the Delaware River and returned to Philadelphia. Washington thereupon ordered Greene back to Whitemarsh before the reunited British assailed the other half of the divided American army. Greene returned on 1 December in time to help Washington frustrate a brief British sortie against his camp four days later. Greene regretted that he had not accomplished more, but Washington reassured him of his continued confidence and support. None of this, though, negated the fact that the Americans had lost their last chance to win the campaign.[107]

Command Changes

Washington had on a number of occasions complained to Congress that he needed additional generals to run his main army. On 7 October, three days after the Battle of Germantown, Washington again asked Congress to appoint more generals. He noted that once all the reinforcements he had summoned from the Hudson Highlands arrived, he would have thirteen brigades at his disposal. To adequately lead them, he needed six major generals and thirteen brigadiers. However, he would have only four major generals (Greene, Stephen, Stirling, and Sullivan) and eleven brigadiers (Conway, Huntington, Maxwell, McDougall, Muhlenberg, Nash, Scott, Varnum, Wayne, Weedon, and Woodford) to command all these units. One of the brigadiers, Anthony Wayne, was running a division, and a number of colonels were commanding brigades. Washington disliked placing colonels in temporary charge of brigades because the transitory nature of their assignment made it difficult for them to exert and exercise their authority. Moreover, the number of available generals declined as the year went on. Francis Nash died from the wounds he sustained at Germantown the same day Washington wrote to Congress, and Stephen was dismissed from the army the following month. Although Generals Glover, Learned, Paterson, and Poor reached Washington's army that autumn from northern New York, they brought their brigades with them and therefore did little to alleviate Washington's shortage of generals.[108]

In his 7 October 1777 letter to Congress, Washington suggested one man for promotion to major general: Alexander McDougall. Born in Scotland in 1731, McDougall immigrated to New York with his family nine years later. He commanded privateers during the Great War for Empire and then made a living as a merchant. He also committed himself to the patriot cause by joining the Sons of Liberty and speaking out against British authority. Indeed, the New York assembly imprisoned him for writing fiery pamphlets denouncing its decision to quarter British troops in New York City. He was commissioned a colonel and regimental commander when the war began and was promoted to brigadier in August 1776. He participated in the New York City campaign and fought valiantly at the Battle of White Plains. In the spring of 1777 Washington sent McDougall to the Hudson Highlands to help Israel Putnam run that department and a few months later summoned him to Pennsylvania for the Battle of Germantown. Despite a stutter and talkative nature, McDougall impressed almost everyone, including the irascible Charles Lee, with his combativeness, sensibleness, and commitment. He also possessed an unusual amount of modesty, honesty, and discernment for a Revolutionary War officer. For example, while in the Hudson Highlands he quarreled with and eventually arrested Col. Henry Livingston for traducing his character. Although a court-martial found Livingston guilty of disrespecting a senior officer, McDougall argued against dismissing Livingston because he believed that he might make a good officer someday. On the other side of the ledger, McDougall was also self-pitying and often felt unappreciated. His biggest problem, though, was his fragile health. A bout with rheumatism in

December 1776 almost convinced McDougall to resign his commission, and he became so ill in late November 1777 that he nearly died. Even so, Washington saw something in McDougall from early in the conflict and therefore supported and encouraged him. In his letter to Congress recommending McDougall's appointment to major general, Washington wrote:

> This gentleman from the time of his appointment as brigadier, from his abilities, military knowledge, and approved bravery has every claim to promotion. If I mistake not, he was passed over in the last appointments of major generals and younger officers preferred before him; but his disinterested attachment to the service prevented his acting in the manner, that is customary in like circumstances. This, I think, gives him a peculiar title to esteem, and concurs with the opinion I have of his value as an officer, to make me wish it may appear advisable to Congress, to promote him to one of the vacancies.[109]

Congress responded to Washington's request by appointing two major generals on 20 October. The first appointee, McDougall, was undoubtedly the result of Washington's strong recommendation. The second appointee was Robert Howe, commander of the Southern Department. Congress had passed over Howe the previous February because the North Carolina delegation failed to lobby effectively for him. Howe had resented the oversight and pressured both congressmen and Washington for redress, though he insisted that he never let his disgruntlement interfere with his duties or commitment to the cause. Howe's difficulties extended beyond his rank. Unclear lines of authority, questions about his competency and character, and personality conflicts with civil and military officials hindered his efforts to run the Southern Department. In an attempt to harmonize the department, Congress had already authorized him to relieve one troublesome general, Brig. Gen. Lachlan McIntosh, and send him to Washington's army, which would also help alleviate Washington's shortage of generals. Congress's original intention was to remove Howe and assign him to Washington's army as well, but it decided that promoting him instead would give him the power he needed to do his job well. By the time word of Congress's decision reached the Southern Department, though, another disgruntled general stationed there, Christopher Gadsden, had resigned his commission.[110]

In addition to Howe and McDougall, Congress also appointed three brigadiers that autumn: Kazimierz Pułaski (15 September), John Stark (4 October), and Louis Lebègue de Presle Duportail (17 November). As with the major generals, Congress acted for specific reasons. Stark owed his promotion to his Bennington victory. The Polish-born Pułaski gained fame by unsuccessfully combating Russian domination of his homeland in the 1760s. He escaped to France and then traveled to America in July 1777 because of his commitment to fight for liberty everywhere.

Although he did not speak English, he possessed a letter of recommendation from Benjamin Franklin. More importantly, he had considerable experience leading cavalry, a branch in which the Continental army was notably deficient. Pułaski impressed people with his intrepidness, self-confidence, martial skill, and courage. Congress put him in charge of the Continental army's small cavalry corps, and in that capacity he saw action at Brandywine and Germantown. As for Duportail, he was a thirty-four-year-old French army engineer whom the French government dispatched to America at Franklin's behest. Like Pułaski, Duportail compensated for his limited English with knowledge of a vital skill few Americans possessed. Duportail reached America in March 1777, and in late summer Congress made him a colonel and the Continental army's engineering chief. His ability, sound judgment, and common sense impressed Washington. When Duportail complained that Congress was dragging its feet in making good its promise to elevate him to brigadier, Washington on 3 November lobbied Congress to do so, adding that Duportail's engineering talents made him practically irreplaceable. Congress's positive response two weeks later was a tribute not only to Washington's influence but also to Duportail's contribution to the American war effort.[111]

Congress's decision to appoint only five generals that autumn was attributable to a number of factors. For one thing, Philadelphia's fall disrupted operations and scattered the congressional membership. Reconvening at York was time-consuming, distracting, and difficult. Under such circumstances, Congress attended to only the most pressing business and left everything else on the backburner. In addition, some state delegations proved unwilling or unable to effectively lobby for their officers. One Maryland congressman, for example, estimated that his state deserved one major and two brigadier generals, but it had only Brig. Gen. William Smallwood on the Continental army's roster. Considering Congress's precarious situation, though, the Maryland delegation decided not to press the issue. Francis Nash's death at the Battle of Germantown opened up a slot for an additional North Carolina general. Col. Alexander Martin was the North Carolina brigade's senior colonel, but many of the brigade's officers disliked him because of his alleged substandard performance at Germantown, and they made their views known to the state's congressmen. In response to this information, on 15 December North Carolina's state assembly instructed its congressmen to nominate Cols. Thomas Clark and Jethro Sumner as brigadiers. Although the North Carolina delegation submitted their names on 19 February 1778, Congress failed to act until the following January. In the meantime, Washington put Lachlin McIntosh in command of the brigade when he finally arrived from Georgia. The Pennsylvania and South Carolina delegations also asked for more brigadiers, but nothing immediately came of their requests either.[112]

Before the Continental army went into winter quarters, Washington made one more important change to its command structure. Adam Stephen's dismissal left his division leaderless. To replace him, Washington turned not to one of the army's innumerable veteran generals but rather to Marquis de Lafayette. Lafayette had started badgering Washington for a combat command commensurate with his rank as soon as he recovered from his Brandywine wound. As far as he was concerned, his participation in Brandywine as an observer was sufficient military education for the job. It never occurred to him that witnessing a battle was not the same thing as leading large units under fire. He instead saw division command as a means to attain the glory that was every bit as important to him as securing American independence. On 1 November Washington wrote to Congress about Lafayette. Considering Lafayette's significant connections and commitment to the American cause, Washington believed that giving him Stephen's division was a good idea. Besides, noted Washington, Lafayette had already done much to promote the war effort by, for example, dissuading several disgruntled foreign officers from badmouthing the United States when they returned to Europe. Finally, Washington referenced the courage Lafayette demonstrated at Brandywine to buttress his case. When Lafayette distinguished himself in an otherwise insignificant skirmish along the Delaware later in the month, Washington was quick to pass along the information to Congress in another letter arguing for Lafayette's appointment. He said little about Lafayette's youthfulness, inexperience, unfamiliarity with American culture and traditions, or the impact that his selection might have on the fractious American officer corps. Despite all the reasons he provided Congress, it seems obvious that Washington was motivated primarily by his personal affinity for the young Frenchman. So was Congress, which on 1 December informed Washington that it had no objection to Washington choosing a twenty-year-old Frenchman with no combat leadership experience as head of one of the half dozen most crucial posts in the main Continental army.

Lafayette's appointment to division command should have outraged an American officer corps inordinately sensitive to matters of honor and seniority, but it did not. For one thing, Lafayette had Washington's backing. Almost all high-ranking officers esteemed the commander in chief and were therefore reluctant to second-guess him on such a personnel issue. For another, Lafayette's glamor, image, fortune, and friendliness blinded officers to his limitations and their honor. Even the hard-bitten de Kalb, for instance, wrote of Lafayette, "The friendship with which he has honored me since I made his acquaintance and that which I have vowed to him because of his personal qualities oblige me to have that deference for him. No one is more deserving than he of the consideration he enjoys here. He is a prodigy for his age; he is the model of valor, intelligence, judgment, good conduct, generosity, and zeal for the cause of liberty for this continent."[113] Other supporters included such well-respected officers as George Clinton, Greene, and Knox. When at the end of the year John Sullivan and Enoch Poor complained to Washington about officers promoted without sufficient seniority or merit, they explicitly omitted Lafayette from their critique: "Under this exception [promotion out of line for extraordinary reasons] we are happy to mention the Marquis de Lafayette, whose sacrifices to our cause, and personal merit, highly deserve the honors bestowed upon him."[114] As a result, Lafayette leaped over two dozen generals without creating the resentment that such situations had previously generated. It was an accomplishment that surpassed anything he had yet done on the battlefield.[115]

Conclusions

Congress's biggest personnel accomplishment in 1777 was its Baltimore Resolution. By codifying seniority, a state's contribution to the Continental army, and merit, Congress established a standard that brought some clarity to the hitherto opaque and perplexing procedure of choosing generals. Even so, Congress failed to define its terms and assign weight to each one, thus preserving a large measure of subjectivity to the process that continued to undermine officer morale and cohesion. The introduction of foreign volunteers further confused the newly established criteria for promotion because they did not fit easily into the Baltimore Resolution rubric. The fact was, though, that as much as some people wanted to make the selection of generals as objective and transparent as possible, legislative decisions were inherently political, biased, and messy. From this perspective, the Baltimore Resolution, while a step forward, was more aspirational than attainable.

In terms of creating generals, 1777 was a banner year for Congress. Indeed, Congress was far more successful in conjuring up generals than troops for them to lead. That year Congress appointed twelve major and twenty-one brigadier generals, so that by December 1777 the Continental army contained a total of seventeen major and twenty-four brigadier generals in service, as well as two held prisoner (Lee and Thompson). Of the active generals still present at year's end, Massachusetts provided the most with seven (Heath, Lincoln, Nixon, Knox, Glover, Paterson, and Learned), followed by Virginia (Gates, Woodford, Muhlenberg, Weedon, and Scott) and Connecticut (Spencer, Arnold, Parsons, Putnam, and Huntington) both with five. New York (Schuyler, McDougall, James Clinton, and George Clinton) and Pennsylvania (Mifflin, St. Clair, Wayne, and Hand) each had four generals. New Hampshire boasted of three generals (Sullivan, Poor, and Stark), New Jersey (Stirling and Maxwell) and Rhode Island (Greene and Varnum) of two, and Maryland (Smallwood), North Carolina (Howe), South Carolina (Moultrie), and Georgia (McIntosh) had one apiece.

Only tiny Delaware did not have a general. There were also five foreign generals (Lafayette, de Kalb, Conway, Pułaski, and Duportail).

On the other side of the ledger, the Continental army lost thirteen generals that year. Three were killed in action (Mercer at Princeton, Wooster during the Danbury raid, and Nash at Germantown), two died of accidents or illness (Morris and du Coudray), seven resigned or refused to accept their appointments (Armstrong, Cadwalader, Lewis, De Haas, Gadsden, Preudhomme de Borre, and Reed), and one was dismissed (Stephen). Congress promoted another eight brigadiers to major general (Arnold, Stirling, Mifflin, St. Clair, Stephen, Howe, McDougall, and Conway) and appointed three others directly to that rank (Lincoln, Lafayette, and du Coudray). All these changes indicate that there was a good deal of movement and turnover at the Continental army's highest levels, but much of it was due to circumstances and seniority rather than any deliberate plan to push the best men to the top of the command structure.

Unfortunately for Congress, the quality of the generals it appointed fell short of the quantity. Indeed, the record of American major and brigadier generals in 1777 ran the gamut from mediocre to poor. Arnold and Stark fought well in the Saratoga campaign—Stark's successes, however, occurred before Congress promoted him to brigadier—but none of the remaining Continental generals distinguished himself on the battlefield in such a way as to make a significant and positive difference in the outcome. Most of them showed plenty of physical courage, but they lacked the tactical initiative, deftness, and sophistication victory usually required. They were also handicapped by poorly trained and ill-equipped soldiers who could not march, deploy, and maneuver as quickly or efficiently as their British and Hessian counterparts. Unless they were situated in terrain conducive for defense, such as northern New York's forests or northern New Jersey's hills, they repeatedly lost their open field engagements whether on the offensive (Germantown) or the defensive (Brandywine). Moreover, these defeats generated recriminations and controversy that undermined civil-military relations and esprit de corps, as Maxwell, Schuyler, St. Clair, Stephen, Sullivan, and Wayne all discovered. Fortunately for America's prospects in the war, Washington's reluctance to scapegoat failing generals helped keep such dissension within bounds. Finally, disputes over rank and seniority caused by Congress's unclear promotion rules and the influx of foreign officers continued to roil the officer corps. Although these problems were bad enough in 1777, they got worse before they got better.

CHAPTER 4

Rebirth

1777–1778

The Conway Cabal

On 19 December 1777 Washington ended the campaign season by marching his army to winter quarters at Valley Forge, Pennsylvania. Situated on the Schuylkill River's south bank about twenty miles northwest of Philadelphia, Valley Forge was far enough from the city for the American army to guard against a surprise enemy attack, but close enough for it to contest British foraging parties scouring the surrounding countryside. Although the weather that winter was comparatively mild, American troops faced plenty of other problems that made their lives miserable. Inadequate clothing forced soldiers to wear filthy rags that became infested with lice and spawned typhus. Without enough food and shelter, they became vulnerable to innumerable other diseases as well. There was no shortage of the basic necessities among the civilian population, but poor logistics and the country's decentralized political structure prevented supplies and equipment from reaching the army in suitable quantities. Because Congress lacked the power to tax, farmers hesitated to accept its increasingly worthless currency. In addition, quartermaster Thomas Mifflin's 8 October resignation due to poor health meant that there was no one with sufficient authority to coordinate the purchase and transfer of materials to the army. As a result, around two thousand men died that winter at Valley Forge from hunger, disease, exposure, and exhaustion. That the army did not completely dissolve was a tribute to the rank and file's devotion to the cause and to Washington's leadership. Washington resorted to desperate measures to keep the army together that included impressing supplies from local farmers and pleading with governors for emergency out-of-channels help. Such ad hoc measures, though, would not sustain the army in the long run.

Unlike many of his generals, Washington stayed at Valley Forge the entire winter to share his troops' miseries. Despite his outward confidence, he had a difficult time remaining upbeat and optimistic. After all, he was a competitive and proud man who had lost two major battles and the city in his charge. These failures, as well as the unending responsibilities of command, wore him down. He sometimes felt unappreciated, put-upon, and misunderstood because of people's unrealistic expectations. As he explained to the president of Congress, Henry Laurens, "I can assure those gentlemen [in Congress], that it is a much easier and less distressing thing, to draw remonstrances in a comfortable room by a good fireside, than to occupy a cold, bleak hill, and sleep under frost and snow without clothes or blankets."[1] Although he fared better than the rank and file that winter, Washington was not immune to the army's shortages and physical sufferings. At one point he noted to a correspondent that he was writing on his only piece of paper, and that he did not possess a whole stick of wax either. Fortunately for him, in early February Martha Washington arrived to raise his spirits and those of the people around her. Washington also took comfort in the camaraderie of his staff and generals, and in his unyielding faith in the American cause.[2]

Congress spent the winter of 1777–78 in York, Pennsylvania. Cooped up in a cramped and backwater town without cosmopolitan Philadelphia's amenities, some delegates could not help but reflect on the unfortunate series of events that had resulted in their internal exile. Their present circumstances, along with persistent reports of the main American army's poor discipline, quarreling officers, and chronic shortages, led some to conclude that Washington was the ultimate source of the current unhappy military situation. Congress's high turnover and low attendance rates—at one point in January, there were only fifteen delegates present—further undermined support for Washington because so few of the delegates present had participated in his selection, and they therefore lacked a proprietary interest in his professional survival. One delegate complained, "We want a general; thousands of lives and millions in property are yearly sacrificed to the insufficiency of our commander in chief. Two battles he has lost for us by two such blunders as might have disgraced a soldier of three months standing: and yet we are so attached to this man that I fear we shall rather sink with him than throw him off our shoulders. And sink we must under his management."[3] It was consequently unsurprising that some concluded that the country could do better with someone other than Washington as commander in chief. Although no one publicly expressed such sentiments, the small number of congressmen present at York amplified the whispers of the discontented.[4]

Moreover, those dissatisfied with Washington's military performance that winter had a high-ranking successful general with whom to unfavorably compare him. Horatio Gates's victory at Saratoga seemed to show that well-led American troops could not only beat the British, but destroy them. To some, Gates possessed the magic military touch the Americans needed to win the war. Comparing the two generals, one congressman elaborated:

> General Gates's unparalleled success gave me great pleasure, but it has not obliterated the remembrance of the disorders I have seen in the army in this [Washington's] department. . . . I have heard several officers who have served under General Gates compare his army to a well regulated family. The same gentlemen have compared General Washington's imitation of an army to an unformed mob. Look at the characters of both! The one on the pinnacle of military glory, exulting in the success of schemes planned with wisdom and executed with vigor and bravery, and above all see a country saved by their exertions. See the other outgeneraled and twice beaten, obliged to witness the march of a body of men only half their number through 140 miles of thick settled country, forced to give up a city the capital of a state, and after all outwitted by the same army in a retreat.[5]

There were some obvious flaws in this assessment, not the least of which were unfounded and exaggerated assumptions about Gates's military prowess. Considering the military situation that winter, though, it was unsurprising that some people concluded that perhaps Gates might make a better commander in chief than Washington.[6]

These whisperings against Washington had already begun when on 28 October Col. James Wilkinson strode into a tavern in Reading, Pennsylvania. Wilkinson, a twenty-year-old Marylander, had studied medicine before the war. He fought in Canada, was with Charles Lee when the British captured him—he supposedly escaped by hiding in the fireplace—and served as Gates's deputy adjutant general during the Saratoga campaign. He was a sly, unscrupulous, and quarrelsome man who owed his rise through the ranks more to unbounded ambition than to any real ability. Gates had sent him to York to deliver official news of Burgoyne's surrender, but he decided to take a detour to visit his girlfriend. At the tavern he met William Alexander, Lord Stirling and his staff whiling away the dreary and rainy day drinking and yacking. All the alcohol loosened tongues and lowered inhibitions. In the course of swapping war stories, Wilkinson told Stirling's aide, Maj. William McWilliams, that one of Stirling's brigade commanders, Brig. Gen. Thomas Conway, had badmouthed Washington in a recent letter to Gates. McWilliams passed this information along to Stirling. Stirling and Conway did not get along. As far as Conway was concerned, Stirling was an incompetent amateur. Stirling, for his part, considered Conway an insubordinate troublemaker. Stirling saw this piece of gossip McWilliams handed him as a means with which to poison the commander in chief against Conway. On 3 November Stirling wrote to Washington. Saying nothing about his recent daylong drinking session, he added in a postscript his third-hand account of Conway's comments. Washington responded to this information by penning an icily brief note to Conway to show him that he knew of his machinations:

> Sir: A letter which I received last night, contained the following paragraph. "In a letter from Gen[era]l Conway to Gen[era]l Gates he says: 'Heaven has been determined to save your country; or a weak general and bad counselors would have ruined it.'"[7]

Thomas Conway's name became attached to the series of confusing and peculiar events his letter to Gates set in motion: the Conway Cabal. Born in Ireland in 1733, Conway's family moved to France when he was six years old. He entered the French army in 1749 and rose to the rank of colonel. Like many other French officers, he saw the Revolutionary War as an opportunity to make a name for himself, so he got in touch with Silas Deane and offered his services. Deane was sufficiently impressed with Conway's long record, stance on military discipline, and fluency in English to recommend him to Congress. When Conway reached America in April 1777, he told Congress that he did not want any particular rank or position. The delegates liked Conway's apparent selflessness and résumé enough to appoint him a brigadier general and send him to Washington. Washington appreciated Conway's candidness and obvious military expertise and was in need of brigadiers. He assigned Conway command of a Pennsylvania brigade in Stirling's division. Conway's success in turning the brigade into the best-trained outfit in the army paid dividends at both Brandywine and Germantown. Sullivan spoke highly of him, and Lafayette called him brave, active, and intelligent. Unfortunately for Conway, he squandered all this goodwill his military skills accrued for him. He was openly contemptuous of generals he considered unqualified, incompetent, or drunk—men like Stirling. He also criticized Washington for heeding Knox's bad advice to assail Chew House during the Battle of Germantown. Nor was he happy that Congress appointed de Kalb a major general over his head. As a result, officers increasingly interpreted his forthrightness as arrogance. In fact, the more they got to know Conway, the more convinced they became that he was ambitious, intriguing, and self-aggrandizing. Some even questioned his courage. Rumor had it that at Germantown John Cadwalader and Joseph Reed had found a distraught Conway cowering in a barn because his horse had been wounded in the neck. Whatever the truth of such allegations, the upshot was that most officers considered Conway a troublemaker of dubious character. This included Washington, who on 16 October wrote a congressman recommending against Conway's promotion, adding, "General Conway's merit then, as an officer, and his importance in this army, exists more in his own imagination than in reality; for it is a maxim with him to leave no service of his own untold nor to want anything which is to be obtained by importunity."[8]

As far as Washington and his supporters were concerned, Stirling's fortuitous discovery of the contents of Conway's letter to Gates exposed a developing conspiracy to shear the commander in chief of his power and authority. Although the details changed in the ensuing months, these men had no doubt that a conspiracy existed. Conspiracy theories ran deep in the American psyche, and indeed a sincere and widespread belief among many colonists that the British government was scheming to strip them of their liberties contributed to the revolution itself. Conway was just a minor, albeit aggravating, player whose correspondence pointed toward a bigger fish: Gates. Washington felt that Gates had for some reason disrespected and denigrated him in word and deed ever since the siege of Boston. Gates's subsequent appointment to command the Northern Department and his army's victory at Saratoga turned him from a disgruntled subordinate into a powerful rival. Many of Washington's officers had been stung by the unfavorable comparisons between the northern and southern armies and concluded that Philip Schuyler, Benjamin Lincoln, and Benedict Arnold deserved most of the credit for victory at Saratoga, not Gates. From this perspective, it was not surprising that these men were inclined to close ranks and think the worst of Gates on the slimmest of evidence. Gates's reluctance to dispatch reinforcements to Washington after Saratoga provided more evidence that he was predisposed against Washington's position as commander in chief.

Even Gates, though, was not necessarily the center of the conspiracy. Washington's friends ascribed that role to Thomas Mifflin. Mifflin was a prominent Pennsylvania politician, army officer, and outgoing quartermaster general. He had a knack for charming people and bringing them around to his perspective, so he knew which levers to pull to get his way. One person wrote of Mifflin, "He is plausible, sensible, popular, and ambitious, takes great pains to draw over every officer he meets with to his own way of thinking and is ever engaging."[9] He had the previous summer spoken out against Washington's decision to march to Pennsylvania and leave New England unprotected and felt that Washington listened too much to his less able lieutenants. According to Washington's supporters, Mifflin was so disgusted with Washington's military blunders that he had decided to use his influence to remove him from his post—or anyhow to reduce his power. He was therefore employing his persuasive skills to build a faction in and out of Congress whose tentacles extended not only to officers such as Gates and Conway, but also to delegates such as Benjamin Rush, James Lovell, John and Sam Adams, and Richard Henry Lee. Worst of all, Mifflin's critics argued that Mifflin and his coconspirators were motivated not by patriotism, but rather by a desire for power that would enable them to control both the army and the revolution.[10]

That fall Washington and his supporters identified various pieces of evidence that, in their minds, confirmed the existence of a conspiracy against the commander in chief. The first was the relationship between Conway and Gates revealed by Wilkinson's indiscretion. If Washington's chief rival and his most disgruntled subordinate were communicating, then deposing the commander in chief was likely a frequent correspondence topic. Then, on 17 October, Congress established a new Board of War with a vaguely defined job of overseeing the army. On 7 November Congress named its members, one of whom was Thomas Mifflin. Three weeks later, Congress, at Mifflin's request, unanimously appointed Gates president of the board, but with the condition that he could still serve in the field if necessary. Considering its makeup and mission, Washington's allies not surprisingly viewed it as an attempt to clip Washington's wings and perhaps even ease him out of his post. Moreover, on 13 December Congress promoted Conway to major general and appointed him the Continental army's new inspector general. In doing so, Congress ignored both seniority and Washington's strong objections. To some, the only possible explanation for Conway's elevation was as a reward for some nefarious and clandestine service rendered, and an expectation of similar deeds in the future. Put together, then, it seemed to many of Washington's allies that shadowy and sinister forces in and out of Congress were planning to separate the commander in chief from the army he had directed for more than three years.[11]

The truth of the matter was that no conspiracy against Washington existed—except in the minds of the commander in chief and his boosters. There were certainly prominent people who griped about Washington's recent lack of success and compared him unfavorably with Gates, but there was no secret, coordinated plan among them to remove him from his command. Gates's, Conway's, and Mifflin's dislike of Washington's generalship did not mean that they were actively colluding against him. There were logical and innocuous reasons behind Congress's actions that Washington's supporters incorrectly interpreted as threads to the conspiracy. Congress formed the new Board of War to help the commander in chief, not to strip him of his power. The old board consisted solely of delegates who lacked sufficient time and expertise to make it very useful, but Congress hoped that putting on it professional soldiers such as Mifflin and Gates would increase its effectiveness. Delegates expected the board to find and fix problems with the various departments, thus freeing Washington from the logistical busywork that took up so much of his time so he could focus on beating the British. Gates had successfully held an important independent command and could thus best understand Washington's problems, so it only made sense to put him in charge of the board. Congress promoted and appointed Conway inspector general because his primary duty would be training troops, and for all his faults the French officer had a proven track record in this area. Moreover, generals such as Sullivan and Lafayette had vouched for Conway, so many of the delegates were unaware of the growing hostility toward him.[12]

To expose and defuse the conspiracy they sincerely believed existed, Washington's allies vehemently denounced Conway, Gates, and Mifflin to their friends, family, and colleagues in their conversations and correspondence. They took their cue from Washington. Although Washington was ordinarily discreet about such matters, he made no effort to discourage his friends from deprecating the alleged plotters. Indeed, he indulged in some deprecation himself. Washington's officers portrayed Conway, Gates, and Mifflin as duplicitous, disloyal, unscrupulous, and power-hungry troublemakers who owed whatever successes they enjoyed to happenstance, not ability. They questioned Conway's character, the extent Gates contributed to victory at Saratoga, and Mifflin's record as quartermaster. Alexander Hamilton, for example, wrote to George Clinton on 13 February 1778:

> You and I had some conversation when I had the pleasure of seeing you last with respect to the existence of a certain faction. Since I saw you, I have discovered such convincing traits of the monster, that I cannot doubt its reality in the most extensive sense. I dare say, you have seen and heard enough to settle the matter, in your own mind. . . . Have you heard anything of Conway's history? He is one of the vermin bred in the entrails of this chimera dire [a classical monster], and there does not exist a more villainous calumniator and incendiary.[13]

By so ferociously rebuking Conway, Gates, and Mifflin, Washington and his associates forced the officer corps and congressmen to take a stand on the supposed conspiracy. For most it was an easy decision to side with Washington. On the one hand, Washington's officers were united by their loyalty to their commander in chief, their resentment of unfavorable comparisons with Gates's army, and their anger with Congress for promoting Conway over the heads of twenty-three other brigadiers. On the other hand, the only thing Washington's critics had in common was a vague frustration with his generalship. They had no organization or plan—or even an awareness that they were part of a conspiracy to depose Washington. People who had expressed friendship for the accused conspirators or had criticized Washington's generalship—a list that included de Kalb, Lafayette, Sullivan, and Wayne—hastened to reaffirm their loyalty to the commander in chief. Congressmen, for their part, were caught unawares by the outrage some of their decisions had created. They too rushed to acknowledge their support for Washington. By mid-January 1778, Henry Laurens, the president of Congress, assured Lafayette that Congress was solidly behind Washington. Small wonder that in a moment of unguarded clarity, Greene wrote, "The late faction that has been the subject of speculation for some time past vanishes like a mist before the warming beams of the sun in a summer's morning. It begins to be a doubt whether there ever was any such thing if the party charged were to be credited."[14]

Given the circumstances, it was no surprise that Washington and his allies so easily succeeded in cowering or disgracing the officers they targeted for condemnation. The accused plotters' initial response to these conspiracy charges was to run for cover and attempt to demonstrate their innocence, but their often clumsy efforts to prove a negative usually deepened their guilt in their enemies' eyes. For all of Gates's shortcomings, he was not the kind to engage in cabals. His big sin was that he was a successful general who had received an unsolicited letter from one of Washington's most vocal critics. Gates learned of the developing scandal from Mifflin on 3 December. Naturally enough, his initial reaction was outrage that someone had pilfered his private correspondence, so he focused his attention on uncovering the culprit. Wilkinson disingenuously suggested that perhaps Gates's aide, Lt. Col. Robert Troup, had inadvertently blurted something to Alexander Hamilton during the latter's recent visit to Albany. When Gates learned the truth about Wilkinson's drunken gossiping from Conway, he angrily reprimanded him. Wilkinson responded by challenging Gates to a duel in York on 24 February 1778, but Gates managed to soothe Wilkinson's ruffled feathers and avoid the planned shoot-out. As for his relationship with the commander in chief, Gates explained to Washington that he and Conway were not friends, and in any case the French officer's letter did not contain the purported sentence. Gates admitted that Conway had criticized the army but noted that officers did that sort of thing all the time in their private correspondence.[15]

Unfortunately for Gates, Washington was not about to let him off the hook so easily. Washington responded that Gates's account did not ring true to him and suggested that releasing the relevant correspondence was the best way for Gates to clear his name and bring this unpleasant episode to an end—unless he had something to hide. Gates wanted to appease Washington, but he also believed in protecting Conway's privacy. He assured Laurens and others who had Washington's ear that he had no relationship, conspiratorial or otherwise, with Conway, and that he did not want to quarrel with the commander in chief. In a 21 February 1778 letter to Washington, Gates wrote plaintively, "I solemnly declare that I am of no faction."[16] Washington replied that he was satisfied with Gates's explanations, as he well might be now that his chief rival was so eager to placate him. However, in a letter to another officer several weeks later, Washington indicated that he remained suspicious despite Gates's protestations of innocence: "G[ate]s has involved himself in his letters to me, in the most absurd contradictions. . . .

I have a good deal of reason to believe that the machinations of this junto will recoil upon their own heads, and be a means of bringing some matters to light which by getting me out of the way some of them thought to conceal."[17]

Gates at least managed to survive the episode professionally. The same, though, could not be said of the man who gave his name to the whole sordid affair. Conway was well aware that most of Washington's officers despised him as a malcontent and coward. He left Whitemarsh in November 1777 under the assumption that his military career in America was over, and Washington wished him Godspeed back to France. Congress's surprising decision to promote him and appoint him inspector general, however, offered him the opportunity for resurrection, or at least for a stay of execution. Unfortunately for him, his letter to Gates—or, more accurately, Wilkinson's inebriated and erroneous retelling of it—destroyed whatever slim chances he had for redemption. Conway had not kept a copy of the letter, so he was unsure whether or not he had used the incriminating phrase, but he knew full well that he had criticized Washington. In an awkward series of letters to Washington in November, December, and January that were at once beseeching and condescending, he explained that his comments were meant to be constructive, and that anyway officers frequently communicated with each other in such an open and blunt manner. He denied any role in a cabal to remove Washington. Instead, he stated that he respected Washington's honesty, patriotism, and common sense but believed that Washington often let his less capable lieutenants influence him. If such backhanded comments were not sufficiently insulting, he also cynically compared Washington to Frederick the Great. Finally, he complained, truthfully enough, that Washington's supporters were out to dishonor him.[18]

Reading Conway's dissembling letters did nothing to improve Washington's negative opinion of the man. As far as Washington was concerned, even if Conway's purported quotation was not exact, the general gist was probably on target. In his response to Conway, Washington coolly and deceptively insisted that he had nothing to do with his subordinates' angry efforts to discredit him. Instead, he attributed their resentment to Congress's decision to elevate Conway over the heads of so many worthy brigadiers. By way of reference, Washington asked Conway to remember his bitterness when Congress gave de Kalb seniority over him. Even so, Washington assured Conway that army officers would treat him with all professional courtesy. Conway discovered otherwise when he visited Valley Forge just before the new year to talk with Washington about his new responsibilities as inspector general. He received such a frosty reception there that he recognized that he could not adequately fulfill his new duties, so he returned to York and submitted his resignation as inspector general. The next month, Conway finally got a copy of his letter, and he wrote to Washington on

27 January that it did not contain the alleged damning phrase. Although he refrained from divulging the letter's contents, the following month Washington through his own sources discovered that Conway had actually written to Gates, "What a pity there is but one Gates! But the more I see of this army the less I think it is fit for general action under its actual chiefs and actual discipline. I speak to you sincerely and freely and wish I could serve under you."[19] Conway thought about publishing the letter to clear his name, but Henry Laurens dissuaded him because it might alert the British to discord in the American camp.[20]

In the meantime, Congress transferred Conway to New York to get him out of the way, but later that spring Conway wrote to Laurens and threatened to quit unless he received an independent command. To his surprise, the crafty Laurens submitted the letter to Congress, which took advantage of the opportunity to rid itself of the troublesome Frenchman by accepting his resignation forthwith on 28 April. Strife followed Conway out of the army. Because Cadwalader had accused him of cowardice at Germantown, Conway challenged him to a duel that they fought on 4 July. Cadwalader severely wounded Conway in the face, and for a while it looked like the French officer might not survive. While on his supposed deathbed, Conway wrote one last letter to Washington to apologize for all the trouble he had caused. He eventually recovered, however, and returned to France later that year.[21]

Finally, Thomas Mifflin paid a professional price for supposedly masterminding the alleged conspiracy. Even before the Conway Cabal, critics had taken Mifflin to task for his failings as army quartermaster. Rumors that he was the leader of an anti-Washington plot, though, ruined what remained of his reputation in the army. Laurens, for example, wrote of Mifflin, "His fawning mild address and obsequiousness, procured him toleration from great men on both sides, a sort of favoritism from some; his idleness, duplicity and criminal partialities in a certain circle laid the foundation of our present deplorable state."[22] Washington agreed with this assessment and never trusted Mifflin again. When Mifflin asked for a field command that spring, Washington noted that giving him one would be unfair to those generals who had remained at their posts and done their duty that winter. Although Mifflin retained his major generalship even after he resigned as quartermaster, he saw no further action. He submitted his resignation in August 1778, but Congress did not get around to accepting it until the following February. He returned to politics, albeit with diminished influence, and became a congressman before the war ended. He later said to an inquiring historian of his role in that winter's purported intrigues:

> I declare to you, with the greatest sincerity and solemnity, that I never formed a plan or a party to injure General Washington's command. I never desired to have

> any person whomsoever, take the command of the American army from him; nor have I said or done anything of, or respecting him, which the public service did not require; and which I would not have said, with the greatest freedom to you, as his friend and as a friend to American independency. I never aspired, in thought, to the command of the army; and always would have deprecated the idea as improper and dangerous to myself and to America had that idea occurred, which it never did to me.[23]

The Conway Cabal may have been more imagined than real, but it still had a profound impact on the Revolutionary War. Washington and his supporters' disproportionate and synchronized responses to the incident secured Washington's position as commander in chief by demonstrating to everyone in and out of the army the high political and professional costs of challenging—or, more accurately, being perceived as challenging—his authority. Indeed, in this respect it is closer to the truth to refer to it as the Washington Cabal. Congress continued to question Washington's decisions and even on occasion to overrule him, but after the winter of 1777–78 there were no more rumblings about removing him. Washington's enhanced status benefited the war effort because he now had more freedom to formulate strategy and deal with officers without constantly looking over his shoulder at a Congress ready to second-guess him. The episode turned Washington into the untouchable and indispensable man, a potentially dangerous combination for a young republic struggling to secure its independence and freedom. The Conway Cabal also solidified Washington's bond with his army, though it did not end the backbiting and discord that periodically roiled the officer corps. This undoubtedly made for a more effective army in the years to come, but it also increasingly separated the officers from the society they were charged to protect. Indeed, the officer corps gradually developed the mind-set of a standing professional army in a society that historically viewed such a force as a threat to liberty.

Generals at Valley Forge

Rank had its privileges even in the comparatively egalitarian Continental army. This did not, however, mean that life was necessarily easy for Continental generals in the winter of 1777–78. Although they had better rations, quarters, and clothing than the rank and file, they were just as susceptible to boredom, loneliness, frustration, disease, and exhaustion. They were also burdened with the responsibility for their units' well-being. Infighting and disruptive transfers sapped generals' morale and damaged esprit de corps. Unreliable wages and inflation made it increasingly difficult for generals to support their military and biological families. Small wonder that so many of Washington's generals asked him for leave to return home for the winter. There they could pass the season in comfortable dwellings in front of warm fires with their friends and loved ones. Washington often found it difficult to refuse such requests from men who had served so faithfully for so long, even though fewer generals in camp increased the workload for the rest and set a bad example for soldiers who had no say in where they were situated. At one point there were only three brigadiers left at Valley Forge: Paterson, Poor, and Varnum. When Varnum asked for a furlough in April 1778 to see his wife and make arrangements for his finances, Washington finally drew a line and said no.[24]

Once a general reached home, getting him back to camp sometimes proved difficult. On 8 January 1778, for instance, Washington asked John Glover to return to Valley Forge from his Marblehead home to prepare his brigade for the next campaign and alleviate some of the burdens under which the remaining generals in camp labored. Glover replied that he wanted to comply with Washington's orders, but could not. For one thing, he was busy overseeing the transfer of Burgoyne's defeated army to Cambridge, Massachusetts. Moreover, runaway inflation made it next to impossible for him to afford staying in the army and supporting his motherless children. Finally, and most importantly, three years of active service had broken down Glover's health. He did not believe he was physically capable of withstanding the rigors of army life, so he intended to ask Congress's permission to resign his commission. Washington greatly valued Glover and did not want to lose him. The previous year he had successfully overcome Glover's reluctance to rejoin the army by appealing to his sense of duty. Washington resorted to a similar stratagem this time, writing, "I have too high an opinion of your value as an officer to do anything that may contribute to your relinquishing that character. My earnest wish is that you may continue in it. The spirit of resigning, which is now become almost epidemical, is truly painful and alarming."[25] This time the best he got from Glover was his promise to visit Valley Forge as soon as he felt up to it so Washington could see for himself that he was in no condition to take over his brigade.[26]

The same day Washington summoned Glover, he also wrote to Brig. Gen. Ebenezer Learned in Oxford, Massachusetts, to ask him to return as soon as possible to Valley Forge to resume command of his brigade. Learned had given up his commission after the siege of Boston after sustaining a serious injury in a fall, but Congress appointed him a brigadier anyway in April 1777. He led a brigade in the Saratoga campaign, marched south with it to reinforce Washington's army, and then secured a leave to visit his home. Once there, he was in so much pain that he could scarcely ride a horse, so he decided to step down again. William Heath, though, persuaded him to consult Washington first. Learned did so in a letter that included a surgeon's certificate testifying to his poor health. Although

Washington did his best to dissuade Glover from quitting, he made no effort to keep Learned in the army. Learned possessed neither Glover's sterling combat record nor his close relationship with Washington, so it was not surprising that the commander in chief was willing to cut him loose. Congress accepted Learned's resignation on 24 March 1778, and he played no further part in the conflict.[27]

Moreover, some of those generals who remained in camp at Valley Forge failed to pull their weight or caused more trouble than they were worth. No one doubted Kazimierz Pułaski's physical courage, but his leadership of the cavalry corps that winter left much to be desired. The basic problem was that he was not sufficiently familiar with American language and culture to overcome his officers' ingrained hostility toward foreigners. His inability to do so undermined unit cohesion and morale. Pułaski himself recognized his shortcomings and in March 1778 voluntarily surrendered his command. He did not, though, give up his commission. Instead, he secured Congress's and Washington's permission to organize an independent cavalry corps. Although Washington chastised him for recruiting British deserters into his new outfit, he continued to value Pułaski's zealousness and initiative.[28]

William Maxwell also came under fire from his own men that winter. On 2 March a group of officers from his brigade presented a visiting congressional committee to Valley Forge with a *Memorial of Jersey Field Officers Ag[ains]t Gen. Maxwell.* In it they criticized Maxwell's lack of fortitude and industry, his unfamiliarity with military discipline, and his ignorance of his military responsibilities. Although they acknowledged the unorthodox manner of their complaint, they insisted that they acted out of the purest patriotic motives. They explained away their failure to follow the chain of command by noting that Washington was too busy to involve himself in such minutiae and Stirling had never seen Maxwell in battle. In all likelihood, though, they probably felt that neither general would listen to their grievances. They said nothing about Maxwell's excessive consumption of alcohol, probably because a court-martial the previous autumn had more or less absolved him of that particular military sin, but instead focused on the impact of his drinking. In this case, the congressional committee washed its hands of the affair. Perhaps because the officers provided no specific evidence to back up their claims, Washington did not act either, so Maxwell retained his command.[29]

Dissension among Virginia brigadier generals Peter Muhlenberg, Charles Scott, George Weedon, and William Woodford constituted a more complicated, protracted, and serious problem for the Continental army that winter. Congress had appointed Muhlenberg, Weedon, and Woodford brigadiers on 21 February 1777 to give Virginia more representation in the roster of generals, allotting their seniority based on their previous ranks. Because Woodford was not in the Continental army when Congress acted, he became the most junior brigadier of the three officers. After the army encamped at Valley Forge, Woodford formally complained that he deserved to be senior to Muhlenberg and Weedon. Woodford had served as a colonel in the Continental army in 1775–76 before resigning in a dispute over rank with Hugh Mercer. During his first stint in the service, Woodford had been senior to both Muhlenberg and Weedon. By that logic, Woodford believed that Congress erred in its original rankings. He had not made an issue of it during the campaign, but now that the army was in winter quarters, he threatened to resign unless he got his way. Meanwhile, Scott, who had become a brigadier eight days after his other three Virginia colleagues, made a similar claim against Weedon.[30]

Washington was ordinarily sympathetic to matters of honor, yet even he found this one exasperating. At the same time, though, he understood the four officers' thinking and was more inclined to blame congressional carelessness than the officers themselves for the imbroglio. He explained to Laurens:

> When rank is once given, no matter upon what principle, whether from mistake or other causes, the party in possession of it in most cases is unwilling to give it up, though the most obvious principles of justice or even the public good should require it. Such is the general ambition of men and attachment to their own private preferment. It is a truth, that it will ever be found more easy to prevent, than to remedy difficulties after they have happened.[31]

Washington valued all four officers for their contributions during the recent campaign and worried that at least one of them would resign no matter how the issue was resolved. He therefore focused most of his energy into persuading them all to remain in the service regardless of the outcome of the dispute. Because of the complexities involved, neither Congress, Washington, nor the various committees and boards constituted to look into the dispute was willing to make a final determination, but they instead kicked the responsibility back and forth to each other throughout the winter of 1777–78. Most officers, though, sided with Woodford because of their commitment to seniority. Finally, on 19 March 1778, Congress canceled the four officers' commissions and issued new ones. Listening to the squeaky wheels, it made Woodford the most senior brigadier, followed by Muhlenberg, Scott, and Weedon.

Congress's decision satisfied Scott and Woodford, but Muhlenberg and Weedon understandably felt differently. Weedon was on leave at his Fredericksburg, Virginia, home when he got the news. He resented that Congress did not give him the opportunity to present his side of the issue, and he felt that Woodford was being mean and petty. Although Washington asked him to remain in the army, Weedon replied that as a gentleman he had no choice but to relinquish his commission. Congress agreed to let Weedon stay home but insisted that he retain his rank in case he ever changed his mind and returned to duty. Muhlenberg's response was refreshingly altruistic. As a Lutheran preacher, his sense of duty and Christian forbearance overcame his resentment. He told Washington that he did not enter the army for either ambition or honor, so he would not let those traits determine his actions. His main concern was that Congress's verdict might cost him his officers' respect and hurt his military effectiveness.[32]

During the winter there were a number of transfers that had an impact on the American army's command structure. Maj. Gen. Joseph Spencer spent 1777 in Rhode Island in command of a small force tasked with keeping an eye on the British garrison in Newport. It was a thankless job that promised little glory or recognition, but plenty of logistical headaches. Considering his army's low priority, Spencer had considerable difficulty provisioning his two thousand or so troops. In addition, his inability to pry the British out of their Newport stronghold alienated local authorities so much that Spencer asked for a court of inquiry into his conduct, which ultimately cleared him of any responsibility for his failure to take the port. Even so, he did not impress people with his military prowess. One observer noted, "Spencer might make a good deacon or selectman, but never can serve his country as a major general."[33] Frustrated with the insufficient resources at his disposal and Congress's refusal to provide sufficient help, Spencer submitted his resignation in December. No one expressed much regret at his departure, including Washington, who had sent Spencer to Rhode Island in the first place to get him out of the main army and into a post where his shortcomings were less likely to injure the American cause.[34]

Congress directed Washington to replace Spencer with another major general. Because Washington grumbled that he did not have any major generals in his main army to spare for Rhode Island, he initially thought about transferring Putnam or Heath there. Then, however, he recognized an opportunity to kill two birds with one stone. That winter John Sullivan was as usual a disgruntled and discontented man. Part of his problem was financial. After three years in the army without much by way of compensation, Sullivan was so deeply in debt that he could not afford new clothes. He wanted to go home to New Hampshire to get his fiscal house in order, but Washington refused his permission because he needed Sullivan at Valley Forge to help keep the army from dissolving. There was, though, more to Sullivan's despondency than that. He felt unappreciated and put-upon. He had fought as long and as hard as anyone, but Congress seemed more interested in investigating than rewarding his actions. Sullivan wanted an independent command that would give him the chance to prove his value as a general. Spencer's resignation enabled Washington to reward a loyal, albeit troublesome, subordinate, so he issued the necessary orders on 10 March 1778. Sullivan happily accepted the new job and packed his bags. Considering the dissension and controversy that followed Sullivan everywhere, public response to his appointment was surprisingly positive. Congressmen in particular hoped that Sullivan could inject more energy and initiative into the small army guarding Rhode Island.[35]

To lead Sullivan's old division, Washington appointed Brig. Gen. William Smallwood. Born in 1732 into a family of Maryland planters, Smallwood participated in the Great War for Empire before serving ten years in the colony's assembly. He was wounded at the head of a regiment at the Battle of White Plains five days after Congress promoted him to brigadier general. Although he subsequently commanded a brigade in Sullivan's division, he spent most of 1777 recruiting, organizing, and leading the Maryland militia, in which capacity he fought at Germantown. Washington probably selected him to take over Sullivan's division because he was familiar with the outfit. Smallwood was a steady and loyal comrade-in-arms who counted Sullivan and Greene among his friends. He was a lifelong bachelor in an era when the overwhelming majority of men married. One person wrote that he was "a worthy man and good officer, a firm American, and much devoted to the cause."[36] Washington liked him enough to chide him in a letter about spending too much time with British ladies. Washington's rare stab at humor, though, exposed one of Smallwood's less admirable traits. Smallwood was so hurt by Washington's jest that the commander in chief felt compelled to apologize for it. Indeed, Smallwood could be hypersensitive, petty, haughty, and quarrelsome. When the Maryland government sent a stock of coffee, tea, sugar, and cognac to its officers serving with Washington, Smallwood placed a guard over it with orders to keep de Kalb away from partaking in the goodies because he was not a Marylander. For these reasons he was not very popular among the officers in the Maryland brigade. He cut a fine figure but was more stolid and stately than dashing and aggressive. Smallwood's division spent the winter of 1777–78 garrisoning Wilmington, Delaware, and therefore did not suffer quite as much as the soldiers at Valley Forge.[37]

In April 1777 Congress had sent Brig. Gen. Edward Hand to Fort Pitt in western Pennsylvania as head of the Western Department. Hand's inability to protect American settlers from American Indians provoked considerable criticism, so he asked Congress to relieve him from his post. Congress obliged on 2 May 1778 and assigned Washington the task of finding Hand's replacement. After mulling it over, Washington gave the job to Brig. Gen. Lachlan McIntosh. McIntosh emigrated from Scotland to Georgia when he was a small boy. He grew up in a Savannah orphanage and secured an education thanks to James Oglethorpe's intervention.

In 1748 he moved to Charleston, South Carolina, and got employment in Henry Laurens's countinghouse. When the Revolutionary War began, Georgia commissioned McIntosh a militia colonel, and in September 1776 Congress appointed him a brigadier general. The following May he killed Declaration of Independence signatory Button Gwinnett in a duel over Georgia's political and military leadership. Although a jury found McIntosh not guilty of murder, his allies persuaded Congress to order him northward to Washington's army to keep him out of further trouble. He arrived after the Philadelphia campaign concluded, and Washington put him in charge of the North Carolina brigade. That winter he impressed Washington with his good conduct, common sense, attention to duty, and efforts to maintain camp discipline. The more Washington thought about it, the more convinced he became that McIntosh possessed the necessary qualities to run the remote and distant Western Department. As Washington put it, "I have great expectations from his prudence, good sense, and knowledge of negotiation in Indian affairs, in which I imagine he has been conversant during his long residence in Carolina and Georgia."[38] Unfortunately, McIntosh was more effective in a subordinate role than the top spot. He lacked the initiative and determination for such an independent command and struck some as lazy. Moreover, he did not seem particularly enthusiastic about a mission that promised little more than excessive paperwork, congressional neglect, and tedium out on the war's periphery.[39]

Dispatching Sullivan as Spencer's replacement and McIntosh as Hand's were simple personnel transactions. However, that winter Washington also faced more complicated matters that disrupted the main army's command structure. Some congressmen wanted to follow up on Burgoyne's surrender at Saratoga by mounting another invasion of Canada. To lead it, Congress selected Lafayette, with Conway and John Stark as his chief lieutenants. Lafayette owed his appointment to his continuing popularity in Congress and its hope that his French background would attract French Canadian support. Lafayette was as usual looking for ways to contribute to the war effort and achieve personal glory—not necessarily in that order—so he jumped at the opportunity for an independent mission. He was flattered and honored by Congress's offer and determined to succeed. Although he was initially amenable to Conway's participation in the operation because he respected the French officer, he soon jettisoned the idea when he learned that the officer corps detested the man. He insisted that either McDougall or de Kalb, or both, accompany him instead. When Congress balked, he threatened to decline the appointment and return to France if he did not get his way. Congress did not want to lose or antagonize its shiniest French ornament, so it gave in to Lafayette's demand.

When Lafayette reached Albany to begin preparations for the invasion, he discovered discontented militiamen, insufficient funds, and a dearth of supplies, equipment, and manpower. There were, however, plenty of generals there, including Arnold, Conway, Lincoln, and Schuyler. They all told him that a successful campaign was impossible with the available resources. Faced with failure from the get-go, an embarrassed Lafayette felt as if he had been played for a fool. He was so frustrated and angry that he wished he had never left France, and he suspected that villainy and treason were at the root of his woes. Congress finally canceled the operation on 7 March. By that point no one in Congress could seem to recall the logic behind it or who had initiated it. Fortunately for Lafayette, the fiasco did not hurt his reputation. In fact, congressmen appreciated the time and energy he invested in the project. Washington, who had taken a hands-off approach to the plan from the start, reassured Lafayette of his continued confidence and welcomed him back to the main army. In the end, Lafayette's natural cheerfulness and optimism reasserted itself, and he returned to his division.[40]

People respected Israel Putnam for his patriotism, past service, and physical courage, but by the winter of 1777–78 there was an emerging consensus that whatever his positive attributes, he lacked the wherewithal to command American forces in the strategically vital Hudson Highlands. Prominent officials in and out of Congress argued that he was too ineffective and lazy for his job. For example, New York's governor, Brig. Gen. George Clinton, warned Washington that Putnam had completely alienated the local militia, suppliers, and the state legislature. One of Putnam's subordinates, Brig. Gen. Samuel Parsons, was so unhappy with the confusion, unclear lines of authority, and disgruntled civilians in the area that Washington had to talk him out of resigning his commission. There were even persistent rumors that Putnam seized property for his own personal use without compensating either the owner or the state. Putnam seemed unwilling or unable to respond to such complaints. Washington was well aware of these problems and shared the prevailing view of Putnam's abilities. He wanted to replace Putnam more for general inefficiency than for any specific military sin, but relieving an officer still popular in some circles was politically tricky. Fortunately for Washington, Congress provided a means for him to do so. Congress had ordered a court of inquiry into Putnam's conduct after the British so easily seized Forts Clinton and Montgomery during a thrust up the Hudson River the previous October. Washington seized on this as an excuse to remove Putnam on 16 March 1778, explaining to him: "My reason for making this change is owing to the prejudices of the people which whether well or ill grounded must be indulged, and I should think myself wanting in justice to the public and candor towards you were I to continue you in a command after I have been almost in direct terms informed that the people of the state of New York will not render the necessary support and assistance while you remain at the head of that department."[41] Washington ordered Putnam to report to

Connecticut to help raise troops. Although Washington intended to replace him with Alexander McDougall, in mid-April Congress directed Horatio Gates to take over the Hudson Highlands.[42]

Thomas Mifflin's untimely resignation as quartermaster compounded Washington's logistical woes. Among other responsibilities, the quartermaster provided the army's transportation. Because Mifflin was unable to secure and maintain enough horses, Washington's army at Valley Forge soon ran short of the provisions and equipment it needed to function. Washington and a congressional committee that visited camp that winter recognized that the army required a strong and capable new quartermaster to bring order out of the chaos Mifflin had left behind. Without one, the army would most likely dissolve before winter ended. There was some talk of appointing Philip Schuyler to the post. Schuyler had proven his logistical talents as commander of the Northern army, was currently unemployed, and possessed Washington's confidence. However, some congressmen still bore a grudge against him for his arrogant patrician manner, believed that he lacked the necessary temperament for the job, and blamed him for Fort Ticonderoga's fall.

With Schuyler out of the picture, Washington and the congressmen at Valley Forge put their heads together and decided that Nathanael Greene was the right man for the position. Greene was Washington's most trusted lieutenant, had a business background, and understood the army's logistical difficulties. The problem was persuading Greene to accept the assignment. Greene had wanted to return home on leave that winter to see his family and get a handle on his personal finances, but Washington denied him permission because he valued Greene too much. Nor was Greene successful in his efforts to get home to Rhode Island by persuading Washington to appoint him Spencer's replacement. When Washington and the congressional committee asked him to become quartermaster, Greene hesitated because it promised little by way of glory and fulfillment. Greene believed that Mifflin had caused so much damage as quartermaster that no one could straighten things out. Besides, Greene saw himself first and foremast as a combat commander. In the end, though, Washington's persuasive abilities and Greene's sense of duty prevailed. Greene agreed to accept the post on the conditions that he could select his immediate subordinates and that he retained his rank and seniority.

Greene took over as quartermaster on 23 March 1778 and immediately started putting the army's logistical house in order in time for spring campaigning. Although he knew that he had his work cut out for him, within days he complained that the obstacles he faced were almost insurmountable because he lacked the necessary time and resources. Indeed, he could not even get enough information from Mifflin to figure out what the army had and needed. Nevertheless,

Greene got things done. He established or refurbished a chain of magazines and supply depots for the army to draw on from Head of Elk in Maryland up to the Hudson River. He repaired the broken roads to Valley Forge to make it easier for wagons to bring supplies to camp. To combat theft, he authorized branding the army's livestock, and he tapped Maryland as a source of horses and wagons to ease the burden on war-ravaged Pennsylvania. He paid his deputy quartermasters by commission to motivate them, despite the opportunities for corruption this represented, and he compensated citizens with whom the army did business in printed certificates redeemable in a short period of time to limit inflation's impact on them. Unlike his predecessor, Greene had the advantages of improved weather, a good relationship with Washington, and Congress's willingness to sacrifice economy and spend whatever was necessary to supply the army, so he got results. By mid-May Washington noted that although army logistics were still not up to par because of the neglect and incompetence under which they had suffered the previous winter, they were in good enough shape to permit the army to wage war that spring. For this Washington credited Greene, writing later that summer:

> And in justice to General Greene, I take occasion to observe that the public is much indebted to him for his judicious management and active exertions in his present department. When he entered upon it, he found it in a most confused, distracted, and destitute state. This by his conduct and industry has undergone a very happy change. . . . In a word he has given the most general satisfaction and his affairs carry much the face of method and system.[43]

On 26 September 1777, the same day the British army marched into Philadelphia, a German officer named Friedrich Wilhelm von Steuben disembarked at Portsmouth, New Hampshire. Steuben was the last, and in some respects the most important, of the foreign volunteer officers who became Continental army major generals. He was born in Magdeburg in 1730, the son of an army engineer, spent part of his youth in Russia, and received a Jesuit education. He was commissioned in the Prussian army at age seventeen and served in the Great War for Empire. Discharged as a captain at the end of the conflict, Steuben fell on hard times and accumulated considerable debts over the course of the next fourteen years as he tried with mixed success to find employment in a European army. He saw the Revolutionary War as an opportunity to ply his trade and jumpstart his career. The shrewd Benjamin Franklin saw something worthwhile in the down-on-his-luck forty-seven-year-old German, so he dispatched him to America with a letter introducing him inaccurately as a Prussian lieutenant general. Steuben was discouraged with the poor reception he initially received in America, but stifling his disappointment, he traveled southward to York to present himself and his credentials to Congress. Although Steuben was as ambitious as the next man, he won congressmen over with his altruistic attitude.

On 27 February Steuben rode to Valley Forge to meet Washington. Washington was his usual formal and cordial self, but by now he had had enough experience with foreign officers to know that all that glittered was not gold. Nevertheless, Washington was impressed with Steuben's obvious military experience, and even more so with his willingness to serve as a volunteer major general in any capacity Washington saw fit until he proved himself enough to warrant a regular commission. Washington initially toyed with the idea of appointing Steuben quartermaster, but he ultimately decided that Steuben could best serve the cause by drilling the Continentals. This was an inspector general's job, but Washington did not want to reopen Conway Cabal wounds by asking Congress to assign Steuben to the position. Instead, he gave Steuben an inspector general's mandate and authority, but without the title. With his marching orders in hand, Steuben got to work.[44]

Washington had long recognized that insufficient training was one of the American army's biggest shortcomings. By the winter of 1777–78 plenty of American officers and men had combat experience, but this did not mean that the army functioned as a professional eighteenth-century military force. Most American soldiers had not mastered close-order marching, rapid deployment, efficient maneuvering out in the open, mass volley firing, and the bayonet. There was no armywide training regimen. Although some officers, such as Conway, did train their outfits, they were the exceptions. It was therefore unsurprising that the well-disciplined British army repeatedly defeated its American counterpart in open field engagements from Long Island to Germantown. Washington wanted Steuben to rectify this problem by establishing a simple and uniform system of drill for the army. Fortunately for the Americans, Steuben possessed the proper character and personality for the job. He quickly wormed his way into Washington's inner circle with his gregariousness and kindheartedness. On one occasion, when introduced to a young and vivacious woman named Miss Sheaf, Steuben said, "I have from my youth been cautioned to guard against mischief, but I had no idea that her attractions were so powerful." His impulsive generosity explained his chronic indebtedness. He once gave his last dollar to a crippled, distraught, and discharged black soldier unable to afford the toll across the Hudson River.[45]

Steuben organized a model company and personally trained them, setting an example for an officer corps that frequently disdained such mundane work. There was nothing easy about it; Steuben's English was poor and his temper short, but both improved rapidly over the next few weeks with the help of translators and his growing understanding of American society. His rough-and-ready style, tireless commitment, theatrical tirades, and multilingual cussing amused the men and invariably drew a crowd as he put his company through its paces. Because time was limited, he focused on teaching the troops to do a few things very well. Washington created brigade inspectors to carry Steuben's training to the rest of the army, and soon Valley Forge echoed with the clomp of boots and the barking of commands as Continentals drilled and paraded from dawn until midafternoon.[46]

Steuben's efforts helped to transform Washington's army into a well-drilled and disciplined force. Washington was particularly pleased and happily gave Steuben the credit, writing to Congress in late April 1778: "I should do injustice if I were to be longer silent with regard to the merits of the Baron de Steuben, his knowledge of his profession added to the zeal which he has discovered since he began upon the functions of his office, lead me to consider him as an acquisition to the service and to recommend him to the attention of Congress."[47] Congress took the hint and on 5 May appointed a grateful Steuben both inspector general and major general. By doing so, Congress elevated Steuben over all the brigadiers. Such a dramatic departure from the seniority principle would ordinarily have outraged the hypersensitive American officer corps, but not in this case. For one thing, officers liked Steuben and appreciated his accomplishment. For another, most saw Steuben as a staff officer who would never lead troops into battle. Steuben still managed to ruffle a few feathers. On the same day Congress promoted him, starchy Brig. Gen. James Varnum complained to Washington about Steuben. Varnum respected Steuben and supported a uniform system of drill, but he grumbled that Steuben was abusing his power by issuing orders to brigade officers on his own authority and without consulting brigade commanders. Washington responded the next month by spelling out and curtailing Steuben's responsibilities. By then, however, the spring campaign had begun, relegating questions about Steuben's clout to the backburner.[48]

The Battle of Monmouth Courthouse

The Revolutionary War did not take place in an international vacuum but was instead part of a wider geopolitical conflict within a broader British-dominated Eurocentric world. Ever since its defeat in the Great War for Empire, the French government had sought an opportunity to knock the upstart British down a peg or two. The French were well aware of Britain's problems with its North American colonies, so they were quick to grasp the possibilities the American rebellion offered. If British prosperity depended on commerce within its empire, then breaking the political links between London and its colonies in North America might undermine British power and enable France to regain military and economic superiority. As it was, the Americans were more than willing to accept France's clandestine aid that flowed across the Atlantic in 1776 and 1777, but they did not push for a military alliance until after their disastrous defeats around New York City. Throughout 1777 American commissioners in Paris lobbied for France's entry into the war, but the French hesitated in part because they questioned American resolve. Victory at Saratoga and Washington's determined resistance around Philadelphia, however, cleared up such doubts and convinced the French that the Americans were in their war for the long haul. On 6 February 1778 the United States and France signed treaties of commerce and alliance that bound the two countries to wage war together until American independence was won. France's recognition of the United States made conflict between it and Britain inevitable, and by mid-June the two countries were at war.

France's imminent entry into the war forced the British government to recalibrate its grand strategy. French involvement transformed what had been a regional conflict into a world war, compelling the British to disperse their limited resources to defend their possessions in Europe, India, the West Indies, and on the West African coast. To deal with the developing French threat, the British government adopted a two-pronged approach. First, it dispatched a commission led by the Earl of Carlisle to end the rebellion by offering the Americans self-government within the British Empire. The Americans would probably have accepted such a proposal at the war's start, but by 1778 Congress concluded that it was too little too late. In addition, the British decided to simultaneously retrench in America while undertaking offensive operations against French islands in the West Indies. Doing so meant abandoning Philadelphia and concentrating British forces in easily defended New York City. The British government left the specific details up to Howe's replacement, Gen. Henry Clinton. Clinton opted to send Philadelphia's loyalist population and the army's baggage to New York City by sea. As for his eleven thousand redcoats, provincials, and Hessians, Clinton planned to march them overland through New Jersey to New York City.

Washington was impressed with the changes Steuben had brought about in the army's rank and file, but he had reason to question the quality and quantity of their generals. Although his army contained sufficient major generals, there were as usual not enough brigadiers for all the brigades. Indeed, Washington was so short of them that he declined to transfer the troublesome James Varnum to Rhode Island to help John Sullivan. Of the seventeen Continental brigades at his disposal, Washington had brigadiers for only nine of them: Huntington (Connecticut), Maxwell (New Jersey), Muhlenberg (Virginia), Paterson (Massachusetts), Poor (New Hampshire), Scott (Virginia), Varnum (Rhode Island), Wayne (Pennsylvania), and Woodford (Virginia). As a result, Washington needed brigadiers for two of Massachusetts's three brigades, two of Pennsylvania's three, both of Maryland's, one of Virginia's, and North Carolina's. There was nothing new about the dearth of brigadiers for the Maryland, North Carolina, and Pennsylvania brigades, but Glover's, Learned's, and Weedon's absences explained the deficits in the Massachusetts and Virginia lines. Washington had repeatedly explained to Congress that brigades ran most efficiently with a brigadier at their helm. He believed that relying on a brigade's most senior colonel to lead it did not provide enough stability and continuity for an effective outfit, making it difficult to get things done. Consolidating units was a possible solution because brigades rarely exceeded five hundred men. Doing so, though, was so politically tricky that Washington did not attempt it until after the campaign was over. Until then, Washington's army remained shortchanged at the brigade level.

Things were more complicated at the division level. Because Washington hoped to reorganize the army, he refrained from making final decisions as to division leaders until a congressional committee arrived for consultations. Among other changes, Washington wanted to form the divisions into wings under lieutenant generals that could maneuver more easily in combat. Creating lieutenant generals was Congress's prerogative, though, so Washington had to wait on it. He could have simply organized the wings and placed them under the command of major generals, but there were not enough major generals on hand for the divisions, let alone for divisions and wings. Although Washington was unhappy with the resulting uncertainty, he figured that the army was sufficiently familiar with all the major generals that he could make his assignments at the last minute without disrupting the army.[49]

The quality of those major generals was another question mark. He had at his disposal six major generals: Greene, de Kalb, Lafayette, Mifflin, Stirling, and Steuben. Two of them—Greene and Steuben—were busy with staff responsibilities. De Kalb came down with a violent fever in early May that placed him on death's door until he recovered in mid-July. Of the remaining three, plodding mediocrity characterized Stirling's combat record. Even so, he had more battle experience than Lafayette and Mifflin. The army's other major generals were not readily available. The two Washington respected the most, Benedict Arnold and Benjamin Lincoln, were still recovering from their Saratoga wounds. Although Washington also thought a lot of Philip Schuyler and Arthur St. Clair, they were awaiting courts-martial for their roles in Fort Ticonderoga's fall. Gates, Heath, Howe, and Sullivan were busy running their departments, but McDougall was on his way. Washington worried that Congress might send Putnam to join the main army since he was currently underemployed in Connecticut. Washington, though, considered Putnam more a hindrance than an asset and asked his congressional allies to make sure that did not happen. Washington could have used his brigadiers to lead divisions, but that would mean fewer brigadiers for his brigades. Besides, none of them had demonstrated much tactical finesse in the war so far. Most were sturdy enough fighters, but it remained to be seen whether they could intelligently maneuver the units Steuben had trained.[50]

Washington's efforts to construct an effective command structure that spring were complicated by one final addition: Charles Lee. A British cavalry patrol had captured the eccentric and quarrelsome Lee on 13 December 1776 in Basking Ridge, New Jersey. Because Lee was a former redcoat officer, some Americans feared that the British would put him on trial for treason. Indeed, Congress threatened retaliation if they did so. In the end, though, the British decided to treat him as a prisoner of war. His conduct in captivity was as peculiar as his personality. He concluded that neither side could win the war, so he presented himself as a reasonable middleman who could bring the belligerents together for a compromise peace that would satisfy everyone. He even drew up military plans for both the British and the Americans to use that he believed would advance negotiations. No sooner had the British seized Lee than the Americans sought to secure his release. On 10 July 1777 an American raiding party kidnapped Brig. Gen. Richard Prescott, the British commander of the garrison at Newport, Rhode Island, in his bedroom in a daring midnight raid. Prescott had sufficient rank to warrant an exchange for Lee. While British and American prisoner commissioners worked out the final details, the British released Lee on parole in early April 1778.

On 5 April 1778 Washington, his main lieutenants, and their aides rode four miles from Valley Forge to welcome Lee from Philadelphia. Lee arrived with his usual retinue of dogs yipping behind him. Washington dismounted, greeted Lee warmly, and escorted him past the Continentals drawn up to pay their respects. That evening Washington hosted an elegant dinner complete with music for Lee, and the next morning he delayed breakfast because Lee slept late. Lee's natural sourness was exacerbated not only by a bout of gout, but also because British soldiers had stolen a cache of liquor William Howe generously gave him before he left Philadelphia. Despite his previous difficulties with Lee, Washington was pleased to have him back with the American army. He not only valued Lee's military expertise, but he needed as many generals as he could to lead his divisions and brigades. Lee's opinion of Washington, though, had not changed for the better. A week after he reached Valley Forge, Lee wrote to Washington from York criticizing Washington's strategic thinking, but if this raised doubts in Washington's mind about Lee's cooperativeness, he did not express them. Washington was not the only officer still entranced by the Lee mystique. Greene, for example, distrusted Lee's assertion that the British planned to attack Maryland and worried that Washington's enemies might co-opt Lee, but he did not question Lee's basic competency. Greene wrote of Lee, "He is undoubtedly a good officer and a great scholar. But he is not a little unhappy in his temper."[51] As a result of this continuing forbearance, Lee had a rare second chance to contribute to the war effort as a combat commander.[52]

After visiting Washington at Valley Forge, Lee traveled to York to visit Congress. Before his capture, Lee's eccentric mannerisms and opinions had been one of his strengths, conveying as they did an enchanting authenticity, but now they raised eyebrows among the delegates. For one thing, he seemed all too eager for Congress to reach an accommodation with the British to end the war short of American independence. There were already plenty of rumors circulating that the British planned to offer the Americans self-government within the British Empire, so some delegates saw Lee's lobbying as part of a British public relations campaign to sell their scheme. Whether Lee was a conscious or unconscious tool in this British strategy was beside the point; either way, he was interfering with American efforts to secure independence. Lee also urged Congress to elevate him to lieutenant general. Lee explained that plenty of officers who had once been his juniors now shared his rank because his captivity had prevented him from distinguishing himself on the battlefield. It was only fair, he said, for Congress to bestow on him the promotion he would most certainly have earned had not that British patrol seized him, so he could maintain his seniority. Finally, Lee expressed contempt for Washington, his army, and his strategy. Lee argued that any attempt to mold the Continentals into professional soldiers capable of standing up to the redcoats and Hessians was bound to fail. Rather, he advocated relying on the militia to wage partisan warfare. As for Washington and his lieutenants, Lee had seen nothing to persuade him that they were sufficiently competent for their responsibilities. He told one person that Washington was not qualified to command a sergeant's guard. In a letter to Henry Laurens, Lee wrote, "I am well and hope always shall be well with General Washington. And to speak again vainly I am persuaded (considering how he is surrounded) that he cannot do without me." Unfortunately for Lee, Congress had already made up its mind about Washington's leadership and about independence, and was in no mood to revisit either issue. As a result, he received such a frosty reception that he noted that "the odd humor in which I found some of the members almost frightened me from giving my opinion on any subject."[53] His social obtuseness prevented him from understanding that to espouse such freewheeling and unpopular opinions was unlikely to enhance his reputation or generate much sympathy.[54]

So long as the British maintained their naval supremacy in America, there was little Washington could do to pry them out of their Philadelphia and New York City strongholds. Henry Clinton's decision to abandon Philadelphia and march his army overland through New Jersey to New York City, however, gave Washington a chance to strike the extended and exposed British away from their naval support. The questions for Washington were whether and how to take advantage of this opportunity. As evidence mounted that the British army's days in Philadelphia were numbered, Washington on 17 June summoned his generals to council to consider their options. The consensus was to pursue and harass the British through New Jersey, but Washington did not commit to challenging them in full-scale battle. When Washington learned the next day that the British had evacuated Philadelphia, he put his soldiers on the road to New Jersey. American troops reached the Delaware River at Corryell's Ferry, north of Trenton, on 20 June, and then took two rainy days to get to the other side. Although the British had the shorter route, their baggage train, alternating heavy rains and oppressive heat, and opposition from local militia and William Maxwell's detached brigade slowed them down. On 24 June Washington's army paused at Hopewell township, five miles short of Princeton, to take a breather and give its generals time to consider their next move.

Some of Washington's generals, such as Anthony Wayne, spoke in favor of aggressively challenging the British, but Lee argued forcefully and persuasively against such action. He did not believe that the Continentals could stand up against the redcoats, so any confrontation was bound to end in a defeat that would be all the more unfortunate and unnecessary now that significant French aid was in the offing. Although some of Washington's officers already doubted Lee's judgment, no one was willing to speak up against him—yet. Instead, the council recommended that Washington dispatch another 1,500 men to cooperate with Maxwell and the New Jersey militia in hindering the British march while the rest of the army acted according to circumstances. No one wanted to provoke a full-fledged battle, but hopefully these reinforcements might make the British bleed more as they crossed through New Jersey. It was an imperfect compromise that accomplished little more than to commit the army piecemeal to an undefined mission. However, it also fit Washington's strategic inclinations. After all, harassing the enemy's flanks had worked well in stymieing Howe's New Jersey incursion the previous year. On the other hand, provoking a major battle might lead to another Brandywine, with all its unfortunate consequences. There may have been a logic to the council's recommendation, but it is small wonder that Washington's aide, Alexander Hamilton, later wrote dismissively that the conference "would have done honor to the most honorable society of midwives, and to them only."[55]

Hamilton was not the only one who thought so. Talking among themselves, many of Washington's generals regretted their timid and half-hearted recommendations. Greene, Lafayette, and Wayne each wrote to Washington to urge more aggressive action. Greene lamented that they were missing an opportunity to strike the vulnerable British column because of unfounded and exaggerated fears of failure, adding that he was confident the army could win any big battle that might grow out of a more aggressive strategy. Lafayette stated that he, Greene, Duportail, Paterson, Steuben, and Wayne all wanted to send more troops after the British. Washington was persuaded, and the next morning he issued new orders. He had already dispatched Col. Daniel Morgan's riflemen and 1,500 men under Charles Scott—but not Scott's brigade—to pursue the British, but now he upped the ante by directing Wayne to join them with another 1,000 troops. Together with Maxwell's brigade, Scott's men, and other miscellany, this advanced corps totaled somewhat less than 5,000 men.[56]

Because he had always been supportive of the seniority concept, Washington offered command of the advanced corps to Lee as the main army's ranking major general. Lee, however, turned down the job because he did not understand its size and significance. Stirling was next in line, but sources disagree whether he declined the honor or Washington passed him over. The opportunity now devolved on Lafayette, who leaped at the chance to command troops in what might turn into a major battle. Although Lafayette was a major general with an outsized reputation and self-image to match, the truth was that he had minimal combat leadership experience. His status in the army was based more on his aristocratic lineage, Washington's partiality, and his good-naturedness than on his fighting prowess. A little more than a month earlier, the British had nearly captured Lafayette and 2,400 troops Washington dispatched across the Schuylkill to reconnoiter. Lafayette managed to slip away and return to Valley Forge, but it had been a close call. Fortunately for Lafayette, most officers focused on the coolness he displayed in escaping rather than the carelessness that had put him in the predicament in the first place. Washington, for example, wrote, "Upon the whole the Marquis came handsomely off, and the enemy returned [to Philadelphia] disappointed and disgraced."[57] Another officer, lower in the food chain and apparently less susceptible to the Lafayette mystique, was closer to the mark when he noted, "It was a very lucky affair on our side, that we did not lose our whole detachment."[58] Whatever Lafayette's qualifications, Washington had confidence in him. Washington ordered Lafayette to strike the British rear guard if possible and promised to support him with the rest of the army.[59]

When Lee realized the advanced corps' size and significance, he had a change of heart. On 25 June Lee wrote to Washington asking for the command. Lee stated that it would look bad for everyone if he did not get the job. Lee's request put Washington in a quandary because he did not want to anger either Lafayette or Lee. In an effort to square this circle, Washington reinforced the advanced corps with Varnum's and Scott's brigades—but not Scott, who was already with the advanced corps—and placed Lee in charge of the augmented force. Washington, however, told Lee not to interfere with Lafayette if he had already committed his soldiers to battle. In coming up with such a convoluted and unclear solution, Washington placed his officers' honor above military common sense. In any event, Lafayette graciously agreed to surrender command of the advanced corps for the good of the cause and out of respect for Lee. Besides, he was having a difficult time locating and coming to grips with the British army. American logistics, intelligence, and coordination were breaking down under the stress of active operations, and Lafayette lacked the experience to rectify these problems. Increasingly jumpy and apprehensive, Lafayette was relieved to turn over responsibility to Lee.[60]

On the evening of 26 June American intelligence located the British army near Monmouth Courthouse. On the next day the advanced corps concentrated at nearby Englishtown, and Washington brought up the main body three miles behind it at Manalapan. The two armies were now less than five miles apart, but Washington worried that the British might get away unscathed because they were only a day's march from the safety of the easily defended hills around Middletown. If he wanted to strike a blow, he had to do so soon. With this in mind, on 27 June Washington met with Lee, Lafayette, Maxwell, Scott, and Wayne to plot strategy. Washington instructed Lee to assail the British rear guard the next day if possible and promised to bring up the balance of the army in support. Maxwell, Scott, and Wayne all later testified that Washington's orders were discretionary, but they also asserted that he clearly expected aggressive action even if it led to a full-scale battle with the entire enemy force. As Wayne later convolutedly put it, "The idea I conceived from General Washington's conversation was, that we should attack the enemy, and that he should be near to support us with the main body of the army, which, in its consequences, must, if we were pushed, inevitably, I think, have brought on a general action."[61] Lee, however, saw things differently. He still wanted to avoid any major engagement with the British army and believed that the recent conferences at Valley Forge and Hopewell confirmed this policy. He failed to realize that Washington had gradually come around to the idea of provoking a major battle if necessary. Much of the subsequent confusion grew out of this fundamental misunderstanding between the two men.

On the morning of 28 June, Lee pushed his advanced corps toward Monmouth Courthouse. When he identified the British rear guard, he dispatched Wayne to fix it in position while he readied the balance of his troops to outflank and cut off the enemy. At this point, however, he spotted the remainder of the British army streaming down the Middletown road toward Monmouth Courthouse. Lee suddenly recognized that the British intended to do to the American advanced corps what he had hoped to do to the British rear guard—gobble it up before the rest of the army arrived to reinforce it. The hunter, it seemed, had become the hunted. Lee reacted to this disconcerting realization by reorienting his units to avoid the trap he feared was snapping shut on him. However, he failed to make his intentions clear to his subordinates, most of whom he was unfamiliar with. In the ensuing confusion, some American outfits fell back. A confused Scott and Wayne sent to Lee for orders but received no response. As the redcoats approached his exposed right flank, Scott on his own authority ordered his soldiers to retreat. Once Scott pulled out, the rest of the American line caved in. Wayne directed his men to withdraw, followed by Maxwell. Despite the mix-up, the Americans did not flee in panic but instead remained in formation as they marched away. Lee was furious at this unanticipated turn of events, for which he blamed Scott. "Then, by God, you have ruined me!" he exclaimed when he met Scott. Thus, by firing scarcely a shot, and suffering few casualties, the advanced corps removed itself from the field.

While Lee's advanced corps engaged the British, Washington put the rest of the American army in motion toward Monmouth Courthouse. He sent Lee orders to assail the British rear guard unless there was good reason not to, promising to support him as soon as possible. Washington was in such a hurry that he ordered his men to chuck their packs and blankets to increase their pace. Soon, however, evidence mounted that things were not going according to plan. Washington encountered a frightened fifer within two and a half miles of Monmouth who told him that Lee was retreating. As he approached the battlefield, Washington met entire units falling back in good order or sitting down along the roadside, with livid officers condemning Lee's withdrawal. Washington had seen more than his share of military debacles in the course of his three defeat-studded years as commander in chief, but familiarity did not mask the anger, frustration, and disappointment he invariably felt in such circumstances. Whatever his emotions, he kept his mind focused on the issue at hand as he rode across the field to survey the situation with a spyglass as British cannonballs landed around him. After consulting several officers, including Wayne, he started sorting out and redeploying his soldiers.

As Washington struggled to restore order, Lee rode up at the head of another column of backtracking troops. A frustrated Washington asked angrily, "What is all this?" Lee did not quite hear the question over the din of battle, so he hesitated and stammered, "Sir? Sir?" until Washington repeated himself and expressed astonishment at this "unaccountable retreat." Lee thought that he had done a fairly good job salvaging the advanced corps from the trap he believed the British had baited for him. He responded to Washington's irate query by blaming contradictory intelligence, battlefield confusion, superior British cavalry, and insubordination among too many officers. He singled out Scott in particular for condemnation and reminded Washington that he had always opposed attacking the British army. Washington replied that Lee should never have taken command of the advanced corps if he was unwilling to obey orders. The argument was necessarily brief as the British were fast approaching, so Washington directed Lee to help delay the British while he positioned the main body. Lee did as he was told, and afterward Washington sent him back to Englishtown to collect stragglers.[62]

Although Henry Clinton's primary objective was shepherding his British army safely across New Jersey, he decided to take advantage of American confusion by assuming the offensive in an effort to inflict a serious defeat on Washington's army. Unfortunately for Clinton, Washington improvised his defenses well. Washington divided his army into two wings under the two most senior generals still on the battlefield. He assigned Stirling command of one of them and ordered him to secure the American left flank. He gave the other to Nathanael Greene and posted him on the American right flank. Greene may have been the army's quartermaster, but he had persuaded Washington a few days earlier to let him have a temporary combat command. Besides, Washington valued Greene more than any other of his generals. Successive British attacks in the stifling heat on the American positions failed to displace the Steuben-trained Continentals. Washington ordered Greene to dispatch Woodford's brigade to unoccupied Comb's Hill, about a mile south of the American lines overlooking the British left flank. Cannons placed there helped turn back the British assaults. As dusk approached, Washington prepared to assail the British with three brigades, but bad terrain prevented them from getting into position on time. Despite this setback, Washington intended to resume the battle the next morning, so he had his troops sleep on their arms. When the sun rose, though, the British were gone. Clinton opted to cut his losses and continue his march through New Jersey to Sandy Hook, from where the Royal Navy on 5 July shipped his men across the Lower Bay to New York City, thus ending their eleven-month-long sojourn to and from Philadelphia.

Although the British made good their escape, Washington was quick to declare victory because the Americans retained control of the battlefield. The British sustained 358 casualties, including 65 killed in combat, 59 dead from heatstroke, 170 wounded, and 64 missing. American figures were probably about the same, though Washington reported only 196 lost. As the overall army commander, Washington of course received the bulk of the credit for this success. Congress voted him its official thanks, and officers extolled him for almost singlehandedly turning the battle's tide. Alexander Hamilton wrote, "I never saw the general [Washington] to so much advantage. His coolness and firmness were admirable. He instantly took measures for checking the enemy's advance, and giving time for the army, which was very near, to form and make a proper disposition."[63] Greene added, "The commander in chief was everywhere, his presence gave spirit and confidence and his command and authority soon brought everything into order and regularity."[64] Washington was, for his part, generous in doling out praise to his officers. He was one of many who singled out Wayne for his ferocious combativeness in repelling the British attacks. He also lauded Knox's skillful handling of the artillery. Others commended Greene and Stirling for their steadfastness. Of course, once Washington arrived and redeployed his units, American officers required little tactical sophistication to repulse the British assaults. They instead relied on their Steuben-trained Continentals to stand in place and fight.[65]

Lee's presence marred Americans' efforts to celebrate their marginal victory. To be sure, Lee's actions in recognizing and reacting to the British trap probably saved the advanced corps from destruction, but that was not how most American officers interpreted things. As far as they were concerned, Lee's performance cost the Americans a decisive victory. Now that Lee had shown himself something less than infallible in combat, officers who had doubted him for one reason or another, but were reluctant to contravene prevailing public opinion by saying so publicly, emerged from the woodwork to condemn him. Besides, he made a convenient scapegoat for those who believed that the Americans mishandled an opportunity to cripple the British during their exposed march through New Jersey. The consensus the officer corps forged soon after the guns cooled was that Lee's timidity, selfishness, inability to control his troops and communicate with his subordinates, and failure to carry out Washington's orders prevented the advanced corps from mangling the British rear guard. As one officer put it, "It is my opinion that if he [Lee] had behaved well we should have destroyed the major part of Clinton's army."[66] Two days after the battle, Scott and Wayne brought the murmurings out into the open by formally complaining to Washington about Lee's generalship at Monmouth Courthouse. Their stated intention was to make it clear that the advanced corps' retreat was not due to insufficient numbers, bad terrain, or the quality of the Continentals, but rather to Lee's failure to command effectively. Left unwritten, but clearly implied, was that Scott and Wayne were in no way responsible for the initial debacle at Monmouth Courthouse.[67]

Washington had never been one to scapegoat his generals. As the author of his share of defeats, he undoubtedly recognized that such a Darwinian policy would sooner or later destroy officer corps morale and undermine his authority as commander in chief. He therefore had no intention of publicly blaming Lee for the advanced corps' difficulties at Monmouth Courthouse. To be sure, he felt that he—or, as he put it, Providence working through him—by rallying the backtracking advanced corps, had saved the day and turned defeat into victory, but he did not criticize Lee for ordering the retreat in the first place. Lee, however, forced Washington's hand. Lee believed, quite accurately, that he had saved the advanced corps from destruction by holding it back. He was outraged by the scuttlebutt around camp that he had almost singlehandedly exposed the American army to catastrophe. On 30 June he wrote to Washington that their battlefield exchange indicated that Washington had not understood the situation. Washington, he continued, seemed to think that he had either disobeyed orders, exhibited cowardice, or fought incompetently. Lee therefore asked Washington to specify which military sin he had committed so he could defend himself before the army, Congress, the country, and the world. Lee's letter finally convinced Washington that Lee was more trouble than he was worth. He responded angrily to Lee, "As soon as circumstances will permit, you shall have an opportunity either of justifying yourself to the army, to Congress, to America, and to the world in general; or of convincing them that you were guilty of a breach of orders, and of misbehavior before the enemy, on the 28th instant, in not attacking them as you had been directed, and in making an unnecessary, disorderly, and shameful retreat."[68] Lee thereupon asked for an immediate court-martial, which Washington granted straightaway.[69]

Lee's court-martial met on and off throughout the summer of 1778. Washington appointed Stirling presiding officer, with Huntington, Poor, Smallwood, and Woodford among its members. Duportail, Knox, Lafayette, Maxwell, Scott, Steuben, and Wayne were among those who testified, and Lee submitted a lengthy defense of his actions. On 12 August the court found Lee guilty of disobeying Washington's orders to attack the British, retreating without cause and skill, and insulting Washington in insolent letters penned after the battle. As for punishment, the court sentenced Lee to a one-year suspension from duty. Lee was of course disgusted with the verdict. He blamed his conviction on a cult surrounding Washington that had no tolerance for a heretic such as himself who did not hold a sufficiently high opinion of the commander in chief's generalship. Lee insisted to all who would listen that his decision to withdraw the advanced corps from the British snare was the source of American success at Monmouth Courthouse, and that he would do it all over again if given the chance. He explained to Laurens, "I am not only guiltless, but that the success of the 28 June ought principally in justice to be ascribed to me."[70] Lee's failure to gracefully accept the court's decision further hardened Washington's heart against him and convinced others that by opposing his commander in chief, he had thrown his support behind the moribund Conway Cabal.

Not surprisingly, Lee sought to overturn the court's verdict. His campaign included appealing to Congress and waging a public relations campaign. He was initially confident of success because he was sure the facts and justice were on his side. On 5 December 1778, though, after two months' vacillation, Congress voted seven states to two, with two divided, to uphold the court's ruling. Lee blamed the unexpected setback on intraparty strife that had little to do with his case. His PR campaign failed to yield much fruit either. A 3 December article he penned for the Baltimore-based *Dunlap's Gazette* defending his actions at Monmouth Courthouse provoked one of Washington's aides, Henry Laurens's son John, to challenge Lee to a duel for disparaging the commander in chief. After Laurens wounded Lee in the 23 December shoot-out, the seconds successfully insisted that honor had been satisfied and there was no need for another round. Anthony Wayne also wanted to duel Lee for Lee's comments about him in the article, but nothing ever came of it. When Lee's suspension ended, Lee learned that Congress was considering cashiering him to save money, so he forced the issue with a scathing letter that made Congress's decision easier. On 10 January 1780 Congress voted five states to four, with three divided, that it had no further use of Lee's military services. By then Lee was living in Virginia and removed from the conflict. Even so, he maintained his bitterness toward Washington, referring to him in a letter to Gates as a "dark designing sordid ambitious vain proud arrogant and vindictive knave."[71]

Both Lee and Washington contributed to the American army's Monmouth Courthouse woes. Lee undertook an assignment he did not believe in, in order to gratify his own ego, and he neglected to communicate his plans to his subordinates because he had so little confidence in their abilities. However, his decision not to attack the British rear guard was probably correct. Had he done so, the rest of the British army might have destroyed the advanced corps before Washington arrived to reinforce it. Although Lee recognized the danger, it was his lieutenants who avoided it by retreating on their own authority because Lee did not explain to them the threat. As one officer later noted of Lee in his memoirs:

> The truth is, the unfortunate general was only guilty of neglect in not making timely communication of his departure from orders, subject to his discretion, to the commander in chief, which constituted no part of the charges against him. . . . But this offense was different, far different from 'disobedience to orders' or 'a shameful retreat'; neither of which charges were supported by testimony; and both of which were contradicted by fact.[72]

Lee's career-ending mistake occurred not on the battlefield, but in the days that followed. By defying the emerging consensus among the officer corps as to what went wrong, Lee challenged Washington's authority and competency.

Washington's generalship certainly left something to be desired. He committed his forces to an unclear mission in piecemeal fashion, muddied the chain of command by replacing the inexperienced Lafayette with the unenthusiastic and recalcitrant Lee at the last moment, and failed to make clear to everyone his willingness to engage the British army in a major engagement. No doubt Washington redeemed himself by rallying the confused Continentals and skillfully deploying them under pressure, but such actions would not have been necessary had Washington been more decisive and clear in the days before the battle. Whatever Washington's errors, neither Congress nor the officer corps was going to vindicate Lee at Washington's expense. It was therefore unsurprising that they rallied behind their commander in chief and consigned Lee to ignominy.

Conclusions

By the summer of 1778, the Continental army contained seventeen major generals and twenty-five brigadiers, more than enough to meet Washington's needs for his army. This comparatively healthy figure, though, was deceptive. Some of the generals were unavailable for important duties because they were awaiting court-martial (St. Clair and Schuyler), suspended (Lee), prisoners of war (Thompson), recovering from injuries (Arnold and Lincoln), ill (Glover), or inactive (Mifflin and Weedon). Many of the remaining generals were not with Washington's army but were instead serving in other departments or en route from one assignment to another. These included George Clinton, James Clinton, Gadsden, Gates, Hand, Heath, Howe, McDougall, McIntosh, Moultrie, Nixon, Parsons, Pułaski, Putnam, Stark, and Sullivan. Moreover, the chances for adding new generals to the roster were declining. Congress's Baltimore Resolution inadvertently tied the number of generals to the number of soldiers each state produced. As the army's manpower stabilized and then declined, to many people the need for more generals became less urgent. In the winter of 1777–78, Congress appointed or promoted three generals: Conway, Duportail, and Steuben. Although the war continued for another five years, Congress selected only five more major generals and eleven more brigadiers, mostly for the Southern Department. The result was the solidification, if not ossification, of the roster of Continental generals. Adding new generals usually came at the expense of the old, but relieving the older ones was difficult. Lee's experience, for example, showed that removing generals for cause was so time-consuming, arduous, and publicly embarrassing that it was not worth the effort. Change could and did occur through death, injury, and resignation, but such modifications were haphazard and unpredictable—and did not necessarily rid the army of its worst generals. Instead of procuring as generals capable younger officers who had proven themselves in combat, Washington had to work with the men he had.

As the roster of Continental generals congealed, its members united in their devotion to Washington. There was nothing inevitable about this; plenty of officers throughout history have turned their backs on their commander for a host of reasons. For all his aloofness, Washington had a knack for using patience, civility, and expressions of confidence to cultivate fidelity that served him and the American cause well during the war. Indeed, sometimes it seemed that Washington's steadfastness was the only thing holding the army together. Because so many Continental officers saw themselves as part of Washington's team, they were quick to interpret attacks on Washington as attacks on themselves. Conway and Lee, for example, learned to their sorrow that criticizing Washington provoked written and verbal reprisals that ruined their careers. Moreover, Continental generals increasingly saw themselves as a unique caste distinct from the rest of American society, one with its own interests and culture. This cohesion with Washington and with each other somewhat reduced the amount of internal dissension within the officer corps after the winter of 1777–78. The problem was that officers were gradually developing the mind-set of a standing professional army in a society that historically viewed such a force as a threat to liberty. Although this attitude helped win the war, it also threatened the republican principles on which the revolution was based.

Unfortunately for the Americans, this officer corps unity did not translate into improved generalship. Steuben's training helped to turn the rank and file into professional soldiers, but the generals continued to rely on experience as their military teacher. Monmouth Courthouse showed that Continental troops were more proficient at following orders than the generals were at issuing them. After three years of war and innumerable battles, the American army had produced few generals who demonstrated anything beyond courage and stoutness on the battlefield. Most of those who had demonstrated tactical acumen, the ruthless determination to win, and an understanding of the relationship between means and ends—Arnold, Glover, and Stark, for instance—were either indisposed or not in Washington's main army. Whether any of Washington's remaining generals could grow into great combat commanders remained to be seen.

CHAPTER 5

Marking Time

1778–1780

The Siege of Newport

After the Battle of Monmouth Courthouse, Washington marched his army northward to New York and headquartered in White Plains for most of the summer. From there he could keep an eye on the British army in New York City and guard against any British offensive up the Hudson River or toward New England. He could also contemplate future operations in the changed geostrategic environment that French entry into the war had created. As usual, though, Washington had to devote a disproportionate amount of time and energy toward maintaining his ramshackle army, which included myriad personnel matters. He continued to call for more brigadiers. As of 22 July, he had seventeen brigades in his army: four from Massachusetts, three from Virginia, two apiece from Connecticut and Maryland and Pennsylvania, and one each from New Hampshire, New York, North Carolina, and Rhode Island. He needed four additional brigadiers for the Maryland, Massachusetts, North Carolina, and Pennsylvania lines. Washington also noted privately that he could use some more major generals, but he did not ask Congress to appoint any because he figured it was a temporary impediment that he could overcome on his own. Later that summer a visiting congressional committee agreed with his reasoning. As a result, in November Congress authorized five new brigadiers for the deficient state lines, as well as one for a cavalry corps. However, it did not get around to actually selecting them until the following year. In the meantime, Washington had to make do with the generals he had.[1]

Washington also had to deal with innumerable individual personnel problems that summer, some of which came from surprising sources. Friedrich Wilhelm von Steuben had won Washington's and Congress's regards first by agreeing to serve as an honorary major general and then by helping to turn the main army's Continentals into a well-drilled professional force. Congress rewarded him by appointing him a legitimate major general and the main army's permanent inspector general. During the army's march to New York, Washington gave Steuben command of a division because so many generals were busy serving on or testifying in Charles Lee's court-martial. Although Washington considered the assignment a temporary expedient, it angered many of his brigadiers. They had accepted Congress's decision to elevate Steuben over their heads on the assumption that as a staff officer he would have no authority over them. Now, however, he issued orders to some of them as head of a division. Steuben further sabotaged support within the officer corps by ordering the on-the-spot court-martial of a divisional quartermaster whom Steuben accused of treating him disrespectfully. As it was, Steuben was unhappy with his current status in the army. He chafed at the inactivity of the inspector generalship during the campaign season and concluded that he lacked sufficient authority to continue to do his job effectively. Conversely, he enjoyed his combat post and hoped to secure one commensurate with his rank. For these reasons, he told Washington that he would not accept the inspector generalship for the entire army unless he was given more power. Otherwise, he threatened to resign his commission.

On 24 July Washington gave Steuben permission to travel to Philadelphia to consult with Congress and visit friends. Although Steuben's stated mission was to negotiate the duties of the inspector generalship, Washington suspected that Steuben also planned to go over his head and lobby for a combat command. Washington freely acknowledged Steuben's zealousness, intelligence, and ability but was somewhat disgusted that even he had succumbed to the cloying ambition that seemed to seduce most foreign officers—except for, Washington noted, Lafayette. Washington thought that giving Steuben a combat post would undermine morale by alienating brigadiers always touchy about seniority. Instead, Washington hoped that Congress and Steuben could agree on terms for the inspector generalship so Steuben could resume a job for which Washington believed he was uniquely suited. Unhappily for Steuben, Congress was too busy to take up the issue, so it went nowhere. Henry Laurens, though, assured him that the delegates held him in the highest regard. Steuben therefore spent much of the summer fuming and fretting about his future and that of the Continental army.[2]

Nathanael Greene was another of Washington's disgruntled generals that summer. When Washington rebuked Greene for absenting himself from headquarters too often and not locating a new camp for the army quickly enough, Greene penned an angry complaint to his commander in chief. Greene explained that it took him time to find a new camp because he was unfamiliar with the region. Moreover, he could hardly do his job as quartermaster well if he was tied to Washington's headquarters. Such petty grievances, though, were symptomatic of a deeper discontent Greene felt. He had accepted the quartermaster's job reluctantly and at Washington's behest. In doing so, he believed he had exchanged his reputation and any opportunity for future glory for a thankless task. Despite all the obstacles he had faced, Greene thought he had done a good job under worse than trying conditions. To Greene, Washington's criticisms were nitpicky and unfair.

Washington quickly poured oil on these troubled waters. In a letter to Greene, he expressed his deep appreciation for Greene's fidelity, devotion, and especially friendship. One of the advantages of their good relationship, noted Washington, was their freedom to speak candidly about vital issues. Washington had had important logistical matters to address, but he had not seen anyone in Greene's department for several days with whom to discuss them. As for Greene's hurt feelings, Washington wrote, "But let me beseech you my dear sir not to harbor any distrusts in my friendship, or conceive that I mean to wound the feelings of a person whom I greatly esteem and regard. I speak to you freely. I speak the language of sincerity, and should be sorry if any jealousy should be entertained, as I shall ever say more (in matters of this kind) to you, than to others of you."[3] This remedied the immediate crisis, but the basic issue of Greene's dissatisfaction with his post remained unresolved.[4]

In addition to managing personnel difficulties, Washington also faced the never-ending chore of filling holes in his army's organizational chart. Washington had used a light corps on and off since the war's start. This brigade-sized unit of the army's best soldiers was designed to screen the army on the march. Officers considered leading the outfit a great honor because of its quality personnel and important mission. Daniel Morgan's riflemen served as the army's light corps until Washington sent it to northern New York in August 1777 to help stop Burgoyne's invasion. Washington replaced them with a new light corps under William Maxwell, which contested the British march through Maryland and fought at Brandywine. Although Washington disbanded the unit before Germantown, he decided to reconstitute it once he positioned his army outside of New York City in the summer of 1778. He figured that a new light corps could serve as a cushion between the main army and the British by gathering intelligence, harassing the enemy, and sounding the alarm. This time, though, he did not give command to Maxwell, probably because Maxwell was still under a cloud for allegations of drunkenness and incompetence. Instead, on 8 August he assigned the job to Charles Scott. Born in 1739 and orphaned at an early age, Scott enlisted in the Great War for Empire and eventually rose to captain. During the conflict he marched with Edward Braddock toward Fort Duquesne and later served under Washington on the Virginia frontier. Afterward he became a planter, but he joined the army when the Revolutionary War began and fought at the Battle of Great Bridge. In August 1776 he was commissioned a colonel, given a regiment, and sent to join Washington's army. In that capacity he participated in the Trenton-Princeton campaign. After a trip back to Virginia, he returned to Washington's army to lead a brigade at Brandywine and Germantown. The following spring he played a controversial part in the Battle of Monmouth Courthouse, after which he and Anthony Wayne contributed to Charles Lee's discomfiture by committing their criticisms of Lee to paper.

Considering Scott's long and distinguished record, as well as Washington's familiarity with the man, it was no surprise that Washington chose him to command the light corps. In doing so, he passed over more senior brigadiers in his army such as William Maxwell, Peter Muhlenberg, John Paterson, Enoch Poor, Anthony Wayne, and William Woodford. Scott led the outfit for three months, but in late October he wrote to Washington that illness and family problems back home required him to step down. Although Washington had on occasion questioned Scott's alertness as head of the light corps, he was still sorry to lose the services of such a hard fighter. Scott did not resign his commission but instead secured a furlough and returned to Virginia in mid-November. Washington opted to wait until the following year to name Scott's permanent replacement.[5]

On 11 July a French fleet commanded by Adm. Charles Hector, comte d'Estaing and containing 2,500 French troops arrived off Sandy Hook, New Jersey, and secured local naval superiority. Although d'Estaing was too late to interfere with the British evacuation of Philadelphia, Washington hoped to cooperate with the French in a joint assault on New York City. However, d'Estaing concluded that his biggest warships drew too much water to cross the channel into the city's Lower Bay. Thus stymied there, Washington and d'Estaing then decided to assail the 6,700 British soldiers stationed at Newport, Rhode Island. Washington figured that the French fleet could blockade the town while a Franco-American army overwhelmed the isolated garrison on Aquidneck Island. Once the British lost such a large contingent of their army in America, Washington expected the war to end soon thereafter. Because victory seemed so tantalizingly close, Washington strained every nerve to secure the resources necessary to successfully conduct the operation. He sent his two most trusted major generals, Greene and Lafayette, to Rhode Island. Washington expected Lafayette to coordinate with the French and smooth over any misunderstandings and disagreements. As for Greene, Washington believed that his logistical skills, understanding of the local geography and population, and combat prowess would also increase the likelihood of success. Not surprisingly, both generals jumped at the opportunity to escape the tedium of camp life and participate in an active campaign.[6]

Although local Continental units and militia would compose the bulk of the American contribution, Washington dispatched John Glover's and James Varnum's brigades to form the heart of the army. Washington wanted to send more but felt unable to because he was convinced that the British in New York already outnumbered him. Washington had contemplated transferring the starchy and difficult Varnum to Rhode Island the previous May, and his Rhode Island troops undoubtedly had a proprietary interest in liberating Newport. As for Glover, he had recovered from his wintertime ennui and was on duty at West Point, so Washington asked him to resume command of his old brigade. Washington rated Glover highly and no doubt thought that his amphibious experience would prove handy.[7]

Washington chose to remain with his main army and keep an eye on the British in New York City rather than lead the expedition against Newport. He instead entrusted the overall operation to the local department commander, John Sullivan. It was a risky decision for several reasons. Sullivan had seen plenty of combat at Three Rivers, Long Island, Trenton and Princeton, Brandywine, and Germantown, but mostly in subordinate roles. He had comparatively little experience in the top spot. Moreover, Sullivan had generated more controversy and dissension than victories, having at one time or another alienated more than his share of congressmen. His touchiness, tactlessness, and impulsiveness made effective cooperation with the French unlikely. There were, in short, other officers more qualified for such a delicate and important assignment. Washington, however, had his reasons for turning to Sullivan. He had repeatedly defended and vouched for Sullivan when others called for his relief. Replacing Sullivan now would indicate a lack of confidence in him and call into question Washington's long-standing record of support. Doing so would also provoke Sullivan into angrily and loudly resigning his commission, thus creating more discord in the officer corps and making trouble in Congress. Besides, Sullivan possessed the energy and determination the mission needed. Finally, Horatio Gates had hinted that he wanted the job. Washington preferred giving the assignment to the loyal, albeit flawed, Sullivan than to his chief rival, a man who Washington believed had worked to undermine his authority. Washington was well aware of Sullivan's limitations but hoped to compensate for them by giving him detailed advice and surrounding him with talented subordinates such as Greene and Lafayette.[8]

When Sullivan had arrived in Rhode Island the previous May to assume command of American troops there, he was discouraged with the limited resources at his disposal. He counted less than five hundred soldiers with which to confront the British garrison at Newport and repel enemy raids on local coastal communities. Upon receiving Washington's 17 July orders to assail Newport, Sullivan immediately got to work preparing his part in the planned Franco-American assault on the city. He scrounged up all the supplies and equipment he could get his hands on and sorted out the surprisingly large numbers of New England militiamen who turned out for the campaign. Ever the optimist, Sullivan concluded that victory was all but assured once the Franco-American forces exerted themselves. Indeed, his blustery confidence in the operation's chances of success reminded Henry Laurens of John Burgoyne's boasting before his Saratoga downfall. Sullivan got along well with the generals Washington sent him. Sullivan and Greene had worked together on and off since the siege of Boston. Sullivan respected Greene and was pleased to have him on hand. Greene, for his part, was happy to temporarily swap his thankless and tedious quartermaster responsibilities for an active combat assignment. Although Greene occasionally poked fun at Sullivan's pretentiousness, he did so out of affection rather than malice. He had backed Sullivan during Congress's attempts to scapegoat him for the defeat at Brandywine because he respected Sullivan's courage, determination, and common sense. He promised Sullivan his complete support and urged him to trust his judgment. As for Glover and Varnum, both were fellow New Englanders whom Sullivan valued.[9]

Lafayette's role in the Newport operation was more anomalous than Sullivan's and Greene's. He was of course happy to receive a prominent combat assignment that gave him an opportunity for the glory he had craved since he came to America. He was equally pleased to work under Sullivan and with Greene, both of whom he included in his wide circle of friends within the Continental officer corps. French involvement in the proposed assault provided Lafayette with additional and unique parts to play. Washington, d'Estaing, and others expected Lafayette to serve as liaison between the French and the Americans because of his elevated stature and understanding of both cultures. Lafayette's naive eagerness to do so perhaps showed that he failed to recognize the difficulties involved should anything go wrong. Although liaising was obviously crucial to the campaign's success, Lafayette's ambitions extended beyond that. He believed that the French would never consent to placing their soldiers under American command, but that whoever was in charge of them should be familiar with Americans and their ways. As a Frenchman with an American major general's commission, he concluded that he was the logical choice to lead the French contingent in the attack on Newport, as well as his American soldiers, because only he could bridge the cultural divide between the two forces and coordinate their activities. While Washington and d'Estaing were unprepared to go that far, their willingness to entrust a twenty-one-year-old man with so much responsibility was a testament to Lafayette's blithe self-confidence, nobility, and reputation.[10]

Unhappily for Lafayette, he did not get his opportunity to lead a Franco-American army to victory. Sullivan and d'Estaing's plan called for a two-pronged assault on Newport. The French would land at Conanicut Island before crossing over to Aquidneck Island's western coast. At about the same time, the Americans would come ashore on the eastern part of Aquidneck from Tiverton. Once they had consolidated their lodgments, the French and Americans would join forces and besiege Newport while the French fleet prevented the British garrison from receiving outside assistance. Things went wrong from the start. When Sullivan learned that the British had abandoned their positions overlooking the Americans' planned beachhead, he sent his troops across a day earlier than planned, on 9 August. This offended French officers who wanted the honor of planting their flag on Aquidneck Island first. No sooner had the French begun disembarking on Conanicut Island than the British fleet appeared. D'Estaing recalled those troops already ashore and sailed off to confront the Royal Navy, leaving the Americans to commence siege operations on their own. Before the British and French fleets came to blows, though, a tremendous storm swept through the region scattering and damaging warships on both sides. D'Estaing returned on 20 August and informed Sullivan that he was taking his battered fleet to Boston for refitting, thus stranding the Americans on Aquidneck Island.

D'Estaing's inopportune withdrawal alarmed and outraged Americans. Indeed, it provoked a short and intense wave of anti-French sentiment throughout the army and region that cumulated in an 8 September riot in Boston that left a French naval officer dead. It was hardly surprising that the truculent and tactless Sullivan did more to fan than to contain these flames of discontent with the French. Sullivan's initial optimism rapidly evaporated with the deteriorating military situation. The same storm that scattered the British and French fleets also played havoc with Sullivan's army. Heavy winds and rain ruined ammunition stockpiles, ripped tents apart, and left the soldiers exposed, wet, and discouraged. The militia who made up the majority of Sullivan's 8,900-man army began deserting. Sullivan was quick to blame the French for this abrupt and unhappy turn of events. As he saw things, there was no honorable reason for the French fleet to depart for Boston. Sullivan understood that the storm had seriously damaged only one French warship, and he figured it could be repaired as easily in Narragansett Bay as in Boston. His sources told him that French naval officers insisted on abandoning the campaign because they disliked d'Estaing and did not want him to succeed. He sent Greene and Lafayette to try to dissuade d'Estaing from leaving, but to no avail. Sullivan's heavy-handed and undiplomatic ways did, however, alienate French officers who resented American landlubbers passing judgment on their actions. For Sullivan to do so privately was bad enough, but Sullivan did not keep his anger behind closed doors. He not only criticized the French in official orders but also sent d'Estaing an insulting formal protest signed by himself, Greene, Glover, and others. Sullivan as a diplomat was about as contentious as Sullivan the soldier. Small wonder that he wrote to Washington even before his troubles with the French crescendoed, "To combat all these misfortunes and to surmount all those difficulties requires a degree of temper and persevering fortitude which I could never boast of, and which few possess in so ample a manner."[11]

D'Estaing's sudden and unexpected departure left Sullivan's American troops to their own devices on Aquidneck Island. Although on an intellectual level Sullivan knew that without French naval support he could not fulfill his mission and seize Newport, at first he could not bring himself to follow the dictates of logic and abandon the undertaking. He instead contemplated launching a desperate all-out assault on the city, more from a desire to preserve his honor than from any expectation of success, but fortunately for his soldiers he came to his senses and decided against it. In an effort to square the operational circle, he finally opted to retreat to the northern part of the island, dig in, and hope that the French fleet would return so he could restart the siege. His troops withdrew without incident on the night of 28–29 August, but the next day the British sortied out from Newport to disrupt Sullivan's dispositions. Sullivan and his army acquitted themselves well in the ensuing battle and successfully fended off the British attack. Greene in particular distinguished himself. American and British casualties numbered around 200 and 250, respectively. Falling back to the northern tip of Aquidneck Island, though, did not really resolve Sullivan's tactical dilemma; he was still isolated and vulnerable to British naval power cutting him off from Rhode Island proper. When Sullivan realized this and learned that British reinforcements were on their way, he ordered his troops back to the mainland on the night of 30–31 August. The army's departure marked the end of the Newport campaign.[12]

Because the French made such convenient culprits, Americans avoided blaming each other for the botched campaign. Washington as usual refrained from scapegoating anyone. He attributed the campaign's failure primarily to the storm and admitted that d'Estaing may have had little choice but to withdraw his fleet. If he concluded that Sullivan might have been the wrong general for this particular assignment, he kept such thoughts to himself. There was some grumbling about Sullivan in Congress, but not enough to threaten his career. Indeed, most congressmen concluded that in this instance Sullivan was more sinned against than sinner. Congress eventually resolved to thank Sullivan for his fortitude and bravery in repelling the British attack on 29 August. The New Hampshire and Rhode Island legislatures also voted Sullivan their gratitude. The officer corps desisted from criticizing Sullivan too. Greene, for example, stated that Sullivan did all that could be expected of him and ascribed the Newport setback to plain bad luck. Sullivan's generous distribution of praise also helped protect himself from recriminations. He lauded Glover, Lafayette, Varnum, and especially Greene for their actions. To assuage Lafayette's feelings of failure, Congress and Washington commended him for his handling of the rear guard during the evacuation of Aquidneck Island and his efforts to maintain Franco-American relations.[13]

Despite the defeat at Newport and New England's sudden burst of Francophobia, American leaders understood that it was in the United States' best interests to preserve their new alliance with France if they wanted to win the war, so they scrambled to contain the damage the Newport campaign had already caused. This was particularly true of Washington, who as commander in chief had as much to gain from a healthy and productive Franco-American relationship as anyone. When Washington learned of Sullivan's public disenchantment with d'Estaing, he sought to rein him in with another of his patient and encouraging letters to the fractious New Hampshirite. He reminded Sullivan of the new alliance's importance and added that first impressions would play a disproportionate role in its success or failure. Because the French were a proud people with a long military tradition, they were inordinately sensitive to real or perceived slights. He therefore urged Sullivan to go out of his way to work amicably with them and keep any disputes that arose out of the public eye. The best thing to do now, he advised, was to accept d'Estaing's explanation for withdrawing the French fleet and work with him to refit it as soon as possible for future campaigns. It was good advice that would have been more helpful if rendered before the operation began.[14]

Washington may have naively believed that Sullivan could improve his interpersonal skills, but he was not about to rely on that thin reed to restore Franco-American harmony. He also asked Greene and Lafayette to use their influence to soothe the troubled relationship. Doing so, however, placed both officers in awkward positions. Greene had already damaged his credibility with d'Estaing by signing Sullivan's protest letter. In his efforts to make amends, Greene told d'Estaing that the more he thought about it, the more he disliked the content and style of Sullivan's missive. Indeed, Greene claimed that the incriminating letter reflected Sullivan's frustrations more than his true opinion of d'Estaing and the French. He assured d'Estaing that American generals respected the French and appreciated their assistance. To prove his sincerity, Greene promised to speak highly of d'Estaing in his future conversations with Washington. If this explanation of American actions implied poor judgment on Sullivan's part, it was a small price to pay to preserve the Franco-American alliance.[15]

Lafayette's situation was more delicate than Greene's because he was both a patriotic Frenchman and deeply devoted to the American cause. Although his two loyalties had coexisted easily before the Franco-American alliance, the foundering Newport operation threatened to undermine one or the other. Lafayette had eagerly embraced the role of liaison between the French and the Americans as a way to increase his stature with both, but he soon discovered that serving as an honest broker in a losing cause was a difficult and thankless job. Worse yet, he missed the last battle of the campaign because Sullivan had sent him to Boston to again lobby d'Estaing to return to Narragansett Bay with his fleet. As a result, Lafayette lost yet another opportunity to distinguish himself in a combat leadership role. As for the Franco-American dispute, Lafayette remained faithful to his homeland. He declined to sign Sullivan's angry protest letter to d'Estaing out of fear of jeopardizing his future in the French military. He also told Washington that d'Estaing was justified in withdrawing his warships to Boston and complained about the anti-French sentiment that swept the region. Lafayette traced the failure of the offensive against Newport to Sullivan's overconfidence. He made the same points to d'Estaing, albeit in blunter and stronger terms, and assured him that his primary allegiance lay with France: "I told those [American] gentlemen that my country was more dear to me than America, that whatever France did was always right, that M. le Comte d'Estaing was my friend and that I would support those sentiments with a sword that would never have been better employed."[16] At the same time, though, Lafayette stressed to d'Estaing that his difficulties with Sullivan and the New England states did not mean a complete breakdown in the Franco-American relationship so long as Washington and Congress continued to support it. Lafayette's reasoning had its intended effect; on 1 September Lafayette assured Washington that d'Estaing continued to advocate cooperation with the Americans.[17]

Soon after Lafayette did his bit to repair Franco-American relations, he created unnecessary drama in another arena of the war. When Lafayette learned that the Earl of Carlisle had insulted France in a letter to Congress, he took it upon himself to stand up for his country's honor by challenging Carlisle to a duel. Both d'Estaing and Washington thought it was a silly idea. Washington argued to Lafayette that dueling was an archaic concept in the modern world, and that embracing it might expose him to ridicule. Moreover, continued Washington, even if Carlisle accepted Lafayette's offer, the outcome depended more on luck than on righteousness. It therefore made little sense for Lafayette to put his life on the line in this particular instance. Despite Washington's disapproval, Lafayette persisted. In any event, Carlisle casually dismissed Lafayette's challenge for the farce it was. By then Lafayette had decided to return to France. Because the campaign season was over, Lafayette figured he could better serve the cause in Paris lobbying the French government for additional support than as an inactive general in America. Returning to his homeland would also give him the opportunity to bask in the glow of the fame he had accumulated during his year with Washington. Congress and Washington agreed with Lafayette's logic and gave him their blessings. After a bout of fever, Lafayette departed in January 1779 and arrived the following month. He left with a letter from Washington attesting to his continued support and friendship: "I am persuaded, my dear Marquis, there is no need of fresh proofs to convince you either of my affection for you personally or of the high opinion I entertain of your military talents and merit."[18]

After the failed assault on Newport, American intelligence picked up evidence that the British planned to assail Boston in an effort to destroy the French fleet that was refitting there. Washington responded by shifting brigades to New England to confront any British offensive into the region. On 26 September Washington ordered Horatio Gates to command those troops left behind in the strategically vital Hudson Highlands. He informed Gates that he based his decision on various congressional resolutions and other important, albeit unspecified, reasons. Washington did not tell Gates, but those other reasons were that neither he nor many of his lieutenants wanted to work with or under Gates. Although Washington had assured Gates of no hard feelings after the Conway Cabal, he continued to view Gates suspiciously and did not trust him. Leaving Gates in the Hudson Highlands would give him an important and agreeable job that kept him out of the main American army. Gates had hoped to spend the winter at home in Virginia, but he promised to serve wherever ordered. This did not, though, prevent Washington from complaining about Gates's supposedly unsatisfactory and evasive correspondence. Washington added this latest exchange with his chief rival to his thick mental ledger of transgressions Gates had supposedly committed against him.

Although Washington was commander in chief, he still answered to a Congress that on occasion overruled or overlooked him. On 22 October, almost a month after Washington directed Gates to lead troops in the Hudson Highlands, Congress, without consulting Washington, sent Gates to Boston to take over the Eastern Department. Delegates figured that Gates's ability, experience, and rapport with New Englanders made him uniquely suited for the job. Congress's orders surprised, confused, and embarrassed William Heath, the current Eastern Department chief. Heath was a proud man hypersensitive to issues of rank and precedence. He had no problem with Washington superseding him when and if he marched to Boston with the main army, but surrendering his post to Gates was something else. As Heath saw it, Congress's decision to replace him with Gates showed that Congress had lost faith in him. To make matters worse, Congress neglected to reveal to Heath what plans, if any, it had for him now that Gates was replacing him, leaving him in limbo. By the time Gates reached Boston on 12 November, it was obvious that the British had no intention of attacking Boston that season, rendering these command machinations unnecessary. Even so, Congress's directive stood and Gates assumed command. As for Heath, Congress assured him of its continued confidence and promised to clarify his responsibilities by spring.[19]

Maj. Gen. Robert Howe had served as Southern Department commander ever since James Moore succumbed to illness in the spring of 1777. In this capacity he oversaw a series of mostly unsuccessful operations along Georgia's border with

British-controlled Florida. As far as Howe was concerned, his most aggravating problem was not the British, but rather civil authorities who interfered excessively in his efforts to maintain and direct his small army. Civil authorities, for their part, distrusted Howe's character and competence. Howe's differences with former South Carolina general Christopher Gadsden over lines of authority, for example, became so serious that it led to a duel between the two men in August 1778. Neither officer was killed, but the event symbolized Howe's inability to run his department effectively. Moreover, rumor had it that Howe was a philanderer who abused the women with whom he got involved. One woman wrote of him: "This gentleman has the worst character you ever heard through the whole province. . . . He is deemed a horrid animal, a sort of woman-eater that devours everything that comes in his way, and that no woman can withstand him."[20] Whatever the truth of these allegations, they sufficiently alarmed local officials to lobby Congress to remove Howe from his post. Congress complied on 25 September. One delegate explained that Congress recalled Howe because of a "little ridiculous matter he has been concerned with in South Carolina, with regard to a female [which] has induced the delegates of Georgia and South Carolina to desire his recall. Congress complied with their request, but do not intend to enter into the private amours of their generals. I hope our friend (should the war continue) will have an opportunity of displaying his abilities (which Congress acknowledge) in the field of Mars as well as of Venus."[21] News of his relief greatly upset Howe because of its likely impact on his martial reputation. Moreover, Howe feared that this command disruption would make the South even more vulnerable to a British attack. He was right about the latter concern. In late December, while Howe was waiting for his successor, the British attacked Savannah, Georgia. They easily scattered Howe's small army and seized the city on 29 December 1778.[22]

To replace Howe, Congress turned to Maj. Gen. Benjamin Lincoln. Lincoln had sustained a serious leg wound at Saratoga the previous October that required months of convalescence. By the time he rejoined Washington's army in early August 1778, his injuries had healed and he sported a cork-soled shoe to compensate for one leg being shorter than the other. The genial, stuttering, and narcoleptic Lincoln seemed like an unlikely choice to lead the Southern Department. He was a New Englander unfamiliar with southern ways and culture. Although well respected for his courage, gentlemanliness, and ability, he lacked the force of personality necessary to keep difficult people in line. He possessed little combat leadership experience, and his battlefield accomplishments were more apparent than real. Finally, there were more senior major generals available for the post on the Continental army's roster: Philip Schuyler, Israel Putnam, Horatio Gates, William Heath, John Sullivan, Nathanael Greene, Benedict Arnold, Lord Stirling, Thomas Mifflin, and Arthur St. Clair. Despite these rather formidable drawbacks, Congress concluded that he was the right man for the job. Many of his supposed weaknesses, when examined from a different perspective, could easily be interpreted as strengths. Perceiving him as an outsider without an ax to grind, southern politicians and officers might more willingly submit to his authority. His amiable personality would not ruffle feathers but might instead soothe egos and defuse interpersonal tensions. Whatever his record as a combat commander, people were bound to respect his sufferings and sacrifices for the cause. For these reasons, Lincoln's appointment met with widespread approval in the army and in Congress.[23]

George Washington was among Lincoln's biggest boosters. He respected Lincoln as a capable officer who followed orders, did not complain about rank and seniority, and did his job. Lincoln, for example, accepted without rancor Congress's decision to restore Benedict Arnold's seniority, even though it occurred at his expense. When a Frenchman sent Washington three sets of epaulets and sword knots with a request that he give two of them to distinguished officers, Washington forwarded one of them to Lincoln "as a testimony of my sincere regard and approbation of your conduct."[24] Although Washington had looked forward to Lincoln serving under him in the next campaign, he fully approved of Congress's decision to appoint Lincoln the new Southern Department commander.[25]

Lincoln was more ambivalent about his new assignment than were Washington and Congress. He wanted and expected to serve under Washington and was surprised by Congress's decision to appoint him Southern Department commander. He worried that he might not be up to the task, especially physically. As usual, though, Lincoln accepted his orders without complaint, and he headed southward on 24 October. Upon reaching Charleston, South Carolina, in early December, he was shocked by the shortages of manpower, supplies, and equipment in his department. Nor did he much like the amount of control South Carolina authorities exerted over local military affairs. Finally, the unhealthy climate aggravated his wound so much that the following spring Congress authorized him to give up his command and return north if he felt he could no longer do his job. Lincoln opted to stay on after South Carolina's council voiced its support for him. Even so, it was hardly surprising that he summed up his first impressions of his new position by writing Washington, "I have met with almost every disappointment since I came into this department."[26]

Winter Quarters, 1778–1779

On 4 November the French fleet departed Boston for the West Indies, thus ending Washington's hopes of prying the British out of New York City anytime soon. Indeed, French intervention had yielded far fewer strategic benefits than anticipated. The British may have relinquished Philadelphia, but the Americans fumbled opportunities to inflict serious damage on the enemy at Monmouth Courthouse and Newport. With the French fleet gone and the weather turning, Washington put his soldiers into winter quarters. He dispersed his army around New York City by stationing units in Connecticut, West Point and the Hudson Highlands, and Middlebrook, New Jersey. Scattering his brigades would make it more difficult for him to respond to any sudden British offensive, but it also alleviated many of the logistical problems that had plagued his army at Valley Forge and Morristown the previous two winters. At the end of the year, Washington traveled to Philadelphia for consultations with Congress. There he managed to quash Lafayette-inspired talk of another invasion of Canada by pointing out the long-term dangers to American national security should the French succeed in reclaiming the territory. As usual, he pressured Congress to appoint more brigadiers for his brigades. Although Washington's stay lasted forty-two days, he was disenchanted with the low quality of the congressmen and the local population's indifference to the war effort. He was therefore happy to return to the more familiar, albeit spartan, routines of camp life at his Middlebrook headquarters in early February 1779.[27]

Dispersing his army for the winter required Washington to appoint commanders for its several detachments. He could directly control those units at Middlebrook, but he needed generals to oversee the soldiers stationed in Connecticut and the Hudson Highlands. Horatio Gates had led the three brigades Washington eventually deployed in Connecticut until Congress dispatched him to Boston to take over the Eastern Department in October 1778. To replace him, Washington called on a major general already in the state: Israel Putnam. Washington had relieved Putnam as Hudson Highlands chief the previous March for inefficiency and ordered him to Connecticut to help raise troops there. Although almost everyone acknowledged Putnam's courage and commitment, there was a consensus that he was not intellectually and temperamentally suited for high command. Alexander McDougall, for example, had served under Putnam and warned that if he was given control of a sector outside of New York City, traitors and prostitutes would pour out of the city to undermine the army. Moreover, added McDougall, even if Washington issued Putnam specific orders to keep him in line, he probably would not obey them. Washington was under no illusions about Putnam but gave him the assignment anyway. For one thing, Washington did not have many major generals available for the job. Putnam, though, was on hand and underemployed. In addition, Washington greatly respected the seniority principle, and Putnam was second in line on the major general roster. Denying him the post would call into question seniority's relevance. As things turned out, Putnam made no serious mistakes that winter. In fact, he helped defuse a mutiny in Huntington's Connecticut brigade when the men threatened to march on the state legislature in Hartford to express their unhappiness over their lack of basic necessities. Unfortunately for Washington, Putnam's satisfactory performance emboldened him to complain to Washington that he felt sidelined and to ask for a more active mission.[28]

Washington had considerably more confidence in his Hudson Highlands commander, Maj. Gen. Alexander McDougall. The Scottish-born New Yorker had served Washington loyally and effectively in both combat and administrative roles since the war's start. In addition, he was friends with New York governor George Clinton and had previous experience in that department. He was therefore a logical choice for the Hudson Highlands job. Upon assuming his post, McDougall was stunned by the overwhelming logistical challenges he faced. He had almost no money with which to buy tools, tents, firewood, or anything else his soldiers needed. Indeed, at one point he complained that he had two hundred cattle eating their mangers due to a lack of forage. The New York militia turned out grudgingly and did little to stop persistent loyalist raids. Shortages of matériel were of course a way of life for American generals, but McDougall had other, less tangible, grievances. In a nutshell, McDougall believed that Congress was persecuting him for various reasons. He wrote to Washington that he had neither wanted nor asked for what he considered a backwater assignment but accepted it as his duty. In accepting this thankless job, he was exposing himself to congressional vindictiveness. He noted that he had fulfilled his previous responsibilities honorably and well, so he did not understand why Congress was targeting him. He much preferred a combat post in Washington's army so that he might attain glory and advancement.

Washington by now had plenty of experience soothing angry and disgruntled subordinates. He responded to McDougall's letter on 9 February 1779 by assuring him of his continued confidence and friendship. Washington noted that McDougall might not have gotten the assignments he wanted but had received important ones because Washington thought so highly of him. As for Congress, Washington explained that it was not out to get him. What McDougall interpreted as persecution was instead inexperience, carelessness, and inadvertency. Washington added that although he could make no promises, he would probably summon McDougall to join the main army in spring for the next campaign. He concluded by expressing his sympathies for McDougall's logistical woes. Thus comforted and encouraged, McDougall got back to work.[29]

McDougall's kvetching surprised Washington, but Nathanael Greene's did not. Greene had accepted the quartermaster general's post reluctantly and only at the behest of Washington and a congressional committee. He disliked it from the start, and his discontent extended throughout the winter of 1778–79. Like McDougall, he felt unappreciated and put-upon. He resented accusations that he made too much money off the job and had failed to resolve the army's logistical difficulties. Greene argued that inflation caused most of the army's logistical problems, not inefficiency. Although he acknowledged turning a personal profit, he insisted that it was not worth the drudgery and criticism he endured. As far as Greene was concerned, he had served as long and suffered as much for the cause as anyone and therefore deserved better treatment from the public in general and Congress in particular. Indeed, he noted that he had been home only once, briefly, since the war began. Greene's biggest complaint, though, was that in accepting the quartermaster position he had sacrificed any chance of future military glory and advancement. In April 1779 Greene wrote Washington that he wanted to resign as quartermaster. Rumor had it that Benjamin Lincoln's wound required him to surrender command of the Southern Department. If that was the case, Greene hoped to replace him. Washington responded with the usual words of sympathy and encouragement. He promised to support Greene's claim to the Southern Department if it came to that but warned that Congress probably would not consult him on Lincoln's successor. As it was, Lincoln opted to stick it out, shutting the door for now on Greene's continuing hopes for an honorable escape of his thankless quartermaster duties.[30]

Baron von Steuben was another disgruntled general that winter. He had traveled to Philadelphia the previous summer to lobby Congress to endorse his plan for the inspector generalship. Washington suspected that Steuben intended to inveigle a combat command as well, but if he did try to, nothing came of it. As things turned out, Congress did not get around to approving legislation creating an inspector general for the entire army responsible for preparing regulations, conducting inspections, and overseeing the brigade inspectors until 19 February 1779. Steuben passed the winter socializing and finalizing his proposal for a new set of official regulations for the army. The end product became *Regulations for the Order and Discipline of the Troops of the United States*, the so-called Blue Book that the army used as its basis for the training and conduct for soldiers until the War of 1812. Although Congress voted Steuben its official thanks for his efforts in installing a system of order and discipline in the army, Steuben was an unhappy man. For one thing, he felt that Congress was not sufficiently attentive to his projects. Moreover, he grew so frustrated with the long delay in printing and distributing the Blue Book that the Board of War rebuked him for his petulance. He also had to deal with Charles Lee spreading uncomfortably accurate rumors that Steuben had puffed up his résumé to secure his commission in the Continental army. Finally, Steuben increasingly resented his poverty that, among other things, made it impossible for him to regularly pay his aides. He was a spendthrift to begin with, and inflation ate up the purchasing power of whatever money he had left. At a 15 April dinner with Henry Laurens and others, Steuben intimated that Congress should fulfill a promise it made to him when he first offered his services and compensate him for the expenses he had incurred since he arrived in America. When Laurens urged him to drop the issue, Steuben lost his temper and threatened to go home to Europe. He did not follow through, but his unhappiness remained. His tirade, though, caused an unsympathetic Laurens to question Steuben's commitment to the revolution. Laurens noted that Steuben had exaggerated his credentials on his résumé, adding that "the times are distempered and the devils of avarice and ambition are indefatigably improving them to their own advantage."[31]

Greene, McDougall, and Steuben were three of the Continental army's most senior disgruntled officers that winter. There were also a number of discontented brigadiers as well. Although the details varied from person to person, the basic problem was that they all felt unappreciated for one reason or another. Louis Lebègue Duportail, for example, had provided invaluable service as one of the army's few engineers. Indeed, Washington considered him almost irreplaceable. In November 1778 Duportail informed Washington that the furlough he received from the French army to come to America would expire the following February. Duportail threatened to return to France unless Congress created a separate engineering corps and placed him in charge of it. Henry Knox was another unhappy officer. Knox wanted Congress to give him complete control over ordnance and artillery. He complained that sharing control with civilian officials made it impossible for him to do his job effectively. He pointed out that in the previous campaign he did not know from whom to request supplies. William Smallwood, for his part, said he would resign his commission unless Congress promoted him to major general. Smallwood argued that he had done a major general's job on and off during his two years in the army. He claimed that Congress's failure to elevate him reflected poorly on both him and his home state of Maryland. For this Smallwood blamed Congress's fixation on appeasing foreign officers. Finally, Samuel Parsons asked to resign his commission. He believed that he had for some reason lost Washington's confidence. His evidence was his Connecticut brigade's lack of adequate clothing and poor living conditions, for which he blamed Washington. He was also in failing health and having difficulty supporting his family. In the end, Congress and Washington retained the services of all four officers by placating them with words and deeds. Even so, such personnel issues took up Washington's limited time and energy and were an indication of continuing despondency within the officer corps.[32]

Not every general succumbed to Washington's formidable powers of persuasion. Maj. Gen. Philip Schuyler's acquittal by a court-martial of charges of dereliction of duty in Fort Ticonderoga's fall did not prevent him from submitting his resignation in January 1779. Schuyler claimed that he did so because he owed it to his family to devote more attention to his private affairs, but he was also disillusioned by the public scrutiny and criticism that had accompanied his controversial tenure as Northern Department commander. Congress initially refused to accept his resignation because it valued his insight on American Indian affairs. Schuyler, however, insisted and in April Congress acquiesced. Although Schuyler never served directly under Washington, the commander in chief respected the New Yorker for his support, judgment, and wisdom and was sorry to see him leave the army. Their good relationship provided Washington with continued access to Schuyler's shrewd counsel. "I can say with truth," Washington wrote Schuyler, "that I should have been happy to have derived that assistance from you in your military capacity which I shall always take the liberty of asking as from my private friend and a friend of his country."[33]

Washington also lost the services of two long-standing brigadiers that winter, one temporarily and the other permanently. The first was John Glover. On 28 January 1779 Glover wrote Washington from Providence, Rhode Island, that he had to step down and return home to look after his eight motherless children. He had hoped to remain in the army until the war ended, but his family was his top priority. Washington had heard this story before and had previously kept Glover from leaving by appealing to his loyalty. This time, though, Washington opted to let him go. He forwarded Glover's letter to Congress with a note that he regretted losing such a good officer. Congress responded by giving Glover indefinite leave in case he chose to return to duty. He eventually did and served on and off until active hostilities ended. Rhode Island's James Varnum was the other. He submitted his resignation on 12 February. Like Glover, he did so reluctantly in order to look after his private affairs, though in his case the neglect he sought to address was more financial than familial. Both officers were proven and experienced men whose departures showed that rampant inflation and Congress's inability to pay its personnel adequately was undermining the stability of the officer corps.[34]

By the time Glover and Varnum removed themselves from active duty, Congress had already undertaken new efforts to alleviate Washington's continuing shortage of brigadiers. However, political jockeying limited its success. On 9 January 1779 Congress appointed four new brigadiers, in order of seniority: Jethro Sumner (North Carolina), James Hogun (North Carolina), Isaac Huger (South Carolina), and Mordecai Gist (Maryland). Because North Carolina had no brigadiers—Francis Nash had fallen at Germantown and Robert Howe had been elevated to major general—its assembly in December 1777 had instructed its congressional delegates to lobby for the promotions of Cols. Thomas Clark and Jethro Sumner. North Carolina's delegation nominated them on 10 February 1778, but Congress did not act until early the following year. After the North Carolina delegates put forth Clark's and Sumner's names, though, a visiting army officer warned them that Clark's lack of seniority would alienate other

Tarheel officers if Congress advanced him. The North Carolina delegates faced a quandary. On the one hand, they were sufficiently familiar with the dangers of disregarding seniority to know that Clark's selection would cause trouble. On the other hand, they had orders from their assembly to sponsor Clark. When they explained their dilemma to the rest of Congress, someone nominated another North Carolinian, James Hogun, in Clark's place. Hogun was second in seniority among North Carolina's officers behind Sumner and was well respected for his gallantry at Germantown. As a result, Congress opted to appoint Hogun a brigadier instead of Clark. Of the four newly minted brigadiers, three—Gist, Hogun, and Sumner—were available for service in Washington's army.[35]

Four months later, Congress added an additional brigadier to the Continental army's roster. On 11 May a congressional committee appointed to investigate claims that Pennsylvania deserved more generals concluded that based on its military contribution the state should have two major and four brigadier generals. At that time it had only one major general (Arthur St. Clair) and three brigadiers (William Thompson, Anthony Wayne, and Edward Hand). Of the three brigadiers, Thompson was currently a prisoner, and there was some disagreement about whether Hand belonged to Pennsylvania or North Carolina. Doing justice for the Keystone State therefore required at a minimum elevating a brigadier to major general and selecting two new brigadiers. Congress, however, worried that advancing so many Pennsylvanians would provoke other aggrieved delegations into demanding more generals for their states. Such feeding frenzies had in the past caused considerable dissension in and out of Congress and sparked charges of logrolling, horse-trading, and favoritism. To avoid such a time-consuming, contentious, and difficult process, Congress opted to choose only one new brigadier from Pennsylvania. The state's senior colonel, Robert Magaw, was, like Thompson, a prisoner, so Congress picked the next officer in line, William Irvine. The British had captured the Irish-born Irvine at the Battle of Three Rivers in Canada but exchanged him in May 1778. His promotion gave Washington another general to lead one of his Pennsylvania brigades.[36]

The vicissitudes of war also augmented the number of generals available to command Washington's units that winter. Arthur St. Clair had been for nearly a year and a half in professional limbo after ordering Fort Ticonderoga's evacuation in July 1777. An outraged Congress ordered an investigation into St. Clair's conduct, which led to his court-martial in September 1778. The court accepted St. Clair's defense that by abandoning Ticonderoga he saved its garrison for future service and acquitted him of all charges. Like Philip Schuyler, St. Clair discovered that his efforts to clear his name were time-consuming, irksome, and frustrating. Unlike Schuyler, though, St. Clair opted to remain in the army. St. Clair returned to active duty even before Congress ratified the court's verdict on 16 December. Washington had always respected St. Clair and welcomed him back to the main army.[37]

On 19 May 1778 Robert Howe joined Washington's army. Congress had relieved Howe as Southern Department commander the previous September and ordered him to report to Washington's headquarters for reassignment. He carried with him a letter from his replacement, Benjamin Lincoln, to Washington lauding Howe as a "sensible and good officer" who had done all he could to help Lincoln ease into his new position. Unfortunately for Howe, not only was he a stranger to many of the officers in Washington's main army, but he also seriously injured his leg in a fall that hindered him throughout the summer.[38]

Finally, William Heath rejoined the main army. Heath had commanded the Eastern Department until Congress replaced him with Horatio Gates in October 1778. Heath remained in Boston in a redundant capacity through the winter, embarrassed and unhappy with his awkward situation. Although he wrote to Washington for assistance, Washington did not get around to determining Heath's fate until March, when he ordered a relieved and happy Heath to come to his headquarters in May. Once there, Washington assigned him to lead American forces on the east side of the Hudson River. Heath's, Howe's, and St. Clair's arrivals gave Washington three new, albeit mediocre, major generals to lead his divisions.[39]

Stony Point

The absence of French naval support limited Washington's strategic options throughout the 1779 campaign season. Without assistance from a French fleet, the American army could not successfully storm either New York City or Newport. This meant that Washington could only inflict serious losses on the British if they ventured into the interior as John Burgoyne had done in 1777. However, the British limited their operations that year to coastal raids and probes up the Hudson River toward West Point. Despite this strategic frustration, Washington remained hale and hearty throughout the summer and even occasionally indulged his deadpan sense of humor. When one of his cavalry officers, Henry Lee, proposed the immediate beheading of deserters, Washington dryly acknowledged that doing so would probably discourage the practice, but he questioned the propriety of decapitating troopers. Wit aside, the burdens of responsibility sometimes weighed him down. Age, responsibility, and hard experience had sucked all the glory and glamour out of his position, prompting him to write, "I have been more than four years a perfect slave, endeavoring under as many embarrassing circumstances as ever fell to one man's lot to encounter and as pure motives as ever a man was influenced by, to promote the cause, and service I had embarked in."[40]

Washington's army was in reasonably good shape at the start of the 1779 campaign season. It contained approximately 12,000 troops who had been through Steuben's training regimen. Moreover, the army was reaping the benefits of a major organizational overhaul Congress had authorized back in May 1778 and gradually implemented throughout the following year. It included restructuring, consolidating, and condensing regiments to make them more manageable and uniform. On 9 March 1779 Congress reduced the state lines to eighty regiments with an authorized strength of 582 officers and men apiece: Massachusetts (fifteen), Pennsylvania (eleven), Virginia (eleven), Connecticut (eight), Maryland (eight), North Carolina (six), South Carolina (six), New York (five), New Jersey (three), New Hampshire (three), Rhode Island (two), Delaware (one), and Georgia (one). When all was said and done, Washington had seventeen brigades outside of New York City with which to fight the campaign. He divided them into three divisions under de Kalb, St. Clair, and Stirling, with several others under McDougall's command in the Hudson Highlands.[41]

In January 1779 Anthony Wayne secured Washington's permission to leave camp at Middlebrook and travel to Philadelphia. Like his commander in chief, Wayne was dismayed with the city's extravagance, partisanship, and apathy but pleased that the locals treated him so well. While there, Wayne decided to lobby Washington for command of the light corps. Arthur St. Clair had two months earlier returned to duty and replaced Wayne at the head of a division. Wayne disliked his demotion about as much as he disliked serving under St. Clair. Although Wayne assured Washington of his deep respect for St. Clair, he actually despised him because he believed St. Clair had spread unflattering and untrue rumors about his performance at Paoli. As Wayne put it, "To be superseded at this late hour by a man in whose honor, conduct, and candor I can have no confidence, hurts me not a little."[42] Indeed, Wayne was so unhappy he contemplated resigning his commission. Leading the light corps, however, would be a plumb assignment that promised plenty of autonomy and opportunity for glory. Wayne and Washington almost certainly discussed the job while they were both in Philadelphia, and on 10 February Wayne formally asked for it. Washington responded affirmatively six days later. There were other, more senior, brigadiers in the main army than Wayne, but none had his extensive combat leadership experience and record. Washington believed that Wayne's combativeness, initiative, and courage made him uniquely qualified to run the light corps.[43]

Washington's decision to appoint Wayne his light corps commander paid off that summer in one of the brightest American victories of the war. In late May a British expedition ascended the Hudson River and occupied Stony Point and Verplanck's Point. Located on opposing sides of the river about forty miles north of New York City, these outposts could serve as jumping-off points for an advance on the all-important American fortress at West Point. Insufficient manpower prevented the British from continuing their drive to West Point, but they instead opted to fortify both places. Doing so interfered with American defensive and logistical networks and hindered Washington's ability to maneuver his main army and rally the militia. The defenses of Stony Point and Verplanck's Point were so formidable that there did not seem much the Americans could do about it. Washington, however, concluded after reconnoitering the area that Stony Point might be vulnerable to attack, and on 1 July he ordered Wayne, who had recently arrived to lead the light corps, to look into it. Taking a page from his Paoli humiliation, Wayne opted to launch a surprise nighttime bayonet assault on Stony Point's garrison with his light corps. He planned carefully, making sure his men knew their roles and even ordering all dogs on the approach route killed so they could not tip off the enemy with their barking.[44]

After a grueling fourteen-mile hike, Wayne's light corps assailed Stony Point on the night of 15–16 July. They achieved surprise in part because the moonless and cloudy darkness obscured their approach. Although one of the two attacking columns had to wade through several feet of water to get into position, the soldiers got over the abatis surrounding the fort and overwhelmed the garrison after a short but intense fight in which scarcely a shot was fired on the American side. Wayne was wounded at the battle's start by a bullet that grazed his scalp, but it made no difference to the outcome. The Americans captured more than five hundred redcoats, fifteen cannons, and considerable matériel at the cost of around one hundred killed and wounded. The next day Washington ordered Robert Howe to take two brigades and see if he could exploit the resulting enemy confusion by storming Verplanck's Point. Howe decided it was too risky to launch such an assault. After removing everything of value from Stony Point, Washington opted to evacuate the place because he lacked the manpower to hold it permanently. The British reoccupied the site, but they too abandoned it in late October for the same reason.

The consequences of Wayne's Stony Point triumph were marginal. It removed a thorn from the side of Washington's defensive perimeter and showed that the main American army was active during that desultory campaign season, but it did not dramatically change the war's strategic calculus. For Wayne, the victory was sweet revenge for his Paoli humiliation, all the more so because he used similar tactics to achieve it. People throughout the country showered Wayne with praise. They included not only friends such as Greene, Steuben, and Lafayette, but also enemies such as St. Clair and Charles Lee. Lee wrote Wayne, "I do most sincerely declare, that your action in the assault of Stony Point is not only the most brilliant, in my opinion, through the whole course of this war, on either side, but that it is one of the most brilliant I am acquainted with in history."[45] Indeed, it conclusively demonstrated that Wayne was a cut above most American generals. Congress voted Wayne its official thanks but refrained from promoting him to major general, most likely because Washington did not need any more officers of that rank. Robert Howe was just about the only American who participated in the operation, albeit indirectly, who received criticism for his actions by not emulating Wayne's aggressiveness at Verplanck's Point. Washington, though, concluding that Howe had acted prudently, remained focused on the army's accomplishment.[46]

The Iroquois Expedition

The Revolutionary War engulfed the western frontier as well as the Atlantic littoral. Although most American Indian tribes had supported the French during the Great War for Empire, they switched their allegiance to the British after France's expulsion from the continent. American Indians distinguished between ravenous settlers encroaching on their lands and a British government intent on regulating trade and preserving peace. Their understanding of this fundamental reality put Congress and the states at a distinct disadvantage when the war started and their representatives lobbied American Indian tribes for their support or neutrality. Whereas the new United States had little to offer American Indians but dubious promises, the British pledged supplies, weapons, and equipment in exchange for native backing. The British government concluded after some initial hesitation that American Indians were a vital military resource that should be used as such against the rebels. American Indians played an important role in John Burgoyne's unsuccessful invasion of northern New York in 1777. British defeat at Saratoga did not prevent tribes such as the Iroquois from continuing to attack American settlements that dotted the New York and Pennsylvania frontiers. Indeed, the ferocity of such raids increased in 1778. One foray that July into northeastern Pennsylvania's Wyoming Valley, for example, included eight hundred American Indians, loyalists, and redcoats who ravaged the region and terrified the inhabitants. Such marauding hampered Washington's army by destroying the foodstuffs on which it depended. Subsequent retaliatory efforts were localized, ad hoc, unorganized, and ineffective.

Both Washington and Congress were increasingly alarmed with the deteriorating military situation on the New York and Pennsylvania frontiers. In July 1778 the Board of War suggested a campaign against the Iroquois, but Washington rejected the idea because of the lateness of the season and his preoccupation with the Newport operation. However, he did not oppose a punitive expedition so long as it was done right. He believed that the key to stopping the raids on New York and Pennsylvania settlements was to invade the Iroquois homeland. He explained to Laurens, "I am perfectly convinced that the only certain way of preventing Indian ravages is to carry the war vigorously into their own country."[47] That winter, after consulting with Congress and soliciting advice from people he trusted, he decided on a limited, two-pronged offensive against the Iroquois with approximately four thousand troops from four Continental brigades. One prong, consisting of James Clinton's New York brigade, would march southwestward from Canajoharie, New York, down the Susquehanna River. The other, larger prong, comprising three brigades—Edward Hand's, William Maxwell's, and Enoch Poor's—would advance from Easton, Pennsylvania, northwestward up the Susquehanna. After the two forces met at Tioga, Pennsylvania, they would push into the heart of Iroquoia and burn American Indian villages and crops. If the Iroquois warriors resisted, then the Americans could destroy them in battle. By going after the hornets' nest instead of the hornets, Washington hoped to so cripple the Iroquois that they could no longer threaten the frontier.[48]

Washington recognized that the expedition's success depended as much on its commander as on anything else. Selecting the right officer, though, proved problematic. Washington initially wanted Philip Schuyler to lead it. Washington greatly respected the patrician New Yorker and the sage advice he had offered about the Iroquois. Schuyler also had the support of prominent New Yorkers and was the army's most senior active major general. However, Schuyler disqualified himself by submitting his resignation in January. Putnam was next on the roster, but Washington passed him over because he did not believe he was intellectually equal to the job. Gates was after Putnam, and his Saratoga victory gave him a credibility Washington could not ignore. Although Gates had plenty of support, Washington simply did not trust the man. Washington had heard through the grapevine that Gates continued to badmouth him to congressmen, and he found Gates's dissembling and oblique letters exasperating. He explained to Congress's new president, John Jay, "It will not be doing him injustice to say, that, besides the little underhand intrigues, which he is frequently practicing, there has hardly been any great military question, in which his advice has been asked, that it has not been given in an equivocal and designing manner apparently calculated to afford him an opportunity of censuring me on the failure of whatever measures might be adopted."[49] Washington was as usual ascribing motives and actions to Gates that the record simply did not support. Gates may or may not have recognized Washington's grudging offer for what it was, but he saved everyone a lot of consternation by declining because, he said, he did not feel he possessed the necessary youthfulness and vigor. Although William Heath was next in line and currently serving a supernumerary role in the Eastern Department, Washington did not consider him. In all likelihood, Heath simply did not cross Washington's mind.[50]

John Sullivan was the next most senior major general, and the one Washington wanted to lead the campaign against the Iroquois. Even at the time, Washington's continuing confidence in the hard-luck New Hampshire general puzzled some. Sullivan not only had a long record of defeat that extended from Canada to

Newport, but his contentiousness, hypersensitivity, and quarrelsomeness had caused dissension in the army and trouble with Congress. Indeed, when Nathanael Greene informed Pennsylvania governor Joseph Reed of Sullivan's appointment, Reed responded that the expedition was bound to fail with Sullivan at its helm. Despite these reservations, Washington continued to value Sullivan for his loyalty and energy and was inclined to attribute his past failures to chronic misfortune rather than incompetence. Although Washington gave Sullivan yet another opportunity for the glory and distinction he perpetually sought, this time Sullivan hesitated to accept the assignment. He complained that he was too poor and sick for the job because he had not had the chance to go home to restore his health and finances. After mulling things over and procuring a personal loan from a friend, though, Sullivan decided to lead the mission. He left Providence on 29 March.[51]

Washington also envisioned an ancillary operation out of Fort Pitt to support Sullivan's expedition. Fort Pitt was headquarters for the Western Department, headed since May 1778 by Brig. Gen. Lachlan McIntosh. Washington had given the post to McIntosh because McIntosh had impressed Washington with his temperament, common sense, and prudence during their time together at Valley Forge. However, the responsibility of leading such a remote department proved too much for McIntosh. He alienated both military and civil officials with his inefficiency. On 16 January 1779 one of McIntosh's subordinates, Col. Daniel Brodhead IV, wrote Washington that McIntosh was so ineffective that officers no longer wanted to serve under him. Washington responded a month later that although he was concerned about Brodhead's allegations, he needed more specific charges against McIntosh than a general lack of confidence to take action against him. Fortunately for Washington, McIntosh spared everyone a distracting hullabaloo by submitting his resignation to Congress. McIntosh explained to Washington that his lack of resources in the face of increasing American Indian attacks made it impossible for him to do his job. He added that he had lost everything he owned when the British overran Georgia. He concluded that he could be of more use to the American cause anywhere but Fort Pitt. Washington complied by sending him down south to fight for his homeland. All this accumulated stress took a toll on McIntosh; Joseph Reed scarcely recognized him when they crossed paths in Philadelphia in late April. On 5 March Washington appointed Brodhead to replace McIntosh. Brodhead was only a colonel, but Washington thought he had ability and figured that he was more familiar with the region than any general he could send out there. That summer Brodhead led a force of about six hundred men from Fort Pitt up the Allegheny River and back that accomplished little.[52]

In the months after his appointment to lead the expedition against the Iroquois, Sullivan severely tested Washington's long-standing patience and confidence.

Sullivan was generally pleased with the units and brigadiers Washington put at his disposal. Enoch Poor was a veteran commander whose New Hampshire brigade contained many marksmen accustomed to wilderness combat. Despite allegations of excessive drinking, William Maxwell was also an experienced fighter, and his New Jersey brigade seemed solid. Sullivan was unfamiliar with James Clinton and his New York brigade organizing at Canajoharie, and if he formed any opinion about Edward Hand's Pennsylvania brigade, he kept it to himself. Although Washington ordered Greene to give Sullivan top priority in supplies and equipment, even at the expense of the main army, Sullivan was never satisfied. On 25 June, two days after he reached the Wyoming Valley, he grumbled that his army possessed scarcely a barrel of salted meat and that two-thirds of his bread was moldy. Washington's and Greene's assurances that they were doing all they could to provide him with what he needed did little to appease him. Greene was Sullivan's friend and tried to be supportive, but he found Sullivan's complaining frustrating, writing, "He likes to have things in abundance. He is a friend of the soldier although it may be a tax upon the citizen."[53] Moreover, as time went on Greene worried that Sullivan was setting him up as the scapegoat should the expedition fail. Sullivan did not limit his complaints to Greene and Washington. On 21 July he informed the president of Congress, John Jay, that logistical problems and insufficient manpower had prevented him from commencing operations as soon as he wanted. Just to make sure Jay and Congress got his point, he added with his usual heavy-handedness, "But should a defeat take place and the ruin of the army be the consequence, whether I do or do not perish in the action, I call upon the members of Congress to witness to the world that I early foresaw and foretold the danger and used every means in my power, to procure a force sufficient to ensure success but failed to obtain it."[54] An irate Washington responded to Jay that Sullivan was exaggerating his difficulties and that Greene was doing all that could be reasonably expected to support the campaign. As for Sullivan's alleged manpower shortages, Washington noted that if Sullivan had as few soldiers as he claimed, then his inability to count and maintain them showed that he was not a very good officer.[55]

Although Washington wanted the campaign to begin as early in the summer as possible, Sullivan did not feel logistically secure enough to march from the Wyoming Valley until 31 July. He reached Tioga on 11 August and constructed a fort nearby while waiting for James Clinton's brigade to arrive from Canajoharie. A couple years earlier, Schuyler had warned Washington that Clinton was slow and had difficulty maintaining discipline. Whatever the accuracy of that assessment, in this instance Clinton demonstrated considerable conscientiousness and competency. He accumulated supplies and equipment without the drama that accompanied Sullivan's preparations and handled his brigade skillfully. Upon receiving Sullivan's 6 August orders to join him, Clinton got his men under way and reached Tioga sixteen days later. From there the combined expedition plunged northwestward into the heart of Iroquoia against minimal opposition. The British had held back most of their troops in Canada because of rumors of an American invasion, and the American Indians lacked the strength to confront the almost four thousand Continentals rampaging through their territory. On 29 August Sullivan's scouts detected approximately one thousand Iroquois lying in ambush at Newtown. Sullivan directed Hand's Pennsylvanians to assail the American Indian breastworks while his other three brigades hit both enemy flanks. Considering the disparity in numbers and firepower, it was hardly surprising that the American Indians soon broke and ran. American casualties numbered forty-three; the American Indians' losses were somewhat less. From that point the American Indians lacked the means and will to resist Sullivan in any organized fashion, giving him free rein to destroy all the American Indian villages, orchards, and crops within his reach. The expedition reached Seneca Lake on 1 September and the village of Chenussio two weeks later. His confidence growing with each passing day, Sullivan claimed that he could have taken Fort Niagara if he had had sufficient supplies. Because he did not, he turned back, burning as he went, and returned to Tioga at the end of the month.[56]

In many respects Sullivan's march through Iroquoia was remarkably successful. By burning forty American Indian villages, an estimated 160,000 bushels of corn, and countless additional resources, Sullivan's soldiers destroyed so much infrastructure that the Iroquois were transformed from a proud nation into supplicants completely dependent on British largesse for their survival. American settlers therefore received a reprieve from American Indian raids. The campaign also showed that the new United States was capable of organizing and supplying a large-scale expedition into American Indian territory. The fact that the Continentals so easily defeated the American Indians at Newtown was further evidence of their increasing professionalism and skill. The operation accomplished less than Washington and Congress had hoped, though. Sullivan's inability to seize Fort Niagara left the wellspring of American Indian power in the region intact. Nor did the expedition lead to a permanent cessation of American Indian raids on the New York and Pennsylvania frontiers. In fact, the outraged and angry American Indians would return with a vengeance in the following years.

Whatever his expedition's longer-term disappointments, Sullivan still took pride in his first and only independent triumph of the war. Even in victory, though, Sullivan still generated controversy. His accusations to Jay that Greene had not supplied him sufficiently led to a congressional investigation. After examining the evidence, a congressional committee sardonically concluded, "General Sullivan's requisitions have always been indefinite, requiring a large supply, but no certain quantity ever specified by him, previous to the issuing the said general orders, which rendered it impracticable for the Board of War to ascertain what were his wants."[57] But by then such condemnations did not matter much in the warm afterglow of a successful campaign. Congress voted Sullivan its thanks, and Washington added his congratulations privately and in general orders for a job well done. Sullivan, for his part, was generous in his praise for his army and generals, singling out Enoch Poor in particular for his role at the Battle of Newtown.[58]

Sullivan's one major victory was also his last. Throughout his campaign against the Iroquois, he was plagued by a "violent bilious disorder" that sometimes interfered with his generalship. When his illness persisted, Sullivan concluded that he could not recover in the harsh conditions of army camp life, if at all. On 6 November Sullivan informed Washington that he had to step down for his constitution's sake. Washington tried without success to dissuade him. On 30 November Congress accepted Sullivan's resignation with its thanks, thus ending his career with the army. Despite the controversy and strife he spawned during his tenure as general, the officer corps lamented his departure. Even Greene, the most recent high-level target of Sullivan's carping, expressed his regrets. However, the best evidence that Sullivan's contribution to the cause was greater than his military record indicated came from Washington. On 1 December Sullivan wrote to the commander in chief that though he had often worried that Washington might see him as a flatterer, now that his time in the service was over and that was no longer an issue, he wanted to offer Washington assurances: "My public and constant declarations have been, and I now repeat, that in my opinion, you are the savior of this country, and that to your fortitude, bravery, and steady performance, do we owe the independence and freedom we enjoy."[59] Washington responded with kind words all the more gracious because he no longer needed to appease Sullivan to preserve harmony in the officer corps: "I flatter myself it is unnecessary for me to repeat to you how high a place you hold in my esteem. The confidence you have experienced, and the manner in which you have been employed on several important occasions, testify to the value I set upon your military qualifications, and the regret I must feel that circumstances have deprived the army of your services."[60] As it was, Sullivan recovered his health more rapidly than expected, and by early 1780 he was hale enough to go to Congress as one of New Hampshire's representatives.[61]

Tribulations, Transfers, and Treason

In early December 1779 Washington moved his army into winter quarters at Morristown, New Jersey. Being in winter quarters was never easy for the army, but this occasion was the worst so far. For one thing, the weather was abominable. Old-timers insisted that it was the coldest and snowiest winter in living memory. Huge snowdrifts closed roads and isolated the army for days at a time. Even when the roads were clear, it was increasingly difficult to supply the soldiers because inflation had ruined purchasing power and made buying and transporting goods expensive. Indeed, Greene complained that he could not even forward dispatches because there was not enough money to pay couriers. Because the army could not afford to feed its horses, Washington sent most of them away to pastures in warmer climes. This saved the horses at the expense of the army's mobility, which was probably just as well since there was almost no ammunition with which to fight. Congress passed a law in early December that called for each state to maintain its own troops, but this did little to alleviate the logistical crunch. Soldiers went days without bread or meat, and sometimes without both. Although some worried that the army might disband, the troops bore their sufferings with their usual patience and fortitude. Their resilience, though, had its limits. In late May 1780 a Connecticut brigade mutinied over the lack of provisions, but officers persuaded the soldiers to stand down. For many officers and men, the most galling thing about the army's deprivation was that it occurred amid such plenty, which led one congressman to observe, "The country abounds with the necessary resources, but private gain seems the only object of too many individuals without any concern for the public safety."[62]

Personnel problems and management as usual took up a good bit of Washington's time that winter. Almost all of his generals wanted furloughs to go home to visit family and get their personal affairs in order. Washington generously approved most requests, but doing so increased his workload and reduced the army's effectiveness. At one point Washington grumbled that he had only two brigadiers remaining in camp, one of whom wanted to leave. Boredom, frustration, and loneliness frequently created dissension and strife. Those generals still present bickered over and magnified petty annoyances. As quartermaster, Greene was responsible for finding suitable quarters for the generals and their staffs. Unfortunately, a shortage of building materials and dwellings in Morristown made this difficult, so oftentimes generals got smaller and cruder accommodations than they wanted. Indeed, an exasperated Greene griped that there was not an officer in camp satisfied with his quarters. For example, Greene explained to an unhappy Steuben that the reason Knox's lodgings were better than his own was because Knox used his artificers to construct them. Greene also told Samuel Parsons that his quarters were not as good as some more-junior officers' because Washington wanted brigadiers housed close to their brigades. Such squabbles took time away from maintaining the army's efficiency. That winter Washington rebuked Stirling for not carrying out orders quickly enough. He also complained about the deteriorating condition of some of the units. He noted that Maxwell's New Jersey brigade, once one of the army's best, was in terrible shape, as were

James Clinton's New Yorkers. Just because the army was not campaigning and fighting did not mean that it recovered its élan.[63]

Winter did not always bring relaxation and rejuvenation to the generals either. Israel Putnam, for example, in November asked for and received Washington's permission to return to his Connecticut home for a short leave. Once there he suffered a serious stroke that temporarily cost him the use of his right leg and right arm. With the help of his neighbors, he gradually learned to walk again, and even ride a horse, but his days as an active participant in the war were over. Although Washington wished him a speedy recovery, he was undoubtedly relieved by this turn of events. For all the physical courage Putnam had displayed in the conflict, he lacked other qualities a good general needed. His presence on the roster complicated Washington's job by forcing him to work around Putnam in making assignments. To Washington, employing Putnam was simply more trouble than it was worth. Despite the consensus among military and civil officials that Putnam's reputation exceeded his talents, a generous Congress permitted him to retain his rank until the end of the conflict.[64]

There was nothing wrong with Nathanael Greene's health, but his attitude toward his job as the main army's quartermaster general left something to be desired. Despite Washington's continued confidence, Greene remained convinced that serving as quartermaster hurt his chance for distinction. Indeed, Greene sometimes seemed to value glory more than winning the war and securing American independence. His frustration and bitterness infected his professional life. In the summer of 1779, he complained that Congress's recent military reorganization rendered him ineligible for combat command. This contradicted the deal he believed he had made with Congress when he accepted the quartermaster position, a deal that had enabled him to lead men in battle at Monmouth Courthouse and Newport. If he could not command on the battlefield, then he could never gain the military fame he sought but would instead be relegated to the kind of tedious staff work that exposed him to Sullivan's unfair accusations. Greene felt so strongly about the issue that he threatened to quit as quartermaster unless Congress and Washington saw things his way. Not only did he solicit the support of his fellow generals, but he also resorted to passive-aggressive behavior by refusing to attend a meeting to determine rank in the artillery because, he said, he apparently was not worthy of a combat post. On 3 September Washington placated Greene with yet another patient letter. He explained to Greene that as far as he was concerned, although Greene had surrendered his role as a combat officer when he became quartermaster and left his division, Greene need not worry because Washington could still appoint him to a combat command under extraordinary circumstances if necessary. Washington reassured and reminded him:

> The good opinion I have of your abilities and qualifications will make me take pleasure to give you opportunities of rendering service and acquiring military honor in the field as often as it can be done consistent with propriety, the good of the service, and the reasonable pretensions of other officers. The experience you have already had [at Monmouth Courthouse and Newport] may satisfy you of my disposition. You have participated in the only two transactions of importance which have happened since your appointment in which the whole, or a considerable portion of the army has been concerned.[65]

Greene's concerns about his eligibility for combat command, like his earlier disagreement with Washington over campsites, was symptomatic of deeper grievances. Greene deeply regretted his decision to become quartermaster because it deprived him of the opportunity for glory and exposed him to public criticism for his role in the army's increasing logistical problems. On the battlefield Greene could at least face his foes out in the open, but in the political maze in which he now operated his enemies were less obvious and the difficulties more intractable. Greene insisted that inflation, not corruption or incompetency, was responsible for the army's logistical woes. On 12 December a frustrated Greene submitted his resignation to Congress as quartermaster. By now some congressmen were tired of Greene's whining and carping. Greene seemed to think that the quartermaster should be immune from the kind of scrutiny almost every public official faced. Moreover, although Greene was more than willing to condemn others such as Gates for their shortcomings, he seemed incapable of accepting similar treatment. Alluding to Greene, one delegate wrote, "It is surprising too that gentlemen who so loudly complain of cruelty [in] a hasty opinion in others, should be no more careful how they wound those who never in word or deed . . . had injured them."[66] Congress declined to accept Greene's resignation because replacing him would undoubtedly hurt the army. No one, though, bothered to inform Greene of this, so for the next two months he fulfilled his quartermaster duties under the false assumption that his tenure was coming to an end. After he learned the truth, he asked Congress to reaffirm its confidence in his abilities. Congress had already done so the previous June in a unanimous resolution. Doing so again, or whenever Greene felt unappreciated, smacked of emotional blackmail. Even so, one congressman proposed another resolution endorsing Greene's performance as quartermaster, but it became bogged down in amendments and got nowhere. When a congressional committee visited Morristown in early May to discuss the supply situation, Greene refused to cooperate with it until its members acknowledged he was doing a good job. It was Washington who prevented a complete breakdown in Greene's relationship with Congress. He yet again assured Greene of his support and promised to do more to make clear to Congress the burdens under which Greene labored.[67]

The winter also provided Washington with the opportunity to make personnel changes without the distraction of active campaigning. Since he assumed command of the Hudson Highlands in November 1778, Alexander McDougall had found the job thankless, difficult, and exhausting. To make things worse, a painful case of kidney stones inhibited his effectiveness. In November 1779 McDougall asked a sympathetic Washington to relieve him so he could return home to recuperate. Washington agreed, but now he had to find someone else with plenty of rank to take over the Hudson Highlands. He first offered the job to Horatio Gates, then running the Eastern Department in Boston. As a major general credited with winning the Battle of Saratoga, Gates had sufficient cachet for the job. However, Washington neither trusted him nor wanted him serving in the main army. Sending him to the strategically vital Hudson Highlands would keep Gates at a distance without raising eyebrows or hurting feelings. Gates declined the post and instead asked Washington for leave to return to his Virginia home and look after his long-neglected personal affairs. Washington found the request reasonable, all the more so because it got Gates out of the way for the time being. With Gates out of contention, Washington asked William Heath. Heath had spent the summer leading American troops on the eastern side of Hudson River. He had overseen the Hudson Highlands back in 1776, so he was familiar with the region. After Gates he was the most senior major general and was well respected by Congress and New York governor George Clinton. Finally, Heath wanted a more active assignment and had in fact turned down a congressional offer to join the Board of War the previous May to stay in the field.[68]

Two months after Heath took command of the Hudson Highlands, *his* health broke down due in part to the stress and strain of running such an important department with such limited resources. In February he secured Washington's permission to return to Massachusetts to recover. Looking over his roster, Washington discovered that he had in his main army six major generals available to replace Heath: Greene, Stirling, St. Clair, de Kalb, Howe, and Steuben. Greene and Steuben were preoccupied serving as the army's quartermaster and inspector general, respectively, and Washington did not trust Stirling with an independent command. De Kalb's foreign background disqualified him, and St. Clair was busy leading his division and investigating a couple British raids into New Jersey. By process of elimination, that left Howe. Although he had hardly shone as an American general, Washington assigned him to temporarily replace Heath on 21 February 1780.

As commander in chief, Washington was obligated to keep an eye on military events throughout the country. He had initially dismissed the British occupation of Savannah, Georgia, in late 1778 as unimportant to the overall war effort. A failed British attempt to seize Charleston in the spring of 1779 seemed to show that

Benjamin Lincoln, the Southern Department commander, was capable of holding his own. In September Lincoln and d'Estaing's French fleet joined forces to try to retake Savannah. Their 9 October assault on the city was a fiasco, however, that cost nearly a thousand French and American casualties, as opposed to less than one hundred British dead and wounded. Kazimierz Pułaski was among those killed, making him the first American general to fall on the battlefield since Francis Nash went down at Germantown two years earlier. D'Estaing then called off the siege and sailed away with his fleet, leaving behind more hard feelings and another Franco-American defeat.

During the winter of 1779–80, Washington gradually accumulated intelligence that the British planned a major offensive in the southern states. Washington did not, however, know that the British had decided to attack Charleston as part of a southern strategy designed to take advantage of local loyalist support to conquer the Carolinas. As the details of British planning gradually came into focus, Washington in November 1779 dispatched the North Carolina and Virginia lines to bolster Lincoln's small army. He was reluctant to do so because his own force was so weak but felt that Charleston's strategic and psychological importance required the sacrifice. Surprisingly, Washington offered the job of leading them to Stirling. He had over the years refrained from giving the New Jersey general such independent missions, probably because he doubted that Stirling was up to the task, but this time he made an exception. In all likelihood, he guessed that Stirling would decline the honor. Indeed, Stirling replied that although he would cheerfully obey any orders Washington issued, he did not want the job. Stirling explained that since he outranked Lincoln, he would assume overall command of the southern army once he reached Charleston. He had too much respect for Lincoln to replace him at such a crucial time. As a result, Brig. Gens. James Hogun and William Woodford took the North Carolina and Virginia lines, respectively, to Charleston on their own.[69]

On 11 February 1780 eleven thousand British troops landed at Simmons Island and slowly worked their way up to Charlestown Neck, so by late March they were ready to begin siege operations against the South Carolina city. Outnumbered two to one, wracked by indecision, and cowed by local civil authorities, Lincoln was at first unwilling, and then unable, to evacuate the city and save his army. As the British army's coils constricted Charleston, an increasingly concerned Washington sent more aid because he believed the city's loss would be catastrophic to the American cause. On 30 March Washington ordered his chief of engineers, Louis Duportail, to Charleston to assist Lincoln in bolstering the city's defenses. Washington commended Duportail to Lincoln as "a gentleman of whose abilities and merit I have the highest opinion and who, if he arrives in time will be of essential utility to you."[70] Three days later, Washington upped the ante by directing the Maryland and Delaware lines southward. Washington knew that they would probably not arrive in time to make much difference in Charleston's fate, but they would prove useful in defending the rest of the region. Although Smallwood was Maryland's senior brigadier, Washington gave the command to de Kalb because he was a major general and had led the division from which the Maryland and Delaware soldiers were drawn.[71]

On 11 May 1780 Lincoln surrendered Charleston and its defending army to the British. Charleston's conquest was the biggest American defeat of the war. Although the number of killed and wounded during the siege was not great—225 American and 265 British troops, in all—the other statistics were far grimmer for the Americans. The British captured 6,700 American soldiers and sailors, of whom 2,500 were precious Continentals. Indeed, almost the entire North Carolina and Virginia lines marched into captivity. In addition, the Americans lost considerable matériel, including four hundred cannons. The strategic consequences were equally dire. If Savannah's fall had pushed ajar the door to the southern states for the British, then the destruction of the main American army at Charleston blew it wide open. In subsequent weeks British columns fanned out through South Carolina occupying strongpoints, recruiting jubilant loyalists, and intimidating patriots.

Charleston's fall also inflicted significant losses on the Continental army's top leadership. Benjamin Lincoln was, after Charles Lee, the highest-ranking Continental general to fall into British hands during the conflict. Of the army's twenty-five active brigadiers, the British netted six, or a fourth, at Charleston: Louis Duportail, James Hogun, Lachlan McIntosh, William Moultrie, Charles Scott, and William Woodford. After the Charleston garrison surrendered, the only Continental generals still in action in the South were Isaac Huger and Jethro Sumner. Although several of the captured generals eventually returned to service, others did not. Lincoln was exchanged in November and rejoined Washington's army. Duportail, whose specialized engineering skills made him perhaps the most valuable of the six generals taken prisoner, was released on parole the same month and also resumed his duties with Washington. Moultrie, McIntosh, and Scott were eventually exchanged as well, but not until after the fighting had almost ended. Sadly, Woodford and Hogun both died of illness in prison, the former in New York City in November 1780 and the latter in Charleston the following January.

Rumors of Charleston's fall alarmed Congress before official word of the calamity reached Philadelphia. There were few reinforcements available for the South, which meant that de Kalb and his little band of less than one thousand Maryland and Delaware Continentals marching through Virginia were just about the only organized military force left in the region. Congress could, however, do something about reanimating the Southern Department's military leadership.

On 13 June Congress selected Horatio Gates as the new Southern Department commander. Gates was an obvious choice for several reasons. For one thing, as a major general currently on leave in Virginia, he possessed both rank and availability. He also had plenty of experience in independent command and was popular among some New England and Virginia delegates. Most important of all, he had faced an analogous situation three years earlier in northern New York when he took over a demoralized army and led it to victory at Saratoga. Congress hoped he could perform a similar service in the South. As one congressmen explained after Gates got under way, "General Gates seems to possess a thorough understanding of the business he is going upon, and he is proceeding with a wise and well considered system. If he is properly supported, I have little doubt but that he will restore our affairs in that quarter."[72] Congress did not consult Washington on its decision, no doubt because of the press of time and recognition of the poor relationship between the two men. Indeed, Washington had declined to express an opinion about Gates one way or another when Congress appointed him to replace Schuyler after Ticonderoga's fall, and he probably would have done the same thing if asked now. Gates left his Virginia home on 9 July and reached de Kalb's army in Charlotte, North Carolina, at the end of the month.[73]

One of Gates's responsibilities was to assemble a command team for his department. Fortunately for him, part of it was already in place at Charlotte. De Kalb was a steady and experienced officer, but he had not seen much action in the war so far and was, as a foreigner, unfamiliar with the geography and culture of the southern states. Indeed, he concluded that the heat, accommodations, and insects were equally aggravating. He had found the past year of inactivity so disheartening that he considered returning to France, but he was now happy to have an opportunity to participate in an active campaign. De Kalb had two Maryland brigadiers with him: Mordecai Gist and William Smallwood. Unlike de Kalb, both men had plenty of combat experience in the war so far and were equally comfortable leading Continental or militia units. Although Smallwood had started the war as a colonel, Gist had worked his way up from captain, impressing people along the way with his courage, character, and merit.[74]

Gates also hoped to acquire Col. Daniel Morgan's services. Morgan was, like Arnold and Wayne, one of the American army's great combat leaders. Born in New Jersey in 1736, Morgan ran away from home at age sixteen to escape his abusive father and eventually ended up on the Virginia frontier. He possessed no education and was in fact functionally illiterate. What he lacked in formal learning, though, he made up for in character and personality. Morgan was a rough-hewn, combative, and unadorned man full of good sense. He was nicknamed "The Old Wagoner" because he had worked as a teamster early in life. In that capacity he met Washington during Edward Braddock's disastrous expedition to Fort Duquesne at the start of the Great War for Empire. Later in the conflict he was seriously wounded by a musket ball that passed through his left cheek and shattered all the teeth on that side of his jaw. He also bore the scars of five hundred lashes to which he was sentenced after an altercation with a British officer. Morgan later joked that the king owed him one more because the drummer keeping track miscounted. After a youth misspent drinking, gambling, and fighting, he settled down, married, and prospered. He was elected captain of a Virginia rifle company when the Revolutionary War began and participated in the siege of Boston and Benedict Arnold's epic march to Quebec. He was wounded and captured in the assault on that Canadian city but was exchanged in time to help foil the British incursion into New Jersey in the spring of 1777 as the head of Washington's rifle corps. Washington then dispatched him and his riflemen to northern New York to assist first Schuyler and then Gates in repelling the British invasion. The fame he gained at Saratoga was exceeded only by Gates's and Arnold's. He submitted his resignation in 1779 after Congress failed to promote him and Washington passed him over as light corps commander. Congress, though, so respected Morgan's combat prowess that it permitted him to go home with his rank intact just in case he ever opted to return to duty.

Gates was well aware of Morgan's talents. On his way south, Gates stopped at Morgan's farm and asked him to take command of a light corps Gates planned to organize for his army. When Morgan complained about his rank, Gates promised to lobby Congress for his appointment to brigadier. Congress in turn consulted Washington. Although Washington declined to express an opinion one way or another because of his relationship with Gates, he provided enough biased background material to make his views clear. He acknowledged that Virginia probably had enough regiments to justify an additional brigadier, and that Morgan as the most senior colonel was next in line. However, he warned that there might not be enough combat commands to go around if one of Virginia's captured generals were exchanged. He also reminded Congress of the reasons for Morgan's resignation, adding that his grievance that he deserved to lead the light corps was unmerited. In the end, Congress opted to table the issue not because of Washington's reservations, but because some delegates worried that elevating Morgan might provoke other states into submitting more candidates for promotion. As a result, Congress did not get around to making Morgan a brigadier until mid-October, two weeks after Morgan finally joined Gates's army.[75]

While Gates rode south, Washington prepared his army for its sixth campaign season. Good news was in short supply. Although the British had evacuated Newport the previous October, they remained ensconced in their New York City stronghold. There was nothing new about that, but they had also conquered Georgia and were in the process of overrunning South Carolina as well. For all the hope that had attended its birth, the Franco-American alliance had so far generated two defeats, at Newport and Savannah. More ominously, the American war effort was slowly crumbling. Inflation made it increasingly difficult to finance the army, leading to shortages in provisions and clothing even in the summer. Both officers and men complained about inadequate and sporadic pay. Such deprivation, though, seemed limited mostly to the military sphere; civilians outside of the war zones appeared to have most of what they needed to get by. One sympathetic congressional committee wrote:

> Our feelings have more than once been tortured, by seeing the general [Washington], with his little army, involved at a most critical moment in such complicated embarrassments as few generals would have encountered, when at the same time his sensibility must have been greatly wounded by reflecting that this labyrinth of distress was in a great measure owing to the cruel neglect of those whose indispensable duty it was to have supported their cause by furnishing him with an army and supplies equal to the exigency of the time.[76]

Washington as usual did what he could to get by and make do with what he had. He divided his main army into five divisions of two brigades apiece, each under a major general: St. Clair's (Wayne's and Irvine's Pennsylvania brigades), Stirling's (Maxwell's New Jersey and James Clinton's New York brigades), Steuben's (Parsons's and Huntington's Connecticut brigades), Howe's (Nixon's and Glover's Massachusetts brigades), and McDougall's (Paterson's Massachusetts and Poor's New Hampshire brigades). Washington hated surrendering the initiative, but without French naval support there was little he could do to get at the British in New York City. For now all he could do was watch and wait.[77]

Despite its problems, the American army retained its sting. On 6 June five thousand British troops landed at Elizabethtown, New Jersey, and marched inland toward Hobart Gap in an effort to engage Washington's army at Morristown. They ran into Maxwell's New Jersey brigade and New Jersey militia at Connecticut Farms, about five miles outside Elizabethtown. Although outnumbered, the New Jerseyans gave a good account of themselves. In fact, their obstinate defense convinced the British that they would not catch Washington's army by surprise, so they retreated back to Elizabethtown that evening. Two weeks later, on 23 June, the British tried again. This time they encountered Greene and about two thousand Continentals—Maxwell's and Stark's brigades—and New Jersey militia who fought them to a standstill in a series of engagements around Springfield. Once again the British fell back to Elizabethtown and returned to Staten Island. Their two forays into New Jersey resulted in around three hundred casualties. American losses came to about two hundred. No doubt British timidity had much to do with the Americans' success, but that timidity grew out of stout American resistance. Washington gave credit to Maxwell for his stubborn tactics and the New Jersey militia for turning out with alacrity and fighting so tenaciously.[78]

With the exception of the two British incursions into New Jersey that June, Washington's army saw little combat in 1780. Such inaction and the resulting boredom contributed to the infighting, quarreling, and controversy that roiled the officer corps that year at even the highest levels. James Clinton got into a tiff with his officers so serious that he threatened to resign his commission, though it did not come to that. William Irvine decided that he deserved seniority over Edward Hand and waged a prolonged campaign that summer to get it. Washington appointed a board of generals to look into the matter, which concluded unanimously that it lacked the authority and expertise to support Irvine's claims. Finally, Anthony Wayne's relationship with Arthur St. Clair continued to cause difficulties. Washington dissolved the light corps after the 1779 campaign season ended and did not immediately reconstitute it the following spring. Because Washington wanted to gainfully employ the talented Wayne, he asked him to take charge of a Pennsylvania brigade. The problem was that this brigade was part of St. Clair's division. There had been bad blood between St. Clair and Wayne—mostly on Wayne's part—since 1778. Washington's success in persuading Wayne to accept the post did not prevent dissension in the division. The two men bickered over Washington's selection of an officer outside the lines of seniority for a certain post. Wayne sided with the aggrieved officers passed over, whereas St. Clair supported Washington's prerogative to make the appointment. Washington had this and other personnel disputes in mind when he wrote to Wayne: "Let all be as a band of brothers and rise superior to every injury whether real or imaginary and persevere in the arduous but glorious struggle in which we are engaged until peace and independence are secured to our country."[79]

In June Washington received a letter from New York congressman Robert Livingston expressing his concerns about Robert Howe's fitness to lead in the strategically vital Hudson Highlands. Livingston admitted that he did not know Howe, but southerners who did spoke poorly of him. Howe's lackluster record as Southern Department commander, as well as his womanizing reputation, had followed him northward. That being the case, Livingston suggested that Washington find someone else to oversee the Hudson Highlands. Washington responded that he was not sufficiently familiar with Howe's abilities and character to vouch for him. He noted that relieving him of his command outright without cause would injure his pride, but he also promised to assign him to the main army and give the Hudson Highlands to someone else when the time was right.[80]

In the end, Howe, Irvine, St. Clair, and Wayne all stayed in the army despite their various grievances and controversies. The same could not be said of several other generals. William Maxwell had been a mainstay since the war's earliest days, having fought from Canada to the Chesapeake and most everywhere in between. Indeed, he had recently played a prominent role in repelling the British army's recent forays in New Jersey. Maxwell's problem was not his courage or even his somewhat limited intellect, but rather excessive drinking. Although a court-martial back in November 1777 had stated that he had never been so drunk as to disqualify him from doing his duty, the wording clearly implied that he had a problem with alcohol. His brigade officers grew concerned in subsequent operations about his habits, prompting a whispering campaign against him that made Maxwell increasingly unhappy. One officer wrote on 10 July, "Matters with Gen. M[axwe]ll are come to a crisis, what will be the consequences I know not; we have persuaded him to resign and assured him at the same time that if he declines the measure, we must submit his conduct to the judgment of a court martial."[81] Moreover, news that his father and brother had been brutally assaulted and robbed in their farmhouse also weighed heavily on his mind.

Maxwell submitted his resignation to Washington on 20 July. He explained that he had not found commanding the New Jersey brigade as fulfilling as he had hoped. He noted that he had entered the army with the purest of motives and had tried his hardest to do his duty, but he preferred to quit rather than serve under such disagreeable circumstances. Washington forwarded Maxwell's letter to Congress. In his accompanying correspondence, Washington stated that Congress was aware of Maxwell's merits, but he wanted to emphasize Maxwell's patriotism and honesty. He left it at that and made no effort to dissuade Maxwell. In fact, Washington appears to have been disenchanted with Maxwell for some time, going back to Maxwell's court-martial for drunkenness. Despite the New Jersey brigade's fine performance in repelling the most recent British incursion into its state, Washington had complained the previous January that the brigade had gone from one of the army's best outfits to one of its worst. As its commander, Maxwell bore at least some of the blame for that transformation. Congress accepted Maxwell's resignation on 25 July, and he played no further part in the conflict. His departure left Stirling as the state's only general.[82]

Less than two months after Maxwell departed, the army also lost the services of Massachusetts's Brig. Gen. John Nixon. Nixon had fought and been wounded at both Bunker Hill and Saratoga, injuries from which he never fully recovered. In fact, he was so debilitated that he tried to resign in October 1777, but Congress had refused. Despite this implied respect on Congress's part, Nixon remained a brigadier long after the other members of his cohort—St. Clair and McDougall—had been promoted. In fact, his record as a commander was unremarkable. Washington, though, respected his character. In 1778 he gave Nixon leave without a time limit because he knew Nixon would not abuse the privilege. Although Nixon had a large family depending on him, it was his poor health that compelled him to submit his resignation again on 8 September 1780. Congress accepted it four days later, ending his military career.[83]

On the same day Nixon submitted his resignation, the army lost another general: New Hampshire's Enoch Poor. Poor had seen about as much action as anyone in the Continental army. He had participated in the Canadian campaign, Trenton and Princeton, Saratoga, Monmouth Courthouse, and Sullivan's Iroquois expedition. Through it all he built a reputation as a reliable, competent, and low-key officer who skillfully led his New Hampshire brigade. Both Washington and Gates vouched for him, as did Sullivan and John Stark. In late August 1780 he came down with "putrid fever"—probably typhus—and died two weeks later. Washington and most of the main army's high-ranking officers attended his funeral at Hackensack, New Jersey, where he was interred in a mahogany coffin with a pair of pistols and two swords, crossing each other, placed on top. Sullivan called him "a truly brave and valuable officer" and "a great and good man."[84] Washington, for his part, lamented him as "an officer of distinguished merit, who as a citizen and a soldier had every claim to the esteem of his country."[85]

Nathanael Greene remained in the army, but in a different capacity. Although Greene's misery as the army's quartermaster continued in 1780, events that summer finally brought matters to a head. Greene had for some time resented congressional criticism of his work as quartermaster, the tediousness of the job, and the lack of opportunity for glory. To make matters worse, the deteriorating financial situation made it increasingly difficult for Greene to adequately supply the army even in summer. For Greene, the final straw was a congressional proposal to reorganize the Quartermaster Department. Greene thought Congress's plan was good in theory, but not in practice. In particular, Greene worried that he would not be able to work with men he trusted and whose employment Congress had guaranteed as one of Greene's conditions in accepting the job two years earlier. Thoroughly fed up, on 26 July he submitted his resignation as quartermaster, telling Washington in early August:

> I am sensible my conduct has been viewed by many in a very improper light; and I am persuaded many think the business can be done with more method and at a less expense than it has been. I wish it may be the case, but am much mistaken if the nature of the business is capable of more system or will admit of less expense, if the plan of the war continues upon the present scale, and the army on its present footing.[86]

Some congressmen did not appreciate Greene's decision. As far as they were concerned, Greene's resignation was a form of blackmail designed to leave the army in the lurch unless Congress did things his way. Not only was it disrespectful, but it also threatened civilian control of the military. Some delegates were so angry that they introduced a resolution to deny Greene a combat command until he satisfactorily settled his financial accounts as quartermaster. Fortunately for Greene, Washington came to his defense. Washington admitted that he was of two minds about Greene's actions but implored Congress to carefully weigh the pros and cons of attempting to punish him. Doing so without providing Greene the opportunity to defend himself in a court-martial would demoralize other officers. Moreover, Greene had plenty of friends in the officer corps, so targeting him might provoke a firestorm of protests and resignations detrimental to the war effort. Despite his complaining, most congressmen respected Greene and had no stomach for a confrontation with him, Washington, and the army. Indeed, the Connecticut, New Hampshire, Pennsylvania, and Rhode Island delegations remained in his corner throughout the brouhaha. Washington's cautionary words helped dissipate whatever anger remained in Congress. As for Greene, he told his wife that he was happier now that he was no longer quartermaster than ever before in his life. He could also take pride in a letter from Washington attesting to his abilities: "You conducted the various and important duties of it with capacity and diligence entirely to my satisfaction, and as far as I had an opportunity of knowing with the strictest integrity."[87] Greene now looked forward to returning to a combat role and facing his enemies on the battlefield instead of across a table or in the newspapers.[88]

The return to the army of two familiar faces helped offset the departures of Gates, Maxwell, Nixon, and Poor. On 27 April Marquis de Lafayette disembarked from a French frigate at Boston. His unexpected reappearance generated considerable joy among friends and well-wishers who appreciated all that Lafayette had done for the country, including of course Washington. Upon his arrival in Paris in February 1779, Lafayette had basked in the glory he had had gained in the Continental army and focused on lobbying the French government to provide more aid for the United States. The best evidence of his success in this mission was the deployment of 6,500 French troops at Newport later that summer, led by General Jean-Baptiste de Rochambeau with orders to operate under Washington's general direction. With his usual youthful brazenness, Lafayette had proposed himself as leader of the expedition because he understood the American people, had Congress's confidence, and had taken more soldiers into battle than most French officers. French government officials rejected his offer, but his desire to send more help gibed with their own. Washington hoped to use Lafayette as an intermediary to organize a Franco-American combined assault on New York City. He explained to Rochambeau, "As a general officer I have the greatest confidence in him; as a friend he is perfectly acquainted with my sentiments and opinions; he knows all the circumstances of our army and the country at large; all the information he gives and all the propositions he makes, I entreat you will consider as coming from me."[89] After looking things over, Rochambeau and his officers concluded that such an attack could not succeed without more naval support, soldiers, and artillery than were currently available. In the meantime, on 8 August, Washington selected Lafayette to command the newly reconstituted, division-sized light corps. It was a plum assignment befitting Lafayette's stature and Washington's partiality. Lafayette was pleased with the job and spent his own money to properly equip and clothe his soldiers. Unfortunately for Lafayette, his outfit saw little action for the remainder of the campaign season, depriving him of yet another opportunity for glory.[90]

Benedict Arnold was the second addition. The wound Arnold received at Saratoga was so severe that he had been unable to return to active duty for nearly two years. Washington therefore assigned him to command the Philadelphia garrison after the British evacuated the city in June 1778. Considering his temperament, it was unsurprising that Arnold's tenure there was tumultuous and contentious. The basic problem was that the very traits that made Arnold such a magnificent combat leader—his impetuousness, forcefulness, and imperiousness—handicapped his efforts to function in a more administrative role. His personality alienated people hostile toward authority in general and the military in particular. Allegations of speculation and corruption dogged him. Indeed, the appearance that Arnold was living beyond his means implied either that he had gone deeply into debt or that he was turning a penny in clandestine ways that were, if not exactly illegal, then certainly unseemly. Finally, Arnold consorted with wealthy Philadelphians whose loyalty to the patriot cause was suspect, as evidenced by his April 1779 wedding to eighteen-year-old Peggy Shippen. Such activities aroused the suspicion of the Pennsylvania Executive Council, led by Joseph Reed, which waged a prolonged campaign to discredit him and remove him from his post. After the council publicly leveled corruption charges against Arnold, Congress ordered Washington to convene a court-martial to adjudicate them.

Organizing the court took considerable time because Washington and his generals were busy fighting the British, but it finally got under way in earnest in December 1779. Robert Howe chaired it, and Knox, Maxwell, Smallwood, and Stark were among its members. After hearing and weighing the evidence, the court on 26 January 1780 cleared Arnold of all but two minor charges and sentenced him to a reprimand from Washington. Although Washington made the reprimand as mild as possible and in such a way as to appear almost laudatory, it only stoked Arnold's conviction that he was unappreciated and persecuted. He referred to his opponents as "scoundrels in office" and deeply resented the ill treatment to which he was subjected. Long before the verdict he had written to Washington, "Having made every sacrifice of fortune and blood, and become a cripple in the service of my country, I little expected to meet the ungrateful returns I have received of my countrymen, but as Congress have stamped ingratitude as a current coin I must take it."[91] Disgruntled Continental generals were by then a dime a dozen, but Arnold had already set himself apart from the rest by initiating correspondence with the British in the summer of 1779 to explore the possibility of switching sides.[92]

Despite Arnold's innumerable character and personality flaws, Washington still valued his combat prowess and had since the summer of 1778 wanted him for an important post in his army. Now that Arnold's court-martial was over and he had resigned as commander of the Philadelphia garrison, the path finally seemed clear for him to accept Washington's long-standing offer. When Arnold visited Washington's headquarters in June 1780, Washington asked him to lead one of his army's two wings. Arnold surprised those familiar with his aggressiveness and ego by requesting instead to take charge of West Point and the Hudson Highlands. It was an important job, West Point being the key to the Hudson River valley that separated New England from the rest of the country, but not one that provided much opportunity for the glory that had hitherto motivated Arnold. Arnold claimed that he wanted the assignment because his wound disqualified him from active duty in the field. The truth, however, was that Arnold had already struck a deal with the British to use his power to hand West Point over to them in exchange for a brigadier's commission in the British army, command of a loyalist corps, and a substantial sum of money. Arnold's wife Peggy had done her part by inveigling New York congressman Robert Livingston to write Washington to ask him to relieve the current Hudson Highlands commander, the unpopular Robert Howe. Washington had responded by ordering McDougall to replace Howe. To make room for Arnold, McDougall would have to be transferred, but since he saw the post as a backwater, that would not hurt his feelings. Washington remained puzzled by Arnold's curious reticence, but he issued the necessary orders on 3 August. Washington warned Arnold that running the Hudson Highlands was a difficult task but expressed confidence that Arnold would do his best. Indeed, when Arnold assumed his command he discovered that West Point and its environs were in deplorable shape. A fire the previous January had destroyed the quartermaster's barracks, there was no proper guardhouse and powder magazine, and the fortifications left much to be desired. Considering his new loyalties, it was unsurprising that Arnold did little to rectify these deficiencies; instead, he strove to surreptitiously weaken the place further to facilitate the expected British attack on the fortress.[93]

On the night of 22–23 September, Arnold secretly met with Maj. John André, adjutant general to British commander in chief General Henry Clinton, to finalize their plans. Arnold turned over to André detailed diagrams of West Point's defenses to facilitate a British attack on the fortress. Unfortunately for Arnold, local militiamen captured André in civilian clothes on his way back to New York City. Arnold was eating a late breakfast with two of Washington's aides at his headquarters on 24 September when he got word of André's arrest. Recognizing the implications, Arnold excused himself, mounted his horse, rode a couple hundred feet to the Hudson River, boarded a barge, and forced the crew at gunpoint to row him downstream to a British warship. In the meantime, Washington and his entourage arrived at Arnold's headquarters after meeting with Rochambeau at Hartford, Connecticut, to discuss upcoming operations. Although Washington cantered to West Point and back in search of him, Arnold was nowhere to be found. However, when Washington returned to Arnold's headquarters he received word of André's seizure, as well as of the papers in his possession in Arnold's handwriting. This information, along with Arnold's disappearance and accounts of his odd behavior immediately beforehand, led Washington to deduce that Arnold had gone over to the British. Arnold confirmed the theory in a letter to Washington on 25 September. In it Arnold asked Washington to send him his clothes and baggage and claimed that he acted without the knowledge of his wife and staff. He also justified his actions stating, "The heart which is conscious of its own rectitude cannot attempt to palliate a step which the world may censure as wrong; I have ever acted from a principle of love to my country, since the commencement of the present unhappy contest between Great Britain and the Colonies; the same principle of love to my country actuates my present conduct, however it may appear inconsistent to the world, who very seldom judges right of any man's actions."[94]

The short-term military fallout from Arnold's defection was minimal. Washington immediately rushed reinforcements to West Point and summoned the two generals most familiar with the place, William Heath and Alexander McDougall, to go there and strengthen its defenses. Heath had been doing a good job liaising with the French in Newport, but Washington concluded that he would be of more value in the Hudson Highlands and gave him the department in mid-October. Fortunately for the Americans, the British remained buttoned up in New York City and declined to take advantage of this American reshuffling. However, the psychological impact of Arnold's betrayal was significant. Americans were surprised, shocked, and angered by his treachery. For all his problems, Arnold was a military hero, the sparkplug behind the assault on Quebec and victory at Saratoga. In Philadelphia, a crowd burned Arnold in effigy, some clergymen anathematized him, and Congress indignantly struck his name from the army roster. Nathanael Greene wrote, "My pride and feelings are greatly hurt at the infamy of this man's conduct. Arnold being an American and a New Englander, and of the rank of major general, are all mortifying circumstances. The event will be a reproach to us to the latest posterity. Curse on his folly and perfidy."[95] Washington shared these emotions but was also embarrassed for having vouched for and supported Arnold despite evidence that he might be untrustworthy. His fury and shame no doubt contributed to his decision to try John André as a spy and endorse the court's decision to hang him. Of course, there had always been those who had doubted Arnold from the start, or claimed to have done so after the fact. These included Pennsylvania state officials as well as some military officers who had seen Arnold's less attractive side in Canada and northern New York. John Sullivan, for example, wrote, "Arnold has proved himself what I ever knew of him."[96] Anthony Wayne was more candid, stating, "I think that I informed you I had the most despicable idea of him, both as a gentleman and a soldier, and that he had produced a conviction to me in 1776, that honor and true virtue were strangers to his soul; and, however contradictory it might appear, that he never possessed either genuine fortitude or personal bravery."[97] Finally, there was endless speculation as to Arnold's motivations. Some argued that it was greed, others ego, while still others blamed his pride. The truth was that it was a combination of all these factors that overcame and distorted his concept of loyalty.[98]

Arnold's treason added to the prevailing gloom that dismal late summer and autumn. The high hopes placed in Horatio Gates collapsed only two months after Congress appointed him Southern Department commander. Gates took over his army at Charlotte, North Carolina, on 25 July and marched southward with it two days later in an attempt to catch the dispersed British army in South Carolina by surprise. Although Gates had more than 4,000 troops, his army was less impressive than its numbers indicated. For one thing, only 1,400 of them were Continentals—mostly de Kalb's Delawareans and Marylanders. The rest were untrained Virginia and North Carolina militia unlikely to stand up to redcoats in open battle. Moreover, Gates rejected de Kalb's advice and pushed his army through a barren and picked-over region. Many of the soldiers therefore succumbed to diarrhea from consuming a diet of green corn, unripened peaches, and molasses. When Gates approached Camden, South Carolina, he encountered 2,200 British troops under Gen. Charles Cornwallis on 16 August. A British charge scattered the American militia in short order. Gates's efforts to rally them failed, and he was swept along in their flight back to Charlotte. With the militia gone, Cornwallis was free to focus his efforts on de Kalb's now isolated and vulnerable Continentals. De Kalb went down with ten wounds and died in captivity three days later. Gist and Smallwood fought valiantly as well, but their efforts, as well as those of the rank and file, could not salvage the situation. Those Continentals who escaped retreated to Charlotte to join the militia. The Battle of Camden cost the Americans eight hundred killed and wounded, as well as another thousand taken prisoner. British losses amounted to only 325. In one fell swoop, the British shattered their second American army in six months, opening the door for their advance through North Carolina to Virginia.[99]

Gates did not lose his command until weeks after he lost his reputation. His crushing defeat exposed him to withering criticism of his generalship, especially from Washington supporters who viewed Gates as a continuing threat to the commander in chief and seized on Camden as an opportunity to neuter him once and for all. Plenty of American generals, including Washington, had lost battles, but Gates's flight from the field before the fighting ended put him in a different, odious, league. Alexander Hamilton, for example, wrote, "But was there ever an instance of a general running away as Gates has done from his whole army? And was there ever so precipitous a flight? One hundred and eighty miles in three days and a half. It does admirable credit to the activity of a man at his time of life. But it disgraces the general and his soldiers."[100] Camden also created dissension within the remnants of the army regrouping at Charlotte. North Carolina militia officers resented Gates's assertion that they were most responsible for the catastrophe. Opposition to Gates among Continental officers coalesced around William Smallwood, whose relationship with Gates rapidly deteriorated because Smallwood had lost confidence in Gates and feared that Gates would relieve him. To complicate matters, Gates's decision to place Smallwood in charge of the North Carolina militia alienated Jethro Sumner.

Gates tried to put the best face on the gloomy situation. He explained to Washington that the British probably captured few militiamen because they broke and ran so quickly. Moreover, the Continentals unquestionably inflicted so many casualties on the British that they were now too weak to immediately exploit their triumph. Finally, Gates claimed that the disaster had prodded North Carolina and Virginia to invest more energy into the war. Despite his efforts to maintain a positive attitude, it was difficult to hide from the reality of the situation. Word of his son's unexpected death added to his demoralization. Washington responded to Gates's letters by approving of Gates's plan to use partisans to tie down the British while he rebuilt his army, snidely observing that Camden shocked people because expectations were so high that Gates would deliver victory. Despite this cutting remark, Washington made no effort to undermine Gates, no doubt because he figured it was not necessary. Congress, for its part, took its time before removing Gates from his post. Gates was popular among many New England and Virginia delegates, and firing him might reopen old wounds associated with him. As the weeks passed and the enormity of the Camden debacle became clear, it became obvious that the Southern Department needed fresh leadership. On 5 October, fifty days after Camden, Congress finally acted. Even then, Congress pulled its punches by suspending Gates and ordering

Washington to establish a court of inquiry to investigate his actions at Camden. Congress also directed Washington to appoint a new Southern Department commander while the court did its work.[101]

People in and out of Congress bandied about various names to replace Gates. One possibility was William Smallwood. He was a southerner with military experience in the region. Although he had enemies in the Maryland line, he was popular in Congress. Others suggested Arthur St. Clair, despite the controversy surrounding his abandonment of Fort Ticonderoga in 1777. Some southerners, though, disliked the idea of appointing a Scot because so many North Carolina loyalists came from Scotland, though they failed to explain how the one would impact the other. This same odd logic disqualified another candidate, Alexander McDougall, as did his uncertain health. Interested parties could speculate and advocate all they wanted, but Congress put the final decision in Washington's hands. As far as Washington was concerned, there was only one officer for the job: Nathanael Greene. Greene had been Washington's right-hand man since the siege of Boston and had served with him in every subsequent campaign. He had plenty of experience in combat leadership and logistics and was available now that he had resigned as quartermaster general. To be sure, some congressmen still held a grudge against him because of the messy way he had ended his tenure as quartermaster, but most of the delegates backed him. In fact, three state delegations recommended him to Washington. Greene had impressed Congress with his ability to work well with both Continentals and militia, as evidenced in his success in repelling the recent British incursion into New Jersey. He was also popular within the officer corps. This was all well and good, but the big issue with Greene was his limited success in independent command. For all the know-how he had accrued over the years, he had few sparkling achievements of the kind that differentiated Arnold and Wayne from other officers. Even so, Washington sensed something special in Greene, something that had not yet manifested itself. He appreciated Greene's courage, resourcefulness, fortitude, and coolness. When Washington offered Greene the job on 14 October, he warned him that it was a tough assignment. Greene's desire to perform his duty outweighed his concerns about taking charge of a losing cause and leaving his young family behind. He wrote to a friend, "It is a most difficult command, and hitherto has proved a disgraceful one to all that has gone that way. I wish it may not be my lot."[102] As things turned out, it was perhaps the best personnel decision Washington made in the entire war.[103]

Washington promised to help Greene in any way possible, but the depressing truth was that he could spare little for the Southern Department. However, if he could not send much by way of units, supplies, or equipment, he could send someone with a proven record of creating soldiers. When Washington appointed

Greene to lead the Southern Department, Baron von Steuben was in Philadelphia bickering with Congress over plans to reorganize the office of inspector general. Steuben had done more than anyone else to transform Washington's tatterdemalion men into well-trained soldiers, so Washington hoped he could perform a similar service down south. As Washington explained his thinking to Greene, "His talents, knowledge of service, zeal and activity will make him very useful to you in all respects, and particularly in the formation and regulation of the raw troops, which will principally compose the southern army. You will give him a command suited to his rank, besides employing him as inspector general."[104] Washington also wrote to Steuben to assure him that his transfer was in no way a punishment, but rather an expression of confidence in his abilities. When Greene reached Richmond, Virginia, in mid-November, he ordered Steuben to remain there. Greene figured that Steuben could not only raise, train, and forward levies to the Carolinas but also help repel the latest British invasion of the state. By doing so, he would simultaneously secure Greene's rear and furnish the troops needed to drive the British out of the South.[105]

Greene assumed command of what was left of Gates's army at Charlotte, North Carolina, on 2 December. Conditions were worse than he expected. The troops were demoralized and had lost confidence in Gates. There were shortages of almost everything except misery. To complicate matters, Greene had to deal with some thorny personnel problems. One was William Smallwood. By the time Greene arrived, the relationship between Gates and Smallwood had broken down completely. Smallwood had no faith in Gates and was convinced that Gates was plotting to relieve him. Gates believed that Smallwood was conniving to replace him as head of the Southern Department. Greene's appearance rendered these concerns moot but did not put an end to Smallwood's unhappiness. Although Congress on 15 September unanimously promoted Smallwood to major general in recognition of his courage at Camden and of Maryland's contribution to the army, Smallwood was not satisfied with the honor. For some reason he believed that Congress should backdate his commission so that he would outrank Steuben, even though Steuben had been a major general since May 1778. As a result, Smallwood refused to serve under Steuben and threatened to quit unless Congress saw things his way. Neither Washington nor Greene understood Smallwood's logic. Greene considered Smallwood a good, sensible officer under most circumstances and tried to talk him out of leaving, but to no avail. In the end, Smallwood did not follow through with his threat and remained in the army. Greene eventually ordered him to Maryland, where he joined Gist in recruiting troops for the Maryland line. He remained there for the rest of the war.[106]

Gates was Greene's other big personnel issue. Camden had ruined Gates's reputation and exposed him to ridicule. Indeed, one congressman referred to him as "our runaway general." Washington tasked Greene with convening the court of inquiry Congress had ordered to investigate Gates's actions at Camden because the battle and witnesses were in Greene's new department. To keep the inquiry as impartial as possible, Washington excluded from its membership anyone who had fought at Camden. Whatever Washington's intentions, the upshot was to delay the inquiry indefinitely. Not only was Greene too busy campaigning against the British to organize a court, but it was impossible to locate three generals who had not been at Camden to sit on the inquiry. Gates therefore returned to his Virginia farm to await events. As the weeks turned into months, public anger against Gates cooled. When Greene had met with Gates to assume command of the Southern Department, he was touched by Gates's civility. In fact, Gates told Greene he was happy that Washington had selected Greene as his successor. On 7 December, the day before Gates left for home, Greene wrote Washington that he believed a court of inquiry would clear Gates. The following year, after looking over the Camden battlefield, Greene informed Gates that he believed Gates was more unfortunate than culpable for the disaster there. Others came around as well, especially when word got out that Gates was having trouble paying his taxes because he had spent so much time away from his farm. On 22 May 1781 Congress resolved that Gates was still eligible for active duty while waiting for his court of inquiry and ordered him to report to Washington for reassignment. At about the same time, the president of Congress, Samuel Huntington, asked Washington to find something for Gates to do. Washington responded that he wanted Gates's fate determined as soon as possible, but there was not much he could do about it so long as Greene and his army were preoccupied down south. When Washington and Gates met, Gates stated that he did not want to serve until the court of inquiry cleared his name, so he headed back to Virginia. On 14 August 1782 Congress voted unanimously to repeal its resolution calling for a court of inquiry for Gates. By then no one—not Washington, Greene, or Congress—had much desire to reopen the Camden wounds. After all, the war was almost over and Gates was no longer a threat to Washington. Gates saw this as sufficient justice for him to return to the main army for the remainder of the conflict.[107]

In terms of choosing generals, 1780 was Congress's most uneventful year of the war. Congress appointed only two major generals and one brigadier. William Smallwood's promotion to major general came through on 15 September, followed by Daniel Morgan's to brigadier on 13 October. Ten days later, Congress elevated Samuel Parsons to major general too. There was nothing extraordinary about Parsons. Born in 1737 in Connecticut but raised in Massachusetts, Parsons graduated from Harvard before returning to Connecticut to open his law practice. He served in the Connecticut legislature for eighteen sessions and became one of the colony's political leaders. He was with Ethan Allen and Benedict Arnold when they seized Fort Ticonderoga at the war's start, and later fought at Brooklyn Heights and White Plains. Congress made him a brigadier in August 1776, and since then he had served mostly in Connecticut, fretting about his health and his relationship with Washington. Congress promoted Parsons partly because he had complained that Smallwood had been unfairly advanced over his head and partly because Arnold's treason and Putnam's incapacity left Connecticut without a major general. Washington was not happy about Parsons's appointment. For one thing, he believed he had sufficient major generals. For another, he disliked Congress's selection process. Although he approved of Congress picking a state's most senior colonel as a brigadier if that state had enough men to form a brigade, he was not happy with its opaque criteria for settling on major generals. This lack of transparency and clarity risked angering brigadiers passed over by their juniors. As he put it, "For there is nothing more certain than that the promotion of junior officers over the heads of seniors, unless it is agreeable to some known and established principle, never fails to produce a good deal of discontent, ill blood, and party, which are always injurious."[108] In particular, he worried that the inimitable Knox might resign his commission if Congress elevated a more junior brigadier to major general. As things turned out, Sullivan assured Washington that most congressmen agreed with his logic, so that there would be no more "irregular and unmilitary promotions." Instead, Congress would henceforth stick to seniority.[109]

Conclusions

The number of active Continental generals gradually declined from 1778 to 1780. Eighteen generals left the army for one reason or another in the two and a half years following the Battle of Monmouth Courthouse, including eight major generals (Arnold, Gates, de Kalb, Lee, Mifflin, Putnam, Schuyler, and Sullivan) and ten brigadiers (Hogun, Maxwell, McIntosh, Moultrie, Nixon, Poor, Pułaski, Scott, Varnum, and Woodford). Of these men, two were killed in battle (de Kalb at Camden and Pułaski at Savannah), one became a traitor (Arnold), one died of illness on duty (Poor), three were captured and not exchanged until after the fighting ended (McIntosh, Moultrie, and Scott), two were captured and died in captivity (Hogun and Woodford), six resigned (Maxwell, Mifflin, Nixon, Schuyler, Sullivan, and Varnum), one was incapacitated but retained his rank (Putnam), and two were relieved or suspended from their commands (Gates and Lee). During this same period, Congress promoted only two men to major general (Parsons and Smallwood) and six to brigadier (Gist, Hogun, Huger, Irvine, Morgan, and Sumner). In each case, Congress acted mostly to placate delegations that felt that their states had been shortchanged in the allotment of generals. As a result, at the beginning of 1781 Washington had at his disposal eleven major generals (Greene, Heath, Howe, Lafayette, Lincoln, McDougall, Parsons, Smallwood, St. Clair, Steuben, and Stirling) and fifteen brigadiers (James Clinton, Duportail, Gist, Glover, Hand, Huntington, Irvine, Knox, Morgan, Muhlenberg, Paterson, Stark, Sumner, Wayne, and Weedon). They represented every state except for Delaware and Georgia.

All of the turnover in the two and a half years following the Battle of Monmouth Courthouse did not significantly improve American generalship. This was especially true in the southern states. The reinforcements Congress and Washington dispatched to the region were unable to prevent the British from overrunning Georgia and South Carolina. Robert Howe, the Southern Department commander, could not hold Savannah. His successor, Benjamin Lincoln, not only failed to retake the Georgia city but went on to lose Charleston and its garrison. Finally, Horatio Gates's attempt to redeem American fortunes in the South ended disastrously at Camden. Although Howe, Lincoln, and Gates deserved much of the blame for their defeats, they did not get much help from their subordinate generals. Indeed, poor leadership marked American efforts throughout this period. To be sure, the Americans were plagued by serious logistical and manpower problems, but their replacements faced and overcame these same difficulties later. It is also worth noting that none of the generals who fought so miserably in the South had spent much time under Washington's tutelage.

The generals fought somewhat better in the North. The American failure outside Newport was counterbalanced by several smaller accomplishments elsewhere: the Iroquois expedition, Stony Point, and foiling the British incursions into New Jersey. In each instance, capable American leadership played a major role in American success. Sullivan's successful raid through Iroquoia against the outnumbered and outgunned American Indians helped compensate for his defeat at Newport. He also received solid support from two of his subordinates, Poor and James Clinton. Greene not only fought well in a losing cause outside of Newport, but he and Maxwell led the American forces that repelled the British raid into New Jersey. Finally, Anthony Wayne supplied the dazzling American victory at Stony Point. Conversely, there were few instances of American generals committing the kind of blunders that characterized operations by their counterparts in the South. Keeping the British penned up in New York, though, was due as much to British quiescence as to American generalship.

CHAPTER 6

End of the War

1780–1783

Another Tough Winter

On 6 December 1780 Washington established his headquarters at New Windsor, New York, and placed his army into winter quarters for the sixth time. He deployed the Pennsylvania line in Morristown, the New Jersey brigade at the Clove, New York, the New York brigade in Albany, and the New England units in and around West Point. Washington was by now thoroughly accustomed to disappointment, but the meager results of the last campaign season depressed him. He had hoped that the arrival of Rochambeau's French army as well as Spain's entry into the war against Great Britain, trouble for the British in Ireland, and riots in England might finally bring a victorious end to the conflict. Instead, the American military situation had deteriorated further. In addition to New York City and Georgia, the British had conquered South Carolina and seemed well on their way to overrunning North Carolina and Virginia. Continuing inflation made maintaining the main American army more and more difficult. It had almost no provisions or magazines, and expiring enlistments meant that it might melt away before spring. The population was apathetic and demoralized, and Washington saw nothing on the horizon to change the current situation. The following spring Washington wrote, "It is perhaps, the greatest of the great evils attending this contest, that states as well as individuals, had rather wish well, than act well; had rather see a thing done, than do it; or contribute their just proportion to the doing it. This conduct is not only injurious to the common cause but in the end most expensive to themselves; besides the distrusts and jealousies which are sown by such conduct."[1] Fortunately for the American cause, Washington viewed despair not as a path to defeat and helplessness, but rather as a reminder that God's sovereignty would ultimately deliver victory. "Our affairs," he noted, "are brought to an awful crisis [so] that the hand of providence, I trust, may be more conspicuous in our deliverance."[2]

Continental generals did not face the same challenges as the rank and file, but they too had burdens to bear. Many of them were sick, tired, and broke that winter. Samuel Parsons was wracked by two bouts of fever so severe that at one point he could scarcely walk from his bed to his fire. Arthur St. Clair was afflicted by gout in his right hand, and John Stark's health broke down as well. To make matters worse, inflation and inconsistent compensation left many generals all but penniless. Stark's salary had been in arrears since December 1778, and Glover complained that he had not been paid for more than twenty months. Edward Hand had so little money that he had to ask Congress for funds so he could join Washington's army. Parsons noted that his measly nine dollars was more money than any other officer possessed in his camp. When an officer visited John Paterson at West Point, Paterson could only offer him a miserable glass of whiskey grog. Not surprisingly, once the army settled into winter quarters, many generals asked Washington for leave to go home to see family and attend to neglected personal affairs. Although Washington as usual tried to accommodate them, authorizing a furlough did not necessarily make it so. John Stark, for example, was so poor that he had to borrow money to afford the journey back to New Hampshire.[3]

The war was hard on everyone in one way or another. William Thompson's unhappiness stemmed from his inability to play a more active role in the conflict. Thompson was a well-respected Pennsylvanian whom Congress had made a brigadier in March 1776 and then dispatched at the head of a brigade to Canada, where he was captured at the Battle of Three Rivers in June. Although he was paroled and returned to Philadelphia in October, he could not rejoin the army until he was officially exchanged. Unfortunately for Thompson, this was more easily said than done because at first the Americans held so few high-ranking British officials with which to bargain. However, Thompson remained in limbo even after British generals fell into American hands. Because Washington had assured Thompson that he looked forward to serving with him again, Thompson blamed Congress for his indeterminate status. He could not understand why Congress seemed so eager to secure the release of someone like Charles Lee, who was seized more or less in bed, than someone taken on the battlefield such as himself. To him, the war and its accompanying promotions were passing him by.

On 18 November 1778 the president of Congress, William McKean, ran into Thompson in a Philadelphia coffeehouse. There a frustrated Thompson lashed out at McKean and allegedly called Congress a bunch of "damned rascals." In response, Congress charged Thompson with insulting its collective dignity and ordered a hearing, which lasted on and off for more than a month. Although most witnesses testified that Thompson directed his ire at McKean, not Congress, Thompson decided that in this instance discretion was the better part of valor and apologized if any of his words had given offense. He also asked Congress to keep in mind his situation before rendering its verdict. Just before Christmas, Congress voted to accept Thompson's apology. In 1780 Congress swapped Thompson for Hessian general Friedrich Adolf Riedesel, but by then Thompson was too ill to resume his duties. He submitted his resignation on 30 March 1781 and died in Carlisle five months later.[4]

Washington took advantage of the winter quiescence to make some necessary reassignments. He had appointed a number of ad hoc commanders to run West Point and the Hudson Highlands immediately after Arnold's defection, but on 14 October he put William Heath in charge of the area on a more permanent basis. In addition, at the end of the month he dispatched James Clinton and his brigade to Albany to defend the New York frontier against American Indian, loyalist, and British raids. Washington believed that the locals would have confidence in Clinton, and of course his relationship with his brother the governor would be all for the good. Clinton was predictably appalled by the poor conditions he found in Albany and the lack of supplies available to him. When he complained to Washington about his logistical travails, Washington offered his sympathies but little else. "Under these circumstances," Washington observed, "should the worst evils take place, that may be dreaded, you will have the pleasing consciousness of having faithfully performed your duty to the public and may rely upon their entire approbation and esteem."[5] When Washington's adjutant general, Col. Alexander Scammell, resigned his post in November to take over a regiment, Washington replaced him with Edward Hand and made him inspector general as well. Washington hoped that Hand's rank would give him sufficient clout to do his job well and would add dignity to the position. Hand, however, eventually concluded that he lacked the talent to hold both positions simultaneously because he had been on detached duty for so long that he had never seen Steuben's regimen up close.[6]

Washington also sent recently exchanged Benjamin Lincoln to Massachusetts to help recruit soldiers for the next campaign season. Washington had made no attempt to blame Lincoln for his dismal performance at Charleston and continued to value him. He figured that Lincoln could do more for the cause in his home state than twiddling his thumbs in winter quarters. When spring arrived, Washington summoned Lincoln to the main army and sent William Heath to New England to lobby state legislatures for more supplies. He hoped that Heath's stiff tact and stature as the army's senior active major general made him the right man for such a delicate mission. To replace him, Washington turned to that other Hudson Highlands mainstay: Alexander McDougall. New York had the previous October elected McDougall to Congress. McDougall spent the winter in Philadelphia and there demonstrated the same commitment to the

American cause that characterized his military life. In fact, Congress appointed him secretary of the marine. Through it all, he insisted that his military responsibilities took precedence over his civil ones. When spring arrived McDougall resigned as secretary of the marine and rejoined the army. Washington knew that McDougall would not appreciate yet another tedious stint in the Hudson Highlands, so he bought his acquiescence by assuring him that he would call him to the main army once active operations started.[7]

Considering the wretched circumstances under which they labored, it was remarkable that it took as long as it did for some Continentals to mutiny. On 1 January 1781 the 1,500 men in the Pennsylvania line near Morristown rose up against their officers, killed three of them, and embarked on a march to Philadelphia to present their grievances to Congress. American officers were hardly surprised by the uprising, and some in fact acknowledged the justice of their men's complaints. Indeed, the Pennsylvanians were not only short of food, clothing, and equipment but were also distressed about uncertain enlistment terms that kept some of them in the army longer than they thought was justified. Although the Pennsylvanians kicked St. Clair and Lafayette out of their camp, they permitted Wayne to accompany them. Wayne did so partly to protect the locals, but also to keep the lines of communications with the soldiers open.

Washington was of course deeply concerned when he heard the news. He feared that the Pennsylvanians might go over to the British, disperse and vanish into the countryside, or infect the rest of the army with their rebellious attitudes. His initial inclination was to personally confront the mutineers, but his generals recommended that he remain in New Windsor with the bulk of the army to keep an eye on the British. Washington had confidence in Wayne and urged him to mollify the rebels as much as possible without compromising the army's integrity. In the meantime, he prepared to use force if the more conciliatory approach failed. He shrewdly authorized his officers to inform their men about the Pennsylvanians' actions to give them the opportunity to declare their loyalty and instructed New England units to get ready to march. Parsons wanted to lead the New Englanders, but Howe successfully claimed the command by right of seniority. Before Washington resorted to violence, the Pennsylvanians stopped at Princeton and on 7 January opened negotiations with Wayne and Pennsylvania officials. They also handed over for execution two British emissaries who had slipped into camp. After three days of bargaining, they reached an agreement that permitted the discharge of half the Pennsylvanians and the furlough of the rest. On 20 January two hundred New Jerseyans at Pompton rose up to protest *their* conditions. This time Washington acted decisively and immediately. He sent Howe and his New Englanders to surprise and surround the New Jerseyans, who surrendered without resistance. Howe ordered the three ringleaders court-martialed and shot, and he pardoned everyone else. These incidents demonstrated both the desperation among some Continentals and the continued fidelity among the majority. It also led to the dissolution of the Pennsylvania line. Washington responded by directing Irvine and St. Clair to the Keystone State to organize a new one.[8]

Virginia was the largest, most populous, and most economically powerful of the states. It provided the Continental army not only with its commander in chief but also with a significant number of troops and generals who had participated in just about every campaign of the war. Despite its importance, the British had not paid the state much military attention since the conflict's earliest days. Except for a May 1779 raid by 1,800 redcoats that burned Suffolk, the state had not felt the hard hand of war. All this changed starting in October 1780. That month British general Alexander Leslie and 2,200 British troops raided the Virginia coast before moving southward to join Cornwallis in the Carolinas. No sooner had Leslie pulled up stakes than newly commissioned British general Benedict Arnold and 1,600 mostly loyalist soldiers landed at Westover on the James River in early January to establish a more permanent British presence in the state. Aggressive in any uniform, Arnold seized Richmond on 5 January 1781 without significant opposition. Greatly encouraged, Arnold ordered his men to fan out into the interior and destroy anything of military use to the Americans. After two weeks of pillaging and plundering, Arnold fell back to Portsmouth to await developments and further orders.

Washington saw the latest British invasion of Virginia as an opportunity to snuff out both its traitorous commander and his army. Fairly itching to fit Arnold for a noose, Washington dispatched an expedition to Virginia to cooperate with a French naval squadron in Chesapeake Bay to trap and capture the British force. Although further depleting the main army was dangerous, Washington concluded that the potential benefits outweighed the risks. He opted to substitute quality for quantity by sending Lafayette's light corps to do the job, with reinforcements from the reconstituted Pennsylvania line when they became available. Washington claimed that he put Lafayette in charge of the mission instead of Steuben, who was already on the scene, for political reasons, about which he did not elaborate. In all likelihood, he was motivated more by his affinity for his young French protégé than by anything else. This is not to say that he denigrated Lafayette's military abilities; he later noted that Lafayette "possesses uncommon military talents, is of a quick and sound judgment, persevering, and enterprising without rashness, and besides these, he is of a very conciliating temper and perfectly sober, which are qualities that rarely combine in the same person."[9]

Lafayette was predictably thrilled with the opportunity to escape the wintertime doldrums and gain glory, though he doubted he could snag Arnold. His light corps contained only 1,200 troops, but they were the flower of the American army. Moreover, Lafayette had doted on their elite status by purchasing with his own money elegant swords for the noncommissioned officers and new uniforms for the enlisted men. He had an affable and easy way of interacting with them that won their loyalty and regard. For example, when the stultifying southern heat provoked desertions, he offered to send back to their home regiments in the main army anyone who wanted to leave. Congress's ability to cough up a month's pay certainly helped maintain morale too. With these advantages, Lafayette's light corps made rapid progress southward after Washington issued the necessary orders on 20 February, sometimes marching thirty miles a day on muddy roads. Unfortunately for Lafayette, the French lost naval superiority on the Chesapeake in mid-March as he reached Annapolis, making it impossible for him to snare Arnold. That being the case, Lafayette and his light corps turned around and were trudging back north when he received new orders from Washington directing them to continue their trek southward to join Greene in the Carolinas. Although Greene desperately needed all the troops he could get, he concluded that Lafayette would better serve the American cause by defending Virginia from continued British incursions. Lafayette thereupon made Virginia his destination, entering Baltimore on 16 April, crossing the Potomac River five days later, and arriving in Richmond on 28 April.[10]

While the British raided Virginia, Nathanael Greene was undergoing his own ordeal in the Carolinas. Greene was appalled by the poor state of the army he inherited from Gates when he assumed command at Charlotte, North Carolina, on 2 December 1780. He complained that conditions were worse than he had feared, with chronic shortages of provisions, clothes, tents, discipline, and local goodwill. In fact, the only ray of sunshine was the victory of trans-Appalachian militia over a large loyalist force at the Battle of King's Mountain in western South Carolina on 8 October that compelled Cornwallis to suspend his invasion of North Carolina and retreat to Winnsboro, South Carolina. Mulling things over, Greene concluded that his lack of resources required him to take greater risks. He explained to Washington, "The southern states are in a critical situation, and great exertions and some hazard are necessary to save them."[11] He finally began to demonstrate the military genius that Washington had always suspected he possessed, but which had not fully flowered. Despite his inferiority in numbers, Greene divided his army, sending Daniel Morgan and six hundred troops westward to harass British outposts in that part of the state while he marched his remaining eight hundred soldiers to the Pee Dee River to threaten Charleston. A puzzled Cornwallis responded by splitting his own army of 2,500 men. He dispatched Lt. Col. Banastre Tarleton and 1,100 troops westward to run Morgan to ground while he used the balance of his force to screen Charleston from Greene. Unfortunately for Cornwallis, Morgan decimated Tarleton at the Battle of Cowpens on 17 January in a tactical masterpiece that cost the British over eight hundred killed, wounded, and captured.

When Cornwallis learned of Tarleton's disaster at Cowpens, he immediately marched the rest of his army westward in an attempt to overtake Morgan and his men. Greene, for his part, responded by riding cross-country with a small escort to meet Morgan and his troops on 30 January at Beattie's Ford, and from there they retreated northeastward across North Carolina just ahead of Cornwallis's hard-charging soldiers. The rest of Greene's army joined them at Guilford Courthouse, North Carolina, on 9 February, at which point the arthritic Morgan surrendered his command and returned home. Greene's army crossed the Dan River into southern Virginia on 14 February, leaving the British stranded and boatless on the southern bank.

After dispersing local loyalists and gathering more militia, Greene recrossed the Dan and on 15 March engaged the British in the Battle of Guilford Courthouse. Although Greene's 4,500 men heavily outnumbered Cornwallis's 1,900 soldiers, most of Greene's troops were unreliable militia. In the ensuing clash, superior British discipline carried the day and compelled Greene's withdrawal. Cornwallis's victory, though, cost him a quarter of his force in killed, wounded, and captured, making it impossible for him to remain in central North Carolina. After ten days of fruitless maneuvering, Cornwallis fell back to Wilmington, North Carolina, on 9 April, to secure the Royal Navy's protection and succor. Instead of pursuing, Greene opted to invade South Carolina and liberate it from the British with the help of local partisan forces. In the next six months he fought and lost three battles with the British—Hobkirk Hill (25 April), the siege of Fort Ninety Six (22 May to 19 June), and Eutaw Springs (8 September)—but in each instance he inflicted such heavy casualties on the British that they were obliged to retreat. By autumn British possessions in the South had shriveled to Savannah, Charleston, and Wilmington. Greene's generalship won kudos from within Congress and without.

British reinforcements flowed into Virginia in the spring of 1781. Cornwallis's arrival from Wilmington with his 1,400 tired soldiers on 20 May raised British strength in the state to over 7,000 troops. Cornwallis assumed overall command of British forces in the state and turned his attention to rendering it useless to the American war effort. To oppose him, Lafayette had around a thousand Continentals and some ineffective militia. Worse yet, Virginia's government disintegrated under the weight of British incursions, making it even more difficult than usual for Lafayette to supply and equip his small army. Although outnumbered and outgunned, the twenty-three-year-old Frenchman demonstrated a surprising poise, ability, and composure. He fully recognized the stakes involved and the disadvantages under which he labored, writing, "I have so many arrangements to make, so many difficulties to combat, so many enemies to deal with that I am just that much of a general as will make me an historian of misfortunes, and nail my name upon the ruins of what good folks are pleased to call the army of Virginia."[12] Knowing he lacked the strength to directly confront Cornwallis, but realizing that withdrawing into the interior would demoralize the locals and ruin his army, he therefore resolved to hang on to the British army's flanks and skirmish as much as possible in an effort to harass and annoy them until circumstances hopefully changed for the better. Doing so required considerable alertness and tactical skill to avoid the kind of surprise that brought Wayne to grief at Paoli, but Lafayette managed to maneuver his men with dexterity and aplomb. In particular, he used Virginia's extensive river system to keep just out of Cornwallis's reach. After several weeks of marauding, Cornwallis turned his troops around and headed back toward Portsmouth. Lafayette's pride in his accomplishments, though, was outweighed by his frustration in operating in what he considered a secondary theater that promised little by way of glory. He longed to join Washington and Rochambeau in a climactic assault on New York City. Washington urged him to focus on the matter at hand but also hinted that the war's focus might come to him. In the meantime, Lafayette could do little but await help and hold things together as best he could.[13]

Greene, Lafayette, and Washington all hoped that Baron von Steuben's presence in Virginia would help the state resist the British. However, Steuben proved far less effective in bringing order to Virginia's war effort than he did in training Continentals. Steuben's instincts were sound enough for him to make innumerable reasonable suggestions to state officials for improving the state's defenses. In particular, he urged them to concentrate the militia to either reinforce Greene or resist British incursions. Dispersing it, he insisted, wasted provisions and did little to protect the state. His recommendations often fell on deaf ears. State officials still exercising power were more interested in defending their local communities than in larger national considerations. For all his charm, Steuben lacked the political savvy to make them see the bigger picture. His mercurial temperament and unfamiliarity with Virginia's culture did not help matters. Local officials groused that Steuben meddled too much in minutiae; they even questioned his courage. Indeed, he became a convenient scapegoat for the state's woes. Small wonder that Steuben wrote to Edward Hand in April 1781: "I wish it was in my power to give you a pleasing account of affairs in this part of the continent; but indeed every thing is gloomy, very little in our favor, and appearances entirely against us." Ever the optimist, though, Steuben concluded, "We must do and suffer; and if by any means we may obtain the prize we fight for, the price can scarcely be too great."[14]

Although Lafayette initially praised Steuben's exertions, he became increasingly concerned as the complaints mounted against him. "The conduct of the Baron [Steuben]," Lafayette wrote to Washington, "is to me unintelligible. Every man, woman, and child in Virginia is roused against him. They dispute even on his courage, but I cannot believe their assertions."[15] Lafayette's loyalty to his friends was strong, but not absolute. He eventually concluded that Steuben had become more of a liability than an asset and asked Washington to reassign him. Washington was dismayed by these unexpectedly severe criticisms directed at Steuben but refrained from judging him from four hundred miles away. When the denunciations continued to pour in, though, Washington decided that Steuben's usefulness in Virginia was at an end and on 13 June promised Lafayette he would recall Steuben in such a way as to preserve his honor. As for Steuben, he found his sojourn in Virginia enormously frustrating and miserable. His temper soured and he developed a rash. He grumbled about shortsighted and uncooperative officials, unenthusiastic and surly militia, his lack of authority, and chronic shortages of just about everything a respectable army required. There was more than a little truth in his assertions, and it is quite likely that no one could put the state on a proper war footing. Steuben knew that his inability to do so rendered him supernumerary, so by mid-April he was ready to surrender his post and join Greene in a more purely military role in the Carolinas. By then, though, he had become so ill that he retired to the Charlottesville region until he recovered in September.[16]

Lafayette placed more hope in the reinforcements Congress and Washington promised him. After the January mutiny led to the dissolution of the Pennsylvania line, Washington assigned Arthur St. Clair and William Irvine to work with Pennsylvania authorities to reconstitute the unit. Although both generals complained about the prevailing apathy they encountered, recruits gradually trickled in. On 20 February Congress voted to send them southward to Greene, but Washington redirected them to Virginia instead. He also opted to send the first detachment as soon as possible and then follow up with the rest. Because of recent disciplinary problems with the Pennsylvanians, Washington figured that he better appoint a brigadier to lead and keep them in line. Irvine was one possibility. Washington passed him over, ostensibly because he was busy recruiting, but more likely because his record was not as good as the officer Washington did select: Anthony Wayne. Washington had faith in Wayne, who had proven himself repeatedly as a dynamic combat commander. Wayne had gone home on leave after his role in quelling the Pennsylvania line mutiny, but he hurried to York to organize the levies there. However, a lack of horses and money prevented him from marching southward as soon as he wanted. Both Washington and especially Lafayette lamented what Lafayette termed Wayne's "unaccountable delay." The day before he finally set out, Wayne faced a disciplinary crisis when a few soldiers declined to move until they were paid in specie. Wayne responded by directing his troops to their tents, but when some refused, officers knocked them down and arrested them. Wayne then ordered on-the-spot court-martials that quickly condemned the soldiers to death by firing squads, which sentences were carried out a few hours later. Though pleased with the restoration of order, Wayne was pained by the method necessary to achieve it. On 26 May Wayne and approximately one thousand Pennsylvania Continentals trudged southward. Wayne drove them hard through heavy rains, so they reached the Potomac River on 31 May, crossed over the next day, and joined Lafayette's men on the North Anna River on 10 June.[17]

Cornwallis began withdrawing southeastward a few days after Wayne's Continentals joined Lafayette's little army. Lafayette pursued with about 3,600 men, mostly militia. When Cornwallis reached the James River, he saw an opportunity to cripple the persistent French officer by luring him into a trap. He deployed a small number of men out in the open north of the river as bait and concealed the rest of his army nearby in some woods. When Lafayette approached in midafternoon on 6 July, he sent Wayne and nine hundred Continentals to gobble up what he assumed was the British rear guard before it could scurry across the river. By the time Lafayette discovered the truth, the British had already sprung their trap. Suddenly confronted by two thousand British troops, Wayne ordered a counterattack that compelled the British to recoil. He used the resulting confusion, as well as the gathering darkness, to slip away, ending the Battle of Green Spring Farm. Although the Americans suffered twice as many losses as the British—139 to 70—Lafayette and Wayne managed to paint the action as a success. For one thing, the British retreated across the James the next day, leaving the Americans in control of the field. For another, they claimed to have inflicted more than three hundred casualties on the enemy. Finally, Wayne's bold maneuver against great odds impressed people. The generals' united and deceptive narrative generated kudos from sources who did not know any better, including Washington. In reality, the Americans were lucky to have escaped intact, and the engagement did little to hinder British plans to hole up in Yorktown.[18]

The Siege of Yorktown

On 21 May Washington and Rochambeau met at Wethersfield, Connecticut, to discuss plans for future operations. Washington again lobbied hard for a Franco-American assault on New York City. Rochambeau, though, continued to have reservations about the practicality of such an attack and argued instead for a campaign in Virginia. Washington considered Virginia a secondary theater and figured that the British would evacuate their forces from the state after they lost

New York City. Because he was under orders to defer to Washington, Rochambeau reluctantly agreed to prepare to assail New York City, but he obtained a promise from Washington to operate wherever the French fleet took up position and achieved naval supremacy. Washington was unaware that Rochambeau had already written to the commander of the French fleet, Francois Joseph Paul, comte de Grasse, to urge him to sail to Chesapeake Bay. On 19 June Rochambeau's French troops departed from Newport and after an eighteen-day march reached Washington's army at Dobb's Ferry. While the two armies looked one another over, Washington took stock of the situation. French reluctance and the disinclination of the states to furnish the necessary resources to overrun New York City convinced Washington to take a more flexible view of the strategic situation. He was therefore not terribly disappointed when on 14 August Rochambeau got word from de Grasse that his fleet had left Haiti eight days earlier bound for the Chesapeake, not New York. With that, de Grasse set in motion the chain of events that cumulated in victory at Yorktown two months later.[19]

The Franco-American march to Virginia began on 19 August. Moving 2,500 American and more than 4,000 French soldiers four hundred miles over bad roads past the British garrison in New York City presented innumerable logistical and organizational problems. In terms of personnel, Washington's big challenge was deciding who to take with him. Defending the Hudson Highlands was obviously a vital mission, but it was unsurprising that some generals interpreted orders to stay behind as evidence that Washington lacked confidence in them. Washington appointed William Heath to command those troops remaining in the North. Heath was an obvious choice for a couple reasons. First of all, he was the army's highest-ranking major general and was therefore by right of seniority entitled to such an important job. But there was more to it than that. Although there was nothing outstanding about Heath, whose combat record was undistinguished, Washington had over the years grown to respect him for his devotion, hard work, administrative ability, and diplomatic skills. True to Washington's expectations, Heath uttered no complaints about his assignment.[20]

The other major generals up north responded to their assignments depending on their personal circumstances. Stirling was, after Heath, the army's most senior major general and was therefore a prime candidate to accompany Washington to Virginia, but he was also increasingly infirm. He had never really recovered from a January 1780 raid he led on Staten Island. The freezing rain so injured his already delicate health that he could no longer spend more than an hour at a time in the saddle without enduring great pain. Washington doubted that he could withstand the rigors of a long march to Virginia and opted to leave him behind. Stirling agreed with Washington's assessment of his condition and did not complain.[21]

Arthur St. Clair had written to ask Washington for a more active job even before Washington and Rochambeau determined on their adventure to Virginia. Washington responded that there were not enough troops and units in the main army to accommodate another major general. He urged St. Clair to remain in Pennsylvania for now to focus on his recruiting duties and attend to his sick wife. Of Washington's three division commanders—Howe, Lincoln, and Parsons—Washington chose to take Lincoln to Virginia. For all of Lincoln's military shortcomings, Washington continued to value him for his character. Robert Howe was offended by Washington's decision to keep him outside of New York City. When he complained to Washington, Washington explained that he based his selections on seniority. By that criteria, Lincoln deserved the assignment more. Washington, however, was not being completely honest with Howe. Although Howe outranked Alexander McDougall, Washington had asked McDougall if he wanted to participate in the Virginia campaign. In all likelihood, Washington simply liked and respected McDougall more than Howe and concluded that the former would be more of an asset in the upcoming operation. As it was, McDougall declined the offer, perhaps because of his poor health, choosing instead to continue in charge of the Hudson Highlands.[22]

Choosing brigadiers for the march to Virginia proved an easier task for Washington. He took along Duportail as chief engineer, Hand as adjutant general, and Knox as artillery chief. As for combat units, he selected the New Jersey and New York brigades to participate in the campaign, as well as various miscellany. James Clinton still led the New Yorkers, but New Jersey no longer had a brigadier for its brigade, so command had devolved on Col. Elias Dayton. Leaving the New Englanders behind meant leaving behind their commanders too. As a result, John Glover, John Paterson, Jedediah Huntington, and John Stark did not get the opportunity to march southward. Congress had appointed Stark to run the Northern Department the previous June, but the other three brigadiers spent the campaign under Heath keeping an eye on the British garrison in New York City.

Washington knew from hard and unhappy experience that military plans rarely survived contact with the enemy. Unforeseen events almost always ruined even his most well-thought-out designs. There were, however, exceptions to every rule, and fortunately for him the Yorktown campaign proved one of them. In this instance, almost everything that needed to go right did so. Although Washington attributed his successes to Providence, good planning and British indecision contributed to the outcome as well. The Franco-American army left White Plains on 19 August and arrived at King's Ferry on the Hudson River the next day. A shortage of shipping made traversing the river a long-drawn-out process, so the last men and their baggage did not reach the west bank until 25 August. From there the army skirted Staten Island as if getting into position to assail New York City, but then plunged southward deep into New Jersey. The soldiers put Trenton behind them on 29 August, crossed the Delaware River, and paraded through Philadelphia from 2 to 4 September.

Washington was at Chester, Pennsylvania, the following day when he learned that de Grasse and his French fleet had arrived in the Chesapeake safely, secured naval supremacy, and landed three thousand French troops to help Lafayette trap Cornwallis in Yorktown. After reading the message, he trotted down to the Delaware River shore to frantically beckon a boat carrying Rochambeau and his staff downstream. As soon as Rochambeau disembarked, an overjoyed Washington embraced him and broke the good news. Two days later, he informed Lafayette, "Everything has hitherto succeeded agreeably to my desires and expectations."[23] Meanwhile, the French and American soldiers plodded southwestward to Head of Elk, where some boarded vessels that transported them to the Virginia Peninsula. Others had to continue to Baltimore or Annapolis to find watercraft there. Washington took advantage of proximity to make his first trip in six years to his Mount Vernon home. He spent four days there entertaining Rochambeau and his staff, looking over his property and accounts, and resting. He left on 13 September and rode into Williamsburg the next day. He was greeted by happy locals and an ecstatic and affectionate Lafayette. The first Continentals from New York showed up five days later, and by 25 September the entire Franco-American army was on hand to besiege the British at Yorktown.

Washington reorganized his army for the siege of Yorktown to accommodate its disparate units. As usual, he separated the militia from the Continentals. He divided his Continentals into three divisions of two brigades apiece. He kept the troops he brought from New York under Lincoln, with James Clinton at the head of one brigade and Elias Dayton the other. He assigned the light infantry to a division under Lafayette. Col. Moses Hazen commanded one of its brigades. As for the other, Washington gave it to Peter Muhlenberg, the preacher-turned-soldier who had led a Virginia brigade at Brandywine and Germantown. Washington had sent Muhlenberg to Virginia to help organize the state's militia in the spring of 1780. Washington had always respected Muhlenberg and took advantage of an open slot in Lafayette's outfit to give him a more active position. Finally, Washington created a third division for the recently recovered Steuben, whose usefulness with the Virginia state government was at an end. He fleshed it out with Wayne's Pennsylvania brigade and a new and recently arrived Maryland brigade raised by Mordecai Gist. Although Wayne was recovering from a thigh wound inflicted by one of Lafayette's sentinels, he insisted that he was fit enough to mount a horse and lead troops in an emergency.[24]

After consultations with de Grasse and Rochambeau, Washington marched the Franco-American army from Williamsburg to Yorktown on 28 September to formally open the siege. By then Cornwallis was obviously in serious trouble. His eight thousand troops were cut off from outside help and outnumbered two to one. Moreover, Yorktown was not well situated to withstand a siege, and an abundance of French and American artillery would soon demolish those defenses the British managed to erect. The French and Americans began digging their first parallel, two miles long, on 5 October. Washington was among those on hand to start the process. By 9 October the soldiers had moved enough dirt to emplace cannons, which commenced a brutal bombardment of British lines. The French and Americans twisted the knot tighter by starting construction of a second parallel on 11 October and overrunning a couple of British redoubts three days later that were interfering with operations. All this activity was of course important work and necessary for victory, but the campaign's decisive event had actually occurred more than a month earlier, before the first soldier put his back into shoveling a single speck of earth—and involved not a single American. In early September a British fleet appeared off the Virginia coast to contest de Grasse's control of Chesapeake Bay and relieve Cornwallis's beleaguered garrison. The ensuing Battle of the Virginia Capes on 5 September lasted for four hours. Although tactically a draw—the British lost 336 men and sustained damage to six ships, whereas the French suffered 220 killed and wounded and two crippled ships—the British turned the engagement into a strategic defeat by withdrawing to New York City and leaving Cornwallis to his fate.

As September turned into October, both army officers and civilians grew increasingly confident in victory at Yorktown. This started at the top with Washington, who on 6 October wrote, "I am not apt to be sanguine, but I think in all human probability Lord Cornwallis must fall into our hands."[25] American and French officers agreed. Wayne, for instance, commented, "Unless fortune is uncommonly kind, Lord Cornwallis and his army must submit to our combined forces."[26] Such optimism, along with a commonsense view of the situation, proved contagious. Word spread that the French and Americans were on the verge of a major military success. Virginia militiamen arrived in growing numbers to be in on the kill. Washington complained that all the spectators flocking to view the siege were interfering with soldiers' efforts prosecute it. When St. Clair got word of the unfolding triumph, he hustled to Virginia to participate, only to be disappointed that Washington did not have a command for him commensurate with his rank.[27]

Inevitability, though, did not negate the death, danger, and destruction common to eighteenth-century battlefields. While standing in one of the captured redoubts, Alexander Hamilton and Henry Knox got into an argument over the propriety of soldiers calling out a warning when a shell appeared overhead. Hamilton thought it unmilitary and detrimental to discipline, but the more humane Knox believed it showed concern for the troops' welfare. At that point a soldier yelled, "A shot! A shot!" As Hamilton and Knox scrambled for cover, Hamilton frantically attempted to place Knox's burly frame between him and danger. After the shell exploded, Knox threw Hamilton off and bellowed, "Let me tell you not to make a breastwork of me again!"[28]

On the morning of 17 October, a British drummer and officer mounted a parapet and exposed themselves to the continuous Franco-American bombardment. While the drummer beat for a parley, the officer held up a white handkerchief. The guns gradually fell silent as French and American officers noticed the pair and ordered the artillerymen to cease fire. An American officer jogged over, tied a handkerchief around the eyes of his British counterpart, and escorted him to Washington's headquarters. There the British officer produced a letter from Cornwallis proposing surrender. After more than twelve hours of negotiations by Washington's and Cornwallis's subordinates, the Americans, British, and French agreed to terms. On the nineteenth, the British army, colors furled and accompanied by a band, marched out of Yorktown between two rows of soldiers, the French on the right and the Americans on the left. Lafayette noticed that the British were looking only at the French, so he ordered his division's band to play "Yankee Doodle," which caused British heads to snap toward the Americans. Cornwallis pled illness and remained behind. When his second-in-command, Brig. Gen. Charles O'Hara, attempted to hand his sword to Rochambeau, the French general motioned to Washington. Washington, in turn, directed him to give it to his second-in-command, Benjamin Lincoln, to help compensate his pride for defeat at Charleston. Then the British, Hessian, and loyalist troops grounded their weapons and trudged into captivity. There were around 8,000 of them, not counting the 326 wounded and 309 killed during the siege. The French and Americans, for their part, lost 72 killed and 180 injured.[29]

At three in the morning on 22 October, an express rider galloped into Philadelphia with word of Cornwallis's surrender. Someone brought him to the house of the president of Congress, Thomas McKean. After the rider delivered his dispatches to McKean, an old German watchman started disseminating the exclusive in a loud, sonorous, and accented voice: "Bast dree o'clock and Gornwallis isht taken!" Despite the early hour, the news spread rapidly through the city, so by dawn the rejoicing had already begun. However, the state's executive council delayed the official public celebration until one of Washington's aides arrived on the twenty-fourth to confirm Cornwallis's capitulation. Then citizens illuminated the city to mark the occasion—and broke the doors and windows of the homes of Quakers whose sympathy to the patriot cause they doubted. Congress, for its part, decided to march in procession to the Dutch Lutheran Church to give thanks to God for victory at Yorktown. Five days later, it also resolved its appreciation to Washington, Rochambeau, and de Grasse for their efforts and called for the erection of a marble column at Yorktown to commemorate the triumph there.[30]

It is hard to underestimate the consequences of the Franco-American triumph at Yorktown. Most obviously, it eliminated from the strategic chessboard an entire British field army of eight thousand men. Worse yet, Britain's finite resources and the strains of fighting the Americans and their European allies throughout the globe made these soldiers all but irreplaceable. Without sufficient troops with which to wage the war, the British were reduced to a handful of beachheads along the Atlantic coast at New York City, Wilmington, Charleston, and Savannah. These cities might prove useful as bargaining chips, but they would not win the conflict for the British. Moreover, the same French naval superiority that had doomed Cornwallis's army threatened these remaining British strongholds as well. The victory also raised American morale, proved that fruitful Franco-American cooperation was possible, and demonstrated the American army's growing professionalism. Most important of all, Yorktown convinced British policymakers that there was no way to militarily crush the rebellion and keep their wayward colonies in the British Empire. From that point on, the British focused on extricating themselves from their American quagmire under the best terms they could obtain.

The Yorktown campaign also had an impact on the generals' roster. Although Washington lauded Lafayette, Lincoln, Steuben, Knox, and Duportail in his general orders, the last two officers were most affected by his praise. Duportail had done his usual fine job as chief engineer in laying out siege lines and emplacing artillery, though illness prevented him from witnessing Cornwallis's surrender. Once the British capitulated, Duportail asked Washington to recommend him to Congress both for a promotion to major general and a furlough to travel home to France. The two requests were interrelated because Duportail believed that returning to France with a major general's commission would make his advancement in the French army more likely when he rejoined it. Washington, however, hesitated. He did not doubt Duportail's value or ability and had in fact gone on record as stating that the French officer was indispensable to the army, but he worried that endorsing his appointment to major general would anger more senior brigadiers. By way of compromise, Washington informed Congress of Duportail's outstanding service at Yorktown and his desire for leave. Congress took the hint and on 16 November gave him permission to go to France for six months while elevating him to major general based on his performance at Yorktown, not his seniority. Shortly thereafter Duportail departed for France and did not come back until December 1782.[31]

Knox's journey to major general was more difficult and contentious than Duportail's. The same day Congress elevated Duportail, it rejected Knox's promotion by a seven-to-two state vote. This result was surprising not only because Knox had Washington's backing, but also because most congressmen respected him and recognized his immense contribution to the artillery branch. Congress, however, apparently balked because it was unsure whether Washington believed Knox's actions at Yorktown were sufficiently meritorious. To elevate him for any other reason contradicted Congress's decision the previous May to rely on seniority in selecting major generals. Doing so for reasons other than merit would also alienate those brigadiers senior to Knox: James Clinton, William Moultrie, and Lachlan McIntosh. That being the case, Congress opted not to act.

Knox was predictably unhappy with this turn of events and seriously considered resigning his commission. Friends such as Greene urged patience and opined that Congress would sooner or later do right by him. In the meantime, Washington applied more pressure on Congress on Knox's behalf. He assured Congress that Knox warranted a major generalship based on both his overall abilities and his exemplary performance at Yorktown. In fact, Washington stated that Knox was, if anything, more worthy than Duportail, and that if Knox did not deserve a promotion, then no one did. On 22 March 1782 a congressional committee recommended appointing both Knox and Moultrie to major general. A delegate responded by nominating Clinton, Moultrie, McIntosh, and Knox as major generals, but Congress said no by a seven-to-four state vote. Most congressmen believed that the army already had too many major generals, and that choosing four more simply to placate the egos of some of them was unwise and unsound. A second motion to advance Moultrie and Knox also failed. Finally, Congress decided by nine states to three to advance just Knox and to backdate his commission to 15 November 1781 so he would outrank Duportail. Happily for everyone there, Duportail's absence meant he was in no position to protest. Moultrie and McIntosh, however, were on hand in Philadelphia to register their objections. Neither was pleased to see a more junior officer leap ahead of them. One congressman spelled out and criticized Congress's dilemma in trying to reconcile respect for seniority with its desire to reward excellence: "I am as sensible as any man living of General Knox's merit. But in my opinion no merit whatsoever can justify the promotion of one officer in a way that disgraces another. It is a measure unjust in itself. It is moreover highly impolitic as it gives general uneasiness to the army. In this case there are three brigadiers disgraced, and probably three states affronted."[32] Fortunately for Knox, his unquestioned value, Washington's unwavering support, and worries that he might otherwise quit overcame Congress's ephemeral devotion to seniority.[33]

Denouement

After Yorktown Washington marched most of his Continentals back to the Hudson River to confront the British garrison in New York City. The French army remained in Virginia for the winter and did not return to Newport until the following spring. Despite the ultimately decisive Franco-American victory at Yorktown, the war continued for another two years. In fact, negotiations among American, British, and French diplomats did not begin in earnest until April 1782. During this time, the British left the Americans alone and focused their resources on defending or reclaiming other parts of their empire. Washington wanted to exploit his Yorktown triumph by aggressively assailing the remaining British strongholds along the Atlantic coast, and worried, quite rightly, that Congress and the states would take advantage of British passivity to scale back the American war effort in a premature attempt to save money.[34]

The end of large-scale fighting did not prevent continuing turnover in the army's high command. One important change had been in the works since before Yorktown. In February 1781 Congress decided to replace the cumbersome Board of War with a secretary of war—the official title was "secretary at war"—to oversee the American war effort. Delegates were unable to immediately agree on someone to fill the new post. Washington suggested John Sullivan, but his nomination sparked so much controversy—Sullivan, as it turned out, was as quarrelsome in Congress as in the army—that congressmen opted to table it to avoid a contentious and divisive debate. In the ensuing weeks a consensus emerged that Nathanael Greene was the best man for the job, but everyone also agreed that he was needed more in the Southern Department than in a Philadelphia office. Others proposed Philip Schuyler. Although Congress rejected Schuyler because it concluded that the assignment should go to someone as a reward for performance in the field, the dissension in Congress that had accompanied Schuyler's stint as Northern Department commander was undoubtedly the primary reason for his disqualification. William Heath and Henry Knox were two other possibilities. Knox's genial personality, tremendous work ethic, and familiarity with the army's needs were offset by the difficulty in replacing him as artillery chief. As for Heath, his admirable qualities were negated by a feeling among some delegates that he was too hesitant for such an important responsibility. Finally, Congress zeroed in on Benjamin Lincoln. Despite his ill-starred combat record, congressmen appreciated his integrity, common sense, industriousness, and ability to work well with Washington. These positive traits overcame concerns that he might not possess the sufficient fortitude for a secretary of war. He would, opined one delegate, make a good, but not great, secretary of war. On that rather tepid note, Congress on 30 October made the appointment official.[35]

Victory at Yorktown gave Washington the opportunity to redeploy troops and generals to other departments where they might make a difference. Soon after Cornwallis surrendered, Washington ordered the Pennsylvania, Maryland, and Virginia lines southward either to wrest Wilmington from the British or to reinforce Greene outside of Charleston. Washington originally wanted Marquis de Lafayette to lead the detachment. Lafayette had proven himself a skilled commander in Virginia and was usually eager for a new combat assignment. Moreover, as a Frenchman he was more likely to understand and work well with de Grasse in any combined operations. However, Lafayette declined the offer because he wanted to return to France. Washington then turned to Arthur St. Clair. Despite St. Clair's unremarkable military record, Washington had always respected and supported him, perhaps out of gratitude for St. Clair's astute advice during the Trenton-Princeton campaign. Besides, Lincoln's reassignment and Steuben's unpopularity made St. Clair the only available Continental major general in Virginia for the job. St. Clair got his men under way as soon as possible, but logistical problems stemming from incompetent quartermasters and Virginia's dysfunctional state government so retarded his march that he had only reached Richmond by 14 November. When he learned that the British had evacuated Wilmington on 18 November, St. Clair directed his soldiers to South Carolina. They reached Greene's army on 3 January 1782 after a fifty-seven-day trek. No sooner had they arrived than St. Clair asked Washington for permission to travel to Pennsylvania to attend to his private affairs, which included his wife's deteriorating mental health. As far as St. Clair could tell, there was little chance that the British would venture out of their Charleston and Savannah strongholds anyway. Washington approved St. Clair's request, and he departed in mid-April.[36]

Washington wanted Anthony Wayne to lead the Pennsylvania troops in St. Clair's detachment. Wayne, though, asked for either a short leave of absence or permission to travel to South Carolina independent of St. Clair's march. Although Wayne referenced his wound to justify his requests, in all likelihood he did not want to accompany or serve under St. Clair, toward whom he harbored a long-standing grudge. Washington was ordinarily sympathetic to generals wanting furloughs, but in this case he insisted that Wayne head southward, though he did not object to Wayne traveling separately from St. Clair. Wayne reached Greene's army at Round O, South Carolina, on 4 January 1782. Greene's knowledge of Wayne's antipathy toward St. Clair was probably one reason why he ordered Wayne to take a small contingent of troops to Georgia to keep the British penned in Savannah, hold the loyalists in check, and stop American Indian raids. Wayne was appalled by the logistical problems he faced there and complained that supplying his small force was akin to making bricks without straw. Despite innumerable obstacles, Wayne succeeded in his missions. When the British evacuated Savannah in July, Greene gave Wayne much of the credit for securing the state.[37]

Washington did not initiate all the high-ranking personnel changes that autumn. On 24 September 1781 Congress appointed William Irvine head of the Western Department to replace Daniel Brodhead. Irvine was shocked by the dissension and inefficiency that greeted him at Fort Pitt. Washington, however, was hardly surprised by it, having corresponded with previous department chiefs over the years. Although William Heath did not believe rumors of an impending British attack down Lake Champlain into northern New York, he sent Stirling with an eight-hundred-man detachment to Albany to reinforce the Northern Department commander, John Stark, in mid-November. Heath also told Stirling not to interfere with Stark's dispositions unless there was a military emergency. As it was, Stark was more than happy to get any kind of help and support. Despite Sullivan's successful expedition against the Iroquois in 1779, American Indians and loyalists continued to raid the New York frontier. Stark wrote, "Murder and robberies are committed every day in this neighborhood. So you may judge of my situation, with the enemy on my front, and the devil in my rear."[38] Worse yet, Stark was so short of money, provisions, and equipment that he could not supply the few troops he had. Stark and Stirling got along very well, so the awkward command situation did not have an adverse impact on operations. When the rumored British offensive failed to materialize, Stirling returned southward in late November.[39]

Lafayette's departure from Boston on 18 December marked the last major personnel change among the army's generals for the year. Congress had on 23 November authorized his return to France and asked him to do what he could to facilitate and accelerate the transfer of supplies from France when he arrived. This time, Lafayette came home with real and substantial accomplishments under his belt. Washington was merely the most prominent official who acknowledged his skill in defending Virginia from British depredations earlier in the year. Congress was sufficiently impressed to pass an awkwardly worded resolution addressed to the French king that stated:

> The Marquis de Lafayette has in this campaign so greatly added to the reputation he had before on various occasions acquired and contributed so much with inferior forces to preserve one of the most important states in the union, as well as to the brilliant success at York and Gloucester, that we cannot but wish to procure for him your majesty's favorable attention. And in that view have directed that he should have the honor to present this letter of congratulations to your majesty.

Lafayette continued lobbying and working for the American cause in France, and he remained there for the remainder of the conflict.[40]

Washington spent much of the winter of 1781–82 in Philadelphia, while his Continentals returned to New York and wintered in Newburgh. By the time Washington joined his army in late March, it was increasingly obvious that the war was winding down. Although most of the army's generals stayed on out of a sense of duty and in hopes of securing a pension, two generals took advantage of the quiescence to resign that summer. The first was John Glover. Glover had provided his children with a mother by remarrying in 1781, but then his health broke down. When Glover informed Washington that he could no longer perform his duty, Washington forwarded his letter to Congress with a note suggesting that he be retired with half pay. Glover had not played a major role in the war for several years, but Washington had always valued him for his actions at Long Island, Pell's Point, and Trenton. Samuel Parsons was the other general who resigned in 1782. Like Glover, Parsons had become too ill to remain in the army. Unlike Glover, Parsons initially could not make up his mind whether to step down. He probably worried that if he quit he might lose out on any pension Congress approved, though he claimed that patriotism was behind his reluctance. Parsons had served faithfully but had never had much opportunity to distinguish himself. Washington did not regard Parsons as highly as he did Glover and was frustrated by his indecision. Even so, he respected Parsons's long commitment to the cause, so he recommended that Congress grant him half pay for life as well. Congress initially balked at providing Glover and Parsons such pensions but reversed its decision on 22 July.[41]

The end of serious fighting did not stop the dissension that periodically wracked the army's officer corps. In fact, one of the most serious conflicts erupted that winter and dragged on until late summer 1782. While William Heath kept an eye on the British garrison in New York City during the Yorktown campaign, Alexander McDougall was overseeing the Hudson Highlands. There was long-standing bad blood between the two men. During the New York City campaign, McDougall had mocked Heath's argument that the army should try to hold on to the city, long after the folly of such a strategy became obvious. As far as McDougall was concerned, Heath's chronic micromanaging interfered with the orderly maintenance of his department. On 29 November 1781 an angry McDougall wrote to Heath:

> But permit me at the same time to inform you that it is my determination for the future to disobey every unmilitary and absurd order which may be given by any of your executive officers, and to put them in arrest, however disagreeable it may be to me, if any such are handed to this garrison; *not from any personal dislike of them,* but to have the path of service more fixed and settled than it seems to have been, since I have lately had the honor of serving under your orders.[42]

Whatever his drawbacks and weaknesses, William Heath was hardly the kind of officer to let a subordinate dictate to him. He responded that McDougall had a strange understanding of military prerogatives if he believed he could pick and choose which orders to obey. When Heath subsequently learned that McDougall had been badmouthing him to fellow officers, he placed him under arrest and ordered his court-martial. He accused McDougall of distributing supplies without his consent, failing to report the escape of British prisoners, requisitioning clothing without his approval, insulting him, giving improper orders, and undermining confidence in him by referring to him as a "knave" in front of other officers. McDougall denied the charges and referred to Heath's treatment as "frivolous and vexatious."

Washington was, not surprisingly, unhappy to learn of this distracting clash between two generals whom he respected. Had he been present, he could have settled the dispute quietly and informally as a friend to both men. Now, however, he determined he had no choice but to organize a court-martial for McDougall whose verdict he would feel obligated to respect. As he explained to McDougall, "I will conclude this subject with observing that as you are both gentlemen for whom I have a high and equal esteem, I shall be affected by the decision of the court, in whose ever favor it may terminate."[43] As things turned out, convening the court-martial was not only time-consuming, but also generated more turmoil than Washington expected. When McDougall learned that Washington had assigned Stirling as president of the court, he complained that Stirling was not competent enough for the job and asked for someone else. Stirling replied to Washington that he was happy to withdraw, but he was actually so offended by McDougall's insult that after the court-martial he challenged him to a duel, which, fortunately for both, never occurred. In the end, a court headed by Howe on 28 August acquitted McDougall of seven of the eight charges, finding him guilty only of publicly insulting Heath. By way of punishment, the court sentenced him to a public reprimand from Washington. Washington issued the censure in the gentlest manner possible, stating, "It is with extreme reluctance the commander in chief finds himself under the necessity of carrying the sentence of the court upon the seventh charge into execution more especially as it concerns an officer of so high rank and generally acknowledged merit."[44] To his credit, McDougall accepted the punishment with minimal fuss. To demonstrate his continued confidence in McDougall, Washington also offered him command of a division should his health permit.[45]

On 19 December 1781 Congress resolved that Washington periodically inform Lincoln how many generals he needed for the war. Lincoln in turn would then order the superfluous generals retired on half pay as a cost-cutting measure. Washington responded on 21 March 1782 that he needed every general he had. He explained that the main army contained eight brigades, each of which required a brigadier. Unfortunately, he had only four brigadiers available to lead them: Clinton, Huntington, Paterson, and Stark. Hand was serving as adjutant general, and the rest of the army's brigadiers were either in other departments or on detached duty. As for major generals, Washington had nine slots for them: four divisions, two wings, the light corps, West Point and the Hudson Highlands, and the Northern Department. To occupy these posts, Washington had six major generals on hand: Gates, Heath, Howe, McDougall, Parsons, and Stirling. Duportail, Knox, and Steuben were also present, but they were currently filling specialized positions as chief of engineering, artillery commander, and inspector general. He did not even mention the need for generals in other departments. Finally, Washington wrote that generals were also essential to organizing, training, and commanding the militia when it was called out. Washington noted that he could free up some major generals by eliminating his divisions, but not enough to produce the surplus Congress believed existed.[46]

Secretary at War Lincoln was caught between Congress's desire to save money by jettisoning surplus generals and Washington's conviction that he needed more of them. His solution was to improve the manner in which Congress appointed generals. On 18 January 1782 Lincoln issued a report calling for Congress to repeal its resolution from the previous May fixing the number of generals and relying on strict seniority to supply them. Lincoln believed that Congress's dependence on seniority constituted an abdication of its responsibilities and reduced its flexibility in making important personnel decisions. Moreover, he was convinced that using the seniority principle made it difficult for Congress to retire superfluous generals. He wanted to instead reward states that produced soldiers for the army by giving them additional generals. Congress did not endorse his report until August. Both Lincoln and Washington, though, recognized that this new system penalized good officers from small states. Because these states could not provide enough men to form brigades, it was impossible for their officers to become brigadiers. After consulting with Washington, Lincoln suggested rectifying the problem by combining regiments from smaller states into brigades and promoting the most senior colonel to command each one. As for selecting major generals, Lincoln figured that Congress should continue to rely on seniority. Although Congress declined to transform Lincoln's recommendations into law, it more or less adhered to his proposal for the remainder of the conflict.[47]

In October Congress appointed its last major general of the war: William Moultrie. Congress had the previous March deeply offended James Clinton, Lachlan McIntosh, and Moultrie by promoting Henry Knox over their heads. Indeed, Washington had to dissuade all three officers from resigning their commissions in protest. Clinton and Moultrie responded by pulling every string at their disposal to convince Congress to select them for promotion as well. Clinton secured the backing of the New York delegation, his brother the governor, and William Heath to lobby on his behalf. Moultrie not only rounded up plenty of supporters in and out of Congress but also presented evidence to a congressional committee that Congress had always intended to elevate him to major general, but that the circumstances had never been quite right. He reminded the committee that Congress had voted him its thanks after his successful defense of Charleston Harbor in June 1776, and then three years later had assigned him to lead the Southern Department when it appeared likely that Lincoln would have to give up that post due to illness. On 15 October the South Carolina delegation nominated Moultrie for a major generalship, but Congress rejected the motion by an eight-to-three state vote, with one state divided. Congress also denied a similar motion by the New York delegation on Clinton's behalf. Then, in one of those bizarre turnabouts to which legislative bodies are sometimes prone, Congress reconsidered and decided to make Moultrie a major general after all. The main reason why it picked Moultrie, but not the more senior Clinton, was because New York already had a major general in Alexander McDougall, whereas South Carolina had none. Although Clinton was disappointed, he opted to remain in the army for the rest of the war.[48]

Congress also selected several more brigadier generals in the year before the war ended. The first was Otho Williams. Born in Maryland in 1749 and orphaned at age thirteen, Williams became a government clerk before going into business. He began the war as a company commander outside Boston and was later captured at Fort Washington. Although imprisonment damaged his health, he took over a Maryland regiment after his exchange in early 1778 and led it through the Battle of Monmouth Courthouse. He went south with Gates as his deputy adjutant general and survived the Battle of Camden. He served Greene in both administrative and combat roles during the retreat through North Carolina, and at Guilford Courthouse, Hobkirk Hill, and Eutaw Springs. Through it all he exhibited an elegance, intelligence, and courage that won people's respect. Greene was among those who grew to appreciate Williams's abilities. When Greene recommended Williams's promotion to brigadier in November 1781, Washington seconded it and commented to Congress, "I can assure Congress, that Colonel Williams, as an officer of merit, has ever stood high in my estimation, and that it is my opinion, that his long services, military abilities, and good conduct justly entitle him to the promotion mentioned, provided Congress should think proper, at this time, to fill the vacancy.[49] Washington's initial confidence that his appointment would soon be forthcoming proved premature due to Congress's reluctance to swell the payroll by creating new generals. Greene, however, clinched the deal by telling Congress that he intended to divide the Maryland line into two brigades, for which he needed an additional brigadier. The fact that generals were fewer and farther between in the Southern Department than in Washington's army also probably helped tip the scales. Thus prodded, Congress on 9 May voted to elevate him. In his letter informing Williams of the good news, Greene urged Williams to focus on the result of Congress's actions rather than the somewhat demoralizingly prolonged deliberations required to achieve it.[50]

Although most of the war's fighting was over, Washington continued to argue that he needed more brigadiers for his brigades. Indeed, when he reorganized his army in late August 1782, he had only two brigadiers—Massachusetts's John Paterson and Connecticut's Jedediah Huntington—for his sixteen small brigades. As for Congress, its reluctance to add more generals to its payroll was counterbalanced by the paradoxical desire of some individual delegations to elevate their officers. This was particularly true of the New Jersey delegation, which lobbied hard throughout the year for Congress to appoint Col. Elias Dayton a brigadier so their state would have one officer at that rank. Washington greatly respected Dayton and believed he deserved the promotion but noted that New Jersey had not fielded enough men for its own brigade and brigadier. After consulting with Washington, in July Lincoln recommended that Congress advance three officers to brigadier: Dayton, John Greaton, and Rufus Putnam. The latter two were Massachusetts's senior colonels, whom Lincoln probably chose to compensate the state for losing Learned and Nixon. Lincoln justified Dayton's selection by noting that combining New Jersey's troops with the Delaware line would create a new brigade necessitating an additional brigadier, but Dayton's threat to resign also probably played a role in Lincoln's rationale. On 12 December Congress took up a report based on Lincoln's thinking, but it did not finally promote the three men until 7 January 1783. Seventy-nine days later, on 26 March, Congress at Washington's request made Col. Charles Armand its last brigadier of the conflict. Armand was a French cavalry officer who had seen plenty of combat since he arrived in America in the spring of 1777. He took over Kazimierz Pułaski's legion after the Polish officer was killed trying to storm Savannah in 1779 and fought bravely with Greene in the Carolinas. As a foreigner, Armand's appointment did not give any particular state an advantage.[51]

Washington's dearth of brigadiers was offset by a surplus of major generals. This number, however, declined by one on 15 January 1783 when Stirling succumbed to an acute attack of gout, aggravated by pneumonia, in Albany. Washington had sent him there the previous August to replace the ailing Stark as Northern Department commander. Although Stirling had been ill off and on over the past few years, his death still came as a shock. He was not a great general by any stretch of the imagination, and excessive drinking undoubtedly ruined whatever potential he once had for his calling. Indeed, Washington refrained from giving him important independent missions because he was aware of his intellectual limitations. Despite these and other shortcomings, Washington and the officer corps appreciated Stirling's patriotism, stalwartness, loyalty, and courage. In a letter to Stirling's widow, Washington summed up his feelings for the man:

> It only remains then, as a small, but just tribute to the memory of Lord Stirling, to express how deeply I share the common affliction, on being deprived of the public and professional assistance, as well as the private friendship, of an officer of so high rank, with whom I had lived in the strictest habits of amity, and how much those military merits of his Lordship, which rendered him respected in his lifetime, are now regretted by the whole army. It will doubtless be a soothing consideration in the poignancy of your grief, to find that the general officers are going into mourning for him.[52]

In an equally affected letter to Congress, Washington wrote, "The remarkable bravery, intelligence, and promptitude of his Lordship to perform his duty as an officer, had endeared him to the whole army; and now make his loss the more sincerely regretted."[53] Congress agreed and resolved to remember Stirling for his high sense of duty, meritorious service, and perseverance. He was buried in a vault within the walls of an old Dutch church in Albany.[54]

The Continental army's last great test did not occur on the battlefield but was instead a confrontation with Congress that threatened civilian control of the military. Washington's success in defusing the resulting crisis was an accomplishment as significant to the young republic's survival as any of his military victories. In the winter of 1782–83 army officers in winter quarters in Newburgh, New York, were increasingly unhappy with Congress's inability to provide them with back pay and a pension. Congress was well aware of this discontent even before a delegation led by Alexander McDougall arrived in Philadelphia to articulate the officers' grievances. Although some delegates worried that the officers were trying to dictate to Congress, most wanted to do right by them. The crux of the problem, though, was structural. Under the Articles of Confederation, Congress lacked the power to tax and had to instead rely on voluntary state contributions, which were presently insufficient to support the army. A shadowy group of congressmen decided to use the officers' disgruntlement to scare the states into giving Congress the power to tax. Their plan was to stir up the officers so that it appeared that they might take matters into their own hands if their demands were not met. On 10 March Maj. John Armstrong, one of Gates's aides and son of the namesake former general, circulated an unsigned missive in camp deploring the financial plight of officers and urging them to issue an ultimatum to Congress. Another anonymous letter called for officers to meet the following morning to discuss their options.[55]

Washington was well aware of his officers' unhappiness and sympathized with their predicament. Indeed, he was so worried about their simmering anger that he chose to spend the winter in camp rather than visit Mount Vernon. Even so, he was surprised by the speed with which the crisis came to a head. He recognized immediately that the officers' organized discussions could quickly turn to actions that might endanger the republic. After all, civilian authority over the military would end if the army could intimidate or dictate terms to Congress. Washington strongly suspected that some congressmen were stoking his officers' discontent for their own selfish purposes. And of course he could not help but wonder whether Gates was somehow involved. When he learned of Armstrong's unsigned message, Washington called for a meeting of the officers for 15 March but implied that he would not be there. The officers who gathered in the Temple of Honor building that morning were therefore surprised when Washington showed up and asked to say a few words. He denounced attempts to manipulate the officer corps as unmilitary and subversive to order and discipline. To prove that Congress had their best interests at heart, Washington started to read a letter he had recently received from a Virginia delegate. He paused briefly, reached inside a case for his spectacles, and asked the audience for their indulgence while he adjusted them on his head. As he did so, he noted that he had already grown gray in the service of his country, but now was going blind as well. This offhand comment deeply moved the assembled officers. They suddenly realized that although Washington had sacrificed as much or more than they, he had continued to serve without complaint. One participant noted that eyes welled up throughout the room. Washington went on to condemn the troublemakers as the country's enemies and promised to do all he could to address the officers' grievances.[56]

After Washington departed, Knox took the lead in drafting and securing approval for a resolution censuring efforts to rile up the officer corps and expressing continued confidence in Congress. Three days later, Washington wrote, "The storm which seemed to be gathering with unfavorable prognostics, when I wrote to you last, is dispersed; and we are again in a state of tranquility."[57] For this calm Washington deserved the bulk of the credit. His virtuoso performance quelled officers' disgruntlement and maintained their loyalty to Congress. In the end, Congress voted to compensate the officers with five years' full pay in government bonds, but without a pension.

The Newburgh Conspiracy was the Revolutionary War's last big event. On 15 April 1783 Congress ratified a preliminary peace treaty with Great Britain that, among other things, recognized American independence and provided generous borders for the new country. In June Washington furloughed most of his Continentals. Congress voted to give the troops three months' pay in certificates, which most soldiers redeemed as soon as possible and at far less than face value in order to pay their way home. It was a tawdry and disrespectful way to treat men who had fought for so long under such harsh conditions for little if any pay. On 3 November Congress officially disbanded the Continental army. Most of the generals left for home, so only Washington, Steuben, and Knox remained on the roster to help close up shop. Indeed, when Washington said farewell at the dinner at Fraunces Tavern in early December, the only Continental generals in attendance were Knox, McDougall, Steuben, and James Clinton. By the time a general peace among all the warring nations was signed in Paris in early September, the British had already abandoned Charleston and Savannah, but they waited until they received definitive word of the treaty before evacuating New York City as well.

Conclusions

The number of Continental generals remained stable in late 1780 and into 1781. By the end of the Yorktown campaign, the Continental army contained twelve active major generals (Gates, Greene, Heath, Howe, Lafayette, Lincoln, McDougall, Parsons, Smallwood, St. Clair, Steuben, and Stirling) and fifteen active brigadiers (James Clinton, Duportail, Gist, Glover, Hand, Huger, Huntington, Irvine, Knox, Muhlenberg, Paterson, Stark, Sumner, Wayne, and Weedon). Although Congress selected several additional major and brigadier generals between Cornwallis's surrender and the Treaty of Paris, they had little impact on the war because by then most of the fighting had ended. What was important in that last year of active campaigning was not so much the number of Continental generals, but rather how Washington used them. Washington's challenge was to assign these men to positions best suited to their talents. In this he was largely successful. His most important appointments were of Greene to the Southern Department, Lafayette and Steuben to Virginia, and Heath to New York after Washington and Rochambeau redeployed to Virginia. Of these appointments, Steuben's was the least effective. His rough sensibilities and foreign background were assets in training the Continental army at Valley Forge but proved to be liabilities in his attempts to jumpstart Virginia's war effort. In contrast, putting Greene in charge of the Southern Department was pure genius and demonstrated that Washington's long-held conviction about the Rhode Islander's military abilities was accurate. Despite seemingly insurmountable obstacles, Greene not only stymied Cornwallis's offensive through the Carolinas but then went on to wrest almost the entire South from British control. Similarly, Washington was right to dispatch Lafayette to Virginia. Before that assignment, Lafayette's military accomplishments were more apparent than real. In Virginia, though, he proved himself a canny, astute, and careful general who succeeded in holding off the British until Washington and the French arrived to deliver the coup de grâce at Yorktown. Finally, for all of Heath's limitations, he possessed sufficient stalwartness to hold down the fort and keep the British garrison in New York City in check while Washington and Rochambeau marched southward.

In making his personnel assignments, Washington had to navigate Congress's prerogatives, interpersonal disputes, and the army's commitment to seniority. Here too he acted with considerable skill. When it suited his purposes, he overcame seniority by assigning generals in whom he lacked full confidence to other, less important, jobs. He also tried to keep bickering generals out of each other's hair when he believed it would benefit the war effort. Finally, he had built up enough trust with Congress so that delegates rarely questioned his appointments. For example, he made sure that Wayne got command of the Pennsylvania contingent sent to reinforce Lafayette in Virginia instead of the more senior St. Clair by putting St. Clair in charge of recruiting in Pennsylvania. This kept St. Clair out of Wayne's way and ensured that a proven and veteran combat leader took the Pennsylvanians into battle. Preferring Wayne over St. Clair might have raised eyebrows in Congress several years earlier, but by 1781 none of the delegates saw reason to doubt Washington's decision.

Conclusion

Selection of Generals

Fifteen days after bidding his officers farewell at Fraunces Tavern in New York City, Washington rode into Annapolis to surrender his commission to Congress. Congress understood the event's significance as well as Washington and decided to make an occasion of it. On 22 December 1783 Congress hosted an elegant dinner for Washington, Maryland governor William Paca, state delegates, and local bigwigs. One congressman remembered cheerful voices and happy toasts amid the clang of knives and forks. After the meal Paca invited the attendees to a ball that evening at the statehouse. There Washington spent most of his time dancing with all the women who wanted a turn with the soon-to-be former commander in chief. The next day the statehouse was again packed, this time with people eager to see the ceremony Congress had orchestrated. Women jammed the gallery and men crowded below the stairs. Washington sat opposite the president of Congress, Thomas Mifflin. At around noon, after order had been called and silence obtained, Washington rose and bowed to the assembled delegates. As he began reading his address, his hand shook so much that he brought the other one up to help steady the document. His voice faltered with emotion when he commended the country to God, but after pausing to collect himself he concluded by stating, "Having now finished the work assigned to me, I retire from the great theatre of action; and bidding an affectionate farewell to this august body under whose orders I have so long acted, I here offer my commission, and take my leave of all the employments of public life." With that, he took out his commission and handed it to Mifflin. By then there was scarcely a dry eye in the chamber. After listening to Mifflin's response, Washington withdrew to let Congress wrap up its business, but he returned to say informal goodbyes. Then he headed off to Mount Vernon to enjoy Christmas dinner with his family.[1]

Washington was the highest-ranking and most important general of the Continental army. However, he could not have won the war without the assistance of the seventy-three major and brigadier generals Congress appointed during the conflict to help him. These men implemented Congress's and Washington's orders and maintained the army's institutional machinery. Even the most obscure general had an impact on the war effort one way or another by virtue of his rank if nothing else. Their contributions depended on their locales, duties, talents, and of course happenstance. Although most of the generals worked under Washington at some time during the war, some did not. William Moultrie, for example, spent most of the war in the Southern Department and never took an important direct order from the commander in chief. Others gained fame only after they left Washington's main army. Benedict Arnold did his best work in Canada and northern New York after Washington dispatched him northward. Others made their greatest impact on the army's administration. Baron von Steuben, for instance, did nothing remarkable on the battlefield, but as inspector general he turned the Continentals into well-trained professionals capable of standing up to their British and Hessian counterparts. Other generals served in specialized combat capacities. Louis Duportail and Henry Knox made their marks as chiefs of engineering and artillery, respectively. Finally, some influenced the war's outcome in both subordinate and autonomous capacities. Nathanael Greene and John Sullivan both led independent expeditions and exercised responsibility as division commanders in Washington's main army. It is impossible to evaluate the siege of Boston, the invasion of Canada, the fighting around New York City, Trenton and Princeton, the Philadelphia campaign, the Newport operation, the Iroquois expedition, and the war in the South without taking into account the actions of these two men. For every Greene and Sullivan who cut a wide swathe on and off the battlefield, there were also generals such as Jedediah Huntington, John Paterson, and Enoch Poor who plodded along in relative anonymity as brigade commanders year after year in good times and bad. Their largely unheralded sacrifices and enduring commitment to the cause, as well as their successes and blunders, were part of the Revolutionary War's story too.

Of these seventy-three Continental generals, twenty-nine became major generals and forty-four remained brigadiers. Eleven were foreign officers who crossed the Atlantic Ocean to offer their services to the American cause. As for the remaining sixty-two, sixteen were born outside the Thirteen Colonies—eight in Ireland, five in Scotland, two in England, and one in the Netherlands. The average age of the Continental army's generals at the conflict's start was about forty-one. The oldest and youngest, David Wooster and Marquis de Lafayette, were born in 1710 and 1757, respectively. A little over half of them had prior military experience in King George's War, the Great War for Empire, various encounters with American Indians, or elsewhere. Although almost all of them were sufficiently educated, prosperous, and well connected to attract the attention of their state and congressional delegations to secure commissions, some of them were born into poverty and worked their way up. John Glover started as a cobbler, Alexander McDougall a sailor, Daniel Morgan a teamster, George Weedon an innkeeper and tavern owner, and Otho Williams a clerk. To be sure, these generals did not represent a cross section of American society—they were all white Anglo-Saxon Protestant males—but they were not products of an ossified and exclusive elite either.

Because of their undoubted impact on the war effort, the appointing of Continental army generals was one of Congress's most important responsibilities. In the conflict's first year and a half, Congress selected its generals without any official criteria. Instead, it relied on state delegations to nominate and advocate for individuals who typically reflected the socioeconomic status of their congressmen. These would-be generals, men such as Israel Putnam and David Wooster, tended to be well-respected members of their state's elite, usually with some military experience in the Great War for Empire. Indeed, slightly more than half of the Continental army's generals achieved their rank by this route. Congress chose these men as much for their connections and class as for their military abilities, which were all too often either speculative or based on reputations acquired more than a decade earlier. Because they were the first generals, they gained seniority early, which made it difficult for other generals subsequently picked for somewhat more objective reasons to rise to the top of the army's hierarchy. Although most of them eventually left the army for one reason or another before the war's end, this was generally the result of happenstance, not any congressional effort to systematically evaluate their effectiveness and cull the substandard generals from the army's roster. Moreover, this informal process excluded people with military experience who were not part of their state's ruling class. However, it is hard to envision a more realistic, timely, and efficient manner by which Congress could have created its generals.

As the war went on, Congress systematized its criteria in choosing generals. Generally speaking, Congress increasingly took into account an officer's home state, seniority, and perceived merit in making its selections, standards that it formalized with its Baltimore Resolution of February 1777. There was never much debate in Congress about the validity of these three measures, but the proper definition and weighting of each posed an ongoing problem. The fact was that determining relative merit, calculating how many generals each state warranted, and even parsing the ins and outs of seniority were inherently subjective matters about which honest men could disagree. Was Knox's performance at Yorktown sufficiently meritorious to justify his promotion to major general over the heads of other deserving brigadiers?

If Congress claimed to respect seniority, then why elevate Duportail over James Clinton? Why did Pennsylvania deserve an additional brigadier in the spring of 1779, but not, say, Virginia? In reality, all of Congress's personnel decisions were subject to the usual tools of the legislative trade, such as logrolling, side deals, and favoritism. Indeed, Congress's efforts to systematize this inevitably messy procedure generated hard feelings and charges of hypocrisy. An officer need not possess Benedict Arnold's hypersensitivity to feel slighted by the process. Small wonder that many delegates found picking generals an exhausting, contentious, and disagreeable process. Congress could have mitigated this unpleasantness somewhat early in the war by selecting enough generals to accommodate most interested parties, but even then someone would have invariably been overlooked or snubbed. As time went on, Congress sought to avoid the issue as much as possible by appointing fewer generals. Of the ninety-three appointments to major and brigadier general that Congress made during the war, thirteen occurred in 1775, thirty-two in 1776, thirty-one in 1777, one in 1778, five in 1779, three in 1780, two in 1781, two in 1782, and four in 1783. To be sure, there were other factors that contributed to the dramatic decline in the number of generals Congress chose after 1777, such as its desire to save money and the army's diminishing size, but it is difficult to overlook the delegates' distaste for this particularly tedious chore.

Congress considered seniority in selecting its generals. Congressmen and army officers believed that in the majority of cases the most senior officer should receive the next promotion. There was a logic to it. Seniority was predictable and rational, so every officer knew where he stood, and was likely to stand in the future, in the army's pecking order. Moreover, the most senior officer was usually by definition the most experienced man available, and experience counted for much in the military. Giving the most senior officer the next open slot also rewarded loyalty and service. Congressmen, for their part, liked seniority because it nullified the contentious and time-consuming politicking and backstairs maneuvering that otherwise accompanied such personnel decisions. The problem with advancing officers based on seniority was that it removed incentive from the process. After all, if rising through the army's hierarchy depended mostly on time in rank, then there was no reason for ambitious officers to work hard, take risks, or go the extra mile. Although Congress was always willing to elevate an officer for meritorious conduct, it so narrowly defined the term that few officers could count on it to overcome seniority. It was therefore unsurprising that seniority played the major part in congressional thinking. Whenever it decided that a state deserved a brigadier, it usually gave the post to the state's most senior colonel in the Continental army. It often applied the same principle to choosing major generals. In short, Congress's rule of thumb was to use seniority in promotions unless there was some good reason not to.

Most congressmen saw generalships as both status symbols for their states and forms of patronage, so they tried to make sure that their states got their fair share. During the conflict Congress appointed thirteen generals from Massachusetts (Frye, Glover, Greaton, Heath, Knox, Learned, Lincoln, Nixon, Paterson, Rufus Putnam, Reed, Thomas, and Ward); eleven from Virginia (Gates, Lee, Lewis, Mercer, Morgan, Muhlenberg, Scott, Stephen, Washington, Weedon, and Woodford); eight from Pennsylvania (Armstrong, Haas, Hand, Irvine, Mifflin, St. Clair, Thompson, and Wayne); six from Connecticut (Arnold, Huntington, Parsons, Israel Putnam, Spencer, and Wooster); five each from New York (George Clinton, James Clinton, McDougall, Montgomery, and Schuyler) and North Carolina (Hogun, Howe, Moore, Nash, and Sumner); three apiece from Maryland (Gist, Smallwood, and Williams), New Hampshire (Poor, Stark, and Sullivan), New Jersey (Dayton, Maxwell, and Stirling), and South Carolina (Gadsden, Huger, and Moultrie); two from Rhode Island (Greene and Varnum); one from Georgia (McIntosh); and none from Delaware. A problem, of course, lay in defining "fair share." By 1777 a consensus emerged among delegates that Congress should consider a state's contribution to the Continental army in appointing generals. Therefore, the more soldiers a state pledged to the army, the more generals it should receive. However, it was never that cut-and-dried. Troop numbers fluctuated and there was often a difference between the number of soldiers pledged versus delivered. Moreover, Congress had already appointed a good many generals before it officially decided to take into account an officer's home state. Finally, Congress's other criteria—seniority and merit—could and did distort its effort to dole out generalships based on state contributions.

Despite these problems, on the whole Congress did a good job in fairly allotting generals among the states. On the one hand, Virginia, which contained more people and pledged more regiments to the Continental army than any other state, in return received more generals—eleven—than any other state except Massachusetts. Although Massachusetts promised the second-highest number of regiments, it owed its thirteen generals mostly to the fact that the war began there and it initially supplied more troops than any other state. Similarly, Pennsylvania's eight generals were in line with its third-highest contribution to the army. On the other hand, although Maryland vouchsafed the sixth-highest number of regiments, Congress only appointed three Marylanders generals, the same number as tiny New Hampshire and New Jersey. Maryland, though, was the one glaring anomaly.

The foreign officers who swarmed to America after the war started to offer their services to the patriot cause complicated Congress's efforts to choose generals. During the conflict Congress appointed eleven foreign officers as generals: seven Frenchmen (Armand, Preudhomme de Borre, Conway, du Coudray, Duportail,

Fermoy, and Lafayette), three Germans (de Kalb, Steuben, and Woedtke), and one Pole (Pułaski). Congress picked these men as generals for several interrelated reasons. For one thing, they were all ambitious officers who asked for the rank either blatantly or subtly. In addition, some of them had specialized skills few Americans possessed. Duportail and Fermoy, for instance, owed their generalships to their hard-to-find engineering abilities. Congress elevated others to avoid offending the French government. Securing French support was one of Congress's top foreign policy priorities, and delegates worried that denying generalships to well-connected French officers might alienate influential French government officials. Congress would never have made Lafayette a major general if he had not come from a prominent and well-connected French noble family. Finally, Congress commissioned some of them to fulfill promises made by its overseas representatives. Because Silas Deane had guaranteed du Coudray a major generalship in return for his services and his assistance in facilitating the transfer of war matériel to the Americans, Congress felt obligated to live up to at least some of the commitments made on its behalf.

Congress could of course create as many generals as it wanted to accommodate these men. The problem was that doing so often outraged American officers over whose heads these foreigners were raised. This was especially controversial when Congress promoted foreign officers directly to major general because this gave them authority over American brigadiers who were more than willing to express their displeasure to Washington and congressional delegates. Du Coudray's major generalship, for example, generated considerable opposition among brigadiers who failed to see that he was any more deserving than they. If a foreigner had the support of Washington and the officer corps, his promotion was much less likely to cause dissension. Almost no one protested Lafayette's appointment to major general because he was popular with Washington, his officers, and congressmen. Delegates were more willing to look sympathetically upon the applications of foreign officers such as Woedtke for generalships early in the war when they were easily impressed by glamorous men in search of adventure and employment who claimed military expertise. It did not take long for Congress and Washington to grow disillusioned with foreign officers whose English was often as poor as their soldierly qualities. When France entered the war in 1778, the supply of foreign officers dried up. However, most of those foreign officers who had attained their generalships remained on the Continental army's roster.

Finally, most people agreed that Congress should take merit into account in appointing and promoting generals. Defining the term, though, was a tricky and subjective task that made applying the standard surprisingly problematic. To most delegates, meritorious conduct meant displaying meaningful physical courage in combat—the kind of bravery that turned the tide of battle and delivered victory.

John Stark's performance at the Battle of Bennington, for example, met this criterion and led to his elevation to brigadier general. The difficulty was that this understanding of merit penalized officers who demonstrated exemplary service off the battlefield in training, supplying, supporting, and managing troops. Louis Duportail and Henry Knox contributed enormously to the Continental army's success through their specialized skills, but Congress ordinarily would not have advanced them because neither had shown the requisite gallantry in battle. Washington secured their promotions to major general only by referencing valor at Yorktown that was in actuality no different than that which the two had demonstrated elsewhere prior to the battle. In addition, this narrow understanding of merit hurt hardworking officers who did their duty competently and quietly year after year. Enoch Poor, for instance, probably deserved a major generalship. He capably led his New Hampshire brigade for nearly four years through some of the war's most arduous and important campaigns. Unfortunately for Poor, he never attracted sufficient attention from his superiors to get them to pressure Congress to act on his behalf. And, because Poor was a relatively junior brigadier from a tiny state that contributed few troops to the Continental army, there was no other way for him to rise to a major general.

Seniority, state origins, and merit all contributed to Congress's selection of its generals, but there was one more factor that played an important role: George Washington. Washington wielded considerable clout as commander in chief and was sometimes willing to employ it in personnel matters. Although Washington sympathized with the seniority principle and accepted Congress's focus on state origins of generals, he developed an expansive definition of merit to persuade Congress to promote to general those officers he considered worthy. For example, he convinced Congress to appoint Benjamin Lincoln a major general even though Lincoln had no seniority in the Continental army and had done nothing to distinguish himself on the battlefield. Washington simply concluded that Lincoln was an excellent overall officer worthy of a major generalship. He also pointed to his broad understanding of merit to justify recommending officers such as John Cadwalader, Elias Dayton, Henry Knox, and Alexander McDougall to general. Congress almost always went along with Washington's personnel suggestions because of the respect most delegates had for him. On rarer occasions Washington used his influence to prevent Congress from advancing officers who he believed did not warrant it. He tried unsuccessfully to dissuade Congress from elevating Thomas Conway to major general because he believed Conway was a troublemaker. Later, he came out against Daniel Morgan's promotion to brigadier. Generally speaking, though, he did not stand in Congress's way to create generals because he usually was in need of them to command his brigades and divisions. Either way, it is impossible to discount Washington's impact on Congress in choosing its generals.

Losing Command

Removing Continental generals was often as problematic as selecting them in the first place. The army needed to get rid of substandard generals not only because they cost lives and lost battles, but also because their continued presence on the roster prevented more capable colleagues from rising through the army's hierarchy and securing important commands. However, during the revolutionary conflict the army and Congress stripped only two generals—Charles Lee and Adam Stephen—of their commissions, even though the army's defeat-laden record indicated that there were plenty of others who merited the same fate. There were a couple reasons for this low number. For one thing, purging the army of a general was an onerous, time-consuming, and uncertain process that usually required a court of inquiry, a court-martial, and finally congressional affirmation. A beleaguered general rallied his friends in and out of the army to speak on his behalf, filled the record with positive testimony, and exploited all available loopholes. John Sullivan, for example, survived several attempts to displace him for alleged battlefield failings by using his legal talents to manipulate the system in his favor. Moreover, efforts to relieve generals often became entangled in larger political questions that confused the issue at hand. New England delegates targeted Philip Schuyler as much for his patrician New York background as for his supposed leadership shortcomings. It was therefore hardly surprising that many officers and congressmen concluded that trying to dispose of generals was not worth it.

In addition, Washington was usually reluctant to scapegoat his generals for botched battlefield performances. Washington had, after all, committed his share of tactical and strategic blunders, so for him to try to ruin careers of officers for *their* mistakes would be hypocritical and bad for morale. As a result, he stood by Greene, Sullivan, and other generals despite their bungling. Indeed, he ordered Charles Lee's court-martial for his Monmouth Courthouse actions only because Lee demanded one and refused to let the controversy surrounding his performance there die. Instead, Washington opted to work around deficient generals by transferring them to positions where their limitations would do less harm to the cause or by giving them secondary assignments. For instance, after the Conway Cabal Washington tried to keep Horatio Gates from important posts because he disliked the man and distrusted his military competence. The result was that the army's high command was cluttered with such mediocre generals as Israel Putnam, Gates, and Joseph Spencer who were not so awful as to justify the investment necessary to dislodge them from power, but who were not exactly military assets.

Although there was no organized and systematic way to evaluate and remove inadequate generals, this does not mean that there was no change in the roster.

Far from it. There was plenty of turnover in a war that lasted eight years. None of the original five major generals appointed in 1775 were still active at the end of the conflict. Nor were three of the six major generals selected in 1776 and seven of the twelve chosen in 1777. There were several reasons for this constant churn. Most obviously, a number of generals died before the Treaty of Paris went into effect. Six generals were killed in battle: de Kalb at Camden, Mercer at Princeton, Montgomery at Quebec, Nash at Germantown, Pułaski outside of Savannah, and Wooster during the British raid on Danbury. Another eight—du Coudray, Hogun, Moore, Poor, Stirling, Thomas, Woedtke, and Woodford—succumbed to illness or accident. Their deaths may not have been as valorous as those who fell in combat, but that did not make their sacrifices any less meaningful. Interestingly, only seven of the eleven foreign officers whom Congress picked as generals survived the war. In all, nearly one in five of the Continental generals gave their lives for the patriot cause.

The war was not as hard on Continental generals as on the enlisted men. After all, generals received the privileges of their rank: superior quarters, better food, aides and servants to do much of their physical labor, and authority. Generals also got periodic furloughs, sometimes every winter, to return home to see family and attend to personal affairs. However, generals were burdened with constant responsibilities, the failure of which to fulfill could cost lives. They were also just as vulnerable to loneliness and demoralization as anyone else. Their quarters and rations may have been preferable to those of the rank and file, but they were usually a far cry from what was available to most civilians. As men of means, generals often left behind substantial financial interests that deteriorated due to inflation and neglect, and they went years without little or no pay. Because they tended to be older, generals were more susceptible to illness than most soldiers. As a result, it was unsurprising that during the war a good many of them resigned their commissions or became inactive due to either physical or financial hardship—or both. These included Frye, Glover, Learned, Morgan, Nixon, Parsons, Israel Putnam, Reed, Spencer, Sullivan, Thompson, Varnum, and Ward. These thirteen men made up nearly 18 percent of the Continental army's generals.

Several other generals resigned their commissions not because of any particular physical or financial hardship, but rather out of pique. Two—Armstrong and Lewis—became angry after Congress passed them over by promoting more junior officers to major general and stepped down. Others such as Gadsden, Mifflin, and Schuyler believed that Congress, Washington, or some other authority had wronged them in one way or another. The officers who resigned comprised 8 percent of all generals. Considering the amount of dissension and hurt feelings in the highest ranks of the Continental army, this was a surprisingly small figure.

However, some generals who cited poor health or finances in their decision to quit also had grievances that factored into their thinking.

Subtracting those who died, resigned, were dismissed, or left the army for anomalous reasons—Arnold's treason, for example, or De Haas's refusal to accept his commission—left thirty-four Continental generals still on duty in one capacity or another when the war ended, including only three of the original thirteen major and brigadier generals Congress appointed in June 1775—Horatio Gates, Nathanael Greene, and William Heath. These survivors comprised 45 percent of those generals who served. This was a remarkably high number considering the war's duration and deadliness. It was also a tribute to the dedication these men had for the American cause. They remained at their jobs year in and year out despite Congress's and the public's ingratitude and indifference to their sufferings. They stayed on even when their personal finances evaporated and opportunities for glory disappeared. Few of them intended to use their wartime experience to achieve national ambitions, although some ended up doing so anyway. Indeed, most of them probably agreed with Greene, who wrote in October 1782 that he hoped the war would soon end so he could return to private life and added, "To be with my family is what my soul longs for. I am tired of the bustle of life; and wish to retire to calmer scenes."[2]

Evaluation

Evaluating generals is a tricky and subjective task. Although an army is no better than its leadership, successful generalship often involves factors beyond talent and experience over which a general may have little control, such as available resources, his adversary, geography and terrain, and plain dumb luck. As a result, a superior general can lose a battle or campaign to a mediocre opponent with unmerited advantages. Conversely, a poor general with advantages not of his own making can overcome a more skilled opponent. Even so, assessing the Continental army's generals provides a good means by which to determine whether the United States defeated the British because or in spite of Congress's selection process.

Washington was the war's most prominent general. He led the main American army for eight long years through many of the war's largest and most important campaigns. He certainly made his share of tactical and strategic blunders, especially early in the conflict. His decision to try to defend New York City, for example, nearly resulted in the destruction of his army and a quick end of the revolution. Fortunately for the American cause, he learned from his mistakes and grew into a wily and seasoned commander attuned to the society he was defending. He realized that he needed to separate out his militia and assign them less daunting tasks that they could realistically achieve. Hard experience also taught him to avoid big battles out in the open against the British, but to instead use the local geography to deploy his troops in well-protected positions that the British could not or would not try to overcome. Doing so foiled British incursions in New Jersey in 1777 and 1780 and prevented the British from ascending the Hudson River from 1778 to 1781. Although he bowed to public expectations and attempted unsuccessfully to defend Philadelphia, after the city fell he managed to keep the enemy off balance and tied down at Germantown and along the Delaware River without unduly endangering his army.

Washington's defensive strategy, though, did not mean he surrendered the initiative to the British. As fighter, he sought the opportunity to assume the offensive under the right circumstances. He assailed isolated enemy detachments at Trenton and Germantown, confronted the British army at Monmouth Courthouse, ordered Anthony Wayne to storm Stony Point, and led the Franco-American army to Yorktown. Such attacks did not always work, but they kept the British from dispersing their forces to secure control of the population.

As commander in chief, Washington's responsibilities went beyond managing his own field army. He avoided the parochialism to which many leaders succumb and acknowledged the importance of other theaters to the war effort. For instance, he dispatched Daniel Morgan's elite riflemen to the Northern Department to help repel Burgoyne's invasion in 1777 and later sent his right-hand man, Nathanael Greene, to run the Southern Department. He also understood the significance of naval power and interallied harmony, both of which helped bring about the Franco-American victory at Yorktown. He accomplished his mission without challenging civilian control of the military or undermining the liberties for which the Americans were fighting. By recognizing the enemy's advantages, the constraints imposed by Congress in particular and American political culture in general, and his soldiers' limitations, Washington grew into the war's premier strategist. Congress's appreciation of his talents from the start was a tribute to its ability to appoint quality generals.

Washington outranked the other seventy-three generals Congress appointed during the war. Cultivating a fruitful bond with these men was obviously one of his most important personnel tasks. After all, any mistrust and suspicion between Washington and his generals would inhibit the Continental army's effectiveness and hurt the war effort. Despite his formality, dispassion, and aloofness, Washington inspired intense loyalty and devotion from most of his generals. They grew to admire his integrity, commitment to the cause, sense of honor and fairness, and status. The fact that his bonds with these men were more hierarchical than egalitarian did not make them any less sincere. Washington listened patiently to and sympathized with his generals' complaints, tried his best to redress their grievances, and refused to scapegoat them when they were defeated or criticized. He rarely lost his temper with them and tried within the confines of military propriety to placate them in matters big and small. As a result, both independent-minded aristocrats such as Philip Schuyler and men of more modest means such as Henry Knox revered him. Whatever problems Continental generals had with Congress or each other, most remained ready and willing to obey, support, and cooperate with their commander in chief through thick and thin, as evidenced by their responses to the Conway Cabal and Newburgh Conspiracy. This symbiotic relationship was one reason for the Continental army's remarkable resilience throughout the conflict.

Washington not only led the main American army; he supervised the remaining Continental forces as well. Even so, Congress reserved for itself the power to select department commanders. Sometimes it consulted Washington, but not always. For example, Washington played almost no role in Congress's successive decisions to appoint Lee, Howe, Lincoln, and Gates to lead the Southern Department. As the war progressed and Congress's confidence in Washington grew, it increasingly delegated to him this important job. Washington's ability to cultivate positive relationships with his generals enabled him to choose capable men for these positions. Doing so required an understanding of an officer's character, talents, and potential. He picked Heath and McDougall for the Hudson Highlands, Sullivan for the campaign against the Iroquois, Lafayette to combat Cornwallis in Virginia, and, most famously, Greene for the Southern Department after Gates's defeat at Camden. In each case, he chose strong-willed and intelligent men with whom he had previously worked. All of them performed credibly in their allotted tasks. Of perhaps equal importance, Washington also understood which of his generals he could not entrust to independent commands. Although he liked and respected Stirling, he knew better than to give him an important post of his own. Of course, not all of Washington's selections panned out. His decision to send Steuben to Virginia, for instance, did little to retrieve American fortunes there. Nor could he find an officer to run the Western Department effectively. When Congress permitted him to do so, though, Washington usually used the limited talent at his disposal quite well.

To be sure, not all of Washington's interactions with his generals were smooth and productive. He occasionally failed to form beneficial relationships with officers of similar stature and experience. He harbored a grudge against Horatio Gates out of proportion to whatever sins Gates may have committed during the conflict. His old political rivalry with Adam Stephen may have contributed to Washington's antipathy toward the man. Washington also tolerated ineffective and disruptive generals longer than he should have. Charles Lee, for example, repeatedly denigrated and undermined Washington despite Washington's best efforts to get along with him. Although Washington could not have been unaware of Lee's disdain, he put up with it out of respect for Lee's supposed military acumen and to maintain harmony with Congress and within the officer corps. In the end, it was Lee who terminated the relationship by demanding a court-martial after the Battle of Monmouth Courthouse.

Although most Continental major and brigadier generals served in subordinate roles during the war, a small number had the opportunity to formulate and implement strategy in independent missions. Their records in this area are mixed. Each of the American commanders in Canada—Montgomery, Wooster, Thomas, and Sullivan—was responsible for conducting operations there. Montgomery was smart enough to recognize Quebec's importance and march there as soon as he could after he seized Montreal. After Montgomery's death, Wooster and Thomas were too busy maintaining their tatterdemalion troops to take on the additional burden of making strategic judgments. Sullivan's most important decision was abandoning Canada to save his soldiers.

The following year two more generals had strategic responsibilities as successive Northern Department chiefs: Philip Schuyler and Horatio Gates. Their selections became something of a political football for Congress. Support for each man often broke along geographic lines, and their seniority crowded out others who might have done the job. Congress's inability to settle on one or the other based primarily on military merit demonstrated the difficulties it had in picking generals. Schuyler's critics called him a do-nothing leader who failed to respond vigorously to Burgoyne's invasion of New York. His adherents argued that he preserved his army, delayed the British, and created the logistical network that laid the groundwork for Saratoga. As for Gates, his boosters credited him with establishing and maintaining the position from which his subordinates pummeled the British into submission, whereas his detractors accused him of taking advantage of Schuyler's accomplishments and of letting more aggressive and capable subordinates such as Arnold, Morgan, and Stark fight for him. Whatever the specific criticisms and merits of their actions, both Schuyler and Gates understood that time and geography were on their side and acted accordingly. In the final analysis, though, neither officer rose to the upper ranks as a strategist.

Several generals who served in the southern states also dabbled in strategy with wide-ranging degrees of success. Charles Lee, the original Southern Department commander, justified Congress's faith in him by recognizing Charleston's importance and bringing reinforcements to the city in time to help repel the British amphibious assault in June 1776. Lee's successor, Robert Howe, had less success in holding Savannah in 1778. Nor could he maintain the support of local authorities. Howe's replacement, Benjamin Lincoln, lost both Charleston and its defending soldiers to the besieging British in the spring of 1780. Howe and Lincoln could argue that their strategic hands were tied by their obligation to protect the important cities in their charge, but neither officer showed the kind of initiative, resourcefulness, combativeness, and imagination that enabled Washington to overcome similar challenges. Horatio Gates, the next Southern Department chief, had no such excuse for losing most of his army and reputation at the Battle of Camden three months after Charleston fell. He certainly displayed a pugnaciousness that he had not demonstrated during the Saratoga campaign, but he learned to his sorrow that there was a fine line between aggressiveness and foolhardiness. Fortunately for the Americans, the final head of the Southern Department, Nathanael Greene, proved himself to be one of the great strategists in American history. Despite severe shortages, Greene outmaneuvered the British in a brilliant campaign that resulted in the liberation of much of the Carolinas and Georgia. While Washington pushed for Greene's appointment, Congress's willingness to turn to a New Englander untried in independent command who had recently tested its patience as quartermaster to lead patriot forces in the South did it credit and helped compensate for the generally low quality of the officers it had previously put in charge of the department.

Although only a small number of Continental generals got the opportunity to formulate and implement strategy during the war, far more maneuvered and fought their units on the battlefield. For the most part, they demonstrated more courage than skill. Because these generals usually lacked prewar experience training, managing, and leading their brigades and divisions, it was unsurprising that they made their share of tactical mistakes. There was scarcely a high-ranking commander who did not blunder under fire at some point in the conflict, from Sullivan's clumsy deployments on Long Island to Wayne's foolhardy charge at Green Spring. Indeed, it is easier to count the number of tactical triumphs that Continental generals attained than their defeats. Among the most important were Lee and Moultrie's victory at Charleston, Washington's at Trenton and Princeton, Stark's at Bennington, Gates and Arnold's at Saratoga, Wayne's at Stony Point, Sullivan's at Newtown, Greene's at Springfield, Morgan's at Cowpens, and Washington's at Yorktown. In almost every case, though, American success was due to numerical superiority, geographic advantages, or British errors—or a combination of the three. Other generals performed well even in defeat, such as Weedon at Brandywine and Greene at Guilford Courthouse. Despite their importance, such successes were exceptions to the rule.

Congress did a poor job of rewarding those few officers who proved themselves as well-rounded battlefield commanders. Rather, it tended to promote officers because of their seniority or state origins. With the exceptions of Richard Montgomery, Benedict Arnold, and Alexander McDougall, every officer that Congress advanced to major general was promoted primarily because of reasons other than his record of leading men in battle. Congress did a somewhat better job in elevating skilled battlefield commanders to brigadier generalships, but even these men were a distinct minority. Even worse, Congress overlooked brigadiers who clearly earned promotions to major general for leading their soldiers to victory. Anthony Wayne and Daniel Morgan, for instance, performed brilliantly at, respectively, Stony Point and Cowpens, but both officers remained brigadiers for the remainder of the conflict. Such examples call into question Congress's record in selecting good generals.

Congress was, however, partially responsible for the presence of several generals who contributed to the army's success in more organizational roles. Such generals as Duportail, Knox, and Steuben oversaw no brilliant tactical maneuvers, but without their specialized skills, the Continental army might have disintegrated before it even engaged the British. Although Congress's record in this area was not perfect—Thomas Mifflin, for instance, was such a lackluster quartermaster that the army's logistical system nearly collapsed during his tenure—generals in administrative roles on the whole performed better than those selected for combat assignments. Congress may have appointed such officers on the advice of Washington and others, but the delegates still deserved credit for recognizing their significance and making efforts to vest them with sufficient authority to fulfill their responsibilities.

Successful Generals

The record indicates that the majority of the Continental army's subordinate generals were mediocre at best. Time after time, whether in the top or a subordinate role and regardless of where they fought, they committed strategic and tactical errors that contributed to American defeats. On one level, this is hardly surprising. Although most of them had served in some capacity in the Great War for Empire, they had little experience leading the comparatively large units they commanded during the Revolutionary War. Moreover, they were burdened with poorly trained and ill-equipped soldiers, logistical shortcomings, and administrative snafus. Small wonder that their professional British counterparts repeatedly bested them.

Happily for the American cause, Congress appointed several generals whose command proficiency provided the margin for victory. Some of them, such as Arnold (before his betrayal), Glover, Morgan, Stark, and Wayne, excelled as tacticians. Others—Greene, Lafayette, and Washington—became shrewd strategists. Each of them took advantage of local geography and terrain, the militia's positive attributes, the limited resources at their disposal, and British mistakes to lead their troops to victory. Finally, Knox and Steuben benefited the American military cause in uniquely important ways. Whatever their contributions, it is impossible to explain American success in the war without taking into account the actions of these dozen or so men.

What made these generals different from their less efficacious colleagues? Most of them had several things in common. One was age. Almost all of them were relatively young. At the war's start, Arnold was thirty-four, Greene thirty-three, Glover forty-three, Knox twenty-five, Lafayette eighteen, and Morgan thirty-nine. (At forty-seven, Stark was an outlier.) Their youthfulness gave these successful generals the energy and stamina to fight for years under harsh conditions. By comparison, Gates and Ward were forty-eight, Lee forty-three, Lincoln forty-two, and Putnam and Stephen fifty-seven when the conflict began. Although several of the younger crop of generals fell ill at one point or another, they were healthy enough to return to duty and battle on. Moreover, because their youth, most of these men either had not served in the Great War for Empire, or did so in a minor capacity. As a result, they were less beholden to the British way of doing things than their older comrades who had participated in that conflict and more willing to embrace the unconventional. These generals often avoided major battles with the enemy, used the militia effectively, and molded their tactics to the local geography in ways that were alien to British military practice.

In addition, these officers showed an ability to grow in their jobs and learn from their mistakes. Most of them committed at least one serious blunder early in the war. Greene's foolish commitment to Fort Washington's defense, for example, enabled the British to capture that stronghold along with its defenders. These men took the lessons of failure to heart and became better commanders. Wayne, for instance, employed the same tactics to overrun Stony Point that the British had used so effectively against him at Paoli. In the Carolinas Greene never showed the same obsession with fixed points that he so disastrously demonstrated at Fort Washington. Although the grade of the learning curve varied among these generals, there is no denying its existence.

Successful generals also established good working relationships with Washington. During the war Washington demonstrated a hitherto unknown eye for military talent. He identified most of the war's best American generals early on and did what he could to promote their careers. Washington recognized potential in Arnold, Glover, Greene, Knox, Lafayette, and Wayne from the start. He forgave their mistakes, listened to their gripes, encouraged their efforts, and protected them from congressional retribution. His instincts were not always accurate—he overestimated Lincoln's and Sullivan's abilities, for example, and trusted Arnold far too much—but it is hard to see how the Americans could have won the war without Washington nurturing that small number of talented generals Congress appointed.

Finally, successful American generals shared some of the same character traits. They all possessed a willingness to take calculated tactical and strategic risks, the ability to appeal to Continentals and militia and civilians, resourcefulness, energy, dedication, pride, and a ruthlessness in attaining their objectives. During the conflict they developed an understanding of military affairs that separates great commanders from the ordinary. These qualities manifested themselves in Arnold's actions at Valcour Island and Saratoga, Greene's in the Carolinas, Knox's in securing cannons for Washington's army besieging Boston, Stark's at Bennington, and Wayne's at Stony Point. Although they had different personalities—Knox and Greene were as ingratiating as Stark and Arnold were tetchy, and Morgan and Glover were as roughhewn and plebian as Lafayette was aristocratic and sophisticated—their soldierly instincts were remarkably similar.

The Revolutionary War was an anomaly in American military history for many reasons, including the selection of Continental generals. During the war, the national government's power was concentrated in Congress and severely circumscribed by the states. There was no executive to appoint officers, enforce Congress's laws, implement its policies, and provide a buffer between popular passions and government decisions. Because people are political animals, politics invariably influences the selection of generals in even the most insular system. To its credit, Congress recognized this problem and developed criteria for its selections as an antidote, but politics continued to infect the process throughout the conflict. This resulted in Congress choosing a good many mediocre generals whose presence on the battlefield and in council was often more a hindrance than a help to the war effort. This same system, though, also produced great strategists such as Washington and Greene, aggressive combat leaders such as Arnold and Wayne, and capable administrators such as Steuben. Although the new United States was handicapped by a borderline dysfunctional national government, a large loyalist population, and a mostly preindustrial economy, it still defeated the British and secured its independence. There were of course plenty of reasons for American success in the war—British political and military mistakes, substantial French assistance, geography—but it is impossible to discount the contributions made by the generals picked by Congress in achieving victory.

Notes

Introduction

1. Ebenezer Huntington to Andrew Huntington, 12 August 1783, *Letters Written by Ebenezer Huntington during the American Revolution* (New York: Charles Frederick Heartman, 1914), 106.
2. Most of the information about Washington's stay in New York City is from Benjamin Tallmadge, *Memoir of Col. Benjamin Tallmadge* (New York: Thomas Holman, 1858), 63.
3. William Heath to John Adams, 20 July 1776, "The Heath Papers," *Collections of the Massachusetts Historical Society* (Boston: Massachusetts Historical Society, 1904–5), 2:13.
4. Nathanael Greene to Adams, 2 June 1776, *The Adams Papers Digital Edition*, vol. 4 (Boston: Massachusetts Historical Society), http://www.masshist.org.

Chapter 1. Adopting an Army

1. James Warren to Adams, 7 May 1775, *Adams Papers* 3, http://www.masshist.org; Adams, June and July 1775, *Diary of John Adams*, vol. 3, in *Adams Papers* 3, http://www.masshist.org.
2. It is unclear when Adams made his speech because Congress was at that time meeting as a committee of the whole for which no record of speeches was kept. See Adams, June and July 1775, *Diary* 3, *Adams Papers* 3, http://www.masshist.org.
3. Ibid.; Commission from the Continental Congress, 19 June 1775, *The Papers of George Washington: Revolutionary War Series*, ed. W. W. Abbot, Theodore J. Crackel, Philander Chase, Frank E. Grizzard Jr., David R. Hoth, Edward G. Lengel, and Dorothy Twohig (Charlottesville: University Press of Virginia, 1985–2013) [hereafter cited as *Washington Papers*], 1:6–7; Deane to Elizabeth Deane, 16 June 1775, in Paul Smith, ed., *Letters of Delegates to Congress, 1774–1789* (Washington, D.C.: Library of Congress, 1976–94) [hereafter cited as *Letters of Delegates*], 1:493–95; Dyer to Jonathan Trumbull, 16 June 1775, *Letters of Delegates*, 1:495–96; Dyer to Jonathan Trumbull, 17 June 1775, *Letters of Delegates*, 1:499–500.
4. Address to the Continental Congress, 16 June 1775, *Washington Papers*, 1:1.
5. George Washington to Martha Washington, 18 June 1775, *Washington Papers*, 1:4.

6. Ibid., 1:3–5; Washington to Burwell Bassett, 19 June 1775, *Washington Papers*, 1:12–13; Washington to John Augustine Washington, 20 June 1775, *Washington Papers*, 1:19–20; Adams, June and July 1775, *Diary* 3, *Adams Papers* 3, http://www.masshist.org; Virginia Delegate to [?], 14 June 1775, *Letters of Delegates*, 1:486; Dyer to Jonathan Trumbull, 16 June 1775, *Letters of Delegates*, 1:495–96; Washington to the Captains of Several Independent Companies in Virginia, 20 June 1775, *Letters of Delegates*, 1:527.
7. Washington to Lund Washington, 29 May 1779, *Washington Papers*, 20:688.
8. Marquis de Lafayette to Duc d'Ayen, 16 December 1777, *Lafayette in the Age of the American Revolution: Selected Letters and Papers, 1776–1790*, ed. Stanley J. Idzerda (Ithaca, N.Y.: Cornell University Press, 1977–79), 1:192.
9. For some of the more telling descriptions of Washington during the war, see Abigail Adams to Adams, 16 July 1775, in L. H. Butterfield and Marc Friedlaender, eds., *Adams Family Correspondence* (Cambridge, Mass.: Belknap Press of Harvard University Press, 1963–73) [hereafter cited as *Adams Family Correspondence*], 1:246; Charles Lee to Richard Henry Lee, 19 July 1776, *The Lee Papers* (New York: New-York Historical Society, 1871–73), 1:146–48; Marquis de Chastellux, *Travels in North America in the Years 1780–82* (New York, 1828), 62–63, 72–73; Thomas Burke to the North Carolina Assembly, 29 April 1778, *Letters of Delegates*, 9:533; Francois Barbe-Marbois, 12 September 1779, in Eugene Parker Chase, trans. and ed., *Our Revolutionary Forefathers: The Letters of Francois, Marquis de Barbe-Marbois* (New York: Duttfield, 1929), 113; Lafayette to Friedrich Wilhelm von Steuben, 12 March 1778, *Lafayette in the American Revolution*, 1:353; Benjamin Rush to Thomas Ruston, 29 October 1775, *Letters of Benjamin Rush*, ed. L. H. Butterfield (Princeton, N.J.: Princeton University Press, 1951) [hereafter cited as *Rush Letters*], 1:92; James Thatcher, 20 July 1775 and October 1778, *Military Journal during the American Revolutionary War, from 1775 to 1783* (Boston: Richardson and Lord, 1823), 37, 182–83.
10. Dyer to Jonathan Trumbull, 16 June 1775, *Letters of Delegates*, 1:495–96.
11. John Thaxter to Adams, 28 June 1775, *Adams Family Correspondence*, 1:234.
12. For examples of Congress's self-congratulation, see John Hancock to Joseph Warren, 18 June 1775, *Letters of Delegates*, 1:507–8; Thomas Cushing to James Bowdoin, 21 June 1775, *Letters of Delegates*, 1:530; Samuel Adams to Gerry, 22 June 1775, *The Writings of Samuel Adams*, ed. Harry Alonzo Cushing (New York: G. P. Putnam's Sons, 1907), 3:218–19.
13. Adams to Elbridge Gerry, 18 June 1775, *Letters of Delegates*, 1:503.
14. Adams, June and July 1775, *Diary* 3, *Adams Papers* 3, http://www.masshist.org; Adams to James Warren, 21 June 1775, *Adams Papers* 3, http://www.masshist.org; James Warren to Adams, 7 May 1775, *Adams Papers* 3, http://www.masshist.org; Adams to Gerry, 18 June 1775, *Letters of Delegates*, 1:503–4; Dyer to Joseph Trumbull, 20 June 1775, *Letters of Delegates*, 1:521–22; Samuel Adams to James Warren, 28 June 1775, *Letters of Delegates*, 1:553–54.
15. Samuel Adams to Joseph Warren, 20 June 1775, *Letters of Delegates*, 1:519.
16. William Heath, *Memoirs of Major-General William Heath, by Himself*, ed. William Abbatt (New York: William Abbatt, 1901) [hereafter cited as *Heath Memoirs*], 88; Abigail Adams to Adams, 16 July 1775, *Adams Family Correspondence*, 1:246–47; Washington to John Augustine Washington, 31 March 1776, *Washington Papers*, 3:570; Gerry to the Massachusetts Delegates, 20 June 1775, *Adams Papers* 3, http://www.masshist.org; Charles Lee to Rush, 19 September 1775, *Lee Papers*, 1:206–8; Charles

Lee to John Thomas, 23 July 1775, *Lee Papers*, 1:197–98; John Richard Alden, *General Charles Lee: Traitor or Patriot?* (Baton Rouge: Louisiana State University Press, 1951), 1–16; James Wilkinson, *Memoirs of My Own Times* (Philadelphia: Abraham Small, 1816), 1:107; Richard Henry Lee to Robert Carter Nicholas, 30 April 1776, *Letters of Delegates*, 3:607–8; Alexander Graydon, *Memoirs of a Life Chiefly Passed in Pennsylvania, within the Last Sixty Years* (Edinburgh: William Blackwood, 1822), 337–41; Simeon Alexander, in John C. Dann, ed., *The Revolution Remembered: Eyewitness Accounts of the War for Independence* (Chicago: University of Chicago Press, 1980), 105; Thatcher, n.d., *Military Journal*, 558–66; J. T. Headley, *Washington and His Generals* (New York: Baker and Scribner, 1847), 2:162–69.

17. Dyer to Joseph Trumbull, 20 June 1775, *Letters of Delegates*, 1:521–22; Deane to Joseph Trumbull, 22 June 1775, *Letters of Delegates*, 1:533; Roger Sherman to David Wooster, 23 June 1775, *Letters of Delegates*, 1:539–40; Deane to Elizabeth Deane, 20 July 1775, *Letters of Delegates*, 1:638–40; Sherman to William Williams, 28 July 1775, *Letters of Delegates*, 1:674–75.
18. Adams to Abigail Adams, 18 June 1775, *Adams Family Correspondence*, 1:224–25.
19. Charles Carrollton of Annapolis to Charles Carrollton of Carrollton, 29 June 1775, in Ronald Hoffman, ed., *Dear Papa, Dear Charley: The Peregrinations of a Revolutionary Aristocrat . . .* (Chapel Hill: University of North Carolina Press, 2001) [hereafter cited as *Dear Papa*], 2:830.
20. Adams to Abigail Adams, 18 June 1775, *Adams Family Correspondence*, 1:226; Hancock to Joseph Warren, 18 June 1775, *Letters of Delegates*, 1:507–8; Samuel Adams to Gerry, 22 June 1775, *Writings of Samuel Adams*, 3:218–19; James Warren to Adams, 20 June 1775, *Adams Papers* 3, http://www.masshist.org; Gerry to the Massachusetts Delegates, 20 June 1775, *Adams Papers* 3, http://www.masshist.org.
21. Adams to James Warren, 21 June 1775, *Adams Papers* 3, http://www.masshist.org; James Warren to Adams, 27 June 1775, *Adams Papers* 3, http://www.masshist.org; Adams to Gerry, 18 June 1775, *Letters of Delegates*, 1:503–4; Dyer to Joseph Trumbull, 20 June 1775, *Letters of Delegates*, 1:521–22; Adams to Cotton Tufts, 21 June 1775, *Letters of Delegates*, 1:529; Sherman to David Wooster, 23 June 1775, *Letters of Delegates*, 1:539–40; James Duane to Richard Montgomery, 21 July 1775, *Letters of Delegates*, 1:641–42; Caesar Rodney to Thomas Rodney, 20 June 1775, *Letters to and from Caesar Rodney, 1756–1784*, ed. George Herbert Ryden (Philadelphia: University of Pennsylvania Press, 1933) [hereafter cited as *Rodney Letters*], 60–61.
22. Samuel Adams to James Warren, 28 June 1775, *Letters of Delegates*, 1:553–54; Adams to James Warren, 10 July 1775, *Adams Papers* 3, http://www.masshist.org.
23. For evidence of the American army's plight, see William Tudor to Adams, 19 July 1775, *Adams Papers* 3, http://www.masshist.org; Israel Trask, in Dann, *Revolution Remembered*, 406–13; Samuel Blachley Webb to Deane, 11 July 1775, *Correspondence and Journals of Samuel Blachley Webb*, ed. Worthington Chauncey Ford (New York: Wickersham Press, 1893) [hereafter cited as *Webb Correspondence and Journals*], 1:73–79; Charles Lee to Robert Morris, 4 July 1776, *Lee Papers*, 1:188.
24. The quote is from James Warren to Adams, 7 July 1775, *Adams Papers* 3, http://www.masshist.org. See also Washington to Hancock, 21 September 1775, *Washington Papers*, 2:28; Washington to John Augustine Washington, 13 October 1775, *Washington Papers*, 2:161; Washington to Hancock, 18 and 21 February 1776, *Washington Papers*, 3:335–37; Tudor to Adams, 19 July 1775, *Adams Papers* 3, http://www.masshist.org;

Henry Knox letters, 9 and 11 July 1775, *Life and Correspondence of Henry Knox, Major-General in the American Revolutionary Army*, ed. Francis S. Drake (Boston: Samuel G. Drake, 1873), 18–19; Joseph Trumbull to Deane, 6 July 1775, *The Deane Papers: Correspondence between Silas Deane, His Brothers, and Their Business and Political Associates, 1771–1795* (Hartford: Connecticut Historical Society, 1930), 7–8; Samuel Ward to Samuel Ward Jr., 15 August 1775, *Correspondence of Governor Samuel Ward*, ed. Bernhard Knollenberg (Providence: Rhode Island Historical Society, 1952), 76–77.

25. Washington to Jonathan Trumbull Sr., 18 July 1775, *Washington Papers*, 1:132; Washington to Joseph Reed, 8 November 1775, *Washington Papers*, 2:335.
26. Adams to Greene, 9 March 1777, in *The Papers of General Nathanael Greene*, ed. Richard K. Showman and Dennis M. Conrad (Chapel Hill: University of North Carolina Press, 1976–2000) [hereafter cited as *Greene Papers*], 2:39–40.
27. Charles Thomson to John Dickinson, 29 July 1776, *Letters of Delegates*, 4:562.
28. Washington to Hancock, 10–11 July 1775, *Washington Papers*, 1:85, 89–90; Jonathan Trumbull Sr. to Washington, 13 July 1775, *Washington Papers*, 1:113–14; Washington to Hancock, 21 July 1775, *Washington Papers*, 1:138–39; Washington to Reed, 1 April 1776, *Washington Papers*, 4:9–12; Adams to James Warren, 23 July 1775, *Adams Papers* 3, http://www.masshist.org; James Warren to Adams, 31 July 1775, *Adams Papers* 3, http://www.masshist.org; Deane to Elizabeth Deane, 20 July 1775, *Letters of Delegates*, 1:638–40; Dyer to Joseph Trumbull, 21 and 28 July 1775, *Letters of Delegates*, 1:642–43, 673–74; Webb to Deane, 11 July 1775, *Webb Correspondence and Journals*, 1:79–82.
29. For information on Pomeroy's resignation, Thomas's elevation, and Thomas's character, see Washington to Hancock, 10–11 and 21 July 1775, *Washington Papers*, 1:85, 89–90, 138–39; James Warren and Joseph Hawley to Washington, 4 July 1775, *Washington Papers*, 1:61; Washington to John Thomas, 23 July 1775, *Washington Papers*, 1:159–62; Hancock to Washington, *Washington Papers*, 1:165; Washington to Hancock, 5 August 1775, *Washington Papers*, 1:223; Gerry to the Massachusetts Delegates, 20 June 1775, *Adams Papers* 3, http://www.masshist.org; James Warren to Adams, 27 June and 7, 10, and 31 July 1775, *Adams Papers* 3, http://www.masshist.org; Thatcher, July 1775, *Military Journal*, 32–33; Abigail Adams to Adams, 25 July 1775, *Adams Family Correspondence*, 1:263; Tufts to Adams, 4 and 25 July 1775, *Adams Family Correspondence*, 1:237, 265; Ammi R. Robbins, 15 April 1776, *Journal of the Rev. Ammi R. Robbins, A Chaplain in the American Army* (New Haven, Conn.: B. L. Hamlen, 1850), 8; John Trumbull, *Autobiography, Reminiscences, and Letters of John Trumbull* (New York: Wiley and Putnam, 1841), 18; Charles Carrollton of Carrollton to Charles Carrollton of Annapolis, 8 April 1776, *Dear Papa*, 2:893–95.
30. Washington to Hancock, 4–5 and 31 August 1775, *Washington Papers*, 1:223–30 and 390–91; Hancock to Washington, 26 September 1775, *Washington Papers*, 2:49; George Ross to James Wilson, 15 September 1775, *Letters of Delegates*, 2:16–17; Adams to Samuel Osgood, 15 November 1775, *Letters of Delegates*, 2:349–50; Richard Smith diary, 10 January 1776, *Letters of Delegates*, 3:80–81; Washington to Richard Henry Lee, 26 December 1775, in Peter Force, ed., *American Archives* [hereafter cited as *American Archives*], series 4 (Washington, D.C.: Clerk's Officer of the District Court of the District of Columbia, 1837–53), 4:465–66.
31. Washington to Lund Washington, 20 August 1775, *Washington Papers*, 1:335–36; Washington to Reed, 8 November and 15 December 1775, *Washington Papers*, 2:335, 551–53.

32. Heath, *Heath Memoirs*, 16; Washington to Hancock, 8 and 28 November, 31 December 1775, *Washington Papers*, 2:331, 444–45, 623; Samuel Adams to Gerry, 26 September 1775, *Writings of Samuel Adams*, 3:226–27; Jeduthun Baldwin to Adams, 28 March 1776, *Adams Papers* 4, http://www.masshist.org; Horatio Gates to Adams, 23 April 1776, *Adams Papers* 4, http://www.masshist.org; Committee of Conference Minutes of Proceedings, 23–24 October 1775, *Letters of Delegates*, 2:233–37.
33. The quote is from Washington to Hancock, 31 May 1777, *Washington Papers*, 9:569–70. For evidence of Knox's personality, character, and values, see Heath, *Heath Memoirs*, 16; Greene to Nicholas Cooke, 23 January 1777, *Greene Papers*, 2:13; John Murray to Greene, 21 January 1780, *Greene Papers*, 2:298–300; George Weedon to Greene, 11 November 1781, *Greene Papers*, 9:563–65; Chastellux, *Travels in North America*, 65, 70–71; Alexander McDougall to [?], 3 March 1781, *Letters of Delegates*, 17:10; Washington to John Sullivan, 25 November 1780, *The Writings of George Washington*, ed. John C. Fitzpatrick (Washington, D.C.: Government Printing Office, 1937–39) [hereafter cited as *Washington Writings*], 20:397–98; Knox to Lucy Knox, 2 January 1777, *Life and Correspondence of Knox*, 37–38; William Sullivan, "Familiar Letters," *Life and Correspondence of Knox*, 118–19; James Thatcher, *Life and Correspondence of Knox*, 119–20; Rush to Richard Henry Lee, 6 January 1777, *Rush Letters*, 1:124.
34. John Winthrop to Adams, 5 April 1776, *Adams Papers* 4, http://www.masshist.org.
35. For Washington's response, see Washington to Hancock, 30–31 January and 19 March 1776, *Washington Papers*, 3:216–17, 489–90; Washington to John Augustine Washington, 31 March 1776, *Washington Papers*, 3:569.
36. Washington to Hancock, 31 December 1775, *Washington Papers*, 2:624; Hancock to Washington, 29 January 1776, *Washington Papers*, 3:210–11; Artemas Ward to Washington, 22 March 1776, *Washington Papers*, 3:516; Washington to Reed, 1 April 1776, *Washington Papers*, 4:9–12; Washington to Charles Lee, 9 May 1776, *Washington Papers*, 4:244–46; Adams to Osgood, 15 November 1775, *Letters of Delegates*, 2:349–50; Artemas Ward to Hancock, 12 April 1776, *American Archives*, series 4, 5:872; Greene to Samuel Ward Sr., 4 January 1776, *Greene Papers*, 1:179; Rush to Ruston, 29 October 1775, *Rush Letters*, 1:91–92.
37. Washington to Joseph Spencer, 26 September 1775, *Washington Papers*, 2:55–56; Washington to Reed, 29 February and 9 March 1776, *Washington Papers*, 3:374–75; Joseph Frye to Washington, 18 March 1776, *Washington Papers*, 3:486–87; Washington to Reed, 1 April 1776, *Washington Papers*, 4:9–12; Washington to Charles Lee, 9 May 1776, *Washington Papers*, 4:244–46.
38. Sullivan to New Hampshire Committee of Safety, 8 December 1775, *Letters and Papers of Major-General John Sullivan*, ed. Otis G. Hammond (Concord: New Hampshire Historical Society, 1930–31) [hereafter cited as *Sullivan Letters and Papers*], 1:140–41; Washington to Hancock, 10–11 July 1775, *Washington Papers*, 1:89–90; Washington to John Thomas, 23 July 1775, *Washington Papers*, 1:159–62; Washington to Hancock, 7–9 March 1776, *Washington Papers*, 3:423; Washington to Sullivan, 16 June 1776, *Washington Papers*, 5:10–12; Washington to President of Congress, 7 March 1776, *American Archives*, series 4, 5:106–9; Washington to Hancock, 17 June 1776, *Washington Papers*, 5:20–21.
39. Tench Tilghman to William Duer, 4 October 1776, *American Archives*, series 5, 2:870.
40. For characterizations of Greene and insight into his thinking, see Washington to Henry Laurens, 3 August 1778, *The Papers of Henry Laurens*, ed. David R. Chesnutt and C. James Taylor (Columbia: University of South Carolina Press, 1985–2000)

[hereafter cited as *Laurens Papers*], 14:113; Greene to Cooke, 22 June 1775, *Greene Papers*, 1:89–90; Greene to Jacob Greene, 28 June 1775, *Greene Papers*, 1:92–93; Greene to Samuel Ward Sr., 14 July 1775, *Greene Papers*, 1:98–99; Greene to Adams, 2 June 1776, *Greene Papers*, 1:225–26; Greene to Robert Morris, 21 November 1781, *The Papers of Robert Morris*, ed. E. James Ferguson (Pittsburgh: University of Pittsburgh Press, 1973–77), 3:228–29; Washington to Hancock, 18 March 1777, *Washington Papers*, 8:597; Henry Lee, *Memoirs of the War in the Southern Department of the United States* (New York: University Publishing, 1869), 210–11, 220–21; Washington to George Mason, 22 October 1780, *Washington Writings*, 20:241–42; Headley, *Washington and His Generals*, 2:72–77; Rush, 10 October 1777, "Historical Notes of Dr. Benjamin Rush, 1777," *Pennsylvania Magazine of History and Biography* 27 (1902): 147; Dyer to Sullivan, 23 October 1777, *Letters of Delegates*, 8:162–63; Israel Trask, in Dann, *Revolution Remembered*, 406–14.

41. Wooster to Hector McNeil, 23 April 1776, in Worthington C. Ford, ed., *Some Papers of Aaron Burr* (Worcester, Mass.: Proceedings of the American Antiquarian Society, 1920), 28–29.
42. Washington to Philip Schuyler, 5 November 1775, *Washington Papers*, 2:302; Reed to Washington, 15 March 1776, *Washington Papers*, 3:473–77; Benedict Arnold to Washington, 8 May 1776, *Washington Papers*, 4:229–30; Adams to John Thomas, 7 March 1776, *Adams Papers* 4, http://www.masshist.org; Gates to Adams, *Adams Papers* 4, http://www.masshist.org; Adams to James Warren, 18 March 1776, *Adams Papers* 4, http://www.masshist.org; Gerry to Adams and Samuel Adams, 21 July 1776, *Adams Papers* 4, http://www.masshist.org; Hancock to Wooster, 30 November 1775, *Letters of Delegates*, 2:416; Richard Henry Lee to Charles Lee, 18 May 1776, *Letters of Delegates*, 4:36; Commissioners to Canada to Hancock, 27 May 1776, *Letters of Delegates*, 4:80–84; William Williams to Joseph Trumbull, 7 August 1776, *Letters of Delegates*, 4:636–38; Justus Bellamy, in Dann, *Revolution Remembered*, 379–90; Wooster to President of Congress, 4 May 1776, *American Archives*, series 4, 5:845–46; Charles Carrollton of Carrollton to Charles Carrollton of Annapolis, 17 May 1776, *Dear Papa*, 2:909–10.
43. Hancock to Washington, 6 March 1776, *Washington Papers*, 3:415–16; Duane to Robert Livingston, 6–11 [?] March 1776, *Letters of Delegates*, 3:336–37; Washington to President of Congress, 7 March 1776, *American Archives*, series 4, 5:106–9.
44. Duane to Alexander Stirling, 1 March 1776, *Letters of Delegates*, 3:315–16; Hancock to Stirling, 1 March 1776, *Letters of Delegates*, 3:316; Congressional Resolution, 27 April 1776, *American Archives*, series 4, 5:1340; John Jay to McDougall, 23 March 1776, *The Correspondence and Public Papers of John Jay*, ed. Henry P. Johnson (New York: G. P. Putnam's Sons, 1890–91) [hereafter cited as *Jay Correspondence and Papers*], 1:49–51; Adams to Greene, 22 June 1776, *Greene Papers*, 1:239; Heath to Adams, 20 July 1776, *Adams Papers* 4, http://www.masshist.org; Adams to Heath, 3 August 1776, *Adams Papers* 4, http://www.masshist.org.
45. Samuel Cooper to Adams, 22 April and 15 July 1776, *Adams Papers* 4, http://www.masshist.org; Adams to James Warren, 15 May 1776, *Adams Papers* 4, http://www.masshist.org; Samuel Cooper to Adams, 20 May 1776, *Adams Papers* 4, http://www.masshist.org; General Court to the Massachusetts Delegates, 6 June 1776, *Adams Papers* 4, http://www.masshist.org; Joseph Ward to Adams, 20 June and 28 July 1776, *Adams Papers* 4, http://www.masshist.org; Gerry to Samuel Adams and Adams, 3

August 1776, *Adams Papers* 4, http://www.masshist.org; Hancock to Washington, 16 May 1776, *Washington Papers*, 4:312–13; Artemas Ward to Washington, 9 June 1776, *Washington Papers*, 4:481–82; Artemas Ward to Washington, 23 June 1776, *Washington Papers*, 5:82–83; Hancock to Washington, 29 June 1776, *Washington Papers*, 5:149–50; Washington to Hancock, 4–5 July 1776, *Washington Papers*, 5:199–203; Washington to Artemas Ward, 16 June 1776, *Washington Papers*, 5:13–14; Hancock to Artemas Ward, 26 August 1776, *Letters of Delegates*, 5:64; Artemas Ward to Hancock, 12 April 1776, *American Archives*, series 4, 5:872.

46. Adams to Abigail Adams, 18 February 1776, *Adams Family Correspondence*, 1:349; Arnold to Washington, 14 January and 27 February 1776, *Washington Papers*, 3:81–83, 382; Washington to Hancock, 30–31 January 1776, *Washington Papers*, 3:216–17; Washington to Charles Lee, 30 January and 14 March 1776, *Washington Papers*, 3:222, 467–69; Charles Lee to Washington, 14 February 1776, *Washington Papers*, 3:311; Adams to James Warren, 18 February 1776, *Adams Papers* 4, http://www.masshist.org; Charles Lee to Robert Morris, 9 February 1776, *Lee Papers*, 1:280–81; Charles Lee to Washington, 14 February 1776, *Lee Papers*, 1:295–97; Robert Morris to Charles Lee, 17 February 1776, *Lee Papers*, 1:303–8; Benjamin Franklin to Charles Lee, 19 February 1776, *Lee Papers*, 1:313; Charles Lee to Washington, 19 February 1776, *American Archives*, series 4, 4:1198.

47. The quote is from Washington to John Augustine Washington, 31 March 1776, *Washington Papers*, 3:570. See also Charles Lee to Washington, 3 March 1776, *Washington Papers*, 3:404–5; Washington to Charles Lee, 14 March 1776, *Washington Papers*, 3:467–69; Hancock to Charles Lee, 1 March 1776, *Lee Papers*, 1:342–43; Charles Lee to Robert Howe, 5 April 1776, *Lee Papers*, 1:375–76; Committee of Secrecy for the Province of North Carolina to Charles Lee, 9 April 1776, *Lee Papers*, 1:397; Duane to Stirling, 1 March 1776, *Letters of Delegates*, 3:315–16; Richard Henry Lee to Samuel Purviance, 17 March 1776, *Letters of Delegates*, 3:394–95.

48. Charles Lee to Washington, 5 April 1776, *Lee Papers*, 1:376–78.

49. Charles Lee to Washington, 1 July 1776, *Washington Papers*, 5:168–71; Charles Lee to Pendleton, 1 June 1776, *Lee Papers*, 2:50–51; Rush to Charles Lee, 23 July 1776, *Rush Letters*, 1:103–4; William Moultrie, *Memoirs of the American Revolution* (New York: David Longworth, 1802), 1:141–44; Hugh F. Rankin, *The North Carolina Continentals* (Chapel Hill: University of North Carolina Press, 1971), 71.

50. The poem is from Lewis Beebe, 2 June 1776, "Journal of a Physician on the Expedition against Canada," *Pennsylvania Magazine of History and Biography* 59 (1935): 331–32. See also Hancock to Washington, 6 March 1776, *Washington Papers*, 3:415–16; Adams to John Thomas, 7 March 1776, *Adams Papers* 4, http://www.masshist.org; John Thomas to Washington, 27 April 1776, *Washington Papers*, 4:151–52; Hancock to John Thomas, 6 March 1776, *Letters of Delegates*, 3:341–42; Commissioners to Canada to Hancock, 27 May 1776, *Letters of Delegates*, 4:80–84; Baldwin, 20 May 1776, *Revolutionary Journal*, 44; John Thomas to Commissioners in Canada, 20 May 1776, *American Archives*, series 4, 6:592; Thatcher, 12 July 1776, *Military Journal*, 54–55.

51. Washington to Stirling, *Washington Papers*, 3:553; Schuyler to Washington, 11 May 1776, *Washington Papers*, 4:218–82; Washington to Sullivan, 16 June 1776, *Washington Papers*, 5:10–12; Samuel Chase to Gates, 13 June 1776, *Letters of Delegates*, 4:201–2; Sullivan to Washington, 14 May 1776, *Sullivan Letters and Papers*, 1:199–200; Sullivan

to Hancock, 1 June 1776, *Sullivan Letters and Papers*, 1:212–14; William Thompson, 25 January 1776, "Letters of Two Distinguished Officers of the Revolution," *Pennsylvania Magazine of History and Biography* 35 (1911): 304–5; Washington to President of Congress, 7 March 1776, *American Archives*, series 4, 5:106–9.

52. Abigail Adams to Adams, 10 December 1775, *Adams Family Correspondence*, 1:336.

53. Abigail Adams to Adams, 10 December 1775, *Adams Family Correspondence*, 1:336; Greene to Jacob Greene, 8 May 1778, *Greene Papers*, 2:380–81; Alexander Hamilton to Greene, 22 May 1779, *Greene Papers*, 4:62; Greene to Charles Pettit, 29 July 1779, *Greene Papers*, 4:283–84; Sullivan to Adams, 28 May 1777, *Adams Papers* 5, http://www.masshist.org; Washington to Hancock, 17 June 1776, *Washington Papers*, 5:20–21; Washington to Sullivan, 15 March 1777, *Washington Papers*, 8:580–81; Wilkinson, *Memoirs of My Own Times*, 1:56, 61; William Ellery to William Vernon, 25 April 1778, *Letters of Delegates*, 9:486–88; Thomas Rodney notes, 8 March 1781, *Letters of Delegates*, 17:36–40; Thatcher, n.d., *Military Journal*, 551–55; Headley, *Washington and His Generals*, 2:199–200.

54. Thompson to Washington, 14 May and 2 June 1776, *Washington Papers*, 4:303, 427–29; Sullivan to Washington, 5–6 and 7 June 1776, *Washington Papers*, 4:440–43, 457–58; Sullivan to Hancock, 1 June 1776, *Sullivan Letters and Papers*, 1:212–14; Sullivan's Instructions for General William Thompson, 6 June 1776, *Sullivan Letters and Papers*, 1:225; Sullivan letter, 8 June 1776, *American Archives*, series 4, 6:1036–38.

55. Sullivan to Schuyler, 12 June 1776, *Sullivan Letters and Papers*, 1:234.

56. Sullivan to Hancock, 2 July 1776, *Sullivan Letters and Papers*, 1:276.

57. Sullivan to Washington, 24 and 25 June 1776, *Washington Papers*, 5:92–95, 106–7; Arnold to Washington, 25 June 1776, *Washington Papers*, 5:96–97; Wilkinson, *Memoirs of My Own Times*, 1:61; Arnold to Sullivan, 13 June 1776, *Sullivan Letters and Papers*, 1:237–39; Sullivan to Schuyler, 19, 22, and 25 June 1776, *Sullivan Letters and Papers*, 1:250–54, 257–59, 267–69; Sullivan to Hancock, 2 July 1776, *Sullivan Letters and Papers*, 1:274–77; Address of Field Officers to Sullivan, 8 July 1776, *Sullivan Letters and Papers*, 1:282–83.

58. The quote is from Richard Henry Lee to Washington, 13 June 1776, *Washington Papers*, 4:514. For Congress's decision to appoint Gates and Gates's character and personality, see Chase to Schuyler, 31 May 1776, *Letters of Delegates*, 4:105–6; William Whipple to John Langdon, 14 June 1776, *Letters of Delegates*, 4:219; Gerry to Joseph Trumbull, 18 June 1776, *Letters of Delegates*, 4:263–64; Samuel Adams to Samuel Cooper, 15 July 1777, *Letters of Delegates*, 7:343; Josiah Bartlett to Langdon, 17 June 1776, in Josiah Bartlett, *The Papers of Josiah Bartlett*, ed. Frank C. Meyers (Hanover, N.H.: University Press of New England, 1979) [hereafter cited as *Bartlett Papers*], 75–76; Washington to Hancock, 20 June 1776, *Washington Papers*, 5:55–57; Tudor to Adams, 6 September 1776, *Adams Papers* 5, http://www.masshist.org; McDougall to George Clinton, 5 November 1778, in George Clinton, *Public Papers of George Clinton, First Governor of New York, 1777–1795, 1801–1804* (Albany, N.Y.: J. B. Lyon, 1900–1904) [hereafter cited as *Clinton Papers*], 4:244–49; Thatcher, 18 October 1777 and n.d., *Military Journal*, 128–29, 539–48; Charles Albert Pontgibaud, *A French Volunteer of the War of Independence*, ed. and trans. Robert B. Douglass (Paris: Charles Carrington, 1898), 43; Headley, *Washington and His Generals*, 1:290–92; Charles Carrollton of Carrollton to Charles Carrollton of Annapolis, 28 June 1776, *Dear Papa*, 2:923–24; Washington to Jay, 14 April 1779, *Washington Papers*, 20:57–64.

59. Washington to President of Congress, 17 July 1776, *American Archives*, series 5, 1:389.
60. Adams to Abigail Adams, 27 July 1776, *Adams Family Correspondence*, 2:63; Bartlett to Langdon, 29 July 1776, *Papers of Josiah Bartlett*, 100; Washington to Hancock, 17 June 1776, *Washington Papers*, 5:20–21; Hancock to Washington, 26 and 31 July 1776, *Washington Papers*, 5:473–74, 526–27; Sullivan to Schuyler, 6 July 1776, *Sullivan Letters and Papers*, 1:280–81; Schuyler to Sullivan, 7 July 1776, *Sullivan Letters and Papers*, 1:281–82.
61. Congressional Resolve, 2 October 1776, *Journals of the Continental Congress, 1774–1789* (Washington, D.C.: Government Printing Office, 1905–22), 5:841; Duane to Robert Livingston, 6–11 [?] March 1776, *Letters of Delegates*, 3:336–37; Robert Morris to Reed, 21 July 1776, *Letters of Delegates*, 4:510–13; Chase to Gates, 9 August 1776, *Letters of Delegates*, 4:643; Samuel Adams to Richard Henry Lee, 15 July 1776, *Writings of Samuel Adams*, 3:296–99; Thomas Hartley to Gates, 26 July 1776, *American Archives*, series 5, 1:603–4; Washington to Schuyler, 21 May 1776, *American Archives*, series 4, 6:535; Address of the Committee of Safety and Inspection for Several Towns to Washington, 21 May 1776, *American Archives*, series 4, 6:744–45; Schuyler to Washington, 1 July 1776, *American Archives*, series 4, 6:1199–1201; Adams to John Thomas, 7 March 1776, *Adams Papers* 4, http://www.masshist.org; Schuyler to Washington, 12 April 1776, *Washington Papers*, 4:54–56; Gerry to Adams and Samuel Adams, 21 July 1776, *Adams Papers* 4, http://www.masshist.org.
62. Arnold to Sullivan, 13 June 1776, *Sullivan Letters and Papers*, 1:237–38.
63. Washington to Schuyler, 5 December 1775, *Washington Papers*, 2:498.
64. See, for example, John Thomas Jefferson to John Page, 10 [?] December 1775, *Letters of Delegates*, 2:472–73; Jefferson to Thomas Nelson, 19 May 1776, *Letters of Delegates*, 4:39–40; Charles Carrollton of Carrollton to Charles Carrollton of Annapolis, 30 April and 1 May 1776, *Dear Papa*, 2:901–3; Arnold letter, 26 and 28 March 1776, *American Archives*, series 4, 5:512.
65. For descriptions of Arnold and some of his problems in Canada, see Washington to Hancock, 12 May 1777, *Washington Papers*, 9:396–97; Washington to Hancock, 10 July 1777, *Washington Papers*, 10:240–41; John Joseph Henry, "Journal of the Campaign against Quebec," *Journals and Diaries of the War of the Revolution*, Pennsylvania Archives, series 2 (1893), 15:65–66; Charles Carrollton of Carrollton to Charles Carrollton of Annapolis, 30 April 1776, *Dear Papa*, 2:901; Aaron Burr, *Memoirs of Aaron Burr*(New York: Harper and Brothers, 1836), 1:78; Court of Inquiry of General Arnold, 2 December 1776, *American Archives*, series 5, 3:1042–43; Enoch Poor to Arnold, 9 August 1776, *American Archives*, series 5, 1:802–3; Members of Court Martial to President of Congress, 19 August 1776, *American Archives*, series 5, 1:1072; Sullivan letter, 8 June 1776, *American Archives*, series 4, 6:1036–38; Arnold to Sullivan, 10 June 1776, *American Archives*, series 4, 6:796–97; Philip Van Cortlandt, *The Revolutionary Memoir and Selected Correspondence of Philip Van Cortlandt*, comp. and ed. Jacob Judd (Tarrytown, N.Y.: Sleepy Hollow Restorations, 1976), 37; Lewis Beebe, 13 June 1776, "Journal of a Physician on the Expedition against Canada," *Pennsylvania Magazine of History and Biography* 59 (1935): 334, 341–42; Joseph Ward to Adams, 12 May 1777, *Adams Papers* 5, http://www.masshist.org; Alpheus Parkhurst, in Dann, *Revolution Remembered*, 56–59; John Howland, *The Life and Recollections of John Howland*, ed. Edwin M. Stone (Providence, R.I.: George H. Whitney, 1857),89–90.

66. Address of Field Offices to Sullivan, 8 July 1776, *Sullivan Letters and Papers*, 1:282–83; Members of Court-Martial to President of Congress, 19 August 1776, *American Archives*, series 5, 1:1072.
67. Richard Henry Lee to Jefferson, 3 November 1776, *Letters of Delegates*, 5:431–32; Caesar Rodney to George Read, 25 December 1776, *Rodney Letters*, 141–42; Rush to Thomas Morris [?], 22 October 1776, *Rush Letters*, 1:118–19; Thatcher, 15 October 1776, *Military Journal*, 76.
68. Adams to Washington, 6 January 1776, *Adams Papers* 3, http://www.masshist.org.
69. William Palfrey to Washington, 29 January 1776, *Washington Papers*, 3:212; Washington to Hancock, 13 March 1776, *Washington Papers*, 3:461–63; Washington to Stirling, 14 March 1776, *Washington Papers*, 3:469–71; Washington to Charles Lee, 8 January 1776, *Lee Papers*, 1:236–37.
70. Samuel Shaw to his father, 3 May 1776, *The Journals of Major Samuel Shaw, the First American Consul at Canton*, ed. Josiah Quincy (Boston: Wm. Crosby and H. P. Nichols, 1847), 12.
71. Washington to John Augustine Washington, 22 July 1776, *Washington Papers*, 5:428–29.
72. Greene to Adams, 2 June 1776, *Greene Papers*, 1:226; Congressional Resolve, 23 January 1776, *Journals of the Continental Congress*, 4:81.
73. Washington to Hancock, 11 May 1776, *Washington Papers*, 4:276–80; Washington to Hancock, 5 and 7 August 1776, *Washington Papers*, 5:567–68, 602–4.
74. Adams to Abigail Adams, 21 February 1777, *Adams Family Correspondence*, 2:165; William Williams to Joseph Trumbull, 10 August 1776, *Letters of Delegates*, 4:650–51; Bartlett to Langdon, 11 August 1776, *Bartlett Papers*, 104; Adams to Samuel Parsons, 11 August 1776, *Adams Papers* 4, http://www.masshist.org.
75. Washington to Schuyler, 6 October 1775, *Washington Papers*, 2:120; Washington to Hancock, 17 and 20 June 1776, *Washington Papers*, 5:22, 55–57; Hancock to Washington, 21–22 June 1776, *Washington Papers*, 5:68–69; Richard Henry Lee to Charles Lee, 18 May 1776, *Letters of Delegates*, 4:36; Francis Lightfoot Lee to Landon Carter, 21 May 1776, *Letters of Delegates*, 4:57–58; Commissioners to Canada to Hancock, 27 May 1776, *Letters of Delegates*, 4:80–84; Robert Morris to Deane, 5 June 1776, *Letters of Delegates*, 4:146–48; William Williams to Joseph Trumbull, 7 and 10 August 1776, *Letters of Delegates*, 4:636–38, 650–51; Edward Rutledge to Robert Livingston, 19 [?] August 1776, *Letters of Delegates*, 5:25–27; Wooster to President of Congress, 26 June 1776, *American Archives*, series 4, 6:1081; Congressional Note, 17 August 1776, *Journals of the Continental Congress*, 5:664–65.
76. Adams's comments are in Adams to Parsons, 22 June 1776, *Adams Papers* 4, http://www.masshist.org.
77. Greene to Adams, 2 June 1776, *Greene Papers*, 1:225–26; Parsons to Adams, 24 July 1776, *Adams Papers* 4, http://www.masshist.org; Adams to Parsons, 11 August 1776, *Adams Papers* 4, http://www.masshist.org; Daniel Hitchcock to Adams, 22 August 1776, *Adams Papers* 4, http://www.masshist.org; William Maxwell to Congress, n.d., *American Archives*, series 5, 1:1204; James Varnum to Washington, 25 August 1776, *American Archives*, series 5, 1:1150–51.
78. Adams to Greene, 22 June 1776, *Adams Papers* 4, http://www.masshist.org.
79. Greene to Adams, 2 June 1776, *Greene Papers*, 1:225–26; Adams to Greene, 22 June and 4 August 1776, *Greene Papers*, 1:239, 274; Parsons to Adams, 20 May 1776, *Adams*

Papers 4, http://www.masshist.org; Heath to Adams, 20 July 1776, *Adams Papers* 4, http://www.masshist.org; Rush to Anthony Wayne, 29 September 1776, *Letters of Delegates*, 5:262–63.

80. Adams to Greene, 4 August 1776, *Greene Papers*, 1:273–74; Adams to Hitchcock, 3 August 1776, *Adams Papers* 4, http://www.masshist.org; Joseph Ward to Adams, 8 August 1776, *Adams Papers* 4, http://www.masshist.org; Adams to Parsons, 11 August 1776, *Adams Papers* 4, http://www.masshist.org; Adams to Thomas Mifflin, 15 August 1776, *Adams Papers* 4, http://www.masshist.org; Adams to Joseph Ward, 20 August 1776, *Adams Papers* 4, http://www.masshist.org; Knox to Adams, 21 August 1776, *Adams Papers* 4, http://www.masshist.org; Adams to Hawley, 25 August 1776, *Adams Papers* 4, http://www.masshist.org.
81. Varnum to Washington, 25 August 1776, *American Archives*, series 5, 1:1151.
82. The quote is from Adams to Parsons, 3 August 1776, *Letters of Delegates*, 4:615. See also Tudor to Adams, 19 August 1776, *Adams Papers* 4, http://www.masshist.org; Hitchcock to Adams, 22 August 1776, *Adams Papers* 4, http://www.masshist.org; William Henry Smith, ed., *The Life and Public Services of Arthur St. Clair* (Cincinnati: Robert Clarke, 1882) [hereafter cited as *Life of St. Clair*], 1:372n; Washington to President of Congress, 14 August 1776, *American Archives*, series 5, 1:949–50; Maxwell to Congress, n.d., *American Archives*, series 5, 1:1204; Hitchcock to Washington, 19 August 1776, *American Archives*, series 5, 1:1067–68.
83. Washington to William Livingston, 6 July 1776, *Washington Papers*, 5:223–24.
84. Extract of a Letter from New York, 22 August 1776, *American Archives*, series 5, 1:1111–12.

Chapter 2. Trying Times

1. Greene to Cooke, 22 July 1776, *Greene Papers*, 1:260.
2. Greene to Washington, 25 July 1776, *Greene Papers*, 1:263; Washington to Hancock, 23 August 1776, *Washington Papers*, 6:111–12; Washington to Lund Washington, 26 August 1776, *Washington Papers*, 6:135–37; Reed to his wife, 24 August 1776, in *Life and Correspondence of Joseph Reed*, ed. William B. Reed (Philadelphia: Lindsay and Blakiston, 1847), 1:220; John E. Ferling, *Almost a Miracle: The American Victory in the War of Independence* (Oxford: Oxford University Press, 2007), 133; Reed to William Livingston, n.d., in William Farrand Livingston, *Israel Putnam: Pioneer, Ranger, and Major-General, 1718–1790* (New York: G. P. Putnam's Sons, 1901), 294.
3. John J. Gallagher, *The Battle of Brooklyn, 1776* (New York: Sarpedon, 1995), 133.
4. William Livingston, 31 December 1777, *The Papers of William Livingston*, ed. Carl E. Prince, Dennis P. Ryan, and Mary Lou Lustig (Trenton, N.J.: New Jersey Historical Commission, 1979–87) [hereafter cited as *Livingston Papers*], 2:151–52; Knox to Adams, 21 August 1776, *Adams Papers* 4, http://www.masshist.org; Charles Lee to Rush, 2 November 1776, *Lee Papers*, 2:262–63; John Glover to Washington, 1 April 1777, *Washington Papers*, 9:34–35; Washington to Glover, 26 April 1777, *Washington Papers*, 9:274; Glover to Washington, 26 April 1779, *Washington Papers*, 20:216; Chastellux, *Travels in North America*, 69–70.
5. Edward Hand letter, n.d., *Life and Correspondence of Reed*, 1:229.
6. Knox to Adams, 25 September 1776, *Adams Papers* 5, http://www.masshist.org.
7. Parsons to Adams, 17 September 1776, *Adams Papers* 5, http://www.masshist.org; Washington to Hancock, 29 August and 6 September 1776, *Washington Papers*,

6:155–56, 231–33; Washington to Schuyler, 4 September 1776, *Washington Papers*, 6:218–19; Washington to Massachusetts General Court, 19 September 1776, *Washington Papers*, 6:344–47; Tilghman letter, 8 September 1776, *Memoir of Lieut. Col. Tench Tilghman* (Albany, N.Y.: J. Munsell, 1876) [hereafter cited as *Tilghman Memoir*], 134; Adams to Cooper, 4 September 1776, *Letters of Delegates*, 5:101–2; Adams to Tudor, 20 September 1776, *Letters of Delegates*, 5:200; Committee of Secret Correspondence to Deane, 1 October 1776, *Letters of Delegates*, 5:277–81; John Young to George Clinton, 29 September 1776, *Clinton Papers*, 1:364–65; John Morin Scott to Jay, 6 September 1776, *Jay Correspondence and Papers*, 1:78–83.

8. The quote is from Washington to Hancock, 8 September 1776, *Washington Papers*, 6:249. See also Washington to Hancock, 2 and 4 September 1776, *Washington Papers*, 6:199–201, 215–17.
9. Adams to Abigail Adams, 6 April 1777, *Adams Family Correspondence*, 2:199–200; Greene to Washington, 5 September 1776, *Greene Papers*, 1:294–96; Washington to Hancock, 2, 4, 8, and 14 September 1776, *Washington Papers*, 6:199–201, 215–17, 248–52, 308–9; Council of War, 12 September 1776, *Washington Papers*, 6:288–89; George Clinton to Washington, 12 September 1776, *Washington Papers*, 6:290–92; Heath to Washington, 13 September 1776, *Washington Papers*, 6:302–4.
10. Greene to Cooke, 17 September 1776, *Greene Papers*, 1:300; Greene to Ellery, 4 October 1776, *Greene Papers*, 1:303–4; Washington to Hancock, 16 September and 4 October 1776, *Washington Papers*, 6:313–14, 463–66; Tilghman letter, 19 September 1776, *Tilghman Memoir*, 138–39; George Clinton report, 18 September 1776, *Clinton Papers*, 1:351–54; Knox letter, 23 September 1776, *Life and Correspondence of Knox*, 31–32.
11. Charles Lee to Gates, 14 October 1776, *Lee Papers*, 2:261–62; Richard Henry Lee to John Page, 3 September 1776, *Letters of Delegates*, 5:97–99; James Smith to Eleanor Smith, 7 October 1776, *Letters of Delegates*, 5:314–15; William Hooper to the North Carolina Provincial Convention, 26 October 1776, *Letters of Delegates*, 5:396–403; John Haslet to Caesar Rodney, 10 October 1776, *Rodney Letters*, 137–39; Charles Carrollton of Carrollton to Charles Carrollton of Annapolis, 4 October 1776, *Dear Papa*, 2:952–53; Washington to Hancock, 6 September 1776, *Washington Papers*, 6:231–33; Washington to Massachusetts General Court, 19 September 1776, *Washington Papers*, 6:344–47.
12. Robert Harrison to Hancock, 20 October 1776, *Washington Papers*, 6:592–93; General Orders, 21 October 1776, *Washington Papers*, 7:1; Samuel Adams to Samuel Mather, 26 October 1776, *Letters of Delegates*, 5:389–90.
13. Greene to Adams, 3 March 1777, *Adams Papers* 5, http://www.masshist.org; Charles Lee to Rush, 2 November 1776, *Lee Papers*, 2:262–63; George Clinton to John McKesson, 31 October 1776, *Clinton Papers*, 1:399–401; Knox letter, 1 November 1776, *Life and Correspondence of Knox*, 33.
14. Greene to Washington, 12 October and 9 November 1776, *Greene Papers*, 1:314, 344–45; Greene to Mifflin, 27 October 1776, *Greene Papers*, 1:322–23; Greene to Catharine Greene, 2 November 1776, *Greene Papers*, 1:329–30; Washington to Greene, 7 November 1776, *Greene Papers*, 1:339–40; Greene to Hancock, 12 November 1776, *Greene Papers*, 1:348–49; Greene to Knox, 17 November 1776, *Greene Papers*, 1:351–52; Washington to John Augustine Washington, 19 October 1776, *Washington Papers*, 7:102–5; Washington to Reed, 22 August 1779, *Washington Papers*, 22:224–27; Charles Lee to Reed, 16 November 1776, *Lee Papers*, 2:283–84; Reed to Charles Lee, 21 November 1776, *Lee Papers*, 2:293–94.

15. Greene to Knox, 17 November 1776, *Greene Papers*, 1:351–52.
16. Ibid., 1:352.
17. Charles Lee to Washington, 19 November 1776, *Washington Papers*, 7:187.
18. Washington to John Augustine Washington, 19 November 1776, *Washington Papers*, 7:102–5; Washington to Reed, 22 August 1779, *Washington Papers*, 22:224–27.
19. Thatcher, 20 November 1776, *Military Journal*, 80.
20. The quote is from Washington to Bowdoin, 18 December 1776, *Washington Papers*, 7:365. See also Greene to Christopher Greene, 20 January 1777, *Greene Papers*, 2:8–9; Washington to Charles Lee, 21 and 27 November and 1 December 1776, *Washington Papers*, 7:193–95, 224–25, 249; Washington to Lund Washington, 10/17 December 1776, *Washington Papers*, 7:289–92.
21. Wilkinson, *Memoirs of My Own Times*, 1:126–128; Washington to Arnold, 14 December 1776, *Washington Papers*, 7:331; Washington to Spencer, 14 December 1776, *Washington Papers*, 7:338–39; Washington to Reed, 23 December 1776, *Washington Papers*, 7:423–24; Gerry to James Warren [?], 23 December 1776, *Letters of Delegates*, 5:640–41.
22. Washington to McDougall, 21 December 1776, *Washington Papers*, 7:401.
23. McDougall to Washington, 19 December 1776, *Washington Papers*, 7:376–77; Washington to Hancock, 20 December 1776, *Washington Papers*, 7:381–86.
24. Charles Lee to Gates, 12/13 December 1776, *Lee Papers*, 2:348.
25. The quote is from Washington to Charles Lee, 27 November 1776, *Washington Papers*, 7:224–25. For Lee's attitude and Washington's frustrations, see Heath, *Heath Memoirs*, 80–84; Adams to Abigail Adams, 7 October 1776, *Adams Family Correspondence*, 2:139; Instructions to Major General Charles Lee, 10 November 1776, *Washington Papers*, 7:133–35; Washington to Charles Lee, 21 November 1776, *Washington Papers*, 7:193–95; Charles Lee to Washington, 30 November, 4 and 8 December 1776, *Washington Papers*, 7:235, 259–60, 276–77; Charles Lee to Gates, 14 October and 12/13 December 1776, *Lee Papers*, 2:261–62, 348; Charles Lee to Heath, 21 November 1776, *Lee Papers*, 2:291; Charles Lee to Reed, 24 November 1776, *Lee Papers*, 2:305–6; Thomas Rodney, 16 December 1776, *Diary of Captain Thomas Rodney, 1776–1777* (Wilmington: Historical Society of Delaware, 1888), 12–13; Charles Carrollton of Carrollton to Charles Carrollton of Annapolis, 4 October 1776, *Dear Papa*, 2:952–53.
26. The quote is from Washington to Heath, 30 March 1781, *Washington Writings*, 21:392. See also Hugh Hughes to Adams, 31 March 1776, *Adams Papers* 4, http://www.masshist.org; Greene to Hughes, 17 October 1780, *Greene Papers*, 6:403; Washington to Richard Henry Lee, 24/26 April 1777, *Washington Papers*, 9:255–58; Chastellux, *Travels in North America*, 48–49; Rufus Putnam, *The Memoirs of Rufus Putnam, and Certain Official Papers and Correspondence* (Boston: Houghton, Mifflin, 1903), 57; Thatcher, n.d., *Military Journal*, 500–504; Headley, *Washington and His Generals*, 1:348.
27. Charles Lee to Heath, 26 November 1776, *Lee Papers*, 2:314.
28. Heath, *Heath Memoirs*, 87.
29. Ibid., 80–88; Heath to Washington, 24 November 1776, *Washington Papers*, 7:205–6; Charles Lee to Washington, 24, 26, and 30 November 1776, *Washington Papers*, 7:210–11, 217, 235; Charles Lee to Heath, 21, 23, and 26 November 1776, *Lee Papers*, 2:291, 304, 313–14; Heath to Charles Lee, 21 and 24 November 1776, *Lee Papers*, 2:299–300, 305; Heath to George Clinton, 6 December 1776, *Clinton Papers*, 1:447–48.

30. Wilkinson, *Memoirs of My Own Times*, 105–6; Charles Lee to Washington, 8 December 1776, *Washington Papers*, 7:277; Washington to Charles Lee, 10 December 1776, *Washington Papers*, 7:288.
31. Robert Morris to Deane, 20 December 1776, *Letters of Delegates*, 5:621.
32. The quote is from Rodney, 22 December 1776, *Diary of Thomas Rodney*, 19. See also Abigail Adams to Mercy Otis Warren, January 1777, *Adams Family Correspondence*, 2:150; Greene to Catharine Greene, 16 December 1776, *Greene Papers*, 1:368–69; Washington to Lund Washington, 10/17 December 1776, *Washington Papers*, 7:289–92; Washington to Jonathan Trumbull, 12 December 1776, *Washington Papers*, 7:321; Sullivan to Washington, 13 December 1776, *Washington Papers*, 7:328; Washington to Hancock, 15 December 1776, *Washington Papers*, 7:344–45; Pennsylvania Council of Safety to Washington, 16 December 1776, *Washington Papers*, 7:363; Washington to Samuel Washington, 18 December 1776, *Washington Papers*, 7:369–71; Tilghman letter, 16 December 1776, *Tilghman Memoir*, 147–48; Rush to Richard Henry Lee, 21 December 1776, *Letters of Delegates*, 5:639–40; Hancock to Robert Morris, 23 December 1776, *Letters of Delegates*, 5:642–43; Thatcher, 20 December 1776, *Military Journal*, 80; Howland, *Life and Recollections of John Howland*, 64.
33. Richard Henry Lee to Patrick Henry, 18 December 1776, *Letters of Delegates*, 5:615–16; Benjamin Rumsey to John Hall [?], 19 December 1776, *Letters of Delegates*, 5:617–20; Samuel Adams to James Warren, 25 December 1776, *Letters of Delegates*, 5:660–63; Rodney, 18 December 1776, *Diary of Thomas Rodney*, 14–15; Thomas Fleming, *1776: Year of Illusions* (New York: W.W. Norton, 1975), 416.
34. Rush to Wayne, 29 September 1776, *Rush Letters*, 1:116.
35. Washington to Hancock, 20 December 1776, *Washington Papers*, 7:381–86; Chase to Gates, 13 June 1776, *Letters of Delegates*, 4:201–2; Rush to Richard Henry Lee, 21 December 1776, *Letters of Delegates*, 5:639–40; John Witherspoon to Gates, 30 October 1776, *Letters of Delegates*, 5:419–20; Adam Stephen to Richard Henry Lee, 4 February 1776, *Historical Magazine* 9 (April 1865): 121; Congressional Resolve, 4 September 1776, *Journals of the Continental Congress*, 5:734; Knox to his wife, 2 January 1777, *Life and Correspondence of Knox*, 37–38.
36. Washington to Samuel Washington, 18 December 1776, *Washington Papers*, 7:371.
37. Washington to Robert Morris, 25 December 1776, *Washington Papers*, 7:439–40.
38. Quoted in Wilkinson, *Memoirs of My Own Times*, 131. See also Washington to Hancock, 27 December 1776, *Washington Papers*, 7:454–56; Rush to Richard Henry Lee, 6 January 1777, *Rush Letters*, 1:124.
39. Nicholas Cresswell, 7 January 1777, *The Journal of Nicholas Cresswell, 1774–77* (Port Washington, N.Y.: Kennikat Press, 1968), 179–80.
40. Hancock to Schuyler, 30 December 1776, *Letters of Delegates*, 5:702.
41. Knox to his wife, 28 December 1776, *Life and Correspondence of Knox*, 37.
42. Wilkinson, *Memoirs of My Own Times*, 128–29.
43. Quoted in Harry W. Ward, *Major General Adam Stephen and the Cause of American Liberty* (Charlottesville: University Press of Virginia), 151.
44. Wilkinson, *Memoirs of My Own Times*, 136–37; Washington to Heath, 28 December 1776, *Washington Papers*, 7:468–69.
45. Washington to Hancock, 5 January 1777, *Washington Papers*, 7:519–20.
46. Wilkinson, *Memoirs of My Own Times*, 140–41; Gates to Washington, 29 July 1776, *Washington Papers*, 5:498–500; Arthur St. Clair to Washington, 25 July 1777,

Washington Papers, 10:418–19; *Life of St. Clair*, 1:2–9, 12–16, 36; Wayne to Franklin, 1 September 1776, *The Papers of Benjamin Franklin*, ed. William B. Willcox (New Haven, Conn.: Yale University Press, 1982–83), 22:585–86; Henry Brockholst Livingston to William Livingston, 10 June 1777, *Livingston Papers*, 1:349; Greene to Jacob Greene, 11 August 1777, *Greene Papers*, 2:138; Robert Morris to Charles Lee, 17 February 1776, *Lee Papers*, 1:303–8; Chase to Gates, 13 June 1776, *Letters of Delegates*, 4:201–2; Wilson to Jasper Yates and John Montgomery, 10 August 1776, *Letters of Delegates*, 4:651–53; Headley, *Washington and His Generals*, 2:217–19, 224.

47. Thatcher, 5 January 1777, *Military Journal*, 83.
48. Caesar Rodney to William Killen, 12 January 1777, *Rodney Letters*, 172.

Chapter 3. Turmoil and Strife

1. Washington to Hancock, 20 December 1776, *Washington Papers*, 7:381–86; Washington to Hancock, 20 January 1777, *Washington Papers*, 8:125–28.
2. The quote is from Washington to Hancock, 20 January 1777, *Washington Papers*, 8:128. See also Washington to Reed, 23 December 1776, *Washington Papers*, 7:423–24.
3. Washington to Hancock, 20 December 1776, *Washington Papers*, 7:386.
4. David Mattern, *Benjamin Lincoln and the American Revolution* (Columbia: University of South Carolina Press, 1998), 6–21; William Livingston, 31 December 1777, *Livingston Papers*, 2:151; Robert Morris to Greene, 24 December 1781, *Papers of Robert Morris*, 3:438–39; Cooper to Adams, 15 July 1776, *Adams Papers* 4, http://www.masshist.org; Jeremiah Wadsworth to Greene, 12 December 1782, *Greene Papers*, 12:285–86; Washington to Heath, 18 December 1776, *Washington Papers*, 7:366–67; Washington to Hancock, 20 January 1777, *Washington Papers*, 8:125–28; John Penn to Richard Caswell, 22 October 1778, *Letters of Delegates*, 11:100; Jay to Benjamin Lincoln, 2 April 1779, *Jay Correspondence and Papers*, 1:195; Thatcher, *Military Journal*, 504–17; Samuel Shaw, 1 October 1780, *Journals of Major Samuel Shaw*, 80; Headley, *Washington and His Generals*, 2:123–25.
5. Burke notes, 12–19 February 1777, *Letters of Delegates*, 6:264.
6. Ibid., 6:263–64; Adams to Greene, 9 March 1777, *Adams Papers* 5, http://www.masshist.org; Gouverneur Morris to Washington, 27–28 May 1778, *Washington Papers*, 15:240; Chase to the Maryland Council of Safety, 31 January 1777, *Letters of Delegates*, 6:170; Francis Lewis to the New York Convention, 18 February 1777, *Letters of Delegates*, 6:314–15; Gerry to Knox, 7 February 1778, *Letters of Delegates*, 9:45–47.
7. Congressional Resolve, 19 February 1777, *Journals of the Continental Congress*, 7:133.
8. Gouverneur Morris to Washington, 27–28 May 1778, *Washington Papers*, 15:240.
9. Burke notes, 12–19 February 1777, *Letters of Delegates*, 6:263–64; Adams to Greene, 9 March 1777, *Greene Papers*, 2:36–40.
10. Rush to Richard Henry Lee, 21 December 1776, *American Archives*, series 5, 3:1512–13.
11. For information into Congress's thinking, see Adams to Greene, 9 May 1777, *Greene Papers*, 2:74–75; Adams to Greene, 9 March 1777, *Adams Papers* 5, http://www.masshist.org; Washington to Arnold, 2 April 1777, *Washington Papers*, 9:45–46; Chase to the Maryland Council of Safety, 31 January 1777, *Letters of Delegates*, 6:170; Burke notes, 12–19 February 1777, *Letters of Delegates*, 6:263–64; Francis Lewis to the New York Convention, 18 February 1777, *Letters of Delegates*, 6:314–15; Rush notes, 19 February 1777, *Letters of Delegates*, 6:323–25; Wilson to St. Clair, 20 February 1777, *Letters of Delegates*, 6:333–34; Sherman to Jonathan Trumbull, 6 March 1777, *Letters of*

Delegates, 6:403–5; and Sherman to Jonathan Trumbull, 4 March 1777, *The Trumbull Papers*, pt. 3 (Boston: Collections of the Massachusetts Historical Society), 25–29.

12. Charles Carroll of Carrollton to Charles Carroll Sr., 8 October 1777, *Letters of Delegates*, 8:73.
13. Burke to Caswell, 11 May 1777, *Letters of Delegates*, 7:69. See also Congressional Resolve, 5 February 1777, *Journals of the Continental Congress*, 7:90.
14. Whipple to Josiah Bartlett, 22 February 1777, *Bartlett Papers*, 148; Washington to William Woodford, 3 March 1777, *Washington Papers*, 8:507–8; Washington to Hancock, 14 March 1777 *Washington Papers*, 8:570–72; Executive Committee to Hancock, 25 December 1776, *Letters of Delegates*, 5:684–85; Chase to the Maryland Council of Safety, 31 January 1777, *Letters of Delegates*, 6:170; Hooper to Robert Morris, 4 February 1777, *Letters of Delegates*, 6:208–9; Francis Lewis to the New York Convention, 18 February 1777, *Letters of Delegates*, 6:314–15; Whipple to Joseph Whipple, 28 February 1777, *Letters of Delegates*, 6:392–93; Sherman to Jonathan Trumbull, 6 March 1777, *Letters of Delegates*, 6:403–4; Sherman to Jonathan Trumbull, 4 March 1777, *Trumbull Papers*, pt. 3, 25–29; Congressional Resolve, 22 February 1777, *Journals of the Continental Congress*, 7:141–42; Tudor to Adams, 16 March 1777, *Adams Papers* 5, http://www.masshist.org; Greene to Washington, 12 August 1776, *Greene Papers*, 1:284; Washington to President of Congress, 14 August 1776, *American Archives*, series 5, 1:949–50; Gates to President of Congress, 30 September 1776, *American Archives*, series 5, 2:615.
15. Washington to John Cadwalader, 3 March 1777, *Washington Papers*, 8:493–94; Reed to Washington, 8 March 1777, *Washington Papers*, 8:541–42; Washington to Thomas Jefferson, 3 September 1777, *Washington Papers*, 11:137–38; John Cadwalader to Washington, 27 April 1778, *Washington Papers*, 14:658; John Cadwalader to Washington, 4 December 1778, *Washington Papers*, 18:360.
16. Gates to Washington, 23 February and 7 March 1777, *Washington Papers*, 8:423, 533–34; Washington to Gates, 1 March 1777, *Washington Papers*, 8:471; Washington to Richard Henry Lee, 24/26 April 1777, *Washington Papers*, 9:255–58; Washington to Gates, 28 April 1777, *Washington Papers*, 9:292; Washington to Hancock, 10 May 1777, *Washington Papers*, 9:373–74; Andrew Allen to Schuyler, 17 March 1777, *Letters of Delegates*, 3:393–94.
17. Glover to Washington, 1 April 1777, *Washington Papers*, 9:34–35; Heath to Washington, 16 April 1777, *Washington Papers*, 9:176–78; Washington to Glover, 26 April 1777, *Washington Papers*, 9:274.
18. Washington to Andrew Lewis, 3 March 1777, *Washington Papers*, 8:500.
19. Washington to Hancock, 31 August 1775, *Washington Papers*, 1:390–91; Washington to John Parke Custis, 24 July 1776, *Washington Papers*, 5:441; Washington to Poor, John Paterson, and Glover, 3 March 1777, *Washington Papers*, 8:503–4; Andrew Lewis to Washington, 8 August 1778, *Washington Papers*, 16:272–74; Adams to Sullivan, 3 June 1777, *Adams Papers* 5, http://www.masshist.org; John Stark letter, 22 March 1777, *Documents and Records Relating to the Province of New-Hampshire from 1764 to 1776*, comp. and ed. Nathan Bouton (Nashua, N.H.: Orren C. Moore, 1873–74), 8:518.
20. The quote is from Arnold to Washington, 11 March 1777, *Washington Papers*, 8:352. See also Adams to Greene, 9 May 1777, *Greene Papers*, 2:74–75; Joseph Ward to Adams, 12 May 1777, *Adams Papers* 5, http://www.masshist.org; and Sherman to Jonathan Trumbull, 6 March 1777, *Letters of Delegates*, 6:403–5.

21. Washington to Arnold, 2 April 1777, *Washington Papers*, 9:46.
22. Ibid., 9:45–46; Joseph Ward to Adams, 12 May 1777, *Adams Papers* 5, http://www.masshist.org; Washington to Arnold, 3 March 1777, *Washington Papers*, 8:493; Washington to Richard Henry Lee, 6 March 1777, *Washington Papers*, 8:523; Washington to Richard Henry Lee, 24/26 April 1777, *Washington Papers*, 9:255–58.
23. Washington to Hancock, 5 and 12 May 1777, *Washington Papers*, 9:349–50, 396–97; Gerry to Joseph Trumbull, 26 March 1777, *Letters of Delegates*, 6:493–94; Adams to Abigail Adams, 30 April 1777, *Letters of Delegates*, 7:12; Sherman to Jonathan Trumbull, 26 May 1777, *Letters of Delegates*, 7:133–34; James Lovell to Whipple, 8 August 1777, *Letters of Delegates*, 7:443; Henry Laurens to John Rutledge, 12 August 1777, *Laurens Papers*, 11:448.
24. Robert Howe to Henry Laurens, 9 June 1777, *Laurens Papers*, 11:355; Washington to Hancock, 7 October 1777, *Washington Papers*, 11:416–19; Robert Howe to Washington, 2 November 1777, *Washington Papers*, 12:88–89; McDougall to Washington, 10 December 1778, *Washington Papers*, 18:389–93.
25. For Heath's travails, see Tudor to Adams, 7 March 1777, *Adams Papers* 5, http://www.masshist.org; Washington to Heath, 4 February and 3 March 1777, *Washington Papers*, 8:240–41, 498; Washington to Richard Henry Lee, 24/26 April 1777, *Washington Papers*, 9:255–58; Washington to Hancock, 28 April 1777, *Washington Papers*, 9:293–94; Washington to Heath, 10 May 1777, *Washington Papers*, 9:376–77; Heath to Washington, 6 February 1777, in Charles S. Hall, ed., *Life and Letters of Samuel Holden Parsons: Major General of the Continental Army and Chief Judge of the Northwestern Territory, 1737–1789* (Binghampton, N.Y.: Otseningo, 1905) [hereafter cited as *Life and Letters of Parsons*], 84; Timothy Pickering to his wife, 7 February 1777, in Octavius Pickering, *The Life of Timothy Pickering* (Boston: Little, Brown, 1867) [hereafter cited as *Life of Pickering*], 1:109; and Adams to Abigail Adams, 21 February 1777, *Adams Family Correspondence*, 2:165.
26. Deane to Elizabeth Deane, 20 July 1775, *Letters of Delegates*, 1:638–39.
27. For characterizations of Putnam's and Washington's thinking, see Adams to Abigail Adams, 21 February 1777, *Adams Family Correspondence*, 2:165; Washington to Hancock, 30–31 February 1776, *Washington Papers*, 3:216–17; Washington to McDougall, 16 May 1777, *Washington Papers*, 9:441–42; Graydon, *Memoirs of a Life*, 176; George Clinton to Gates, 17 December 1777, *Clinton Papers*, 2:589; William Livingston to George Clinton, 28 March 1778, *Clinton Papers*, 3:90; Simeon Alexander, in Dann, *Revolution Remembered*, 106; Francois, Marquis de Barbe-Marbois, n.d., in Chase, *Our Revolutionary Forefathers*, 107; Washington to Reed, 14 and 15 January 1777, *Life and Correspondence of Reed*, 1:292–93, 293–94; and Thatcher, 8 September 1778, *Military Journal*, 176–77.
28. Wayne to Gates, 4 February 1777, *Life of St. Clair*, 1:385–86; Wayne to Sharp Delany, 20 February 77, in Charles J. Stille, *Major-General Anthony Wayne and Pennsylvania Line in the Continental Army* (Philadelphia: J. B. Lippincott, 1893), 49–50; Washington to St. Clair, 18 April 1777, *Life of St. Clair*, 1:392–93; Hancock to St. Clair, 30 April 1777, *Life of St. Clair*, 1:393; Washington to Gates, 28 April 1777, *Washington Papers*, 9:292; Washington to Hancock, 28 April and 3 May 1777, *Washington Papers*, 9:293–94, 333–35.
29. The complaint and quote is from Sullivan to Washington, 9 March 1777, *Washington Papers*, 8:547. See also Sullivan to Washington, 13 February 1777, *Sullivan Letters and Papers*, 1:320–22.

30. The quotes and details of Washington's response are in Washington to Sullivan, 15 March 1777, *Washington Papers*, 8:580–81. See also Massachusetts Legislature Respecting General Sullivan, 18 April 1777, *Sullivan Letters and Papers*, 1:330–31.
31. Adams to Greene, 4 August 1776, *Greene Papers*, 1:273.
32. The quote is from Chastellux, *Travels in North America*, 64. See also Adams to Abigail Adams, 13 February 1776, *Adams Family Correspondence*, 1:347; William Livingston to Stirling, 17 February 1778, *Livingston Papers*, 2:233; Charles Lee to Hancock, 5 March 1776, *Lee Papers*, 1:46–48; Wilkinson, *Memoirs of My Own Times*, 1:331–32; Charles Carroll of Carrollton to Washington, 27 September 1777, *Washington Papers*, 11:330; Albigence Waldo, 4 January 1778, "Valley Forge, 1777–1778: Diary of Surgeon Albigence Waldo, of the Connecticut Line," *Pennsylvania Magazine of History and Biography* 21 (1897): 320; Rush, 10 October 1777, "Historical Notes of Dr. Benjamin Rush, 1777," *Pennsylvania Magazine of History and Biography* 27 (1902): 147; Charles Lee to Washington, 19 February 1776, *American Archives*, series 4, 4:1198; and Thatcher, 22 August 1780, *Military Journal*, 245–46.
33. Washington to Stirling, 6 May 1777, *Washington Papers*, 9:358–59; Stirling to Washington, 6 May 1777, *Washington Papers*, 9:359–60.
34. Washington to Stephen, 26 April 1777, *Washington Papers*, 9:282.
35. Ward, *Major General Adam Stephen*, 1–22, 43; Rush to Richard Henry Lee, 21 December 1776, *Letters of Delegates*, 5:639–40; Washington to Stephen, 12 May 1777, *Washington Papers*, 9:406.
36. Hamilton to New York Committee of Correspondence, 14 April 1777, in *The Papers of Alexander Hamilton*, ed. Harold C. Syrett (New York: Columbia University Press, 1961–62) [hereafter cited as *Hamilton Papers*], 1:231; Hamilton to Lincoln, 26 April 1777, *Hamilton Papers*, 1:239–40; Greene to Adams, 13 April and 2 May 1777, *Greene Papers*, 2:55–56, 64–65; Joseph Ward to Adams, 19 April 1777, *Adams Papers* 5, http://www.masshist.org; Mann Page to John Page, 15 April 1777, *Letters of Delegates*, 6:385–86; Committee of Foreign Affairs to the Commissioners, 18 June 1777, in Jared Sparks, ed., *The Diplomatic Correspondence of the American Revolution* (Boston: N. Hale and Gray & Bowen, 1829) [hereafter cited as *Diplomatic Correspondence*], 1:306–8.
37. Washington to Hancock, 18 March 1777, *Washington Papers*, 8:597.
38. Hamilton to Gouverneur Morris, 12 May 1777, *Hamilton Papers*, 1:251; Greene to Christopher Greene, 20 January 1777, *Greene Papers*, 2:8–9; Greene to Nicholas Greene, 23 January 1777, *Greene Papers*, 2:10–11; Greene to Catharine Greene, 20 May 1777, *Greene Papers*, 2:85–86; Washington to Greene, 18 March 1777, *Greene Papers*, 2:44–45; Greene to Washington, 25 March 1777, *Greene Papers*, 2:46–48; Washington to McDougall, 11 May 1777, *Washington Papers*, 9:388.
39. Jacques Barbeu-Dubourg to Franklin, n.d., *American Archives*, series 4, 5:410.
40. Graydon, *Memoirs of a Life*, 137.
41. Sullivan to Washington, 25 June 1776, *Washington Papers*, 5:106–7; Gates to President of Congress, 6 August 1776, *American Archives*, series 5, 1:796; Rush to Barbeu-Dubourg, 16 September 1776, *Rush Letters*, 1:110–12; John Carroll to Eleanor Darnall Carroll, 1 May 1776, *The John Carroll Papers*, ed. Thomas O'Brien Hanley (Notre Dame, Ind.: University of Notre Dame Press, 1976), 1:47–48; Robbins, 18 and 24 July 1776, *Journal*, 31, 32; Richard Smith diary, 13 March 1776, *Letters of Delegates*, 3:375; Whipple to Joshua Brackett, 17 March 1776, *Letters of Delegates*, 3:395; Hancock to

Baron Frederick William de Woedtke, 19 March 1776, *Letters of Delegates*, 3:406; Oliver Wolcott to Andrew Adams, 22 March 1776, *Letters of Delegates*, 3:427–28; Whipple to Joseph Whipple, 6 May 1776, *Letters of Delegates*, 3:633–35; Charles Carrollton of Carrollton to Charles Carrollton of Annapolis, 12 March 1776, *Dear Papa*, 2:869–70.

42. Deane to the Secret Committee, 3 December 1776, *American Archives*, series 5, 3:1051–53.

43. The quote is from Washington to Hancock, 11 February 1777, *Washington Papers*, 8:305. See also Washington to Hancock, 7 October 1776, *Washington Papers*, 6:498–99; Washington to Hancock, 20 January and 20 February 1777, *Washington Papers*, 8:114–15, 381–82, 390–91; Washington to Hancock, 9 and 16 May 1777, *Washington Papers*, 9:371, 438–39; Washington to Richard Henry Lee, 17 May 1777, *Washington Papers*, 9:453–54; and Washington to Franklin, 17 August 1777, *Washington Papers*, 10:647–48.

44. Henry Laurens to John Rutledge, 12 August 1777, *Laurens Papers*, 11:448; Henry Laurens to Louis Fleury, 28 April 1778, *Laurens Papers*, 13:206–7; Adams to Greene, 2 June 1777, *Greene Papers*, 2:101; Hancock to Washington, 17 March 1777, *Washington Papers*, 8:591–92; Lovell to Washington, 24 July 1777, *Washington Papers*, 10:386–89; Lovell to Whipple, 29 July 1777, *Letters of Delegates*, 7:391–92; Henry Laurens to Washington, 31 July 1778, *Letters of Delegates*, 10:377–80; Richard Henry Lee to Deane, 22 [?] January 1779, *Letters of Richard Henry Lee*, ed. James Curtis Ballagh (New York: Macmillan, 1911–14), 2:11–26; Chevalier Dubuysson memoir, *Lafayette in the American Revolution*, 1:77; Secret Committee of Congress to Deane, 2 March 1776, *Deane Papers*, 19; Deane to the Secret Committee, 6 December 1776, *American Archives*, series 5, 3:1089–91; Deane to the Committee of Secret Correspondence, 28 November 1776, *Diplomatic Correspondence*, 1:69–74; Congressional Resolves, 18 February and 19 March 1777, *Journals of the Continental Congress*, 7:131, 185.

45. The quote is from Deane to Committee of Secret Correspondence, 18 August 1776, *American Archives*, series 5, 1:1020. See also Jonathan Williams Jr. to the American Commissioners, 27 January 1777, *Papers of Benjamin Franklin*, 23:239; Agreement between Deane and Philippe Charles Tronson du Coudray, 11 September 1776, *American Archives*, series 5, 2:284–85; Deane to Jay, 3 December 1776, *Jay Correspondence and Papers*, 1:97–102; and Franklin and Deane to the President of Congress, 9 February 1777, *Diplomatic Correspondence*, 1:264.

46. Adams to Greene, 7 July 1777, *Greene Papers*, 2:111–12; Adams to James Warren, 19 June 1777, *Adams Papers* 5, http://www.masshist.org; Heath to Washington, 19 May 1777, *Washington Papers*, 9:472–73; Washington to Heath, 1 June 1777, *Washington Papers*, 9:579; Lovell to Washington, 24 July 1777, *Washington Papers*, 10:386–89; Charles Carroll of Carrollton to Charles Carroll Sr., 13 June 1777, *Letters of Delegates*, 7:189–90; Lovell to Franklin, 4 July 1777, *Letters of Delegates*, 7:292–93; William Williams to Jonathan Trumbull, 5 July 1777, *Letters of Delegates*, 7:301–3; Marquis de Lafayette's Memoir of 1779, *Lafayette in the American Revolution*, 1:11; Dubuysson memoir, *Lafayette in the American Revolution*, 1:79; Deane to Committee of Secret Correspondence, 18 August 1776, *American Archives*, series 5, 1:1011–21; Committee of Foreign Affairs to the Commissioners, 1 December 1777, *Diplomatic Correspondence*, 1:346–49.

47. Greene to Jacob Greene, 4 June 1777, *Greene Papers*, 2:104; Greene to Hancock, 1 July 1777, *Greene Papers*, 2:109.

48. Hancock to Washington, 8 July 1777, *Washington Papers*, 10:227.
49. Adams to Greene, 7 July 1777, *Greene Papers*, 2:111–12; Dyer to Joseph Trumbull, 7 and 8 July 1777, *Letters of Delegates*, 7:312–14, 321–22; Lovell to Whipple, 7 July 1777, *Letters of Delegates*, 7:315–17; Congressional Resolve, 7 July 1777, *Sullivan Letters and Papers*, 1:407.
50. Adams's quote is from Adams, 18 September 1777, *Diary and Autobiography of John Adams*, ed. L. H. Butterfield (Cambridge, Mass.: Belknap Press of Harvard University Press, 1961), 2:263. See also Hancock to Washington, 17 September 1777, *Washington Papers*, 11:254; Lovell to Whipple, 7 August and 17 September 1777, *Letters of Delegates*, 7:437–38, 687–88; Jacob Hiltzheimer, 16 September 1777, *Extracts from the Diary of Jacob Hiltzheimer*, ed. Jacob Cox Parsons (Philadelphia: William F. Fell, 1893), 35; Marquis de Lafayette's Memoir of 1779, *Lafayette in the American Revolution*, 1:11; Dubuysson memoir, *Lafayette in the American Revolution*, 1:79; Committee of Foreign Affairs to the Commissioners, 1 December 1777, *Diplomatic Correspondence*, 1:346–49; Congressional Resolves, 12 and 21 July 1777, *Journals of the Continental Congress*, 8:540, 569.
51. Henry Laurens to John Rutledge, 30 January 1778, *Laurens Papers*, 12:379–80; Lafayette to Washington, 14 October 1777, *Washington Papers*, 11:505–7; Lafayette to Henry Laurens, 18 October 1777, *Lafayette in the American Revolution*, 1:124–26; Thatcher, 27 November 1778, *Military Journal*, 186.
52. Greene to Griffin Greene, 22 October 1780, *Greene Papers*, 6:422–23.
53. The quote is from Lafayette to Adrienne de Noailles de Lafayette, 1 October 1777, *Lafayette in the American Revolution*, 1:116. See also Henry Laurens to John Lewis Gervais, 5 August 1777, *Laurens Papers*, 11:423; Washington to Henry Laurens, 1 November 1777, *Laurens Papers*, 12:8; Greene to Catharine Greene, 20 November 1777, *Greene Papers*, 2:200; Samuel Otis to Greene, 30 April 1780, *Greene Papers*, 5:538; Chastellux, *Travels in North America*, 66–67; Gouverneur Morris to Henry Laurens, 26 January 1778, *Letters of Delegates*, 8:658; Francis Lewis to the New York Convention, 30 March 1778, *Letters of Delegates*, 9:354–56; Henry Laurens to Lafayette, 29 May 1778, *Letters of Delegates*, 9:768–69; Henry Laurens to the King of France, 21 October 1778, *Letters of Delegates*, 11:95; Richard Henry Lee to Arthur Lee, 27 October 1778, *Letters of Richard Henry Lee*, 1:445–46; Pickering letter, 20 August 1777, *Life of Pickering*, 1:151; Marquis de Lafayette's Memoir of 1779, *Lafayette in the American Revolution*, 1:11–12; Congressional Resolve, 31 July 1777, *Lafayette in the American Revolution*, 1:88; Johann Kalb to Pierre de Saint-Paul, 7 November 1777, *Lafayette in the American Revolution*, 1:145–49; Thatcher, *Military Journal*, 531–38; and Pontgibaud, *French Volunteer*, 41–42.
54. Washington to Lafayette, 25 September 1778, *Washington Papers*, 17:129.
55. Washington to Henry Laurens, 1 November 1777, *Laurens Papers*, 12:8; Washington to Benjamin Harrison, 19 August 1777, *Washington Papers*, 11:4–5; Lafayette to Washington, 14 October 1777, *Washington Papers*, 11:505–7; Washington to Gouverneur Morris, 24 July 1778, *Washington Papers*, 10:153–55; Washington to Franklin, 28 December 1778, *Washington Papers*, 18:521; Washington to Lafayette, 29 December 1778, *Washington Papers*, 18:526; Barbe-Marbois, 12 September 1779, in Chase, *Our Revolutionary Forefathers*, 116; Washington to Joseph Jones, 10 July 1781, *Washington Writings*, 22:352–55; Thatcher, 27 November 1778, *Military Journal*, 186.
56. Deane to the Committee of Secret Correspondence, 6 November 1777, *Diplomatic Correspondence*, 1:62.

57. Robert Morris to Hancock, 17 February 1777, *Letters of Delegates*, 6:309; Richard Henry Lee to Mann Page, 15 September 1777, *Letters of Delegates*, 7:666–67; Lovell to Whipple, 17 September 1777, *Letters of Delegates*, 7:687–88; Henry Laurens to Gervais, 9 October 1777, *Letters of Delegates*, 8:92; Burke to Sullivan, 12 October 1777, *Letters of Delegates*, 8:110–13; Deane to Hancock, 16 [?] March 1777, *Lafayette in the American Revolution*, 1:33–34; Kalb to Pierre de Saint-Paul, 7 November 1777, *Lafayette in the American Revolution*, 1:145–49; Deane to the Secret Committee, 28 November and 6 December 1776, *American Archives*, series 5, 3:882–85, 1089–91; Friedrich Kapp, *The Life of John Kalb: Major-General in the Revolutionary Army* (New York: privately printed, 1870), 85, 114–19.
58. Lee, *Memoirs of the War*, 577.
59. Ibid., 575–77; Lafayette to Henry Laurens, 26 January 1778, *Laurens Papers*, 12:352–53; Lafayette to Washington, 14 October 1777, *Washington Papers*, 11:505–7; Washington to Richard Henry Lee, 16 October 1777, *Washington Papers*, 11:529–30; Washington to Richard Henry Lee, 28 October 1777, *Washington Papers*, 12:40–42; Lovell to Whipple, 17 September 1777, *Letters of Delegates*, 7:687–88; Headley, *Washington and His Generals*, 2:320.
60. General Orders, 22 June 1777, *Washington Papers*, 10:103–4; Washington to Hancock, 22 June 1777, *Washington Papers*, 10:104–5; Washington to Reed, 23 June 1777, *Washington Papers*, 10:113–15; Washington to Jonathan Trumbull, 23 June 1777, *Washington Papers*, 10:116–17; Duane to Robert Livingston, 28 June 1777, *Letters of Delegates*, 7:260–62; Parsons to his wife, 22 June 1777, *Life and Letters of Parsons*, 103–4.
61. The quote is from St. Clair to Washington, 17 July 1777, *Life of St. Clair*, 1:429. See also Heath, *Heath Memoirs*, 111–12; Henry Laurens to Gervais, 12 September 1777, *Laurens Papers*, 11:520; Adams to Abigail Adams, 20 July 1777, *Adams Family Correspondence*, 2:285; Greene to Jacob Greene, 13 July 1777, *Greene Papers*, 2:119; Washington to Heath, 13 July 1777, *Washington Papers*, 10:271–72; Washington to Schuyler, 18 July 1777, *Washington Papers*, 10:323–24; and Thatcher, 6 July and [?] October 1777, *Military Journal*, 102, 183–84.
62. Washington to Hancock, 10, 12, and 18 July 1777, *Washington Papers*, 10:240–41, 252–53, 320; Washington to Schuyler, 18 July 1777, *Washington Papers*, 10:323–24; Schuyler to Washington, 22 July 1777, *Washington Papers*, 10:365–66.
63. Washington to Schuyler, 24 July 1777, *Washington Papers*, 10:397.
64. Washington to Lincoln, 24 July 1777, *Washington Papers*, 10:385; Washington to Jonathan Trumbull, 31 July 1777, *Washington Papers*, 10:471–72; Schuyler to Washington, 1 August 1777, *Washington Papers*, 10:482–83.
65. Henry Laurens to Gervais, 5 August 1777, *Laurens Papers*, 11:417–18; George Frost to Bartlett, 19 August 1777, *Bartlett Papers*, 169; Greene to Varnum, 14 August 1777, *Greene Papers*, 2:140–41; Schuyler to Washington, 13 August 1777, *Washington Papers*, 10:606–7; New York Delegates to the New York Convention, 9 May 1777, *Letters of Delegates*, 7:50–51; Duane to Schuyler, 23 August 1777, *Letters of Delegates*, 7:535–36; Samuel Adams to Richard Henry Lee, 22 July 1777, *Writings of Samuel Adams*, 3:389–92; Samuel Adams to James Warren, 31 August 1777, *Writings of Samuel Adams*, 3:395–97; Thatcher, 5 July 1777, *Military Journal*, 102.
66. Washington to Hancock, 3 August 1777, *Washington Papers*, 10:492–93; Duane to Schuyler, 20 February 1779, *Letters of Delegates*, 12:97–98; Delegates to Congress to George Clinton, 19 February 1779, *Clinton Papers*, 4:580–82; Congressional Resolve,

1 and 3 August 1777, *Journals of the Continental Congress*, 8:596, 600; Washington to Schuyler, 18 January 1779, *Washington Papers*, 19:18–19; New England Delegates to Washington, 28 July 1777, *Adams Papers* 5, http://www.masshist.org.

67. Hamilton to Robert Livingston, 7 August 1777, *Hamilton Papers*, 1:307–8; Henry Laurens to Gervais, 5 August 1777, *Laurens Papers*, 11:417–18; New England Delegates to Washington, 28 July 1777, *Adams Papers* 5, http://www.masshist.org; Henry Dearborn, 19 August, *Revolutionary War Journals of Henry Dearborn, 1775–1783* (Chicago: Caxton Club, 1939), 102; Gates notes, 18 June 1777, *Letters of Delegates*, 7:213–15; Duane to Schuyler, 19 June 1777, *Letters of Delegates*, 7:224–27; Duer to Schuyler, 19 June 1777, *Letters of Delegates*, 7:228–31; Samuel Adams to Richard Henry Lee, 15 July 1777, *Letters of Delegates*, 7:343–44; Jonathan Trumbull Jr. to Jonathan Trumbull, 9 June 1777, *Trumbull Papers*, pt. 3, 55–56.
68. Washington to Gates, 7 May 1777, *Washington Papers*, 9:362; Washington to Hancock, 15 September 1777, *Washington Papers*, 11:236–37; Wayne to Gates, 4 February 1777, *Life of St. Clair*, 1:385–86.
69. Washington, *Washington's Opinion of His General Officers*, https://archive.org/stream/washingtonsopinioowash#page/no/mode/2up, 2.
70. George Lux to Greene, 3 November 1781, *Greene Papers*, 9:524–25; Greene to Wayne, 9 January 1782, *Greene Papers*, 10:175–76; Charles Lee to Wayne, 11 April 1779, *Lee Papers*, 3:356–57; Chastellux, *Travels in North America*, 71–72; Robert Morris to Wayne, 8 September 1778, *Letters of Delegates*, 10:609; Graydon, *Memoirs of a Life*, 293–95; Lee, *Memoirs of the War*, 420, 595–96; Washington to William Gordon, 2 August 1779, *Washington Papers*, 22:11–12; Headley, *Washington and His Generals*, 1:338–40; John Lacey, "Memoirs of Brigadier-General John Lacey, of Pennsylvania," *Pennsylvania Magazine of History and Biography* 25 (1901): 353.
71. Israel Putnam to Washington, 21 July 1777, *Washington Papers*, 10:346–47; Washington to Sullivan, 25 July 1777, *Washington Papers*, 10:420; Washington to Philippe Hubert Preudhomme de Borre, 3 August 1777, *Washington Papers*, 10:495; Sullivan to Washington, 7 August 1777, *Washington Papers*, 10:547–50; William Smallwood to Washington, 15 August 1777, *Washington Papers*, 10:626–27; Washington to Smallwood, 23 August 1777, *Washington Papers*, 11:55; Washington to Sullivan, 27 August 1777, *Washington Papers*, 11:80; Hancock to Washington, 3 September 1777, *Washington Papers*, 11:134–35; Washington to Hancock, 3 September 1777, *Washington Papers*, 11:135–36; Duane to George Clinton, 25 August 1777, *Letters of Delegates*, 7:547–48; Sullivan to Washington, 5 and 10 July, 12 August 1777, *Sullivan Letters and Papers*, 1:404–5, 413–14, 428–29; Washington to Sullivan, 7 July 1777, *Sullivan Letters and Papers*, 1:408–9; Smallwood to Sullivan, 7 September 1777, *Sullivan Letters and Papers*, 1:501–2.
72. It is unclear when or how Stirling hurt himself. Washington wrote him a letter on 27 August, probably to express his condolences for his injuries, but the letter has been lost. Nor is it clear exactly when that summer Stirling complained to Washington about Conway's behavior. See also Greene to Catharine Greene, 17 July and 10 September 1777, *Greene Papers*, 2:121, 154–56; Greene to Jacob Greene, 31 August 1777, *Greene Papers*, 2:147; Report of a Court of Enquiry, 1 November 1777, *Greene Papers*, 2:188–89; Stirling to Washington, 30 August and [?] August or September 1777, *Washington Papers*, 11:97–98, 105; Thomas Conway to Washington, 1 September 1777, *Washington Papers*, 11:106–7; General Orders, 25 October 1777, *Washington Papers*, 11:604–6.

73. Quoted in Harry W. Ward, *General William Maxwell and the New Jersey Continentals* (Westport, Conn.: Greenwood Press, 1997), 113.
74. Wilkinson, *Memoirs of My Own Times*, 1:51; Washington to Hancock, 30 August 1777, *Washington Papers*, 11:93; Washington to Maxwell, 5 September 1777, *Washington Papers*, 11:153–54; General Orders, 26 October 1777, *Washington Papers*, 12:1–2; Chase to Gates, 13 June 1776, *Letters of Delegates*, 4:201–2; Abraham Clark to Elias Dayton, 7 March 1777, *Letters of Delegates*, 6:411–14; Washington to President of Congress, 20 July 1780, *Washington Writings*, 19:218–19; Maxwell to Gates, 16 November 1776, *American Archives*, series 5, 3:731; Extract of a Letter from the Camp at the Mouth of the Sorel, 12 June 1776, *American Archives*, series 4, 6:826–28; Robbins, 18 September 1776, *Journal*, 40.
75. Hancock to Washington, 26 March 1777, *Washington Papers*, 8:636–37; George Clinton to Washington, 18 April 1777, *Washington Papers*, 9:199–200; Washington to George Clinton, 20 April 1777, *Washington Papers*, 9:216–17; George Clinton to the Council, 11 July 1777, *Clinton Papers*, 2:105–6; Washington to Council of Safety, 22 July and 4 August 1777, *Clinton Papers*, 2:122–23, 170–75.
76. Parsons to Adams, 15 August 1776, *Adams Papers* 4, http://www.masshist.org; Washington to Hancock, 13 March 1776, *Washington Papers*, 3:461–64; Washington to Hand, 14 March 1777, *Washington Papers*, 8:572–73.
77. Washington to Hancock, 20 January 1777, *Washington Papers*, 8:125–28; Washington to Richard Henry Lee, 24/26 April 1777, *Washington Papers*, 9:255–58; Richard Henry Lee to Washington, 29 April 1777, *Washington Papers*, 9:301; Sherman to Jonathan Trumbull, 6 March 1777, *Letters of Delegates*, 6:403–5; Adams to Abigail Adams, 30 April 1777, *Letters of Delegates*, 7:12; Congressional Resolution, 11 April and 13 May 1777, *Journals of the Continental Congress*, 7:256, 349; Reed, *Life and Correspondence of Reed*, 295–300.
78. Washington to Hancock, 11 September 1777, *Washington Papers*, 11:200–201.
79. Burke to Caswell, 17 September 1777, *Letters of Delegates*, 7:680–81.
80. Washington to Hancock, 15 September 1777, *Washington Papers*, 11:236–37; Burke to Caswell, 11 May, 10 and 17 September 1777, *Letters of Delegates*, 7:69, 640, 678–83.
81. Hamilton and John Laurens to Sullivan, 21 September 1777, *Hamilton Papers*, 1:329–30; Sullivan to Adams, 28 September 1777, *Adams Papers* 5, http://www.masshist.org; Sullivan to Washington, 24 October 1777, *Washington Papers*, 11:600–601; Stephen to Sullivan, 20 September 1777, *Sullivan Letters and Papers*, 1:455–56; William Willcocks to Sullivan, 25 September 1777, *Sullivan Letters and Papers*, 1:457–58; Sullivan to Hancock, 27 September, 6 and 17 October 1777, *Sullivan Letters and Papers*, 1:460–70, 475–78, 537–39; Conway statement, 20 September 1777, *Sullivan Letters and Papers*, 1:555–56; Charles Cotesworth Pinckney statement, 24 September 1777, *Sullivan Letters and Papers*, 1:557; William Richardson to Sullivan, 13 October 1777, *Sullivan Letters and Papers*, 1:560–61; Lafayette to Sullivan, 1 November 1777, *Sullivan Letters and Papers*, 1:564–65; Sullivan letter, 5 November 1777, *Documents and Records of New Hampshire*, 8:743–45.
82. Washington to Sullivan, 24 October 1777, *Washington Papers*, 11:602.
83. Washington to Sullivan, 20 and 23 September 1777, *Washington Papers*, 11:277, 308–9; Sullivan to Washington, 6 and 24 October 1777, *Washington Papers*, 11:414–15, 600–601; Washington to Hancock, 7 October 1777, *Washington Papers*, 11:416–19; Chase to Thomas Johnson, 16 September 1777, *Letters of Delegates*, 7:669–70; Lovell

to Whipple, 17 September 1777, *Letters of Delegates*, 7:687–88; Dyer to Sullivan, 23 October 1777, *Letters of Delegates*, 8:162–63.

84. Henry Laurens to John Laurens, 10 October 1777, *Laurens Papers*, 11:550; Dyer to Sullivan, 11 and 23 October 1777, *Letters of Delegates*, 8:104–5, 162–63; Sullivan to Burke, *Sullivan Letters and Papers*, 1:565–68; Sullivan to Burke, 18 April 1778, *Sullivan Letters and Papers*, 2:35.

85. Washington to Hancock, 5 April 1777, *Washington Papers*, 9:68; Washington to Heath, 18/19 April 1777, *Washington Papers*, 9:205–6; Washington to Richard Henry Lee, 24/26 April 1777, *Washington Papers*, 9:255–58; Instructions for Brigadier General Preudhomme de Borre, 20 May 1777, *Washington Papers*, 9:490; Washington to Hancock, 13 September 1777, *Washington Papers*, 11:213–14; Preudhomme de Borre to Washington, 12 October 1777, *Washington Papers*, 11:494–95; Chase to Thomas Johnson, 12 and 16 September 1777, *Letters of Delegates*, 7:649, 669–70; Richard Henry Lee to John Page, 25 November 1777, *Letters of Delegates*, 8:322–24; Court of Inquiry, 10–12 October 1777, *Sullivan Letters and Papers*, 1:482–501; Congressional Revolve, 11 April 1777, *Journals of the Continental Congress*, 7:256; Congressional Resolve, 4 October 1777, *Journals of the Continental Congress*, 9:763.

86. Greene's orders, 13 September 1777, *Greene Papers*, 2:156; Greene to Henry Marchant, 25 July 1778, *Greene Papers*, 2:470–72; William Williams to Jonathan Trumbull, 13 September 1777, *Letters of Delegates*, 7:657–60; Burke to Caswell, 17 September 1777, *Letters of Delegates*, 7:678–81; Gerry to James Warren, 17 September 1777, *Letters of Delegates*, 7:678–83; Sullivan to Hancock, 27 September 1777, *Sullivan Letters and Papers*, 1:460–70; Sullivan to Mr. Powars and Mr. Winters, n.d., *Sullivan Letters and Papers*, 1:472–75; Lee, *Memoirs of the War*, 68, 89; Pickering diary, 11 September 1777, *Life of Pickering*, 1:154–56; Knox to Artemas Ward, 13 September 1777, *Life and Correspondence of Knox*, 48–50; Marquis de Lafayette, *Memoirs of Gilbert M. Lafayette*, ed. H. L. V. DuCoudray-Holstein (Geneva: John Greves, 1835) [hereafter cited as *Lafayette Memoirs*], 41–42.

87. Wayne to Washington, 27 September 1777, *Washington Papers*, 11:336.

88. Wayne to Washington, 2, 19, and 21 September and 22 October 1777, *Washington Papers*, 11:131–32, 273, 286–87, 582–83; General Orders, 1 November 1777, *Washington Papers*, 12:74–75; Stephen R. Taaffe, *The Philadelphia Campaign* (Lawrence: University Press of Kansas, 2003), 86–87.

89. The quote is from Lee, *Memoirs of the War*, 96. See also Charles Carroll of Carrollton to Charles Carroll Sr., 8 October 1777, *Letters of Delegates*, 8:72–73; Duane to Schuyler, 9 October 1777, *Letters of Delegates*, 8:89–90; Penn to Caswell, 10 October 1777, *Letters of Delegates*, 8:101–2; North Carolina Delegates to Caswell, 20 October 1777, *Letters of Delegates*, 8:154–55.

90. Report of Court of Enquiry, 1 November 1777, *Greene Papers*, 2:188–89; Stephen to Washington, 9 October 1777, *Washington Papers*, 11:468–69; General Orders, 25 October 1777, *Washington Papers*, 11:604–6; General Orders, 20 November 1777, *Washington Papers*, 12:327–28; Charles Carroll of Carrollton to Charles Carroll Sr., 12 October 1777, *Letters of Delegates*, 8:110–13; Henry Laurens to John Wells, 20 October 1777, *Letters of Delegates*, 8:151–52; Rush, 10 October 1777, "Historical Notes of Dr. Benjamin Rush," *Pennsylvania Magazine of History and Biography* 27 (1902): 147.

91. General Orders, 26 October and 4 November 1777, *Washington Papers*, 12:1–2, 113; Heath to Daniel Morgan, 30 September 1777, in William Heth, *The Diary of*

Lieutenant William Heth while a Prisoner in Quebec, 1776, ed. B. Floyd Flickinger (Winchester: Virginia Historical Society, 1931), 30–31.

92. Greene's Orders, 7 October 1777, *Greene Papers*, 2:171; Greene to McDougall, 28 January 1778, *Greene Papers*, 2:259–61; Wilkinson, *Memoirs of My Own Times*, 1:352–53; Charles Carroll of Carrollton to Charles Carroll Sr., 8 October 1777, *Letters of Delegates*, 8:75–76; Lee, *Memoirs of the War*, 95.
93. Washington to Hancock, 5 October 1777, *Washington Papers*, 11:395.
94. Joseph Ward to Adams, 9 October 1777, *Adams Papers* 5, http://www.masshist.org.
95. Hancock to Dorothy Hancock, 8 October 1777, *Letters of Delegates*, 8:76–78; Charles Carroll of Carrollton to Charles Carroll Sr., 9 October 1777, *Letters of Delegates*, 8:86–88; Lee, *Memoirs of the War*, 95.
96. Henry Laurens to Gates, 5 November 1777, *Laurens Papers*, 2:21.
97. Quoted in Ward, *Major General Adam Stephen*, 194.
98. Hamilton to Washington, 6 and 10 November 1777, *Hamilton Papers*, 1:353–54, 357–58; General Orders, 18 October 1777, *Washington Papers*, 11:541; Washington to Patrick Henry, 13 November 1777, *Washington Papers*, 12:242–43; Gates to Washington, 7 November 1777, *Webb Correspondence and Journals*, 1:376n; John Lamb, *Memoir of the Life and Times of General John Lamb*, ed. Isaac Q. Leake (Albany, N.Y.: Joel Munsell, 1857), 190.
99. Hamilton to Washington, 12 November 1777, *Hamilton Papers*, 1:361.
100. Hamilton to Washington, 10 and 12 November 1777, *Hamilton Papers*, 1:358–60, 361; Washington to Israel Putnam, 19 October 1777, *Washington Papers*, 11:558; Washington to Israel Putnam, 19 November 1777, *Webb Correspondence and Journals*, 1:391; Israel Putnam to Washington, 16 December 1777, *Webb Correspondence and Journals*, 1:401–2.
101. Greene to Catharine Greene, 20 May 1777, *Greene Papers*, 2:85.
102. Thomas Rodney notes, 8 March 1781, *Letters of Delegates*, 17:37.
103. Adams to Greene, 4 August 1776, *Greene Papers*, 1:273–74; Greene to Washington, 12 August 1776, *Greene Papers*, 1:284; Varnum to Greene, 10 February 1781, *Greene Papers*, 7:277–79; Robert Morris to William Greene, 29 December 1781, *Robert Morris Papers*, 3:466; Gouverneur Morris to Washington, 23 May 1778, *Washington Papers*, 15:202; Greene to Samuel Ward Sr., 16 October 1775, *Correspondence of Governor Samuel Ward*, 102–6.
104. Varnum to Washington, 3, 8, 9, 11, 12, 14, 15, and 16 November 1777, *Washington Papers*, 12:111–12, 176–77, 185–86, 217, 218, 233, 261–62, 273, 283–84.
105. Washington to Greene, 24 November 1777, *Greene Papers*, 2:210; Stirling to Washington, 3 November 1777, *Washington Papers*, 12:110–11.
106. Greene to Washington, 24 November 1777, *Greene Papers*, 2:209.
107. Greene to Washington, 26 November 1777, *Greene Papers*, 2:218–19; Washington to Greene, 26 November 1777, *Greene Papers*, 2:220–21.
108. Washington to Hancock, 7 October 1777, *Washington Papers*, 11:416–19.
109. The quote is from ibid., 11:418. See also Jay to McDougall, 17 October 1775, *Letters of Delegates*, 2:197–98; Daniel Roberdeau to Gerry, 6 December 1777, *Letters of Delegates*, 8:385; Lafayette to Henry Laurens, 26 January 1778, *Laurens Papers*, 12:352–53; Washington to Schuyler, 20 August 1775, *Washington Papers*, 1:331; Israel Putnam to Washington, 10 June 1777, *Washington Papers*, 9:667–71; McDougall to Washington, 10 December 1778, *Washington Papers*, 18:389–93; and Charles Lee to Rush, 2 November 1776, *Lee Papers*, 2:262–63.

110. Robert Howe to Henry Laurens, 9 June 1777, *Laurens Papers*, 11:355; Washington to George Walton, 9 August 1777, *Washington Papers*, 10:538–39; Robert Howe to Washington, 2 November 1777, *Washington Papers*, 12:98–99; Henry Laurens to John Rutledge, 19 October 1777, *Letters of Delegates*, 8:144–45; Henry Laurens to Robert Howe, 20 October 1777, *Letters of Delegates*, 8:149–51; E. Stanley Godbold Jr. and Robert H. Woody, *Christopher Gadsden and the American Revolution* (Knoxville: University of Tennessee Press, 1982), 178–81.
111. Richard Henry Lee to Mann Page, 15 September 1777, *Letters of Delegates*, 7:666–67; Washington to Richard Peters, 3 November 1777, *Washington Papers*, 12:106; Washington to Henry Laurens, 10 November 1777, *Washington Papers*, 12:199–201; Washington to Henry Laurens, 16 November 1778, *Washington Papers*, 18:168–69; Washington to Casimir Pulaski, 24 November 1778, *Washington Papers*, 18:284; John Laurens to Henry Laurens, 22 March 1778, *Laurens Papers*, 13:15–25; Henry Laurens to John Laurens, 29 March 1778, *Laurens Papers*, 13:52; Albigence Waldo, 4 January 1778, "Valley Forge, 1777–1778: Diary of Surgeon Albigence Waldo, of the Connecticut Line," *Pennsylvania Magazine of History and Biography* 21 (1897): 320–21.
112. Rumsey to Benedict Edward Hall, 4 November 1777, *Letters of Delegates*, 8:231–32; Cornelius Harnett to Burke, 13 and 20 November 1777, *Letters of Delegates*, 8:254–56, 289–90; Duer to Wilson, 30 November 1777, *Letters of Delegates*, 8:345–46; Harnett to Caswell, 27 August 1778, *Letters of Delegates*, 10:506–9.
113. Kalb to Pierre de Saint-Paul, 7 November 1777, *Lafayette in the American Revolution*, 1:146.
114. From Certain General Officers to Washington, 31 December 1777, *Washington Papers*, 13:81.
115. For Washington's decision to appoint Lafayette and the officer corps' reaction, see Washington to Henry Laurens, 1 November 1777, *Laurens Papers*, 12:8; Henry Laurens to John Laurens, 30 November 1777, *Laurens Papers*, 12:113; Lafayette to Henry Laurens, 14 December 1777, *Laurens Papers*, 12:151; Henry Laurens to Lafayette, 20 December 1777, *Laurens Papers*, 12:163–64; Greene to Catharine Greene, 20 November 1777, *Greene Papers*, 2:200; Greene to Washington, 26 November 1777, *Greene Papers*, 2:218–19; Duer to Wilson, 30 November 1777, *Letters of Delegates*, 8:345–46; Lafayette to Monsieur Duboismartin, 23 October 1777, *Lafayette in the American Revolution*, 1:128–31; Washington to Henry Laurens, 26 and 29 November 1777, *Lafayette in the American Revolution*, 1:158–59, 160–61; Cadwalader to Reed, 30 November 1777, *Life and Correspondence of Reed*, 1:348n–49n; Henry Laurens to Adams, 3 December 1777, *Adams Papers* 5, http://www.masshist.org; Lafayette to Washington, 14 October 1777, *Washington Papers*, 11:505–7; Lafayette to Washington, 30 December 1777, *Washington Papers*, 13:68–70; Congressional Resolve, 1 December 1777, *Journals of the Continental Congress*, 9:982–83; Lafayette, *Lafayette Memoirs*, 43–45; and George Clinton to Lincoln, 14 February 1778, *Clinton Papers*, 2:753.

Chapter 4. Rebirth

1. Washington to Henry Laurens, 23 December 1777, *Laurens Papers*, 12:195.
2. Ibid.; Washington to Greene, *Greene Papers*, 2:220–21; Washington to John Clark, 16 December 1777, *Washington Papers*, 12:614; Washington to Gordon, 23 January 1778, *Washington Papers*, 13:322–23.

3. Jonathan Dickinson Sergeant to Lovell, 20 November 1777, *Letters of Delegates*, 8:296.
4. John Clark Jr. to Greene, 10 January 1778, *Greene Papers*, 2:249–51; Adams to Rush, 8 February 1778, *Adams Papers* 5, http://www.masshist.org; James Clark to Washington, 6 January 1778, *Washington Papers*, 13:160–61; Burke to Caswell, 4 [?] November 1777, *Letters of Delegates*, 8:226–28; Lovell to Gates, 27 November 1777, *Letters of Delegates*, 8:329; Henry Laurens to John Laurens, 8 January 1778, *Letters of Delegates*, 8:545–49; Lovell to Samuel Adams, 13 January 1778, *Letters of Delegates*, 8:579–80; Henry Laurens to Spencer, 14 January 1778, *Letters of Delegates*, 8:593–94; Rush to Adams, 1 October 1777, *Rush Letters*, 1:154–57; Benjamin Rush, 10 October 1777, "Historical Notes of Dr. Rush, 1777," *Pennsylvania Magazine of History and Biography* 27 (1902): 147.
5. Rush to Adams, 21 October 1777, *Rush Letters*, 1:160.
6. Henry Laurens to Gates, 5 November 1777, *Laurens Papers*, 12:21; William Livingston under alias of "De Lisle," 31 December 1777, *Livingston Papers*, 2:150–51; Adams to Samuel Savage, 26 October 1777, *Letters of Delegates*, 8:188; Lovell to Gates, 27 November 1777, *Letters of Delegates*, 8:329; Marquis de Lafayette's Memoir of 1779, *Lafayette in the American Revolution*, 1:171.
7. The quote is from Washington to Conway, 5 [?] November 1777, *Washington Papers*, 12:129. See also Wilkinson, *Memoirs of My Own Times*, 1:330–32, 383–84; Stirling to Washington, 3 November 1777, *Washington Papers*, 12:110–11; and Washington to Gates, 5 January 1778, *Washington Papers*, 13:138–39.
8. The quote is from Washington to Richard Henry Lee, 16 October 1777, *Washington Papers*, 11:529. See also Greene to Jacob Greene, 3 January 1778, *Greene Papers*, 2:242–45; Rush to Adams, 13 October 1777, *Adams Papers* 5, http://www.masshist.org; Sullivan to Adams, 10 November 1777, *Adams Papers* 5, http://www.masshist.org; Washington to Hancock, 9 May 1777, *Washington Papers*, 9:370; Stirling to Washington, [?] August or September 1777, *Washington Papers*, 11:105; Conway to Washington, 1 September 1777, *Washington Papers*, 11:106–7; Lafayette to Washington, 14 October 1777, *Washington Papers*, 11:505–7; Jedediah Huntington to Jabez Huntington, 29 December 1777, "Huntington Papers: Correspondence of the Brothers Joshua and Jedediah Huntington, during the Period of the American Revolution," *Collections of the Connecticut Historical Society* (Hartford: Connecticut Historical Society, 1923), 20:390–91; Deane to the Secret Committee, 29 November 1776, *American Archives*, series 5, 3:555–58; Sullivan to Hancock, 27 September 1777, *Sullivan Letters and Papers*, 1:460–70; Sullivan to Meshech Weare, 25 October 1777, *Sullivan Letters and Papers*, 1:542–47; Graydon, *Memoirs of a Life*, 318; Lee, *Memoirs of the War*, 95; and Kapp, *Life of John Kalb*, 8.
9. James Craik to Washington, 6 January 1778, *Washington Papers*, 13:161.
10. John Laurens to Henry Laurens, 1 and 5 January 1778, *Laurens Papers*, 12:231, 418; Lafayette to Henry Laurens, 5 January 1778, *Laurens Papers*, 12:253–56; Henry Laurens to John Laurens, 8 January 1778, *Laurens Papers*, 12:269–71; Greene to McDougall, 25 January 1778, *Greene Papers*, 2:259–61; Greene to Jacob Greene, 3 January and 7 February 1778, *Greene Papers*, 2:242–45, 277; Greene to William Greene, 7 March 1778, *Greene Papers*, 2:300–304; Adams to Rush, 8 February 1778, *Adams Papers* 5, http://www.masshist.org; Joseph Jones to Washington, 22 January 1778, *Washington Papers*, 13:310–11; Washington to Gouverneur Morris, 18 May 1778, *Washington*

Papers, 15:156–57; Washington to Landon Carter, 30 May 1778, *Washington Papers*, 15:267–70; Washington to Jay, 14 April 1779, *Washington Papers*, 20:57–64; Marquis de Lafayette's Memoir of 1779, *Lafayette in the American Revolution*, 1:171; Tilghman to Cadwalader, 18 January 1778, "Selections from the Military Papers of General John Cadwalader," *Pennsylvania Magazine of History and Biography* 32 (1908): 167–70; Wilkinson, *Memoirs of My Own Times*, 330–31.

11. Henry Laurens to Gates, 28 November 1777, *Laurens Papers*, 12:103–4; Lafayette to Henry Laurens, 5 January 1778, *Laurens Papers*, 12:253–56; Washington to Henry Laurens, 31 January 1778, *Laurens Papers*, 12:488–89; Greene to Jacob Greene, 3 January 1778, *Greene Papers*, 2:242–45; Greene to McDougall, 5 February 1778, *Greene Papers*, 2:275–76; From Certain General Officers to Washington, 31 December 1777, *Washington Papers*, 13:79–81; Washington to Thomas Nelson, 8 February 1778, *Washington Papers*, 13:480–81; Washington to John Fitzgerald, 28 February 1778, *Washington Papers*, 13:694; Washington to Patrick Henry, 28 March 1778, *Washington Papers*, 14:336–37; Washington to Landon Carter, 30 May 1778, *Washington Papers*, 15:267–70.
12. Lafayette to Henry Laurens, 18 October 1777, *Laurens Papers*, 11:568; Henry Laurens to John Rutledge, 1 December 1777, *Laurens Papers*, 12:116–17; Richard Henry Lee to Washington, 20 October 1777, *Washington Papers*, 11:562–63; Richard Henry Lee to Washington, 20/22 November 1777, *Washington Papers*, 12:330–32; Abraham Clark to Stirling, 15 January 1778, *Letters of Delegates*, 8:597–98; Sullivan to Adams, 10 November 1777, *Adams Papers* 5, http://www.masshist.org.
13. Hamilton to George Clinton, 13 February 1778, *Hamilton Papers*, 1:428.
14. The quote is from Greene to Smallwood, 16 March 1778, *Greene Papers*, 2:316. See also Henry Laurens to John Laurens, 1 January 1778, *Laurens Papers*, 12:231; Lafayette to Henry Laurens, 4, 5, and 26 January 1778, *Laurens Papers*, 12:253–56, 256–57, 351; Henry Laurens to John Laurens, 8 January 1778, *Laurens Papers*, 12:269–71; Lachlin McIntosh to Henry Laurens, 8 January 1778, *Laurens Papers*, 12:278–79; Henry Laurens to Lafayette, 12 January 1778, *Laurens Papers*, 12:285; Greene to Henry Laurens, 12 January 1778, *Laurens Papers*, 12:291–92; Henry Laurens to Lafayette, 24 March 1778, *Laurens Papers*, 13:27–30; Greene to Jacob Greene, 3 January 1778, *Greene Papers*, 2:242–45; Greene to McDougall, 25 January 1778, *Greene Papers*, 2:259–61; Greene to William Greene, 7 March 1778, *Greene Papers*, 2:300–304; Abraham Clark to Stirling, 15 January 1778, *Letters of Delegates*, 8:597–98; Washington to Lafayette, 31 December 1777, *Washington Papers*, 13:83–84; Washington to Gouverneur Morris, 18 May 1778, *Washington Papers*, 15:156–57; Protest of General Officers to Congress, 31 December 1777, *Sullivan Letters and Papers*, 1:606–9; Jedediah Huntington to Jabez Huntington, 29 December 1777, "Huntington Papers," 390–91; Wayne to Gates, November 1777, *Life and Correspondence of Reed*, 1:342; Wayne to Mifflin, 10 November 1777, in Kenneth R. Rossman, *Thomas Mifflin and the Politics of the American Revolution* (Chapel Hill: University of North Carolina Press, 1952), 101–2; Kalb to Comte de Broglie, 24 September and 25 December 1777, and Kapp, *Life of Kalb*, 127, 137.
15. Gates to Henry Laurens, 8 December 1777, *Laurens Papers*, 12:135–36; Wilkinson, *Memoirs of My Own Times*, 1:372–76, 384–89; Gates to Washington, 8 December 1777, *Washington Papers*, 12:576–77; Gates to Washington, 23 January 1778, *Washington Papers*, 13:319–21.

16. Gates to Washington, 19 February 1778, *Washington Papers*, 13:590.
17. The quote is from Washington to Fitzgerald, 28 February 1778, *Washington Papers*, 13:694. See also Henry Laurens to John Rutledge, 30 January 1778, *Laurens Papers*, 12:378; Henry Laurens to John Laurens, 3 February 1778, *Laurens Papers*, 12:393; Lux to Greene, 28 April 1778, *Greene Papers*, 2:367; Gates to Washington, 23 January and 19 and 24 February 1778, *Washington Papers*, 13:319–21, 590, 654–55; Washington to Gates, 9 February 1778, *Washington Papers*, 13:484–87; Washington to Gouverneur Morris, 18 May 1778, *Washington Papers*, 15:156–57; and Washington to Landon Carter, 30 May 1778, *Washington Papers*, 15:267–70.
18. Conway to Washington, 5 and 16 November 1777, *Washington Papers*, 12:130–31, 276–77; Conway to Washington, 31 December 1777 and 10 and 27 January 1778, *Washington Papers*, 13:77–78, 195–96, 359–60; Washington to Conway, 16 November 1777, *Washington Papers*, 12:277; Conway to Sullivan, 3 January 1778, *Sullivan Letters and Papers*, 2:2–3.
19. Fitzgerald to Washington, 16 February 1778, *Washington Papers*, 13:556n.
20. Henry Laurens to John Laurens, 28 January 1778, *Laurens Papers*, 12:368; Henry Laurens to Lafayette, 5 June 1778, *Laurens Papers*, 13:404–7; Washington to Conway, 16 November 1777, *Washington Papers*, 12:277; Washington to Conway, 30 December 1777, *Washington Papers*, 13:66–67; Washington to Henry Laurens, 2 January 1778, *Washington Papers*, 12:238–39.
21. Gates to Henry Laurens, 27 May 1778, *Laurens Papers*, 13:348; Henry Laurens to Washington, 28 April 1778, *Washington Papers*, 14:669; Washington to Gouverneur Morris, 18 May 1778, *Washington Papers*, 15:156–57; Conway to Washington, 23 July 1778, *Washington Papers*, 16:140.
22. Henry Laurens to John Laurens, 8 January 1778, *Laurens Papers*, 12:270–71.
23. The quote is from Mifflin to Jared Sparks, 4 [?] April 1782, in Rossman, *Mifflin and Politics*, 136. See also Henry Laurens to John Laurens, 8 January 1778, *Laurens Papers*, 12:269–71; Henry Laurens to Rawlins Lowndes, 12 June 1778, *Laurens Papers*, 13:447; Greene to Jacob Greene, 3 January and 7 February 1778, *Greene Papers*, 2:242–45, 277; Lux to Greene, 24 October 1778, *Greene Papers*, 3:14–15; Cadwalader to Greene, 5 December 1778, *Greene Papers*, 3:103–4; Wilkinson, *Memoirs of My Own Times*, 1:330–31; Washington to Richard Henry Lee, 29 August 1775, *Washington Papers*, 1:372–75; Richard Henry Lee to Washington, 20/22 November 1777, *Washington Papers*, 12:330–32; Craik to Washington, 6 January 1778, *Washington Papers*, 13:160–61; Washington to Gouverneur Morris, 18 May 1778, *Washington Papers*, 15:156–57; and Ellery to Whipple, 21 December 1777, *Letters of Delegates*, 8:453–57.
24. Washington to Varnum, 9 April 1778, *Washington Papers*, 14:434–44.
25. Washington to Glover, 18 February 1778, *Washington Papers*, 13:579–80.
26. Washington to Glover, 8 January 1778, *Washington Papers*, 13:172–73; Glover to Washington, 27 January 1778, *Washington Papers*, 13:362–63; Washington to Glover, 15 March 1778, *Washington Papers*, 14:188–89; Glover to Washington, 29 March and 10 April 1778, *Washington Papers*, 14:350–51, 454–55; Glover to Washington, 15 May 1778, *Washington Papers*, 15:124–25.
27. Washington to Ebenezer Learned, 8 January 1778, *Washington Papers*, 13:172–73; Heath to Washington, 7/10 February 1778, *Washington Papers*, 13:469–70; Learned to Washington, 7 February 1778, *Washington Papers*, 13:471–72; Washington to Heath, 27 February 1778, *Washington Papers*, 13:682; Washington to Learned, 5 March 1778, *Washington Papers*, 14:69.

28. Wayne to Washington, 5 March 1778, *Washington Papers*, 14:72–74; William Livingston to Washington, 9 March 1778, *Washington Papers*, 14:115; Washington to Henry Laurens, 14 March 1778, *Washington Papers*, 14:174–75; Henry Laurens to Washington, 30 March 1778, *Washington Papers*, 14:359; Washington to Pulaski, 1 May 1778, *Washington Papers*, 15:7.
29. Ward, *General William Maxwell*, 88–91.
30. For the tedious details of the dispute, see Weedon to Henry Laurens, 29 December 1777, *Laurens Papers*, 2:219–20; Greene to Weedon, 27 April 1778, *Greene Papers*, 2:362–65; Washington to Henry Laurens, 26 December 1777, *Washington Papers*, 13:5; Wayne to Washington, 28 December 1777, *Washington Papers*, 13:34–35; Woodford to Washington, 19 and 21 February 1778, *Washington Papers*, 13:601–2, 637; Washington to Woodford, 21 February 1778, *Washington Papers*, 13:636–37; Board of General Officers, 4 March 1778, *Washington Papers*, 14:59; Washington to Weedon, 15 March 1778, *Washington Papers*, 14:190–91; Washington to Henry Laurens, 10 April 1778, *Washington Papers*, 14:459–62; Committee at Camp Statement, 2 March 1778, *Letters of Delegates*, 9:197–98; Congressional Resolve, 19 March 1778, *Journals of the Continental Congress*, 10:269; and Congressional Resolve, 18 August 1778, *Journals of the Continental Congress*, 11:807.
31. Washington to Henry Laurens, 22 December 1777, *Washington Papers*, 12:179–80.
32. Weedon to Washington, 30 March and 13 April 1778, *Washington Papers*, 14:361–62, 503–5; Peter Muhlenberg to Washington, 10 April 1778, *Washington Papers*, 14:466; Muhlenberg to Congress, 7 March 1778, in Henry A. Muhlenberg, *The Life of Major-General Peter Muhlenberg of the Revolutionary Army* (Philadelphia: Carey and Hart, 1849), 129–31.
33. Tudor to Adams, 7 March 1777, *Adams Papers* 5, http://www.masshist.org.
34. Spencer to Washington, 7 January 1778, *Washington Papers*, 13:169–70; Rhode Island Council of War to Washington, 15 January 1778, *Washington Papers*, 13:252–53; Dyer to Jonathan Trumbull, 14 January 1778, *Letters of Delegates*, 8:583–84; Ellery to Cooke, 1 March 1778, *Letters of Delegates*, 9:185–86; Greene to Christopher Greene, 5 January 1778, *Greene Papers*, 2:247.
35. Greene to Jacob Greene, 7 February 1778, *Greene Papers*, 2:277; Greene to Smallwood, 16 March 1778, *Greene Papers*, 2:315–16; Cooke to Greene, 19 April 1778, *Greene Papers*, 2:345–47; Sullivan to Adams, 13 November 1777, *Adams Papers* 5, http://www.masshist.org; From Certain General Officers to Washington, 31 December 1777, *Washington Papers*, 13:79–81; Sullivan to Washington, 14 February 1778, *Washington Papers*, 13:539–41; Washington to Sullivan, 14 February 1778, *Washington Papers*, 13:341–42; Washington to Henry Laurens, 27 February 1778, *Washington Papers*, 13:686–88; Washington to Continental Congress Camp Committee, 1 March 1778, *Washington Papers*, 14:5; Sullivan to Washington, 2 March 1778, *Washington Papers*, 14:40–41; Ellery to Vernon, 25 April 1778, *Letters of Delegates*, 9:486–88; Henry Laurens to John Rutledge, 19 May 1778, *Letters of Delegates*, 9:718–19; Sullivan to Washington, February 1778, *Sullivan Letters and Papers*, 2:20–21; Jedediah Huntington to Jabez Huntington, 13 March 1778, "Huntington Papers," 404–5.
36. Matthew Tilghman to President of Congress, 12 July 1776, *American Archives*, series 5, 1:215.
37. Lux to Greene, 28 April and 26 May 1778, *Greene Papers*, 2:367, 409–12; Washington to Hancock, 13 December 1776, *Washington Papers*, 7:324–25; Washington to Smallwood,

6 March 1778, *Washington Papers*, 14:79–80; Rumsey to Benedict Edward Hall, 4 November 1777, *Letters of Delegates*, 8:231–32; Greene to Reed, 9 January 1781, *Life and Correspondence of Reed*, 2:344–46; Kapp, *Life of Kalb*, 185.

38. Washington to William Russell, 19 May 1778, *Washington Papers*, 15:167.

39. Henry Laurens to John Laurens, 21 June 1777, *Laurens Papers*, 11:383–84; Henry Laurens to John Wells Jr., 31 May 1778, *Laurens Papers*, 13:381; Washington to Henry Laurens, 12 May 1778, *Laurens Papers*, 13:297; Greene to Daniel Brodhead, 21 February 1779, *Greene Papers*, 3:283; Brodhead to Greene, 26 May 1779, *Greene Papers*, 4:81; Walton to Washington, 5 August 1777, *Washington Papers*, 10:513–14; Washington to McIntosh, 26 May 1778, *Washington Papers*, 15:228; Washington to Brodhead, 15 February 1779, *Washington Papers*, 19:199; Brodhead to Washington, 16 March 1779, *Washington Papers*, 19:497; Washington to Gouverneur Morris, 20 March 1779, *Washington Papers*, 19:545.

40. Henry Laurens to Lafayette, 25 January 1778, *Laurens Papers*, 12:341; Lafayette to Henry Laurens, 26 and 31 January, 19 February, and 6 March 1778, *Laurens Papers*, 12:350–53, 387–88, 468–70, 519–21; Duane to Henry Laurens, 18 February 1778, *Laurens Papers*, 12:463; Henry Laurens to John Rutledge, 11 March 1778, *Laurens Papers*, 12:543–44; Henry Laurens to Duane, 7 April 1778, *Laurens Papers*, 13:85; Greene to McDougall, 5 February 1778, *Greene Papers*, 2:275–76; Lovell to Adams, 8 February 1778, *Adams Papers* 5, http://www.masshist.org; Washington to Gates, 27 January 1778, *Washington Papers*, 13:361; Lafayette to Washington, 19 and 23 February 1778, *Washington Papers*, 13:594–96, 648–50; Washington to Lafayette, 10 March 1778, *Washington Papers*, 14:132–33; Lafayette to Adrienne de Noailles de Lafayette, 3 February 1778, *Lafayette in the American Revolution*, 1:274–76; Henry Laurens to Lafayette, 24 March 1778, *Lafayette in the American Revolution*, 1:376–77; Henry Laurens to John Rutledge, 3 February 1778, *Letters of Delegates*, 9:18–20.

41. Washington to Israel Putnam, 16 March 1778, *Washington Papers*, 14:203.

42. Hamilton to George Clinton, 22 December 1777, *Hamilton Papers*, 1:368; George Clinton to Hamilton, 28 December 1777, *Hamilton Papers*, 1:371; Lafayette to Henry Laurens, 4 March 1778, *Laurens Papers*, 12:514; Robert Livingston to Washington, 14 January 1778, *Washington Papers*, 14:234–37; Ann Hawkes Hay to Washington, 28 February 1778, *Washington Papers*, 13:695–96; Continental Congress Camp Committee to Washington, 6 March 1778, *Washington Papers*, 14:76–77; Washington to Robert Livingston, 12 March 1778, *Washington Papers*, 14:163–64; George Clinton to Washington, 5 March 1778, *Washington Papers*, 14:62–63; Washington to Henry Laurens, 17 March 1778, *Washington Papers*, 14:210–11; Lovell to Gates, 5 October 1777, *Letters of Delegates*, 8:57–58; Henry Laurens to Jacob Christopher Zinn, 28 April 1778, *Letters of Delegates*, 9:517–20; George Clinton to Gates, 17 December 1777, *Clinton Papers*, 2:586–89; Parsons to Washington, 7 March 1778, *Life and Letters of Parsons*, 153–55; Israel Putnam to Washington, 16 December 1777, *Webb Correspondence and Journals*, 1:401–2.

43. The quote is from Washington to Henry Laurens, 3 August 1778, *Laurens Papers*, 14:113. See also Greene to Henry Laurens, 26 March 1778, *Laurens Papers*, 13:42–44; Greene to Susanna Livingston, 11 November 1777, *Greene Papers*, 2:194–96; Greene to Marchant, 17 November 1777, *Greene Papers*, 2:199; Greene to Jacob Greene, 2 and 3 January 1778, *Greene Papers*, 2:242–45; Greene to Cooke, 5 February 1778, *Greene Papers*, 2:274; Greene to Knox, 26 February 1778, *Greene Papers*, 2:293–94; Greene

to William Greene, 7 March 1778, *Greene Papers*, 2:300–304; Greene to Weedon, 7 March 1778, *Greene Papers*, 2:304–6; Reed to Jonathan Bayard Smith, 13 February 1778, *Letters of Delegates*, 9:92–93; Jonathan Bayard Smith to Reed, 24 February 1778, *Letters of Delegates*, 9:176–79; and Jedediah Huntington to Jabez Huntington, 13 March 1778, "Huntington Papers," 404–5.

44. Henry Laurens to Steuben, 14 January 1778, *Laurens Papers*, 12:304; John Laurens to Henry Laurens, 28 February 1778, *Laurens Papers*, 12:483–84; Steuben to Henry Laurens, 12 March 1778, *Laurens Papers*, 12:552–53; Washington to Henry Laurens, 30 April 1778, *Laurens Papers*, 13:222–24; Lovell to Adams, 8 February 1778, *Adams Papers* 5, http://www.masshist.org; Steuben to Washington, 6 December 1777, *Washington Papers*, 12:567; Gordon to Washington, 9 January 1778, *Washington Papers*, 13:187–88; Washington to Steuben, 9 January 1778, *Washington Papers*, 13:193–94; Washington to Henry Laurens, 27 February 1778, *Washington Papers*, 13:686–88; Washington to Peter Scull, 19 March 1778, *Washington Papers*, 14:231; Roberdeau to Thomas Wharton, 16 January 1778, *Letters of Delegates*, 8:606–7; Robert Morris to Henry Laurens, 4 February 1778, *Letters of Delegates*, 9:22; Gerry to Samuel Adams, 7 February 1778, *Letters of Delegates*, 9:43–44; Henry Laurens to Washington, 19 February 1778, *Letters of Delegates*, 9:133–34; Congressional Resolve, 14 January 1778, *Journals of the Continental Congress*, 10:50; Steuben to Gates, 27 December 1777, *The Papers of General Friedrich Wilhelm von Steuben, 1777–1794*, ed. Edith von Zemenszky (Millwood, N.Y.: Kraus International Publications, 1982) [hereafter cited as *Steuben Papers*], reel 1.

45. Friedrich Kapp, *The Life of Frederick William Von Steuben, Major General in the Revolutionary Army* (New York: Mason Brothers, 1859), 639.

46. John Laurens to Henry Laurens, 25 March and 1 April 1778, *Laurens Papers*, 13:34–37, 68; Washington to Henry Laurens, 24 July 1778, *Laurens Papers*, 14:69–70; Washington to McDougall, 23 May 1777, *Washington Papers*, 9:506–7; Washington to Henry Laurens, 27 February 1778, *Washington Papers*, 13:686–88; Washington to Henry Laurens, 26 July 1778, *Washington Papers*, 16:172–73; Washington, *Washington's Opinion*, 2; Thatcher, *Military Journal*, 517–31; Headley, *Washington and His Generals*, 1:309–13; Lafayette to Henry Laurens, 14 April 1778, *Steuben Papers*, reel 1.

47. Washington to Henry Laurens, 30 April 1778, *Laurens Papers*, 13:224.

48. Hamilton to Duer, 18 June 1778, *Hamilton Papers*, 1:497–99; Henry Laurens to Duane, 7 April 1778, *Laurens Papers*, 13:77; John Laurens to Henry Laurens, 18 April and 14 June 1778, *Laurens Papers*, 13:140, 457; Steuben to Henry Laurens, 16 May 1778, *Laurens Papers*, 13:307; Washington to Henry Laurens, 24 July 1778, *Laurens Papers*, 14:69–70; James Warren to Adams, 7 June 1778, *Adams Papers* 5, http://www.masshist.org; Varnum to Washington, 5 May 1778, *Washington Papers*, 15:54–56; Washington to Henry Laurens, 18 June 1778, *Washington Papers*, 15:448–49; Alexander Scammell to Sullivan, 8 April 1778, *Sullivan Letters and Papers*, 2:32–33; Varnum to Sullivan, 28 April 1778, *Sullivan Letters and Papers*, 2:41–43; Jedediah Huntington to Jabez Huntington, 10 June 1778, "Huntington Papers," 409; Lafayette to Lazare-Jean Theveneau de Francy, 10 April 1778, *Lafayette in the American Revolution*, 2:20–22.

49. Washington to Charles Lee, 15 June 1778, *Lee Papers*, 2:402–5.

50. Washington to Henry Laurens, 3 August 1778, *Laurens Papers*, 14:111–12; Washington to Gouverneur Morris, 29 May 1778, *Washington Papers*, 15:260–62; Kapp, *Life of Kalb*, 160.

51. Greene to Griffin Greene, 25 May 1778, *Greene Papers*, 2:406.
52. Washington to Henry Laurens, 4 April 1778, *Laurens Papers*, 13:75; John Laurens to Henry Laurens, 5 April 1778, *Laurens Papers*, 13:77; Greene to Pettit, 18 June 1778, *Greene Papers*, 2:442; Washington to Charles Lee, 27 January and 22 April 1778, *Lee Papers*, 2:378, 390–91; Charles Lee to Washington, 13 and 28 April and 15 June 1778, *Lee Papers*, 2:382–89, 391–92, 399–402; Elias Boudinot, *The Life, Public Services, Addresses, and Letters of Elias Boudinot*, ed. J. J. Boudinot (Boston: Houghton, Mifflin, 1896), 1:142–46.
53. The two quotes are from Charles Lee to Henry Laurens, 17 April 1778, *Lee Papers*, 2:390.
54. For Lee's actions and interactions, see Henry Laurens to Duane, 17 April 1778, *Laurens Papers*, 13:130; Charles Lee to Henry Laurens, 14 May 1778, *Laurens Papers*, 13:302–3; Hancock to Washington, 6/7 January 1777, *Washington Papers*, 8:3–4; Charles Lee to Primrose Kennedy, n.d., *Lee Papers*, 2:356; Charles Lee, 29 March 1777, "Scheme for Putting an End to the War, Submitted to the Royal Commissioners," *Lee Papers*, 2:361–66; Charles Carroll of Carrollton to Charles Carroll Sr., 17/18 May 1778, *Letters of Delegates*, 9:691–92; and Boudinot, *Life of Boudinot*, 1:139–47.
55. The quote is from Hamilton to Elias Boudinot, 5 July 1778, *Lee Papers*, 2:468. See also Henry Dearborn, 23–26 June 1778, *Revolutionary War Journals*, 124–25; Council of War, 24 June 1778, *Greene Papers*, 2:444–45; and Charles Lee's testimony, 9 August 1778, *Lee Papers*, 3:174–77.
56. Greene to Washington, 24 June 1778, *Greene Papers*, 2:447; Lafayette to Washington, 24 June 1778, *Washington Papers*, 15:528–29; Wayne to Washington, 24 June 1778, *Washington Papers*, 15:534–35.
57. Washington to Gouverneur Morris, 29 May 1778, *Washington Writings*, 11:485.
58. Dearborn, 20 May 1778, *Revolutionary War Journals*, 121.
59. Hamilton to Boudinot, 5 July 1778, *Hamilton Papers*, 1:511; Charles Lee to Washington, 25 June 1778, *Lee Papers*, 2:417–18; Washington to Lafayette, 25 June 1778, *Washington Papers*, 15:539.
60. Hamilton to Boudinot, 5 July 1778, *Hamilton Papers*, 1:510–11; Charles Lee to Washington, 25 June 1778, *Lee Papers*, 2:417–18; Lafayette to Washington, 26 June 1778, *Lee Papers*, 2:418–19; Washington to Charles Lee, 26 June 1778, *Lee Papers*, 2:421–22; Washington to Lafayette, 25 and 26 June 1778, *Washington Papers*, 15:539, 555; Greene to Jacob Greene, 2 July 1778, *Greene Papers*, 2:449–52.
61. Wayne testimony, 4 July 1778, *Lee Papers*, 3:5.
62. Taaffe, *Philadelphia Campaign*, 214–18.
63. Hamilton to Boudinot, 5 July 1778, *Hamilton Papers*, 1:512.
64. Greene to Jacob Greene, 2 July 1778, *Greene Papers*, 2:451.
65. John Laurens to Henry Laurens, 30 June and 2 July 1778, *Laurens Papers*, 13:532–37, 543–45; Hamilton to Boudinot, 5 July 1778, *Hamilton Papers*, 1:511–12; Charles Lee to Isaac Collins, 3 July 1778, *Lee Papers*, 2:452–53; General Orders, 29 June 1778, *Washington Papers*, 15:583–84; Knox to William Knox, 3 July 1778, *Life and Correspondence of Knox*, 58–59; Wayne to his family, 1 July 1778, in *Life and Services of Gen. Anthony Wayne*, ed. H. N. Moore (Philadelphia: Leary, Getz, 1845), 61–63; Congressional Resolve, 7 July 1778, *Journals of the Continental Congress*, 11:673.
66. John Cilley to Bartlett, 3 July 1778, in Dennis Ryan, ed., *A Salute to Courage* (New York: Columbia University Press, 1979), 132–33.

67. Hamilton to Boudinot, 5 July 1778, *Hamilton Papers*, 1:510–11; John Laurens to Henry Laurens, 30 June 1778, *Laurens Papers*, 13:532–37; Wayne and Charles Scott to Washington, 30 June 1778, *Lee Papers*, 2:438–40; Wayne to his family, 1 July 1778, *Life and Services of Wayne*, 61–63.
68. Washington to Charles Lee, 30 June 1778, *Lee Papers*, 2:435.
69. Charles Lee to Richard Henry Lee, 29 June 1778, *Lee Papers*, 2:430; Charles Lee to Washington, 30 June 1778, *Lee Papers*, 2:435–36, 437–38, Washington to Charles Lee, 30 June 1778, *Lee Papers*, 2:437; Charles Lee to Robert Morris, 3 July 1778, *Lee Papers*, 2:457–59; Washington to John Augustine Washington, 4 July 1778, *Lee Papers*, 2:459–61; Washington to Reed, 12 December 1778, *Lee Papers*, 3:273–74; Washington to Custis, 4–8 August 1778, *Washington Papers*, 16:242.
70. Charles Lee to Henry Laurens, 30 October 1778, *Laurens Papers*, 14:460.
71. The quote is from Charles Lee to Gates, 19 December 1779, *Lee Papers*, 4:401. For details of Lee's court-martial, see Proceedings of a General Court Martial, 1 July to 12 August 1778, *Lee Papers*, 3:1–208. See also John Laurens to Hamilton, 5 December 1778, *Hamilton Papers*, 1:593; Hamilton and Evan Edwards, 24 December 1778, "Account of a Duel between Major General Charles Lee and Lieutenant Colonel John Laurens," *Hamilton Papers*, 1:602–3; Charles Lee to Reed, 22 July 1778, *Lee Papers*, 2:478–80; Charles Lee to Rush, 29 September 1778, *Lee Papers*, 3:236–37; Charles Lee to Aaron Burr, October 1778, *Lee Papers*, 3:238–39; Charles Lee to Congress, 13 October 1778, *Lee Papers*, 3:239–40; General Lee's Vindication to the Public, 8 December 1778, *Lee Papers*, 3:255–65; Walter Stewart to Wayne, 6 December 1778, *Lee Papers*, 3:271–72; Washington to Reed, 12 December 1778, *Lee Papers*, 3:273–74; Charles Lee to John Laurens, 22 December 1778, *Lee Papers*, 3:283; Wayne to Charles Lee, 7 January 1779, *Lee Papers*, 3:291; Charles Lee to Wayne, 11 April 1779, *Lee Papers*, 3:356–57; Penn to Woodford, 6 December 1778, *Letters of Delegates*, 11:295; Henry Laurens to Lowndes, 7 December 1778, *Letters of Delegates*, 11:296–97; Duane to Schuyler, 20 March 1779, *Letters of Delegates*, 12:211; Washington to Reed, 12 December 1778, *Washington Papers*, 18:396–98; Congressional Resolve, 5 December 1778, *Journals of the Continental Congress*, 12:1195–96; and Congressional Resolve, 4 December 1779, *Journals of the Continental Congress*, 15:1348.
72. Lee, *Memoirs of the War*, 115–16.

Chapter 5. Marking Time

1. Washington to Henry Laurens, 3 August 1778, *Laurens Papers*, 14:110–11; Committee on Arrangement to Henry Laurens, 7 September 1778, *Laurens Papers*, 14:284–85; General Orders, 22 July 1778, *Washington Papers*, 16:121–22; Thatcher, 3 July 1778, *Military Journal*, 163–64; Congressional Resolve, 24 November 1778, *Journals of the Continental Congress*, 12:1158.
2. For Steuben's travails see Hamilton to Boudinot, 26 July 1778, *Hamilton Papers*, 1:528–29; Washington to Henry Laurens, 24 July 1778, *Laurens Papers*, 14:69–70; Henry Laurens to Washington, 28 August 1778, *Laurens Papers*, 14:242; Gouverneur Morris to Washington, 2 August 1778, *Letters of Delegates*, 10:383; Henry Laurens to Steuben, 12 October 1778, *Letters of Delegates*, 11:51; Washington to Gouverneur Morris, 24 July 1778, *Washington Papers*, 16:153–56; Steuben to Washington, 24 July 1778, *Washington Papers*, 16:157–58; Washington to Henry Laurens, 26 July and 12 September 1778, *Washington Papers*, 16:172–73, 582–83; Washington to Henry

Laurens, 13 November 1778, *Washington Papers*, 18:139; Washington to Steuben, 19 December 1778, *Washington Papers*, 18:468–69; Steuben to Conrad-Alexandre Gerard, 24 September 1778, *Steuben Papers*, reel 1; and Congressional Resolve, 28 August 1778, *Sullivan Letters and Papers*, 2:271–72.

3. Washington to Greene, 21 July 1778, *Greene Papers*, 2:464.
4. For Greene's tribulations see ibid., 2:464–65; Greene to Washington, 21 July 1778, *Greene Papers*, 2:461–63; and Greene to William Greene, late September 1778, *Greene Papers*, 2:529–30.
5. For Washington's decision to resurrect the light corps and appoint Scott as commander, see General Orders, 8 August 1778, *Washington Papers*, 16:266–67; Washington to Charles Scott, 8 and 21 October 1778, *Washington Papers*, 17:308, 660–61; and Charles Scott to Washington, 21 and 29 October 1778, *Washington Papers*, 17:513–14, 635–36.
6. Washington to Sullivan, 31 July 1778, *Sullivan Letters and Papers*, 2:160–61; Washington to Gouverneur Morris, 29 May 1778, *Washington Papers*, 15:260–62; Washington to Lafayette, 27 July and 10 August 1778, *Washington Papers*, 16:185–86, 284; Washington to Sullivan, 27 July 1778, *Washington Papers*, 16:187–88; Washington to Jonathan Trumbull, 28 July 1778, *Washington Papers*, 16:194; Washington to John Augustine Washington, 23 September 1778, *Washington Papers*, 17:110–11; Committee at Camp to Henry Laurens, 14 February 1778, *Letters of Delegates*, 9:95.
7. Washington to Henry Laurens, 22 July 1778, *Washington Papers*, 16:127–30.
8. Henry Laurens to Gervais, 22 August 1778, *Laurens Papers*, 14:200; Greene to Sullivan, 23 July 1778, *Greene Papers*, 2:466–67; John Matthews to Thomas Bee, 26 August 1778, *Letters of Delegates*, 10:502–3; Washington to Sullivan, 17 and 31 July 1778, *Sullivan Letters and Papers*, 2:88–90, 160–61.
9. Sullivan to Henry Laurens, 1 August 1778, *Laurens Papers*, 14:106–7; Henry Laurens to Gervais, 22 August 1778, *Laurens Papers*, 14:200; Greene to Sullivan, 23 July 1778, *Greene Papers*, 2:466–67; Greene to John Brown, 6 September 1778, *Greene Papers*, 2:507–13; Sullivan to Greene, 5 October 1778, *Greene Papers*, 2:541–43; Sullivan to Henry Laurens, 16 May 1778, *Sullivan Letters and Papers*, 2:52; Sullivan to William Greene, 26 May 1778, *Sullivan Letters and Papers*, 2:54–55; Sullivan to Washington, 26 July 1778, *Sullivan Letters and Papers*, 2:126–27; Heath to Sullivan, 26 July 1778, *Sullivan Letters and Papers*, 2:122–24; Sullivan to Heath, 28 July 1778, *Sullivan Letters and Papers*, 2:137–41; Varnum to Washington, 7 July 1778, *Washington Papers*, 16:36–37; Sullivan to Washington, 1 August 1778, *Washington Papers*, 16:219–20.
10. John Laurens to Henry Laurens, 22 August 1778, *Laurens Papers*, 14:200–204; Greene to Washington, 28/31 August 1778, *Greene Papers*, 2:499–503; Lafayette to Sullivan, 22 July 1778, *Sullivan Letters and Papers*, 2:101–2; Washington to Sullivan, 27 July 1778, *Washington Papers*, 16:187–88; Lafayette to Washington, 6 August 1778, *Washington Papers*, 16:261.
11. The quote is from Sullivan to Washington, 13 August 1778, *Sullivan Letters and Papers*, 2:206. See also Sullivan to Henry Laurens, 17 and 23 August 1778, *Laurens Papers*, 14:184–85, 210–12; A Protest of the General Officers on Rhode Island to d'Estaing, 22 August 1778, *Greene Papers*, 2:487–89; Sullivan to Henry Laurens, 16 August 1778, *Sullivan Letters and Papers*, 2:218–20; and Sullivan to Washington, 23 August 1778, *Sullivan Letters and Papers*, 2:264–65.
12. Sullivan to Greene et al., 23 August 1778, *Greene Papers*, 2:492–93; Greene to Sullivan,

23 August 1778, *Greene Papers*, 2:493–96; Sullivan to Washington, 13 and 28 August 1778, *Sullivan Letters and Papers*, 2:205–7, 275–76; Sullivan to Henry Laurens, 16 August 1778, *Sullivan Letters and Papers*, 2:218–20; Sullivan to Jeremiah Powell, 26 August 1778, *Sullivan Letters and Papers*, 2:266–67; Sullivan to William Greene, 29 August 1778, *Sullivan Letters and Papers*, 2:273–75.

13. Sullivan to Henry Laurens, 31 August 1778, *Laurens Papers*, 14:248–53; Henry Laurens to William Smith, 12 September 1778, *Laurens Papers*, 14:302; Greene to Washington, 28/31 August 1778, *Greene Papers*, 2:499–503; Greene to Brown, 6 September 1778, *Greene Papers*, 2:507–13; Sullivan to Greene, 5 October 1778, *Greene Papers*, 2:541–43; Greene to Reed, 26 October 1778, *Greene Papers*, 3:18–19; Reed to George Bryan, 2 September 1778, *Letters of Delegates*, 10:552; Henry Laurens to Lowndes, 6 September 1778, *Letters of Delegates*, 10:583–84; Marchant to the Rhode Island Assembly, 12 September 1778, *Letters of Delegates*, 10:630; Henry Laurens to Sullivan, 13 September 1778, *Letters of Delegates*, 10:635–36; Congressional Resolve, 9 September 1778, *Sullivan Letters and Papers*, 2:326–28; Sullivan to John Wendell, 23 September 1778, *Sullivan Letters and Papers*, 2:355–56; William Livingston to Sullivan, 25 September 1778, *Sullivan Letters and Papers*, 2:362–64; New Hampshire General Court, 21 November 1778, *Sullivan Letters and Papers*, 2:441; Resolution of the Rhode Island General Assembly, March 1779, *Sullivan Letters and Papers*, 2:523; Washington to John Augustine Washington, 23 September 1778, *Washington Papers*, 17:110–11; Washington to Lafayette, 25 September 1778, *Washington Papers*, 17:128–31; Daniel Lyman to Heath, 23 August 1778, "Heath Papers," 2:258; Trumbull, *Autobiography, Reminiscences, and Letters*, 57; Thatcher, 4 September 1778, *Military Journal*, 174–75.

14. Washington to Greene, 21 August and 1 September 1778, *Greene Papers*, 2:486–87, 505–6; Washington to Sullivan, 28 August and 1 September 1778, *Sullivan Letters and Papers*, 2:270–71, 289–90; Washington to Custis, 4–8 August 1778, *Washington Papers*, 16:242; Washington to John Augustine Washington, 23 September 1778, *Washington Papers*, 17:110–11; Washington to Lafayette, 1 September 1778, *Lafayette in the American Revolution*, 2:164–65.

15. Greene to Heath, 27 August 1778, *Greene Papers*, 2:497; Greene to Washington, 28/31 August 1778, *Greene Papers*, 2:499–503; Washington to Greene, 1 September 1778, *Greene Papers*, 2:505–6; Greene to Count d'Estaing, 23 September 1778, *Greene Papers*, 2:526–27.

16. Lafayette to d'Estaing, 22 August 1778, *Lafayette in the American Revolution*, 2:139.

17. Sullivan to Henry Laurens, 31 August 1778, *Laurens Papers*, 14:248–53; Lafayette to Washington, 25–26 August and 1 September 1778, *Washington Papers*, 16:369–74, 461–63; Lafayette to d'Estaing, 24 August 1778, *Lafayette in the American Revolution*, 2:142–46.

18. The quote is from Washington to Lafayette, 29 December 1778, *Washington Papers*, 18:526. See also Lafayette to Washington, 24 and 25 September 1778, *Washington Papers*, 17:118, 128–31; Washington to Henry Laurens, 6 October 1778, *Washington Papers*, 17:281; Washington to d'Estaing, 24 October 1778, *Washington Papers*, 17:551–52; Washington to d'Estaing, 5 November 1778, *Washington Papers*, 18:48–49; Lafayette, *Lafayette Memoirs*, 59–61; and Lord Carlisle to Lafayette, 11 October 1778, *Lafayette in the American Revolution*, 2:189.

19. Greene to Washington, 19 and 22 September 1778, *Greene Papers*, 2:523–24, 525; Henry Laurens to Heath, 21 November 1778, *Letters of Delegates*, 11:236; Samuel Adams to

Charles Chauncy, 25 December 1778, *Letters of Delegates*, 11:377–78; Gates to Washington, 23 and 27 September 1778, *Washington Papers*, 17:89, 148–49; Washington to Gates, 26 September 1778, *Washington Papers*, 17:141; Heath to Washington, 1 December 1778, *Washington Papers*, 18:355; Washington to Jay, 14 April 1779, *Washington Papers*, 20:57–64; Gates to Heath, 3 November 1778, "Heath Papers," 2:286–87; Heath to Washington, 12 November 1778, "Heath Papers," 2:290–91.

20. Quoted in Rankin, *North Carolina Continentals*, 18.
21. Quoted in ibid., 173–74.
22. Robert Howe to Henry Laurens, 9 October 1778, *Laurens Papers*, 14:394–95; Harnett to Caswell, 26 September 1778, *Letters of Delegates*, 10:695–97; Lincoln to Washington, 19 December 1778, *Washington Papers*, 18:466–67; Godbold and Woody, *Gadsden and the American Revolution*, 178–81.
23. Greene to Jacob Greene, 3 January 1778, *Greene Papers*, 2:244; Greene to William Greene, late September 1778, *Greene Papers*, 2:529–30; Lincoln to Washington, 17 March 1778, *Washington Papers*, 14:211–12; Lincoln to Washington, 1 June 1778, *Washington Papers*, 15:291; Harnett to Caswell, 26 September 1778, *Letters of Delegates*, 10:695–97; Richard Henry Lee to Patrick Henry, 21 October 1778, *Letters of Delegates*, 11:96; Penn to Caswell, 22 October 1778, *Letters of Delegates*, 11:100; Henry Laurens to Lowndes, 24 October 1778, *Letters of Delegates*, 11:114.
24. Washington to Lincoln, 7 May 1778, *Washington Papers*, 15:74.
25. Lincoln to Washington, 1 March 1778, *Washington Papers*, 14:13–14; Washington to Edward Rutledge, 5 October 1778, *Washington Papers*, 17:272; Washington to Lincoln, 9 October 1778, *Washington Papers*, 17:317.
26. The quote is from Lincoln to Washington, 5–6 January 1779, *Washington Papers*, 18:576. See also Samuel Holton to the Massachusetts Council, 11 May 1779, *Letters of Delegates*, 12:459–60; Lovell to Adams, 13 June 1779, *Letters of Delegates*, 13:59–60; Lincoln to Washington, 7 July 1779, *Washington Papers*, 21:366–68; and Lincoln to Washington, 5–6 January 1779, *Washington Papers*, 18:576–77.
27. Washington to Henry Laurens, 14 and 27 November 1778, *Laurens Papers*, 14:491–95, 537–39; Duane to Schuyler, 3 January 1779, *Letters of Delegates*, 11:404–5; Remarks for the Continental Congress Committee of Congress, 23–31 January 1779, *Washington Papers*, 19:57–59; Washington to Lafayette, 8/10 March 1779, *Washington Papers*, 19:401–3; Washington to Mason, 27 March 1779, *Washington Papers*, 19:626–28.
28. McDougall to Greene, 12 November 1778, *Greene Papers*, 3:64–65; Parsons to Greene, 11 April 1779, *Greene Papers*, 3:392–94; Washington to Muhlenberg, 2 November 1778, *Washington Papers*, 18:21; Washington to Israel Putnam, 2 November 1778, *Washington Papers*, 18:21; Washington to Israel Putnam, 10 February 1779, *Washington Papers*, 19:166–68; Israel Putnam to Washington, 7 May 1779, *Washington Papers*, 20:368–70; Charles Hall, *Life and Letters of Parsons*, 208.
29. For Washington's decision to appoint McDougall and McDougall's unhappiness, see McDougall to Greene, 12 November 1778, *Greene Papers*, 3:64–65; Washington to McDougall, 23 October 1778, *Washington Papers*, 17:547–48; Washington to McDougall, 8 and 24 November 1778, *Washington Papers*, 18:78–79, 281–82; McDougall to Washington, 10 December 1778, *Washington Papers*, 18:389–93; Washington to McDougall, 9 February 1779, *Washington Papers*, 19:156–60; and McDougall to George Clinton, 15 December 1778 and 20 January and 14 March 1779, *Clinton Papers*, 4:383–87, 501–13, 630–33.

30. Greene to Duane, 16 April 1779, *Greene Papers*, 3:411–14; Greene to Washington, 24 and 26 April 1779, *Greene Papers*, 3:425–28, 429–30; Washington to Greene, 24 April 1779, *Greene Papers*, 3:428–29; Greene to Jacob Greene, 28/30 April 1779, *Greene Papers*, 3:433.
31. The quote and Laurens's narrative of his dinner with Steuben are in Henry Laurens to John Laurens, 18 April 1779, *Letters of Delegates*, 12:347–50. See also Washington to Henry Laurens, 13 November 1778, *Washington Papers*, 18:139; Washington to Steuben, 19 December 1778, *Washington Papers*, 18:468–69; Washington to Jay, 11 March 1779, *Washington Papers*, 19:441–42; Washington to Steuben, 11 March 1779, *Washington Papers*, 19:443; Kapp, *Life of Steuben*, 199–222; and Paul Lockhart, *The Drillmaster of Valley Forge: The Baron de Steuben and the Making of the American Army* (New York: HarperCollins, 2008), 188–89.
32. Parsons to Greene, 11 April 1779, *Greene Papers*, 3:392–94; Parsons to Washington, 26 October 1778, *Washington Papers*, 17:589–90; Washington to Henry Laurens, 16 November 1778, *Washington Papers*, 18:168–69; Knox to Washington, 30 December 1778, *Washington Papers*, 18:531–33; Smallwood to Washington, 30 December 1778, *Washington Papers*, 18:535–37; Washington to Jay, 31 December 1778, *Washington Papers*, 18:542–43; Parsons to Washington, 23 April 1779, *Washington Papers*, 20:180–81; Parsons to Jay, 8 April 1779, in Hall, *Life and Letters of Parsons*, 223–24; Parsons to Greene, 12 March 1779, *Life and Letters of Parsons*, 225.
33. The quote is from Washington to Schuyler, 18 January 1779, *Washington Papers*, 19:19. See also Schuyler to Henry Laurens, 6 October 1778, *Laurens Papers*, 14:389; Duane to Schuyler, 20 February 1779, *Letters of Delegates*, 12:87–98; Duane to George Clinton, 21 March 1779, *Letters of Delegates*, 12:214–16; Jay to Schuyler, 21 March 1779, *Letters of Delegates*, 12:217–18; Delegates to Congress to George Clinton, 19 February 1779, *Clinton Papers*, 4:580–82; and George Clinton to Schuyler, 16 May 1779, *Clinton Papers*, 4:828–29.
34. Glover to Washington, 28 January 1779, *Washington Papers*, 19:95; Washington to Glover, 25 February and 11 March 1779, *Washington Papers*, 19:260, 440; Jay to Washington, 2 March 1779, *Washington Papers*, 19:321; Varnum to Washington, 9 March 1779, *Washington Papers*, 19:426–27; Congressional Resolve, 5 January and 27 February 1779, *Journals of the Continental Congress*, 13:27–29, 259; Washington to Sullivan, 22 February 1779, *Sullivan Letters and Papers*, 2:519–20; Varnum to Sullivan, 18 March 1779, *Sullivan Letters and Papers*, 2:538; James Mitchell Varnum, *A Sketch of the Life and Public Services of James Mitchell Varnum of Rhode Island* (Boston: David Clapp and Son, 1906), 20.
35. Harnett to Burke, 13 November 1777, *Letters of Delegates*, 8:254–56; Burke to Caswell, 10 January 1779, *Letters of Delegates*, 11:442; Whitmell Hill to Caswell, 12 January 1779, *Letters of Delegates*, 11:456–57; Congressional Resolve, 9 January 1779, *Journals of the Continental Congress*, 13:46.
36. Washington to Board of War, 22 May 1779, *Washington Papers*, 20:571–72; Board of War to Washington, 25 May 1779, *Washington Papers*, 20:607–8; Washington to Hand, 31 May 1779, *Washington Papers*, 20:708–9; Congressional Resolve, 11 and 13 May 1779, *Journals of the Continental Congress*, 14:575–76, 578, 585; Wayne to Robert Morris, 5 October 1778, in Stille, *Major-General Anthony Wayne*, 156–58.
37. Washington to Henry Laurens, 1 April 1778, *Washington Papers*, 14:378–79; St. Clair to Washington, 15 November 1778, *Washington Papers*, 18:158–59; St. Clair to Gates,

21 November 1777, *Life of St. Clair*, 1:445–52; Thatcher, October 1778, *Military Journal*, 183–84.

38. Greene to Robert Howe, 27 September 1779, *Greene Papers*, 4:415–16; Washington to Robert Howe, 25 June 1779, *Washington Papers*, 21:250–51; Lincoln to Washington, 28 January 1779, *Washington Papers*, 19:98.
39. Heath to Henry Laurens, 5 December 1778, *Laurens Papers*, 14:563; Heath to Washington, 11 March 1779, *Washington Papers*, 19:440–41; Heath to Washington, 22 April 1779, "Heath Papers," 2:298–99.
40. The quote is from Washington to Reed, 29 July 1779, *Washington Papers*, 21:734. See also Greene to Catharine Greene, 20 July 1779, *Greene Papers*, 4:244; Washington to Henry Lee, 9 July 1779, *Washington Papers*, 21:401; and Barbe-Marbois, 16–17 September 1779, in Chase, *Our Revolutionary Forefathers*, 118.
41. The details of the reorganization are in Robert K. Wright, *The Continental Army* (Washington, D.C.: Government Printing Office, 1983), 146–50.
42. Wayne letter, 14 October 1778, *Lee Papers*, 3:241.
43. Wayne to Washington, 10 February 1779, *Washington Papers*, 19:169–70; Washington to Joseph Jones, 22 July 1780, *Washington Writings*, 19:224–27; Wayne letter, 18 January 1779, *Life and Services of Wayne*, 81–82; Wayne to Washington, 10 May 1779, *Life and Services of Wayne*, 83; Wayne to Stewart, 7 June 1779, *Life and Services of Wayne*, 84–85.
44. McDougall to Washington, 11 June 1779, *Washington Papers*, 21:134–36; Washington to John Augustine Washington, 20 June 1779, *Washington Papers*, 21:198–99; Wayne to Washington, 3 July 1779, *Washington Papers*, 21:341–42; Washington to Wayne, 10 July 1779, *Washington Papers*, 21:432–33; Wayne to Washington, 15 July 1779, *Life and Correspondence of Reed*, 2:111–12.
45. Charles Lee to Wayne, 11 August 1779, *Lee Papers*, 3:357.
46. Greene to Archibald Steel, 20 July 1779, *Greene Papers*, 4:247–48; Burke to Wayne, 19 July 1779, *Letters of Delegates*, 13:244; Jay to Washington, 20 July 1779, *Letters of Delegates*, 13:266–67; Duane to Mary Duane, 21 July 1779, *Letters of Delegates*, 13:275–76; Cyrus Griffin to Burgess Ball, 10 August 1779, *Letters of Delegates*, 13:345–46; Washington to Jay, 21 July 1779, *Washington Papers*, 21:596–600; St. Clair to Wayne, 17 July 1779, *Life of St. Clair*, 1:477; William Irvine to Reed, 23 July 1779, *Life and Correspondence of Reed*, 2:117–18; Lafayette to Wayne, 7 October 1779, *Life and Services of Wayne*, 104–5; Congressional Resolve, 26 July 1779, *Journals of the Continental Congress*, 14:887.
47. Washington to Henry Laurens, 16 November 1778, *Washington Papers*, 18:169–70.
48. Board of War to Washington, 27 July 1778, *Washington Papers*, 16:182–84; Washington to Board of War, 3 August 1778, *Washington Papers*, 16:226–29; George Clinton to Washington, 15 October 1778, *Washington Papers*, 17:385–86.
49. Washington to Jay, 14 April 1779, *Washington Papers*, 20:62.
50. Ibid., 20:57–64; Washington to Schuyler, 11 February 1779, *Washington Papers*, 19:176–79; Gates to Washington, 16 March 1779, *Washington Papers*, 19:501–2.
51. Greene to Washington, 26 April 1779, *Greene Papers*, 3:429–30; John Armstrong to Gates, 12 July 1779, *Letters of Delegates*, 13:194–96; Washington to Sullivan, 6 March 1779, *Sullivan Letters and Papers*, 2:530–31; Sullivan to Washington, 15 April 1779, *Sullivan Letters and Papers*, 3:1–5; Washington to Sullivan, 15 December 1779, *Sullivan Letters and Papers*, 3:173–74; Sullivan to Gates, 17 and 23 March 1779, *Sullivan Letters*

and Papers, 2:535–36, 542; Sullivan to Washington, 16 April 1779, *Washington Papers*, 20:90–93.

52. Brodhead to Washington, 16 January and 16 March 1779, *Washington Papers*, 19:7, 497; Washington to Lachlan McIntosh, 31 January 1779, *Washington Papers*, 19:114–17; Washington to Brodhead, 15 February and 5 March 1779, *Washington Papers*, 19:199, 365–66; McIntosh to Washington, 12 March 1779, *Washington Papers*, 19:451–54; Washington to Gouverneur Morris, 20 March 1779, *Washington Papers*, 19:545; Reed to Washington, 25 April 1779, *Washington Papers*, 20:209–11.
53. Greene to Catharine Greene, 19 July 1779, *Greene Papers*, 4:221.
54. Sullivan to Jay, 21 July 1779, *Sullivan Letters and Papers*, 3:84.
55. Hamilton to Greene, April 1779, *Hamilton Papers*, 2:51–52; Greene to Sullivan, 21 June 1779, *Greene Papers*, 4:175–76; Greene to Pettit, 18 August 1779, *Greene Papers*, 4:327–28; Sullivan to Washington, 10 July 1779, *Sullivan Letters and Papers*, 3:75–77; Sullivan to James Clinton, 11 July 1779, *Sullivan Letters and Papers*, 3:78; Sullivan to Jay, 21 July 1779, *Sullivan Letters and Papers*, 3:80–84; Sullivan to Washington, 16 April 1779, *Washington Papers*, 20:90–93; Washington to Sullivan, 24 May 1779, *Washington Papers*, 20:606–7; Sullivan to Washington, 25 June 1779, *Washington Papers*, 21:253; Washington to Jay, 15 August 1779, *Washington Papers*, 22:124–30.
56. Sullivan to Jay, 15 August and 30 September 1779, *Sullivan Letters and Papers*, 3:95–98, 123–37; Sullivan to Washington, 15 and 30 August 1779, *Sullivan Letters and Papers*, 3:98–100, 107–12; James Clinton to his wife, 6 July 1779, *Clinton Papers*, 5:122–23; James Clinton to George Clinton, 5 and 30 August 1779, *Clinton Papers*, 5:183–84, 224–28; Schuyler to Washington, 15 February 1777, *Washington Papers*, 8:345–46; James Clinton to Washington, 30 June 1779, *Washington Papers*, 21:299–300; Headley, *Washington and His Generals*, 2:178–79.
57. Congressional Resolve, 12 October 1779, *Journals of the Continental Congress*, 15:1163.
58. Bartlett to Nathaniel Peabody, 26 February 1780, *Bartlett Papers*, 277; Greene to Wadsworth, 9 September 1779, *Greene Papers*, 4:373; Harnett to Burke, 9 October 1779, *Letters of Delegates*, 14:49–50; Peabody to Whipple, 9 November 1779, *Letters of Delegates*, 14:171–72; Washington to Sullivan, 15 September 1779, *Sullivan Letters and Papers*, 3:121; Congress Thanks General Washington and General Sullivan, 14 October 1779, *Sullivan Letters and Papers*, 3:148; General Orders, 17 October 1779, *Washington Papers*, 22:741–42.
59. Sullivan to Washington, 1 December 1779, *Sullivan Letters and Papers*, 3:169.
60. Washington to Sullivan, 15 December 1779, *Sullivan Letters and Papers*, 3:173–74.
61. Bartlett to Peabody, 26 February 1780, *Bartlett Papers*, 277; Sullivan to Greene, 30 November 1779, *Greene Papers*, 5:133; Greene to Sullivan, 3 December 1780, *Greene Papers*, 5:144; Sullivan to Washington, 6 November 1779, *Sullivan Letters and Papers*, 3:158; Sullivan to Jay, 9 November 1779, *Sullivan Letters and Papers*, 3:161–62; Action of Congress, 30 November 1779, *Sullivan Letters and Papers*, 3:165–66.
62. The quote is from Samuel Huntington to Jonathan Trumbull, 12 January 1780, *Trumbull Papers*, pt. 4, 10. See also Greene to Weedon, 25 December 1779, *Greene Papers*, 5:209–10; Greene to Benoni Hathaway, 6 January 1780, *Greene Papers*, 5:243; Greene to Reed, 29 February 1780, *Greene Papers*, 5:425–26; Schuyler to Robert Livingston, 7 December 1779, *Letters of Delegates*, 14:254–55; Schuyler to George Clinton, 26 May 1780, *Letters of Delegates*, 15:198–99; Washington to Schuyler, 30 January 1780, *Washington Writings*, 17:464–68; Washington to Lafayette, 18 March

1780, *Washington Writings*, 18:122–25; and Jedediah Huntington to Andrew Huntington, 8 January 1780, "Huntington Papers," 20:436–38.

63. Greene to Parsons, 7 [?] December 1779, *Greene Papers*, 5:153; Greene to Washington, 21 December 1779 and 21 January 1780, *Greene Papers*, 5:192–93, 295–96; Washington to Major Generals and Officers Commanding Brigades, 22 January 1780, *Washington Writings*, 17:425–30; Washington to James Clinton, 24 January 1780, *Washington Writings*, 17:437; Washington to James Clinton, 12 February 1780, *Washington Writings*, 18:4–5; Washington to Stirling, 5 March 1780, *Washington Writings*, 18:71–74; Steuben to George Clinton, 24 December 1779, *Steuben Papers*, reel 2.
64. Israel Putnam to Washington, 29 May 1780, *Life and Letters of Parsons*, 274; Washington to Heath, 18 November 1779, *Washington Writings*, 17:122–23; Washington to Israel Putnam, 26 January 1780, *Washington Writings*, 17:442–43; Washington to Israel Putnam, 5 July 1780, *Washington Writings*, 19:121–22.
65. The quote is from Washington to Greene, 3 September 1779, *Washington Writings*, 16:224. See also Greene to Pettit, 24 July 1779, *Greene Papers*, 4:256; Greene to Robert Howe, 31 July 1779, *Greene Papers*, 4:286–87; and Greene to Washington, 9 July 1779, *Washington Papers*, 21:392–93.
66. Marchant to Nehemiah Hubbard, 31 August 1779, *Letters of Delegates*, 13:437.
67. Washington to Greene, 3 September 1779, *Greene Papers*, 4:358–60; Greene to Samuel Huntington, 12 December 1779, *Greene Papers*, 5:164–67; Greene to Wadsworth, 19 December 1779, *Greene Papers*, 5:187–88; Greene to Washington, 21 January 1780, *Greene Papers*, 5:295–96; Washington to Greene, 22 and 26 January 1780, *Greene Papers*, 5:302–5, 309–12; John Fell diary, 1 July 1779, *Letters of Delegates*, 13:133; Schuyler to Robert Livingston, 7 December 1779, *Letters of Delegates*, 14:254–55; Robert Livingston to Schuyler, 20 December 1779, *Letters of Delegates*, 14:285; Schuyler to Washington, 5 April 1780, *Letters of Delegates*, 15:13–14; Committee at Headquarters to Greene, 5 May 1780, *Letters of Delegates*, 15:81; Congressional Resolve, 7 June 1779, *Journals of the Continental Congress*, 14:695.
68. Washington to McDougall, 13 and 21 November 1779, *Washington Writings*, 17:100–102, 154; Washington to Heath, 18 and 27 November 1779, *Washington Writings*, 17:122–23, 192–96; Washington to Gates, 17 November 1779, *Washington Writings*, 17:116–18; Washington to President of Congress, 27 November 1779, *Washington Writings*, 17:202; Washington to Robert Howe, 5 February 1780, *Washington Writings*, 17:490; McDougall to Heath, 5 December 1779, "Heath Papers," 2:329–30; George Clinton to Heath, 2 December 1779, *Clinton Papers*, 5:392–94; Heath to George Clinton, 25 January and 15 February 1780, *Clinton Papers*, 5:464–67, 491–92; Heath, *Heath Memoirs*, 190.
69. Alan Valentine, *Lord Stirling* (New York: Oxford University Press, 1969), 245–46.
70. Washington to Lincoln, 30 March 1780, *Washington Writings*, 18:178.
71. Washington to Lafayette, 8/10 March 1779, *Washington Papers*, 19:401–3; Washington to Lincoln, 28 September 1779, *Washington Papers*, 22:523–25; Washington to Schuyler, 24 November 1779, *Washington Writings*, 17:176; Washington to President of Congress, 29 November 1779, *Washington Writings*, 17:206–8; Washington to Greene, 26 March 1780, *Washington Writings*, 18:157–58; Council of War, 27 March 1780, *Washington Writings*, 18:164–66; Washington to President of Congress, 2 April 1780, *Washington Writings*, 18:197–200; Washington to John Laurens, 16 April 1780, *Washington Writings*, 18:298–300; Washington to Lincoln, 28 April 1780, *Washington Writings*, 18:306–7.

72. Richard Henry Lee to Henry Laurens, 10 July 1780, *Letters of Richard Henry Lee*, 2:187.
73. Samuel Huntington to Gates, 13 June 1780, *Letters of Delegates*, 15:312; Armstrong to Gates, 15 June 1780, *Letters of Delegates*, 15:319–20; Samuel Huntington to Wolcott, 14 July 1780, *Letters of Delegates*, 15:448–49; Richard Howly to Gates, 28 July 1780, *Letters of Delegates*, 15:517–19; Gates to Jonathan Trumbull, 23 June 1780, *Trumbull Papers*, pt. 4, 54–55; Rush to Adams, 25 August 1780, *Rush Letters*, 1:254–55; Washington to Joseph Jones, 22 July 1780, *Washington Writings*, 19:224–27.
74. Kapp, *Life of Kalb*, 171–72, 199–200.
75. Joseph Jones to Washington, 23 May, 18 July, and 7 [?] August 1780, *Letters of Delegates*, 15:182–83, 468–69, 557–59; Richard Henry Lee to Henry Laurens, 10 July 1780, *Letters of Richard Henry Lee*, 2:186–87; Washington to Joseph Jones, 22 July 1780, *Washington Writings*, 19:224–27; Congressional Resolve, 16 June 1780, *Journals of the Continental Congress*, 17:518–19; Lee, *Memoirs of the War*, 583–84; Henry, "Campaign against Quebec," 15:66, 92n; Headley, *Washington and His Generals*, 2:370–71.
76. Committee at Headquarters to Daniel of St. Thomas Jenifer and Josias Beall, 28 July 1780, *Letters of Delegates*, 15:382.
77. Formation of the Continental Army, n.d., *Washington Writings*, 18:190–91; Washington to Wayne, 18 May 1780, *Washington Writings*, 18:381–83; Washington to Committee of Cooperation, 23 June 1780, *Washington Writings*, 19:57–58; Washington to John Augustine Washington, 6 July 1780, *Washington Writings*, 19:135–37; Washington to Cadwalader, 5 October 1780, *Washington Writings*, 20:121–23; Henry Laurens to Richard Henry Lee, 1 August 1780, *Laurens Papers*, 15:322–23.
78. Washington to Pierre Van Cortlandt, 6 June 1780, *Clinton Papers*, 5:806–9.
79. The quote is from Washington to Wayne, 6 September 1780, *Washington Writings*, 20:1–2. See also Greene to Reed, 29 August 1780, *Greene Papers*, 6:243–45; Armstrong to Irvine, 3 August 1780, *Letters of Delegates*, 15:536–38; Washington to Wayne, 18 May 1780, *Washington Writings*, 18:381–83; General Orders, 7 July 1780, *Washington Writings*, 19:137–39; and George Clinton to James Clinton, September 1780, *Clinton Papers*, 6:185–86.
80. William Livingston to Schuyler, 16 June 1780, *Letters of Delegates*, 15:335–36; Robert Livingston to Washington, 22 June 1780, *Letters of Delegates*, 15:363–64; Washington to Robert Livingston, 29 June 1780, *Washington Writings*, 19:90–92.
81. Ward, *General William Maxwell*, 164–65.
82. Washington to Major Generals and Officers Commanding Brigades, 22 January 1780, *Washington Writings*, 17:425–30; Washington to President of Congress, 20 July 1780, *Washington Writings*, 19:218–19; Maxwell to Washington, 20 July 1780, in Jared Sparks, ed., *Correspondence of the American Revolution* (Boston: Little, Brown, 1853) [hereafter cited as *Correspondence of the American Revolution*], 3:31–32.
83. For Maxwell's travails see McDougall to Washington, 28 October 1778, *Washington Papers*, 17:617; John Nixon to Washington, 28 October 1778, *Washington Papers*, 17:620; Washington to McDougall, 8 November 1778, *Washington Papers*, 18:78–79; Lambert Cadwalader to Margaret Meredith, 7 January 1777, "Selections from the Military Papers of General John Cadwalader," *Pennsylvania Magazine of History and Biography* 32 (1908): 157–59; Congressional Resolve, 12 September 1780, *Journals of the Continental Congress*, 18:819; and Hancock to Nixon, 6 October 1777, *Letters of Delegates*, 8:68–69.

84. Sullivan to Weare, 26 October 1780, *Letters of Delegates*, 16:267.
85. The quote is from Washington to President of Congress, 15 September 1780, *Washington Writings*, 20:51. See also Henry Dearborn, 8 September 1780, *Revolutionary War Journals*, 202; Stark letter, 4 November 1780, *Documents and Records of New-Hampshire*, 8:883–84; and Thatcher, 10 September 1780, *Military Journal*, 253–54.
86. Greene to Washington, 5 August 1780, *Greene Papers*, 6:181.
87. Washington to Greene, 15 August 1780, *Greene Papers*, 6:217.
88. Greene to Hamilton, 15 May 1780, *Hamilton Papers*, 2:323; Greene to Samuel Huntington, 19 and 26 June 1780, *Greene Papers*, 6:26–27, 155–57; Greene to Knox, 18 July 1780, *Greene Papers*, 6:120; Greene to Washington, 27 July 1780, *Greene Papers*, 6:159–60; Committee at Headquarters to Greene, 28 July 1780, *Greene Papers*, 6:162; Ezekiel Cornell to Greene, 29 July and 1 and 13 August 1780, *Greene Papers*, 6:167–68, 176, 203; Jacob Cox to Greene, 7 August 1780, *Greene Papers*, 6:186–89; Pettit to Greene, 11 and 20 August 1780, *Greene Papers*, 6:198–200, 222–26; Greene to Wadsworth, 12 August 1780, *Greene Papers*, 6:201; John Cox to Greene, 21 August 1780, *Greene Papers*, 6:227–28; Committee at Headquarters to Greene, 16 July 1780, *Letters of Delegates*, 15:452–53; Armstrong to Irvine, 3 August 1780, *Letters of Delegates*, 15:536–38; Joseph Jones to Washington, 7 [?] August 1780, *Letters of Delegates*, 15:557–59; Joseph Jones to Washington, 6 September 1780, *Letters of Delegates*, 16:29–31; Washington to Joseph Jones, 13 August 1780, *Washington Writings*, 19:366–69; Congressional Resolve, 5 August 1780, *Journals of the Continental Congress*, 17:697.
89. Washington to Jean-Baptiste Donatien de Vimeur, comte de Rochambeau, 16 July 1780, *Washington Writings*, 19:186.
90. Otis to Greene, 30 April 1780, *Greene Papers*, 5:538; Schuyler to Duane, 13 May 1780, *Letters of Delegates*, 15:122–23; Washington to Lafayette, 18 March 1780, *Washington Writings*, 18:122–25; Washington to St. Clair, 1 August 1780, *Washington Writings*, 19:295; Heath to Washington, 25 July 1780, *Correspondence of the American Revolution*, 3:41–42; Lafayette to Comte de Maurepas, 25 January 1780, *Lafayette in the American Revolution*, 2:344–48; Lafayette to Comte de Vergennes, 2 February 1780, *Lafayette in the American Revolution*, 2:350–52; Vergennes to Lafayette, 5 March 1780, *Lafayette in the American Revolution*, 2:364–67; Lafayette to Steuben, 16 July 1780, *Steuben Papers*, reel 2.
91. Arnold to Washington, 5 May 1779, *Washington Papers*, 20:328.
92. Washington to Henry Laurens, 18 June 1778, *Laurens Papers*, 13:489–90; William Houston to William Livingston, 27 September 1780, *Livingston Papers*, 4:66–68; Greene to Cadwalader, 10 November 1778, *Greene Papers*, 3:56–57; William Paca to the Pennsylvania Council, 9 March 1779, *Letters of Delegates*, 12:178–80; Holton diary, 6–7 October 1779, *Letters of Delegates*, 14:34–35; Arnold to Washington, 19 July 1778, *Washington Papers*, 16:104–5; Arnold to Washington, 19 March 1779, *Washington Papers*, 19:527; Arnold to Washington, 18 April 1779, *Washington Papers*, 20:112–13; Pennsylvania Supreme Executive Council to Washington, 24 April 1779, *Washington Papers*, 20:196–97; General Orders, 6 April 1780, *Washington Writings*, 18:225.
93. Hamilton to John Laurens, 11 October 1780, *Hamilton Papers*, 2:460–70; Greene to William Greene, 2 October 1780, *Greene Papers*, 6:328–30; Schuyler to Arnold, 2 June 1780, *Letters of Delegates*, 15:240–41; Robert Livingston to Washington, 22 June 1780, *Letters of Delegates*, 15:363–64; McDougall to Washington, 10 December 1778, *Washington Papers*, 18:389–93; Washington to Arnold, 28 March 1780, *Washington*

Writings, 18:173–74; Washington to Robert Livingston, 29 June 1780, *Washington Writings*, 19:90–92; Washington to Arnold, 8 August 1780, *Washington Writings*, 19:341–43; Arnold to Washington, 9 August 1780, *Correspondence of the American Revolution*, 3:50–51; Washington to Reed, 18 October 1780, *Life and Correspondence of Reed*, 2:277–79.

94. The quote is from Arnold to Washington, 25 September 1780, *Hamilton Papers*, 2:439. See also Washington to Congress, 26 September 1780, *Clinton Papers*, 6:256n–57n; Alpheus Parkhurst, in Dann, *Revolution Remembered*, 56–59; and Tallmadge, *Memoir*, 35–37.
95. Greene to Catharine Greene, 29 September 1780, *Greene Papers*, 6:321.
96. Sullivan to John Langdon, 4 December 1780, *Letters of Delegates*, 16:412.
97. Wayne letter, 27 September 1780, *Life and Services of Wayne*, 117.
98. Hamilton to Elizabeth Schuyler, 25 September 1780, *Hamilton Papers*, 2:441–42; Houston to William Livingston, 27 September 1780, *Livingston Papers*, 4:66–68; Greene to Catharine Greene, 28 September 1780, *Greene Papers*, 6:319–20; Pettit to Greene, 5–6 October 1780, *Greene Papers*, 6:344–46; Samuel Huntington to Oliver Ellsworth, 2 [?] October 1780, *Letters of Delegates*, 16:129–30; Samuel Adams to Elizabeth Adams, 3 October 1780, *Letters of Delegates*, 16:132–33; Lovell to Peabody, 3 October 1780, *Letters of Delegates*, 16:140; Mathews to Peabody, 3 October 1780, *Letters of Delegates*, 16:143–44; Samuel Richards, *Diary of Samuel Richards: Captain of Connecticut Line, War of the Revolution, 1775–1781* (Philadelphia: Leeds and Biddle, 1909), 69; Washington to Rochambeau, 26 September 1780, *Clinton Papers*, 6:257n; Benjamin Tallmadge to Sparks, 17 February 1834, *Clinton Papers*, 6:261n–64n.
99. Rush to Adams, *Rush Letters*, 1:254–55; Kapp, *Life of Kalb*, 270.
100. Hamilton to Duane, 6 September 1780, *Hamilton Papers*, 2:421.
101. Otho Williams to Hamilton, 30 August 1780, *Hamilton Papers*, 2:386; Schuyler to Hamilton, 10 September 1780, *Hamilton Papers*, 2:425; Greene to Hamilton, 10 January 1781, *Hamilton Papers*, 2:531; Greene to Peabody, 6 September 1780, *Greene Papers*, 6:266–67; Pettit to Greene, 5–6 October 1780, *Greene Papers*, 6:344–46; John Cox to Greene, 6 October 1780, *Greene Papers*, 6:350; Lovell to Peabody, 5 September 1780, *Letters of Delegates*, 16:20–21; Cornell to William Greene, 10 September and 17 October 1780, *Letters of Delegates*, 16:44–45, 212–13; John Hanson to Thomas Sim Lee, 11 September and 3 October 1780, *Letters of Delegates*, 16:51–52, 135–36; Washington to Gates, 8 October 1780, *Washington Writings*, 20:136–38; Gates to Washington, 30 August and 3 September 1780, *Correspondence of the American Revolution*, 3:66–67, 74–77; Rush to Adams, 23 October 1780, *Rush Letters*, 1:255–56; Greene to Reed, 9 January 1781, *Life and Correspondence of Reed*, 2:344–46; Congressional Resolve, 5 October 1780, *Journals of the Continental Congress*, 18:906; Rankin, *North Carolina Continentals*, 255.
102. Greene to Griffin Greene, 22 October 1780, *Greene Papers*, 6:422.
103. Hamilton to Duane, 18 October 1780, *Hamilton Papers*, 2:479; Robert Harrison to Hamilton, 27 October 1780, *Hamilton Papers*, 2:490–91; Clement Biddle to Greene, 6 October 1780, *Greene Papers*, 6:341; Pettit to Greene, *Greene Papers*, 6:344–46; Cornwell to Greene, 19 September 1780, *Greene Papers*, 6:298–300; John Cox to Greene, 6 October 1780, *Greene Papers*, 6:350; Washington to Greene, *Greene Papers*, 6:385–86; Greene to Washington, 16 and 18 October 1780, *Greene Papers*, 6:396, 410; Greene to Catharine Greene, 16–17 October 1780, *Greene Papers*, 6:397–98; Greene to William Greene, 19 October 1780, *Greene Papers*, 6:411; Hanson to Thomas Sim

Lee, 11 September 1780, *Letters of Delegates*, 16:51–52; Daniel of St. Thomas Jenifer to Thomas Sim Lee, 2 October 1780, *Letters of Delegates*, 16:130; Mathews to Washington, 6 and 17 October 1780, *Letters of Delegates*, 16:159, 218–19; Peabody to Richard Henry Lee, 27 October 1780, *Letters of Delegates*, 16:280–82; Hanson to Charles Carroll of Carrollton, 30 October 1780, *Letters of Delegates*, 16:284–85; Washington to Mason, 22 October 1780, *Washington Writings*, 20:241–42; Washington to President of Congress, 22 October 1780, *Washington Writings*, 20:244–45; Washington to Thomas Jefferson, 22 October 1780, *The Papers of Thomas Jefferson*, ed. Julian P. Boyd (Princeton, N.J.: Princeton University Press, 1950–52) [hereafter cited as *Jefferson Papers*], 4:60–61; Greene to Reed, 9 January 1781, *Life and Correspondence of Reed*, 2:344–46.

104. Washington to Greene, 22 October 1780, *Washington Writings*, 20:238–39.
105. Greene to Steuben, 20 November 1780, *Greene Papers*, 6:496–97; Washington to Steuben, 22 October 1780, *Washington Writings*, 20:240–41; Washington to President of Congress, 22 October 1780, *Washington Writings*, 20:244–45; Steuben to Washington, 23 October 1780, *Correspondence of the American Revolution*, 3:126–29; Greene to Steuben, 8 December 1780, *Steuben Papers*, reel 3.
106. Greene to Hamilton, 10 January 1781, *Hamilton Papers*, 2:531; Greene to Washington, 7 December 1780, *Greene Papers*, 6:542–45; Hanson to Thomas Sim Lee, 18 September 1780, *Letters of Delegates*, 16:78–79; Washington to Greene, 9/11 January 1781, *Washington Writings*, 21:86–88; Greene to Reed, 9 January 1781, *Life and Correspondence of Reed*, 2:344–46.
107. Greene to Hamilton, 10 January 1781, *Hamilton Papers*, 2:531; Washington to Greene, 22 October and 7 December 1780, *Greene Papers*, 6:424–25, 542–45; Greene to Gates, 4 October 1781, *Greene Papers*, 9:425–26; Hanson to Philip Thomas, 19 September 1780, *Letters of Delegates*, 16:91–92; Cornell to William Greene, 24 October 1780, *Letters of Delegates*, 16:247–48; Samuel Huntington to Gates, 22 May 1781, *Letters of Delegates*, 17:258; Samuel Huntington to Washington, 26 May 1781, *Letters of Delegates*, 17:268–69; John Rutledge to Gates, 14 August 1782, *Letters of Delegates*, 19:65–66; Washington to President of Congress, 6 June 1781, *Washington Writings*, 22:167–69; Gates to Washington, 22 May 1781, *Correspondence of the American Revolution*, 3:319–20; Congressional Resolve, 21 May 1781, *Journals of the Continental Congress*, 20:521–22; Gates to Jefferson, 2 February 1781, *Jefferson Papers*, 4:501–2.
108. Washington to President of Congress, 20 December 1780, *Washington Writings*, 20:504.
109. Joseph Jones to Washington, 7 [?] August 1780, *Letters of Delegates*, 15:557–59; Sullivan to Washington, 9 November 1780, *Sullivan Letters and Papers*, 3:227–28; Washington to Sullivan, 17 December 1780, *Sullivan Letters and Papers*, 3:244–48; Hall, *Life and Letters of Parsons*, 314–15, 317; Washington to Sullivan, 8 November 1780, *Washington Writings*, 2:397–98; Washington to Duane, 26 December 1780, *Washington Writings*, 21:13–16; Congressional Resolve, 13 October 1780, *Journals of the Continental Congress*, 18:921–22.

Chapter 6. End of the War

1. Washington to Armstrong, 26 March 1781, *Washington Writings*, 21:378–79.
2. Ibid.; Washington to Cadwalader, 6 October 1780, *Washington Writings*, 20:121–23.
3. Sullivan to Stark, 26 November 1780, *Letters of Delegates*, 16:384; Parsons to Wadsworth, 11 January 1781, *Life and Letters of Parsons*, 321–22; Parsons to Washington,

30 April 1781, *Life and Letters of Parsons*, 355–56; Washington to St. Clair, 13 February 1781, *Washington Writings*, 21:216–17; Stark to Washington, 30 November 1780 and 1 January 1781, in Caleb Stark, ed. *Memoir and Official Correspondence of Gen. John Stark* (Concord: Steam Press, 1860) [hereafter cited as *Stark Memoir and Correspondence*], 206, 207–8; Stark to Pickering, 2 January 1781, *Stark Memoir and Correspondence*, 209; Thatcher, 30 April 1781, *Military Journal*, 310; Congressional Resolve, 16 February 1781, *Journals of the Continental Congress*, 19:155; Glover to Washington, 28 January 1781, "Letters Colonial and Revolutionary," *Pennsylvania Magazine of History and Biography* 42 (1918): 81–82.

4. Thomas McKean's Charges against Thompson, 19 November 1778, *Letters of Delegates*, 11:226–27; Charles Thomson's Notes of Proceedings in Congress, 23 November 1778, *Letters of Delegates*, 11:241–49; Washington to Gates, 1 May 1778, *Washington Papers*, 15:3–4; Thompson to Washington, 19 July 1778, *Washington Papers*, 16:106; Washington to Thompson, 23 July 1778, *Washington Papers*, 16:145; Congressional Resolve, 23 November and 24 December 1778, *Journals of the Continental Congress*, 12:1150–52, 1254–55; Congressional Resolve, 30 March 1781, *Journals of the Continental Congress*, 20:508.
5. Washington to James Clinton, 7 May 1781, *Washington Writings*, 22:52.
6. Washington to Sullivan, 17 December 1780, *Sullivan Letters and Papers*, 3:244–48; George Clinton to Schuyler, 2 November 1780, *Clinton Papers*, 6:368–69; Washington to George Clinton, 6 November 1780, *Clinton Papers*, 6:391–92; James Clinton to George Clinton, 29 March 1781, *Clinton Papers*, 6:728; Washington to James Clinton, 28 October 1780, *Washington Writings*, 20:259–60; Washington to Greene, 13 December 1780, *Washington Writings*, 20:469–71; Hand to Steuben, 18 May 1781, *Steuben Papers*, reel 5.
7. Washington to McDougall, 24 October 1780, *Washington Writings*, 20:254; Washington to Lincoln, 8 November 1780, *Washington Writings*, 20:322–23; Washington to President of Congress, 28 November 1780, *Washington Writings*, 20:418–20; Washington to Lincoln, 11 May 1781, *Washington Writings*, 22:72; Washington to McDougall, 21 June 1781, *Washington Writings*, 22:240–41; George Washington, 6 May 1781, *The Diaries of George Washington* (Boston: Houghton Mifflin, 1971), 2:211; Congressional Resolve, 30 March 1781, *Journals of the Continental Congress*, 19:334.
8. Washington to William Livingston, 23 and 27 January 1781, *Livingston Papers*, 4:128, 129; Washington to Greene, 9 January 1781, *Greene Papers*, 7:99–103; Washington to Israel Putnam, 18 January 1779, *Washington Papers*, 19:17–18; Udny Hay to Van Cortlandt, 6 January 1781, *Clinton Papers*, 6:554–55; Hall, *Life and Letters of Parsons*, 320; St. Clair to Reed, 4 January 1781, *Life of St. Clair*, 1:532–33; St. Clair to Washington, 7 and 10 January 1781, *Life of St. Clair*, 1:533–34, 535–36; Washington to St. Clair, 12 January and 3 February 1781, *Life of St. Clair*, 1:537–38, 539–40; Washington to George Clinton, 4 January 1781, *Washington Writings*, 21:58–59; Washington to President of Congress, 6 January 1781, *Washington Writings*, 21:64–66; Washington to Wayne, 8 January 1781, *Washington Writings*, 21:70–71; Washington to Robert Howe, 22 January 1781, *Washington Writings*, 21:128–29; Heath to Parsons, 7 January 1781, "Heath Papers," 3:150–51; Heath to Washington, 6 January 1781, "Heath Papers," 3:152–53; Wayne to Washington, 2 January 1781, *Correspondence of the American Revolution*, 3:192–93; Wayne to Reed, 16 December 1780, *Life and Correspondence of Reed*, 2:315–17.
9. Washington to Joseph Jones, 10 July 1781, *Washington Writings*, 22:353.

10. Lafayette to Hamilton, 23 May 1781, *Hamilton Papers*, 2:643; Washington to Greene, 27 February 1781, *Greene Papers*, 7:363–64; Washington to Greene, 18 April 1781, *Greene Papers*, 8:115–16; Washington to St. Clair, 22 and 26 February 1781, *Life of St. Clair*, 1:540–41, 541–42; Washington to Lafayette, 20 February and 6 and 21 April 1781, *Washington Writings*, 21:253–56, 421–23, 488–89; Washington to Officer Commanding the French Squadron in Chesapeake Bay, 20 February 1781, *Washington Writings*, 21:259–61; Washington to President of Congress, 26 February 1781, *Washington Writings*, 21:300–302; Lafayette to Washington, 2 and 7 March 1781, *Correspondence of the American Revolution*, 3:248–52, 254–57; Greene to Washington, 29 March and 1 May 1781, *Correspondence of the American Revolution*, 3:277–79, 299–300; Thatcher, *Military Journal*, 531–38; Lafayette to Jefferson, 21 February 1781, *Jefferson Papers*, 4:676; Lafayette to Jefferson, 6 March 1781, *Jefferson Papers*, 5:74–76; Lafayette, *Lafayette Memoirs*, 70–71; Lafayette to Steuben, 2 March 1781, *Steuben Papers*, reel 4.
11. Greene to Washington, 13 January 1781, *Correspondence of the American Revolution*, 3:209.
12. Lafayette to Hamilton, 23 May 1781, *Hamilton Papers*, 2:643.
13. Washington to Lafayette, 21 April 1781, *Washington Writings*, 21:488–89; Lafayette to Washington, 4, 8, and 24 May 1781, *Correspondence of the American Revolution*, 3:303–6, 306–7, 320–22; Lafayette, *Lafayette Memoirs*, 71–75; Lafayette to Greene, 18 May 1781, *Steuben Papers*, reel 5.
14. Quoted in Kapp, *Life of Steuben*, 421–22.
15. Lafayette to Washington, 18 June 1781, *Steuben Papers*, reel 5.
16. Washington to Greene, 18 April 1781, *Greene Papers*, 8:114–16; Joseph Jones to Washington, 29 June 1781, *Letters of Delegates*, 17:336–38; Washington to Steuben, 4 April 1781, *Washington Writings*, 21:414–15; Washington to Joseph Jones, 10 July 1781, *Washington Writings*, 22:352–55; Washington to Lafayette, 13 July 1781, *Washington Writings*, 22:367–69; Lafayette to Washington, 15 March 1781, *Correspondence of the American Revolution*, 3:264–65; Steuben to Washington, 15 April 1781, *Correspondence of the American Revolution*, 3:290–94; Greene to Washington, 1 May 1781, *Correspondence of the American Revolution*, 3:299–300; Steuben to Jefferson, 27 November and 16 and 30 December 1780, *Jefferson Papers*, 4:163, 212–14, 250–51; Jefferson to Washington, 10 January 1781, *Jefferson Papers*, 4:333–35; Jefferson to John Walker, 18 January 1781, *Jefferson Papers*, 4:400; George Muter to Jefferson, 2 March 1781, *Jefferson Papers*, 5:45–46; Steuben to Jefferson, 5 March 1781, *Jefferson Papers*, 5:66–70; Walker to Jefferson, 9 March 1781, *Jefferson Papers*, 5:108; Peters to Pickering, 16 January 1781, *Steuben Papers*, reel 3; Steuben to Lafayette, 29 March 1781, *Steuben Papers*, reel 4; Lafayette to Chevalier de la Luzerne, 16 June 1781, *Steuben Papers*, reel 5; Lafayette to Washington, 18 June 1781, *Steuben Papers*, reel 5; Steuben to Peters, 23 July 1781, *Steuben Papers*, reel 5.
17. Washington to St. Clair, 26 February 1781, *Life of St. Clair*, 1:541–42; St. Clair to Washington, 8 and 15 April and 16 June 1781, *Life of St. Clair*, 1:545–46, 546–48, 549–50; Washington to Wayne, 26 February and 8 April 1781, *Washington Writings*, 21:296–97, 433–34; Washington to Jefferson, 4 April 1781, *Washington Writings*, 21:417–18; Lafayette to Washington, 24 May 1781, *Correspondence of the American Revolution*, 3:320–22; Wayne to Reed, 26 May 1781, *Life and Correspondence of Reed*, 2:361; Ebenezer Denny, 1 May 1781, *Military Journal of Major Ebenezer Denny, an Officer in the Revolutionary and Indian Wars* (Philadelphia: J. B. Lippincott, 1859),

34; William Livingston to Webb, 28 May 1781, *Webb Correspondence and Journals*, 2:341–42; Wayne letter, n.d., *Life and Services of Wayne*, 130–32.

18. Wayne to Robert Morris, 12 July 1781, *Papers of Robert Morris*, 1:278–79; Wayne to Greene, 7 August 1781, *Greene Papers*, 9:148; Washington to Lafayette, 30 July 1781, *Washington Writings*, 22:431–32; Washington to Wayne, 30 July 1781, *Washington Writings*, 22:435–36; Wayne to Washington, 8 July 1781, *Correspondence of the American Revolution*, 3:347–50.
19. Washington, 14 August 1781, *Diaries*, 2:254; Washington to Jefferson, 8 June 1781, *Jefferson Papers*, 6:82–83; Washington to Greene, 6 October 1781, *Greene Papers*, 9:429.
20. Washington to Heath, 19 August 1781, *Washington Writings*, 23:20–23; Heath, *Heath Memoirs*, 275–78.
21. Washington to Stirling, 14 July 1781, *Washington Writings*, 22:374; Valentine, *Lord Stirling*, 249.
22. Washington to St. Clair, 10 July 1781, *Life of St. Clair*, 1:552–53; Washington to Lincoln, 7 September 1781, *Washington Writings*, 23:98–101; Washington to Robert Howe, 24 September 1781, *Washington Writings*, 23:131–32.
23. Washington to Lafayette, 7 September 1781, *Washington Writings*, 23:97.
24. William Feltman, 2 September 1781, *The Journal of Lieut. William Feltman, of the First Pennsylvania Regiment, 1781–82* (Philadelphia: Historical Society of Pennsylvania, 1853), 11–12; Wayne to Robert Morris, 14 September 1781, *Life and Correspondence of Reed*, 2:365–66.
25. Washington to McKean, 6 October 1781, *Washington Writings*, 23:189.
26. Wayne to Robert Morris, 14 September 1781, *Life and Correspondence of Reed*, 2:365.
27. St. Clair to Irvine, 6 September 1781, *Life of St. Clair*, 1:556–57; St. Clair to his wife, 16 October 1781, *Life of St. Clair*, 1:560.
28. William Livingston to Heath, 15 September 1781, *Livingston Papers*, 4:294; Rhode Island Delegates to William Greene, 17 September 1781, *Letters of Delegates*, 18:50–51; General Orders, 15 September and 16 October 1781, *Washington Writings*, 23:114–15, 233–34; Washington to David Forman, 24 September 1781, *Washington Writings*, 23:132–33; Knox to Lucy Knox, 3 August 1781, *Life and Correspondence of Knox*, 66; Feltman, 14 September 1781, *Journal of William Feltman*, 13–14; *The Western Literary Messenger* 19 (October 1852): 62.
29. Feltman, 19 October 1781, *Journal of William Feltman*, 22; Denny, 17 October 1781, *Military Journal*, 44; Charles Carrollton of Carrollton to Charles Carrollton of Annapolis, 25 October 1781, *Dear Papa*, 3:1489–90; Thomas Fleming, *The Perils of Peace: America's Struggle for Survival after Yorktown* (New York: HarperCollins, 2007), 9–10.
30. Anna Rawle, "A Loyalist's Account of Certain Occurrences in Philadelphia after Cornwallis's Surrender at Yorktown," *Pennsylvania Magazine of History and Biography* 16 (1892): 103; Congressional Resolve, 24 and 29 October 1781, *Journals of the Continental Congress*, 21:1071–72, 1080; Hiltzheimer, 24 October 1781, *Diary of Jacob Hiltzheimer*, 46.
31. Washington to Louis Lebegue de Presle Duportail, 26 October 1781, *Washington Writings*, 23:268–69; Washington to President of Congress, 31 October 1781, *Washington Writings*, 23:307–8; Congressional Resolve, 16 November 1781, *Journals of the Continental Congress*, 21:1121; Duportail to Washington, 27 October 1781, in Elizabeth S. Kite, *Brigadier-General Louis Lebegue Duportail: Commandant of*

Engineers in the Continental Army, 1777–1783 (Baltimore: Johns Hopkins University Press, 1933), 215–17.

32. John Morin Scott to George Clinton, 27 March 1782, *Letters of Delegates*, 18:425.
33. Weedon to Greene, 11 November 1781, *Greene Papers*, 9:563–65; Greene to Knox, 14 April 1782, *Greene Papers*, 11:60–61; Wolcott to Samuel Huntington, 3 December 1781, *Letters of Delegates*, 18:227–28; John Morin Scott to George Clinton, 27 March 1782, *Letters of Delegates*, 18:425; New York Delegates to George Clinton, 29 March 1782, *Letters of Delegates*, 18:427–29; General Orders, 20 October 1781, *Washington Writings*, 23:244–47; Washington to Lincoln, 5 December 1781, *Washington Writings*, 23:371–72; Washington to Bee, 8 March 1782, *Washington Writings*, 24:50–51; Congressional Resolve, 16 November 1781, *Journals of the Continental Congress*, 21:1120; Congressional Resolve, 29 January and 22 March 1782, *Journals of the Continental Congress*, 22:61, 144–46.
34. Washington to Greene, 16 November 1781, *Greene Papers*, 9:379–80; Washington to Alexander Martin, 30 October 1781, *Washington Writings*, 23:302–3; Washington to Bartholomew Dandridge, 20 April 1782, *Washington Writings*, 24:139–44.
35. Robert Morris to Greene, 24 December 1781, *Robert Morris Papers*, 3:438–39; Biddle to Greene, 11–18 November 1781, *Greene Papers*, 9:586–88; Wadsworth to Greene, 12 December 1782, *Greene Papers*, 12:285–86; Varnum to Washington, 20 August 1781, *Letters of Delegates*, 17:539–44; Varnum to Washington, 2 October 1781, *Letters of Delegates*, 18:107–8; Varnum to Greene, 30 October 1781, *Letters of Delegates*, 18:171–73; Lovell to Abagail Adams, 4 December 1781, *Letters of Delegates*, 18:228–30; Rhode Island Delegates to William Greene, 6 December 1781, *Letters of Delegates*, 18:237–41; Reed to Greene, 1 November 1781, *Life and Correspondence of Reed*, 2:370–76.
36. Washington to St. Clair, 29 October and 30 November 1781, *Life of St. Clair*, 1:561–62, 567–68; St. Clair to Washington, 14 November 1781 and 4 February 1782, *Life of St. Clair*, 1:563–64, 568–69; Washington to President of Congress, 27/29 October 1781, *Washington Writings*, 23:294–96; Washington, 21 October 1781, *Diaries*, 2:270.
37. Wayne to Greene, 28 February 1782, *Greene Papers*, 10:423–24; Greene to Biddle, 1 September 1782, *Greene Papers*, 11:614–16; Washington to Wayne, 4 November 1781, *Washington Writings*, 23:329.
38. Stark to President of New Hampshire Congress, 28 June 1781, *Stark Memoir and Correspondence*, 173.
39. Washington to Irvine, 18 December 1781, *Washington Writings*, 23:396–97; Stark to George Clinton, 31 August 1781, *Clinton Papers*, 7:278; Stirling's Order of Commendation, 3 November 1781, *Clinton Papers*, 7:480; Stark to Stirling, 21 October 1781, William Alexander Duer, ed. *The Life of William Alexander, Earl of Stirling* (New York: Wiley and Putnam, 1847), 214–15; Heath to Stark, 25 October 1781, *Stark Memoir and Correspondence*, 280–81; Heath's General Orders, 9 November 1781, *Stark Memoir and Correspondence*, 290–91.
40. James Madison to Pendleton, 13 November 1781, *Letters of Delegates*, 18:194–95; Hanson to Lafayette, 24 November 1781, *Letters of Delegates*, 18:212; Washington to Lafayette, 15 November 1781, *Washington Writings*, 23:340–42; Congressional Resolve, 23 November 1781, *Journals of the Continental Congress*, 21:1134–35.
41. Abraham Clark to Dayton, 29 July 1782, *Letters of Delegates*, 18:672–73; Washington to Glover, 22 May 1782, *Washington Writings*, 24:278; Washington to Parsons, 28 May 1782, *Washington Writings*, 24:298–99; Washington to Lincoln, 10 July 1782,

Washington Writings, 24:416; Congressional Resolve, 18 and 22 July 1782, *Journals of the Continental Congress*, 22:397–99, 405–6; Samuel Parsons' Division Orders, 3 April 1782, *Life and Letters of Parsons*, 412–23; Parsons to Washington, 17 May and 5 June 1782, *Life and Letters of Parsons*, 414–15.

42. McDougall to Heath, 29 November 1781, "Heath Papers," 3:318.
43. Washington to McDougall, 3 February 1782, *Washington Writings*, 23:482–83.
44. General Orders, 28 August 1782, *Washington Writings*, 24:83.
45. Lincoln to Greene, 16 August 1782, *Greene Papers*, 11:551; Duane to McDougall, 28 August 1782, *Letters of Delegates*, 19:101; Washington to Stirling, 4 April 1782, *Washington Writings*, 24:102–3; Washington to McDougall, 24 and 28 August 1782, *Washington Writings*, 24:59, 73–74; McDougall to Heath, 7 November and 19 December 1781, "Heath Papers," 3:301–3, 328–30; Heath to McDougall, 18 January 1782, "Heath Papers," 3:338–40; Heath to Washington, 18 January 1782, "Heath Papers," 3:340–41.
46. Congressional Resolve, 20 November and 19 December 1781, *Journals of the Continental Congress*, 21:1127, 1179–80; Washington to Lincoln, 21 March 1782, *Washington Writings*, 24:83–86.
47. Washington to Cornell, 13 February 1782, *Washington Writings*, 23:497–99; Congressional Resolve, 19 January and 25 June 1782, *Journals of the Continental Congress*, 22:38–39, 349; Congressional Resolve, 14 and 30 October and 4 December 1782, *Journals of the Continental Congress*, 23:650–51, 698–99, 762–63.
48. John Morin Scott to George Clinton, 27 March 1782, *Letters of Delegates*, 18:425–26; New York Delegates to George Clinton, 29 March 1782, *Letters of Delegates*, 18:427–29; Duane to George Clinton, 5 December 1782, *Letters of Delegates*, 19:456–57; Congressional Resolve, 22 March 1782, *Journals of the Continental Congress*, 22:144–47; Congressional Resolve, 14 and 15 October and 30 December 1782, *Journals of the Continental Congress*, 23:648–49, 653–56, 836; Heath to George Clinton, 5 December 1782, *Clinton Papers*, 8:55–56; Washington to James Clinton, 8 August 1782, *Washington Writings*, 24:491.
49. Washington to President of Congress, 4 December 1781, *Washington Writings*, 23:370.
50. Washington to Greene, 15 December 1781, *Washington Writings*, 23:389–91; Washington to Otho Williams, 9 July 1781, *Washington Writings*, 24:414–15; Alexander Garden, *Anecdotes of the Revolutionary War in America* (Charleston, S.C.: A. E. Miller, 1822), 59–60; Greene to Reed, 18 March 1781, *Life and Correspondence of Reed*, 2:348–51; Greene to Otho Williams, 7 September 1782, *Life and Correspondence of Reed*, 2:471–72; Congressional Resolve, 22 March and 9 May 1782, *Journals of the Continental Congress*, 22:146, 251–52.
51. Abraham Clark to Dayton, 7 June and 29 July 1782, *Letters of Delegates*, 18:564–65, 672–73; Boudinot to Dayton, 15 October and 25 December 1782 and 7 January 1783, *Letters of Delegates*, 19:257–58, 506, 556; Abraham Clark to Dayton, 11 and 16 December 1782, *Letters of Delegates*, 19:478, 484; Washington to Lincoln, 17 June 1782, *Washington Writings*, 24:354–55; Washington to Heath, 17 June 1782, *Washington Writings*, 24:355–56; Washington to Lincoln, 11 November 1782, *Washington Writings*, 25:329; Congressional Resolve, 5 June 1782, *Journals of the Continental Congress*, 22:318; Congressional Resolve, 4, 12, and 30 December 1782, *Journals of the Continental Congress*, 23:763–64, 790–91, 836; Putnam, *Memoirs*, 94.
52. Washington to Countess of Stirling, 20 January 1783, *Life of Stirling*, 260.

53. Washington to President of Congress, 20 January 1783, *Washington Writings*, 25:53.
54. Boudinot to Washington, 29 January 1783, *Letters of Delegates*, 19:635–36; Duer, *Life of Stirling*, 258; Congressional Resolve, 28 January 1783, *Journals of the Continental Congress*, 24:96.
55. Washington to Hamilton, 12 March 1783, *Hamilton Papers*, 3:286; Otho Williams to Greene, 22 December 1782, *Greene Papers*, 12:336–38; Lincoln to Greene, 10–12 March 1783, *Greene Papers*, 12:504–5; Madison to Edmund Randolph, 22 October 1782, *Letters of Delegates*, 19:287–88; Madison's Notes of Debates, 7 and 13 January 1783, *Letters of Delegates*, 19:556–57, 578–81; Madison to Benjamin Harrison, 7 January 1783, *Letters of Delegates*, 19:557–58; Hamilton to George Clinton, 12 January 1783, *Letters of Delegates*, 19:577–78; Hamilton to Washington, 13 February 1783, *Letters of Delegates*, 19:688–89; Virginia Delegates to Benjamin Harrison, 18 March 1783, *Letters of Delegates*, 20:54; Washington to Joseph Jones, 14 December 1782, *Washington Writings*, 24:430–31; Washington to President of Congress, 12 March 1783, *Washington Writings*, 25:211–12; Washington to Joseph Jones, 12 March 1783, *Washington Writings*, 25:213–16; Knox to Lincoln, 12 March 1783, *Life and Correspondence of Knox*, 80.
56. Washington to Hamilton, 4 and 12 March 1783, *Hamilton Papers*, 3:278, 286–87; Madison's Notes on Debates, 22 March 1783, *Letters of Delegates*, 20:71–72; Tallmadge, *Memoir*, 53; Washington to Joseph Jones, 14 December 1783, *Washington Writings*, 24:430–31; Washington to President of Congress, 12 March 1783, *Washington Writings*, 25:211–12; Washington to Joseph Jones, 12 March 1783, *Washington Writings*, 25:213–16; Washington to Officers of the Army, 15 March 1783, *Washington Writings*, 25:222–27; Shaw to Reverend Eliot, April 1783, *Journals of Major Samuel Shaw*, 101–5.
57. Washington to Joseph Jones, 18 March 1783, *Washington Writings*, 25:232.

Conclusion

1. James McHenry to Margaret Caldwell, 23 December 1783, *Letters of Delegates*, 21:221–22; David Howell to William Greene, 24 December 1783, *Letters of Delegates*, 21:224–29; Jefferson to Benjamin Harrison, 24 December 1783, *Letters of Delegates*, 21:229–30; James Tilton to Gunning Bedford, 25 December 1783, *Letters of Delegates*, 21:232–33; Abiel Foster to Weare, 26 December 1783, *Letters of Delegates*, 21:233–34.
2. Greene to Weedon, 1 October 1782, *Greene Papers*, 12:4.

Bibliography

Primary Sources

Adams, John. *The Adams Papers Digital Edition*. 11 vols. Boston: Massachusetts Historical Society. http://www.masshist.org/publications/apde/index.php.

———. *Diary and Autobiography of John Adams*. Vol. 2. Edited by L. H. Butterfield. Cambridge, Mass.: Belknap Press of Harvard University Press, 1961.

Adams, Samuel. *The Writings of Samuel Adams*. Vols. 3–4. Edited by Harry Alonzo Cushing. New York: G. P. Putnam's Sons, 1907.

American Revolutionary War Manuscripts. Boston Public Library.

Angell, Israel. *The Diary of Colonel Israel Angell Commanding Officer, 2nd Rhode Island Regiment, Continental Army*. Edited by Edward Field. Providence, R.I.: Preston and Rounds, 1899.

Baldwin, Jeduthan. *The Revolutionary Journal of Col. Jeduthan Baldwin, 1775–1778*. Edited by Thomas Williams Baldwin. Bangor, Maine: De Burians, 1906.

Bangs, Isaac. *Journal of Lieutenant Isaac Bangs*. Edited by Edward Bangs. Cambridge, Mass.: John Wilson and Son, 1890.

Bartlett, John Russell, ed. *Records of the State of Rhode Island and Providence Plantations in New England*. Vols. 7–9. Providence, R.I.: Alfred Anthony, 1862–64.

Bartlett, Josiah. *The Papers of Josiah Bartlett*. Edited by Frank C. Meyers. Hanover, N.H.: University Press of New England, 1979.

Bland, Theodorick. *The Bland Papers: Being a Selection from the Manuscripts of Colonel Theodorick Bland, Jr.* 2 vols. Edited by Charles Campbell. Petersburg, Va.: Edmund and Julian C. Ruffin, 1840–43.

Boudinot, Elias. *The Life, Public Services, Addresses, and Letters of Elias Boudinot*. 2 vols. Edited by J. J. Boudinot. Boston: Houghton, Mifflin, 1896.

Burr, Aaron. *Memoirs of Aaron Burr*. Vol. 1. New York: Harper and Brothers, 1836.

Butterfield, L. H., and Marc Friedlaender, eds. *Adams Family Correspondence*. Vols. 1–4. Cambridge, Mass.: Belknap Press of Harvard University Press, 1963, 1973.

Carroll, Charles. *Journal of Charles Carroll of Carrollton during His Visit to Canada in 1776*. Baltimore: Maryland Historical Society, 1845.

Carroll, John. *The John Carroll Papers*. Vol. 1. Edited by Thomas O'Brien Hanley. Notre Dame, Ind.: University of Notre Dame Press, 1976.

Chase, Eugene Parker, trans. and ed. *Our Revolutionary Forefathers: The Letters of Francois, Marquis de Barbe-Marbois.* New York: Duffield, 1929.

Chastellux, Marquis de. *Travels in North America in the Years 1780–82.* New York, 1828.

Clinton, George. *Public Papers of George Clinton, First Governor of New York, 1777–1795, 1801–1804.* 7 vols. Albany, N.Y.: J.B. Lyon, 1900–1904.

Colonial and State Records of North Carolina. Documenting the American South, University of North Carolina, Chapel Hill. http://docsouth.unc.edu/csr/.

Cresswell, Nicholas. *The Journal of Nicholas Cresswell, 1774–1777.* Port Washington, N.Y.: Kennikat Press, 1968.

Dann, John C., ed. *The Revolution Remembered: Eyewitness Accounts of the War for Independence.* Chicago: University of Chicago Press, 1980.

Deane, Silas. *The Deane Papers: Correspondence between Silas Deane, His Brothers, and Their Business and Political Associates, 1771–1795.* Hartford: Connecticut Historical Society, 1930.

Dearborn, Henry. *Revolutionary War Journals of Henry Dearborn, 1775–1783.* Chicago: Caxton Club, 1939.

Denny, Ebenezer. *Military Journal of Major Ebenezer Denny, an Officer in the Revolutionary and Indian Wars.* Philadelphia: J. B. Lippincott, 1859.

Dewees, Samuel. *A History of the Life and Services of Captain Samuel Dewees.* Edited by John Smith Hanna. Baltimore: Robert Neilson, 1844.

Documents and Records Relating to the Province of New-Hampshire, from 1764 to 1776. Vols. 7–8. Compiled and edited by Nathaniel Bouton. Nashua, N.H.: Orren C. Moore, 1873–74.

Egle, William Henry, ed. *Journals and Diaries of the War of the Revolution.* Harrisburg, Pa.: E. K. Meyers, 1893.

Feltman, William. *The Journal of Lieut. William Feltman, of the First Pennsylvania Regiment, 1781–82.* Philadelphia: Historical Society of Pennsylvania, 1853.

Fogg, Jeremiah. *Orderly Book Kept by Jeremiah Fogg.* Exeter, N.H.: Exeter News-Letter, 1903.

Force, Peter, ed. *American Archives.* Series 4–5. Washington, D.C.: Clerk's Officer of the District Court of the District of Columbia, 1837–53.

Ford, Worthington C., ed. *Some Papers of Aaron Burr.* Worcester, Mass.: Proceedings of the American Antiquarian Society, 1920.

Franklin, Benjamin. *The Papers of Benjamin Franklin.* Vols. 22–23. Edited by William B. Willcox. New Haven, Conn.: Yale University Press, 1982–83.

Graydon, Alexander. *Memoirs of a Life Chiefly Passed in Pennsylvania, within the Last Sixty Years.* Edinburgh: William Blackwood, 1822.

Greene, Nathanael. *The Papers of General Nathanael Greene.* Vols. 1–11. Edited by Richard K. Showman and Dennis M. Conrad. Chapel Hill: University of North Carolina Press, 1976–2000.

Hamilton, Alexander. *The Papers of Alexander Hamilton.* Vols. 1–3. Edited by Harold C. Syrett. New York: Columbia University Press, 1961–62.

Hand, Edward. *The Unpublished Revolutionary Papers of Major-General Edward Hand of Pennsylvania, 1777–1784.* Edited by A. J. Bowden. New York: George H. Richmond, 1907.

Heath, William. "The Heath Papers," vols. 2–3. In *Collections of the Massachusetts Historical Society,* vol. 4, series 7; and vol. 5, series 7. Boston: Massachusetts Historical Society, 1904–5.

———. *Memoirs of Major-General William Heath, by Himself.* Edited by William Abbatt. New York: William Abbatt, 1901.

Heitnam, F. B. *Historical Register of Officers of the Continental Army during the War of the Revolution, April, 1775, to December, 1783.* Washington, D.C.: W. H. Lowdermilk, 1893.

Henry, John Joseph. "Journal of the Campaign against Quebec." *Journals and Diaries of the War of the Revolution.* Pennsylvania Archives, series 2, 15:59–91.

Henry, Patrick. *Patrick Henry: Life, Correspondence and Speeches.* Vol. 1. Edited by William Wirt Henry. New York: Charles Scribner's Sons, 1891.

Heth, William. *The Diary of Lieutenant William Heth while a Prisoner in Quebec, 1776.* Edited by B. Floyd Flickinger. Winchester: Virginia Historical Society, 1931.

Hiltzheimer, Jacob. *Extracts from the Diary of Jacob Hiltzheimer, of Philadelphia, 1765–1798.* Edited by Jacob Cox Parsons. Philadelphia: William F. Fell, 1893.

Hinman, Royal R., ed. *A Historical Collection, from Official Records, Files, &c., of the Part Sustained by Connecticut during the War of the Revolution.* Hartford, Conn.: E. Gleason, 1842.

Hoffman, Ronald, ed. *Dear Papa, Dear Charley: The Peregrinations of a Revolutionary Aristocrat, as Told by Charles Carroll of Carrollton and His Father, Charles Carroll of Annapolis, with Sundry Observations on Bastardy, Child-Rearing, Romance, Matrimony, Commerce, Tobacco, Slavery, and the Politics of Revolutionary America.* Vols. 2–3. Chapel Hill: University of North Carolina Press, 2001.

Howland, John. *The Life and Recollections of John Howland.* Edited by Edwin M. Stone. Providence, R.I.: George H. Whitney, 1857.

Huntington, Ebenezer. *Letters Written by Ebenezer Huntington during the American Revolution.* New York: Charles Frederick Heartman, 1914.

"Huntington Papers: Correspondence of the Brothers Joshua and Jedediah Huntington, during the Period of the American Revolution." In *Collections of the Connecticut Historical Society.* Vol. 20. Hartford: Connecticut Historical Society, 1923.

Jay, John. *The Correspondence and Public Papers of John Jay.* Vols. 1–2. Edited by Henry P. Johnson. New York: G. P. Putnam's Sons, 1890–91.

———. *John Jay: The Making of a Revolutionary, 1745–1780.* Vol. 1. Edited by Richard B. Morris. New York: Harper and Row, 1975.

Jefferson, Thomas. *The Papers of Thomas Jefferson.* Vols. 2–6. Edited by Julian P. Boyd. Princeton, N.J.: Princeton University Press, 1950–52.

Journals of the Continental Congress, 1774–1789. Vols. 1–18. Washington, D.C.: Government Printing Office, 1905–22.

Knox, Henry. *Life and Correspondence of Henry Knox, Major-General in the American Revolutionary Army.* Edited by Francis S. Drake. Boston: Samuel G. Drake, 1873.

Lafayette, Marquis de. *Lafayette in the Age of the American Revolution: Selected Letters and Papers, 1776–1790.* 2 vols. Edited by Stanley J. Idzerda. Ithaca, N.Y.: Cornell University Press, 1977, 1979.

———. *Memoirs of Gilbert M. Lafayette.* Edited by H. L. V. DuCoudray-Holstein. Geneva: John Greves, 1835.

Lamb, John. *Memoir of the Life and Times of General John Lamb.* Edited by Isaac Q. Leake. Albany, N.Y.: Joel Munsell, 1857.

Laurens, Henry. *The Papers of Henry Laurens.* Vols. 10–15. Edited by David R. Chesnutt and C. James Taylor. Columbia: University of South Carolina Press, 1985–2000.

Lea, Russell M. *A Hero and a Spy: The Revolutionary War Correspondence of Benedict Arnold.* Westminster, Md.: Heritage Books, 2006.

Lee, Charles. *The Lee Papers*. Vols. 1–3. New York: New-York Historical Society, 1871–73.

Lee, Henry. *Memoirs of the War in the Southern Department of the United States*. New York: University Publishing, 1869.

Lee, Richard Henry. *The Letters of Richard Henry Lee*. 2 vols. Edited by James Curtis Ballagh. New York: Macmillan, 1911–14.

Lincoln, Benjamin. *The Benjamin Lincoln Papers*. Reel 2. Edited by Frederick S. Allis Jr. Boston: Massachusetts Historical Society, 1967.

Livingston, William. *The Papers of William Livingston*. Vols. 1–4. Edited by Carl E. Prince, Dennis P. Ryan, and Mary Lou Lustig. Trenton: New Jersey Historical Commission, 1979–87.

Marshall, Christopher. *Passages from the Diary of Christopher Marshall*. Vol. 1. Edited by William Duane. Philadelphia: Hazard and Mitchell, 1839–49.

Massachusetts Historical Society. "The Siege of Boston." http://www.masshist.org/online/siege/.

McDougall, Alexander. *Papers of Alexander McDougall, 1757—1795*. Reels 1–5. New York: New-York Historical Society.

Morris, Robert. *The Papers of Robert Morris*. Vols. 1–3. Edited by E. James Ferguson. Pittsburgh, Pa.: University of Pittsburgh Press, 1973–77.

Moultrie, William. *Memoirs of the American Revolution*. Vols. 1–2. New York: David Longworth, 1802.

Pennsylvania Archives, 1st series, vols. 4–9. Edited by Samuel Hazard. Philadelphia: Joseph Serverns, 1853–54.

Pontgibaud, Charles Albert. *A French Volunteer of the War of Independence*. Translated and edited by Robert B. Douglass. Paris: Charles Carrington, 1898.

Putnam, Rufus. *The Memoirs of Rufus Putnam, and Certain Official Papers and Correspondence*. Boston: Houghton, Mifflin, 1903.

Ranzan, David A., and Matthew J. Hollis, eds. *Hero of Fort Schuyler: Selected Revolutionary War Correspondence of Brigadier General Peter Gansevoort, Jr.* Jefferson, N.C.: McFarland, 2014.

Reed, Joseph. *Life and Correspondence of Joseph Reed*. 2 vols. Edited by William B. Reed. Philadelphia: Lindsay and Blakiston, 1847.

Richards, Samuel. *Diary of Samuel Richards: Captain of Connecticut Line, War of the Revolution, 1775–1781*. Philadelphia: Leeds and Biddle, 1909.

Robbins, Ammi R. *Journal of the Rev. Ammi R. Robbins, a Chaplain in the American Army*. New Haven, Conn.: B. L. Hamlen, 1850.

Rodney, Caesar. *Letters to and from Caesar Rodney, 1756–1784*. Edited by George Herbert Ryden. Philadelphia: University of Pennsylvania Press, 1933.

Rodney, Thomas. *Diary of Captain Thomas Rodney, 1776–1777*. Wilmington: Historical Society of Delaware, 1888.

Rush, Benjamin. *Letters of Benjamin Rush*. Vol. 1. Edited by L. H. Butterfield. Princeton, N.J.: Princeton University Press, 1951.

Ryan, Dennis, ed. *A Salute to Courage: The American Revolution as Seen through Wartime Writings of Officers of the Continental Army and Navy*. New York: Columbia University Press, 1979.

Shaw, Samuel. *The Journals of Major Samuel Shaw, the First American Consul at Canton*. Edited by Josiah Quincy. Boston: Wm. Crosby and H. P. Nichols, 1847.

Smith, Paul, ed. *Letters of Delegates to Congress, 1774–1789*. Vols. 1–21. Washington, D.C.: Library of Congress, 1976–94.

Sparks, Jared, ed. *Correspondence of the American Revolution*. Vols. 3–4. Boston: Little, Brown, 1853.

———. *The Diplomatic Correspondence of the American Revolution*. 2 vols. Boston: N. Hale and Gray & Bowen, 1829.

Stark, John. *Memoir and Official Correspondence of Gen. John Stark*. Edited by Caleb Stark. Concord, N.H.: Steam Press, 1860.

Steuben, Friedrich Wilhelm von. *The Papers of General Friedrich Wilhelm von Steuben, 1777–1794*. Reels 1–5. Edited by Edith von Zemenszky. Millwood, N.Y.: Kraus International Publications, 1982.

Stiles, Ezra. *The Literary Diary of Ezra Stiles*. 3 vols. Edited by Franklin Bowditch Dexter. New York: Charles Scribner's Sons, 1901.

Sullivan, John. *Letters and Papers of Major-General John Sullivan*. 3 vols. Edited by Otis G. Hammond. Concord: New Hampshire Historical Society, 1930–31.

Sumner, Jethro, Papers. Southern Historical Collection. Louis Round Wilson Library Special Collection, University of North Carolina, Chapel Hill. http://finding-aids.lib.unc.edu/00705/.

Tallmadge, Benjamin. *Memoir of Col. Benjamin Tallmadge*. New York: Thomas Holman, 1858.

Thatcher, James. *Military Journal during the American Revolutionary War, from 1775 to 1783*. Boston: Richardson and Lord, 1823.

Tilghman, Tench. *Memoir of Lieut. Col. Tench Tilghman*. Albany, N.Y.: J. Munsell, 1876.

Trumbull, John. *Autobiography, Reminiscences, and Letters of John Trumbull*. New York: Wiley and Putnam, 1841.

Trumbull, Jonathan, Sr. *The Trumbull Papers*. Parts 2–4. Boston: Collections of the Massachusetts Historical Society, 1888–1902.

Van Cortlandt, Philip. *The Revolutionary War Memoir and Selected Correspondence of Philip Van Cortlandt*. Compiled and edited by Jacob Judd. Tarrytown, N.Y.: Sleepy Hollow Restorations, 1976.

Ward, Samuel. *Correspondence of Governor Samuel Ward*. Edited by Bernhard Knollenberg. Providence: Rhode Island Historical Society, 1952.

Washington, George. *The Diaries of George Washington, 1748–1799*. Vol. 2. Boston: Houghton Mifflin, 1971.

———. *The Papers of George Washington: Revolutionary War Series*. Vols. 1–22. Edited by W. W. Abbot, Theodore J. Crackel, Philander Chase, Frank E. Grizzard Jr., David R. Hoth, Edward G. Lengel, and Dorothy Twohig. Charlottesville: University Press of Virginia, 1985–2013.

———. *Washington's Opinion of His General Officers*. https://archive.org/stream/washingtonsopinioowash#page/no/mode/2up.

———. *The Writings of George Washington*. Vols. 17–26. Edited by John C. Fitzpatrick. Washington, D.C.: Government Printing Office, 1937–39.

Wayne, Anthony. *Life and Services of Gen. Anthony Wayne*. Edited by H. N. Moore. Philadelphia: Leary, Getz, 1845.

Webb, Samuel Blachley. *Correspondence and Journals of Samuel Blachley Webb*. 2 vols. Edited by Worthington Chauncey Ford. New York: Wickersham Press, 1893.

Weedon, George. *Valley Forge Orderly Book.* New York: Dodd, Mead, 1902.
Wilkinson, James. *Memoirs of My Own Times.* Vol. 1. Philadelphia: Abraham Small, 1816.

Secondary Sources

Alden, John Richard. *General Charles Lee: Traitor or Patriot?* Baton Rouge: Louisiana State University Press, 1951.
———. *A History of the American Revolution.* New York: Alfred A. Knopf, 1969.
Beane, Samuel Collins. "General Enoch Poor." *Proceedings of the New Hampshire Historical Society* 3 (1902): 435–72.
Beeman, Richard R. *Our Lives, Our Fortunes, and Our Sacred Honor: The Forging of American Independence, 1774–1776.* New York: Basic Books, 2013.
Billias, George Athan. *General John Glover and His Marblehead Mariners.* New York: Henry Holt, 1960.
———, ed. *George Washington's Generals.* New York: William Morrow, 1964.
Bodle, Wayne. *The Valley Forge Winter: Civilians and Soldiers in War.* University Park: Pennsylvania State University Press, 2002.
Buchanan, John. *The Road to Valley Forge: How Washington Built the Army That Won the Revolution.* Hoboken, N.J.: John Wiley and Sons, 2004.
Busch, Noel F. *Winter Quarters: George Washington and the Continental Army at Valley Forge.* New York: New American Library, 1974.
Callahan, North. *Henry Knox: General Washington's General.* New York: Rinehart, 1958.
Chadwick, Bruce. *George Washington's War: The Forging of a Revolutionary Leader and the American Presidency.* Naperville, Ill.: Sourcebooks, 2004.
Chidsey, Donald Barr. *The Siege of Boston: An On-the-Scene Account of the Beginning of the American Revolution.* New York: Crown Publishers, 1966.
Coffin, Charles. *Lives and Services of Major General John Thomas, Colonel Thomas Knowlton, Colonel Alexander Scammell, Major General Henry Dearborn.* New York: Robert, Hovey & King, 1845.
Duer, William Alexander, ed. *The Life of William Alexander, Earl of Stirling.* New York: Wiley and Putnam, 1847.
Egleston, Thomas. *The Life of John Paterson: Major-General in the Revolutionary Army.* G. P. Putnam's Sons, 1898.
Ellis, Joseph J. *American Creation: Triumphs and Tragedies at the Founding of the Republic.* New York: Alfred A. Knopf, 2007.
———. *His Excellency: George Washington.* New York: Alfred A. Knopf, 2004.
Ferling, John E. *Almost a Miracle: The American Victory in the War of Independence.* Oxford: Oxford University Press, 2007.
———. *The First of Men: A Life of George Washington.* Knoxville: University of Tennessee Press, 1988.
———, ed. *The World Turned Upside Down: The American Victory in the War of Independence.* New York: Greenwood Press, 1988.
Fischer, David Hackett. *Washington's Crossing.* Oxford: Oxford University Press, 2004.
Fleming, Thomas. *The Forgotten Victory: The Battle for New Jersey—1780.* New York: Reader's Digest Press, 1973.
———. *The Perils of Peace: America's Struggle for Survival after Yorktown.* New York: HarperCollins, 2007.
———. *1776: Year of Illusions.* New York: W. W. Norton, 1975.

———. *Washington's Secret War: The Hidden History of Valley Forge*. New York: HarperCollins, 2005.
Flexner, James Thomas. *Washington: The Indispensable Man*. Boston: Little, Brown, 1974.
Flood, Charles Bracelen. *Rise, and Fight Again: Perilous Times along the Road to Independence*. New York: Dodd, Mead, 1976.
Gabriel, Michael P. *Major General Richard Montgomery: The Making of an American Hero*. Teaneck, N.J.: Farleigh Dickinson Press, 2002.
Gaines, James R. *For Liberty and Glory: Washington, Lafayette, and Their Revolutions*. New York: W. W. Norton, 2007.
Gallagher, John J. *The Battle of Brooklyn, 1776*. New York: Sarpedon, 1995.
Garden, Alexander. *Anecdotes of the Revolutionary War in America*. Charleston, S.C.: A. E. Miller, 1822.
Godbold, E. Stanley, Jr., and Robert H. Woody. *Christopher Gadsden and the American Revolution*. Knoxville: University of Tennessee Press, 1982.
Gottschalk, Louis. *Lafayette and the Close of the American Revolution*. Chicago: University of Chicago Press, 1942.
———. *Lafayette Joins the American Army*. Chicago: University of Chicago Press, 1965.
Graham, James. *The Life of General Daniel Morgan*. New York: Derby and Jackson, 1859.
Hall, Charles S., ed. *Life and Letters of Samuel Holden Parsons: Major General in the Continental Army and Chief Judge of the Northwestern Territory, 1737–1789*. Binghampton, N.Y.: Otseningo, 1905.
Hallahan, William H. *The Day the Revolution Ended, 19 October 1781*. Hoboken, N.J.: John Wiley and Sons, 2004.
Hatch, Robert McConnell. *Thrust for Canada: The American Attempt on Quebec in 1775–1776*. Boston: Houghton Mifflin, 1979.
Headley, J. T. *Washington and His Generals*. 2 vols. New York: Baker and Scribner, 1847.
Henderson, H. James. *Party Politics in the Continental Congress*. New York: McGraw-Hill, 1974.
Hess, Abram. *The Life and Services of General John Philip de Haas, 1735–1786*. Lebanon, Pa.: Lebanon County Historical Society, 1916.
Higginbotham, Don. *War and Society in Revolutionary America: The Wide Dimensions of Conflict*. Columbia: University of South Carolina Press, 1988.
———. *The War of American Independence: Military Attitudes, Policies, and Practice, 1763–1789*. New York: Macmillan, 1971.
Hill, George Channing. *The Life of Israel Putnam*. New York: A. L. Burt, 1903.
Huston, James A. *Logistics of Liberty: American Services of Supply in the Revolutionary War and After*. Newark: University of Delaware Press, 1991.
Hyman, Harold M., ed. *Yorktown: Campaign of Strategic Options*. Philadelphia: J. B. Lippincott, 1975.
Jackson, John W. *Valley Forge: Pinnacle of Courage*. Gettysburg, Pa.: Thomas Publications, 1992.
Kaminski, John P. *George Clinton: Yeoman Politician of the New Republic*. Madison, Wis.: Madison House Publishers, 1993.
Kapp, Friedrich. *The Life of Frederick William Von Steuben, Major General in the Revolutionary Army*. New York: Mason Brothers, 1859.
———. *The Life of John Kalb: Major-General in the Revolutionary Army*. New York: privately printed, 1870.

Kennett, Lee. *The French Forces in America, 1780–1783*. Westport, Conn.: Greenwood Press, 1977.

Ketchum, Richard M. *Saratoga: Turning Point of America's Revolutionary War*. New York: Henry Holt, 1997.

Kite, Elizabeth S. *Brigadier-General Louis Lebegue Duportail: Commandant of Engineers in the Continental Army, 1777–1783*. Baltimore: Johns Hopkins University Press, 1933.

Knollenberg, Bernhard. *Washington and the Revolution, a Reappraisal: Gates, Conway, and the Continental Congress*. New York: Macmillan, 1941.

Leckie, Robert. *George Washington's War: The Saga of the American Revolution*. New York: HarperCollins, 1992.

Lender, Mark Edward, and Garry Wheeler Stone. *Fatal Sunday: George Washington, the Monmouth Campaign, and the Politics of War*. Norman: University of Oklahoma Press, 2016.

Livingston, William Farrand. *Israel Putnam: Pioneer, Ranger, and Major-General, 1718–1790*. New York: G. P. Putnam's Sons, 1901.

Lockhart, Paul. *The Drillmaster of Valley Forge: The Baron de Steuben and the Making of the American Army*. New York: HarperCollins, 2008.

Mahan, John K. *History of the Militia and the National Guard*. New York: Collier Macmillan, 1983.

Martin, James Kirby. *Benedict Arnold, Revolutionary War Hero: An American Warrior Reconsidered*. New York: New York University Press, 1997.

Martin, James Kirby, and Mark Edward Lender. *A Respectable Army: The Military Origins of the Republic, 1763–1789*. Arlington Heights, Ill.: Harlan Davidson, 1982.

Mattern, David B. *Benjamin Lincoln and the American Revolution*. Columbia: University of South Carolina Press, 1998.

McDougall, William L. *American Revolutionary: A Biography of General Alexander McDougall*. Westport, Conn.: Greenwood Press, 1977.

Mintz, Max M. *The Generals of Saratoga: John Burgoyne and Horatio Gates*. New Haven, Conn.: Yale University Press, 1990.

———. *Seeds of Empire: The American Revolutionary Conquest of the Iroquois*. New York: New York University Press, 1999.

Montross, Lynn. *The Reluctant Rebels: The Story of the Continental Congress, 1774–1789*. New York: Harper and Brothers, 1950.

Morpurgo, J. E. *Treason at West Point: The Arnold-Andre Conspiracy*. New York: Mason/Charter, 1975.

Muhlenberg, Henry A. *The Life of Major-General Peter Muhlenberg of the Revolutionary Army*. Philadelphia: Carey and Hart, 1849.

Nelson, Paul David. *Anthony Wayne: Soldier of the Early Republic*. Bloomington: Indiana University Press, 1985.

———. *William Alexander, Lord Stirling*. Tuscaloosa: University of Alabama Press, 1987.

Palmer, John McAuley. *General Von Steuben*. Port Washington, N.Y.: Kennikat Press, 1966.

Papas, Phillip. *Renegade Revolutionary: The Life of General Charles Lee*. New York: New York University Press, 2014.

Philbrick, Nathaniel. *Valiant Ambition: George Washington, Benedict Arnold, and the Fate of the American Revolution*. New York: Viking Press, 2016.

Pickering, Octavius. *The Life of Timothy Pickering*. Vol. 1. Boston: Little, Brown, 1867.

Rakove, Jack N. *The Beginnings of National Politics: An Interpretive History of the Continental Congress*. New York: Alfred A. Knopf, 1979.

Rankin, Hugh F. *The North Carolina Continentals*. Chapel Hill: University of North Carolina Press, 1971.
Rossie, Jonathan G. *The Politics of Command in the American Revolution*. Syracuse, N.Y.: Syracuse University Press, 1975.
Rossman, Kenneth R. *Thomas Mifflin and the Politics of the American Revolution*. Chapel Hill: University of North Carolina Press, 1952.
Royster, Charles. *A Revolutionary People at War: The Continental Army and American Character, 1775–1783*. Chapel Hill: University of North Carolina Press, 1979.
Sanders, Jennings B. *Evolution of the Executive Departments of the Continental Congress, 1774–1789*. Gloucester, Mass.: Peter Smith, 1971.
Schecter, Barnet. *The Battle for New York: The City at the Heart of the American Revolution*. New York: Walker, 2002.
Selby, John E. *The Revolution in Virginia, 1775–1783*. Williamsburg, Va.: Colonial Williamsburg Foundation, 1988.
Shreve, L. G. *Tench Tilghman: The Life and Times of Washington's Aide-de-Camp*. Centreville, Md.: Tidewater, 1982.
Smith, Page. *Reflections on the Nature of Leadership*. Washington, D.C.: Society of Cincinnati, 1982.
Smith, William Henry, ed. *The Life and Public Services of Arthur St. Clair*. Vol. 1. Cincinnati: Robert Clarke, 1882.
Spring, Matthew H. *With Zeal and with Bayonets Only: The British Army on Campaign in America, 1775–1783*. Norman: University of Oklahoma Press, 2008.
Stegeman, John F., and Janet A. Stegeman. *Caty: A Biography of Catharine Littlefield Greene*. Athens: University of Georgia Press, 1977.
Stille, Charles J. *Major-General Anthony Wayne and the Pennsylvania Line in the Continental Army*. Philadelphia: J. B. Lippincott, 1893.
Taaffe, Stephen R. *The Philadelphia Campaign*. Lawrence: University Press of Kansas, 2003.
Tebbel, John. *Turning the World Upside Down: Inside the American Revolution*. New York: Orion Books, 1993.
Treacy, M. F. *Prelude to Yorktown: The Southern Campaign of Nathanael Greene, 1780–1781*. Chapel Hill: University of North Carolina Press, 1963.
Valentine, Alan. *Lord Stirling*. New York: Oxford University Press, 1969.
Van Doren, Carl. *Secret History of the American Revolution*. New York: Viking Press, 1941.
Varnum, James Mitchell. *A Sketch of the Life and Public Services of James Mitchell Varnum of Rhode Island*. Boston: David Clapp and Son, 1906.
Ward, Christopher. *The War of the Revolution*. Vol. 1. Edited by John Richard Alden. New York: Macmillan, 1952.
Ward, Harry W. *Between the Lines: Banditti of the American Revolution*. Westport, Conn.: Praeger, 2002.
———. *General William Maxwell and the New Jersey Continentals*. Westport, Conn.: Greenwood Press, 1997.
———. *Major General Adam Stephen and the Cause of American Liberty*. Charlottesville: University Press of Virginia, 1989.
Wright, Robert K. *The Continental Army*. Washington, D.C.: Government Printing Office, 1983.

Index